In this book, the future of one of the world's most important industries is examined from the perspective of work structures and labor relations policies. The authors examine the restructuring of the world automobile industry in the 1980s, and draw data from in-depth empirical study of three leading car companies in three different countries: the United States, the United Kingdom, and Germany. They demonstrate that the different strategies employed by firms and trades unions in industrial relations, and different national characteristics, have had a major impact on the dismantling of Taylorism and Fordism and the introduction of new structures of work.

This book is an important contribution to the study of change in mass production industries throughout the world. It will be of interest to students of industrial relations and industrial sociology, as well as specialists in government and business.

Breaking from Taylorism

Breaking from Taylorism

Changing forms of work in the automobile industry

Ulrich Jürgens
Thomas Malsch and
Knuth Dohse

CAMBRIDGE
UNIVERSITY PRESS

Published by the Press Syndicate of the University of Cambridge
The Pitt Building, Trumpington Street, Cambridge CB2 1RP
40 West 20th Street, New York, NY 10011–4211, USA
10 Stamford Road, Oakleigh, Victoria 3166, Australia

Originally published in German as *Moderne Zeiten in der Automobilfabrik.*
Strategien der Produktions modernisierung im Länder-und konzernvergleich
by Springer-Verlag Berlin Heidelberg 1989
and © Springer-Verlag Berlin Heidelberg 1989
First published in English by Cambridge University Press 1993 as
Breaking from Taylorism: Changing forms of work in the automobile industry
English translation © Cambridge University Press 1993

Printed in Great Britain at the University Press, Cambridge

A catalogue record for this book is available from the British Library

Library of Congress cataloguing in publication data
Jürgens, Ulrich, 1943–
[Moderne Zeiten in der Automobilfabrik. English]
Breaking from Taylorism / Ulrich Jürgens, Thomas Malsch,
and Knuth Dohse.
p. cm.
Rev. translation of: Moderne Zeiten in der Automobilfabrik.
ISBN 0 521 40544 0
1. Automobile industry and trade – Case studies. 2. Trade-unions–
–Automobile industry workers – Case studies. 3. Industrial
relations – Case studies. 4. Automobile industry and trade – United
States. 5. Automobile industry and trade – Great Britain.
6. Automobile industry and trade – Germany. I. Malsch, Thomas. 1946–
II. Dohse, Knuth. 1948– . III. Title.
HD9710.A2J7813 1993
338.4′76292–dc20 92–26693 CIP

ISBN 0521 40544 0 hardback

Contents

List of illustrations   *page* x
List of tables   xii
Preface   xv
List of abbreviations   xviii

**1 The restructuring of the world automobile industry:
    opportunities for new forms of work**   1
  1.1 The problem posed and the starting situation in the
            industry   1
  1.2 The end of "Modern Times" in the factory?   4
  1.3 Design of the study   7
  1.4 Regarding the contents of this book   16

**2 Changing markets and the rise of Toyotism: the development of
    the national car industries since the 1970s**   21
  2.1 Impulses for change in the 1970s   22
  2.2 The development of the automotive industries of the
            U.S.A., Great Britain and the Federal Republic of
            Germany   24
  2.3 The "Japan Nightmare": A new power in the world
            automobile industry   37
  2.4 "Toyotism" and its prerequisites in work and social
            organization   40

3 Company strategies for answering the challenges   52
  3.1 The world car strategy   53
  3.2 The strategy of product diversification and upgrading 59
  3.3 Strategies of production automation   62

4   Industrial relations in the process of change   92
   4.1   The different "logics" of regulation in the traditional
         industrial relations systems   92
   4.2   Events and impulses for a change in the traditional
         practices in the industrial relations arena   103

**5   Reorganizing quality control – between pressure for efficiency
      and a job enrichment orientation**   126
   5.1   Company strategies for reorganizing quality control and
         their implementation in different industrial relations
         environments   128
   5.2   Computer assisted quality control and its limits   159

**6   Coping with new technology: skilled workers between
      specialization and flexibilization**   173
   6.1   Demarcation rules and skilled labor in production   175
   6.2   New job profiles in the automation areas   184

**7   Regulating work performance and plant efficiency: changes in
      control structures of work**   215
   7.1   Industrial engineering – a change in the role of the
         guardians of Taylorism   217
   7.2   New challenges and approaches to performance
         regulation   238
   7.3   Performance regulation by benchmarking: competing
         for best practices   260
   7.4   Conclusions   279

**8   Comparative achievements in labor productivity and changes in
      personnel structures: trends and development patterns**   281
   8.1   Differences and trends in labor productivity   281
   8.2   Shifting proportions between the direct and indirect
         areas   289

9   Tapping new resources: skill levels and worker participation   306
   9.1   Differences in the systems and emphasis of vocational
         (apprenticeship) training   307
   9.2   Approaches for new work and management concepts   322
   9.3   Programs for worker participation in the context of
         company reorganization   336

10 Is the assembly line obsolete? 345
    10.1 Alternatives within the framework of conventional
        assembly line work 346
    10.2 The risks of venturing into high technology 353
    10.3 The compromise solution with off-line module
        production using AGVs 362

11 Modern times in the automobile factory: trends toward new 370
forms of work (summary and conclusions)
    11.1 Directions of change 371
    11.2 The influence of company strategies 376
    11.3 The influence of national affiliation 379
    11.4 Models for future development 384
    11.5 Outlook for the 1990s 386

Notes 397
Bibliography 409
Index 428

Illustrations

1.1 Explanatory model *page* 15

2.1 The exchange-rate development of selected currencies relative to the U.S. dollar, 1970–86   22

2.2 Production and employment in the U.S. automobile industry   25

2.3 U.S. Auto registration/production and export figures of the U.S. automobile industry (in millions of cars)   27

2.4 Auto production in the U.S. according to manufacturers (in millions of cars)   28

2.5 Profitability of General Motors, Ford, and Chrysler in the U.S. (net profit as a percentage of turnover)   29

2.6 Production and employment in the U.K automobile industry   31

2.7 Production, registered vehicles, and exports of the U.K. (in millions of cars)   32

2.8 Automobile production in Great Britain (in millions of cars)   34

2.9 Profitability of selected British auto companies (net profit as a percentage of turnover)   34

2.10 Production and employment in the automobile industry in the Federal Republic of Germany   35

2.11 Production, registered vehicles, and exports of the Federal Republic of Germany (in millions of cars)   35

2.12 Production and employment at the German mass manufacturers   36

2.13 Profitability of the German mass producers (net profit as a percentage of turnover)   37

2.14 Automobile production and employment in Japan (Index 1970 = 100)   38

2.15 Profitability of Japanese auto companies (net profit as a percentage of turnover)   39

3.1 Network of General Motors' J-car program, 1983 (engine, transmission, and assembly plants) 56

3.2 Turnover per vehicle at four German manufacturers, (1970–85) 60

3.3 The emblem for the "Mutual Growth Program" of Ford and the UAW 89

4.1 Wage differentiation for selected job groups in a comparison between American, British, and German assembly plants 102

6.1 Production teams in a body assembly shop 213

7.1 Production target, actual production and losses caused by strikes at a British plant, 1978–85 273

7.2 Hours of labor per production unit (workers as a whole) 274

8.1 Number of vehicles per worker in three parallel Company A plants 282

8.2 Number of vehicles per worker in each of two parallel plants of Company A and B in North America 283

8.3 Vehicles per worker in parallel Company A and B plants in Great Britain and Germany 284

8.4 Vehicles per worker in three German plants of three different companies 285

9.1 Organizational diagram of the factory management organization at Company B 338

9.2 Organizational diagram of the factory management organization at Company A 339

9.3 Organizational diagram of the factory management organization at Company C 339

10.1 Schematic representation of modular door assembly 364

Tables

1.1 The Taylorist–Fordist regulatory mode and functional alternatives *pages* 5

1.2 The factories studied and their assignment to companies and countries 11

1.3 Factory profile of the core sample 12

1.4 Share of female workers on the blue-collar work force in the factories in the core sample (in %) 14

2.1 Capital investments of selected manufactuers (in millions of the respective national currencies) 24

2.2 Production activity at the assembly plants of GM and Ford in the U.S.A., 1980/6 (as an average per plant and year) 30

3.1 Parallel plants for the production of the same vehicle type for GM and Ford in the U.S. and Europe, (1983) 57

3.2 Number of car models offered by six German companies, 1971 and 1985. 61

3.3 The total time required to build a car in a German company broken down between the different production areas, 1980 and 1985 63

3.4 Robot focal point "body plant" 68

3.5 Computer linkage of companies and suppliers 77

3.6 Delegation of responsibility in the course of the OWL process 86

4.1 Lost time due to strikes in the Hartmoor assembly plant, 1976–85 114

4.2 Illness and disability, (1985) 120

4.3 Average age of the workforce in selected assembly plants, (1985) 120

4.4 Differences in the temporal availability of the workers in a comparison between a German and a U.S. assembly plant, (1985) 121

5.1 Inspection workers as a percentage of direct production
    workers   128
5.2 QUP workers in the factory personnel structure, (1983)   133
5.3 Reduction of QUP workers, inspectors, and repair workers
    at plant Maple City from 1981 to 1983   134
5.4 Inspection workers in the area press/body shop at
    Weinkirchen, (1985)   139
5.5 Categories of production and repair workers in final
    assembly   141
5.6 Personnel structure of quality control at Company C, (1984)   156
5.7 Inspection personnel in selected areas at Heidedorf   157
6.1 Skilled-labor demarcations in welding-electrode
    maintenance in the body shop   178
6.2 Number of skilled-worker classifications in the plant   184
6.3 Maintenance work according to occupational groups for
    hydraulically driven ("old") and electrically driven ("new")
    industrial robots at River City   187
6.4 Deployment patterns on the welding line with fifty
    industrial robots at Mittelort   195
6.5 Skilled-worker utilization on the robotized side panel line –
    a comparison between the British plant Hartmoor and the
    German plant Weinkirchen   200
7.1 The percentage of disabled workers in U.S., British, and
    West German assembly plants   240
7.2 Newly filed grievances in two parallel plants in the U.S.A.   267
7.3 Comparison of the personnel requirements in "man-hours"
    in a U.S. and a Japanese assembly plant (body plant, paint
    shop, trim assembly, and final assembly), 1980   271
7.4 Unemployment rates at selected automobile sites in the
    USA, Great Britain, and the Federal Republic of Germany,
    1980 and 1985   279
8.1 Productivity and personnel development in selected
    assembly plants (total blue-collar workers per 1,000 cars),
    1978–85   287
8.2 Lost days (per worker) as a yearly average according to
    selected criteria in a U.S., a British, and a German assembly
    plant, 1980–4   288
8.3 Development of direct production personnel in selected
    assembly plants, 1978–85   291
8.4 Structure, determination, and developmental tendencies of
    the personnel in direct production   292
8.5 Forms of break-taking in selected factories   295

8.6   "Anlagenführer" and similar jobs in production in the body
      shop of selected German assembly plants   297
8.7   Development of indirect production personnel in selected
      assembly plants, 1978–85   298
8.8   Development of quality inspection personnel in selected
      assembly plants, 1978–85   300
8.9   Development in the number of skilled workers in the
      indirect area in selected assembly plants, 1978–85   301
9.1   Initial vocational training (skilled trade) in selected
      assembly plants   311
9.2   Distribution of the skilled trade apprentices in selected
      assembly plants according to vocational groups   313
9.3   The number of skilled workers, EITs, and apprentices at the
      Greentown plant (1979, 1984, and 1986)   315
10.1 Cycle times on the lines of trim and final assembly in
      minutes, (1985)   347
10.2 Work volumes in the assembly area of Company C
      Heidedorf, (1983)   349
10.3 Comparison of the job classifications in direct assembly in a
      German and an American assembly plant (trim and final
      assembly)   354
11.1 Emphasis of change measures in the individual companies   377
11.2 Emphasis of change measure according to companies and
      countries   380
11.3 Paradigms for the production organization of the future   384

Preface

This study is based on a research project dealing with the work reforms brought about by the restructuring in the world automobile industry in the 1980s. The project was carried out over the course of several years at the "Wissenschaftszentrum Berlin für Sozialforschung" and was a part of "The Future of the Automobile" program, an international research effort coordinated by the Massachusetts Institute of Technology (MIT) and supported financially by the German Science Foundation.

When we developed the concept of our study in 1982, we were not then aware that with our research interests we had touched a nerve of a far-reaching process of change which was just beginning at that time. It was a turbulent period for the factories. Sweeping changes in product and process technology went along with demands for increased performance due to the heightened pressure of competition. The traditional forms of work were being questioned and new forms of work and human resource policies were introduced in many places. There was a widespread awareness that an era of production concepts which had thus far been regarded as "best practice" had come to an end, but there were no answers yet as to the future forms of work and the company strategies in this respect were often vague or controversial. Despite this – or perhaps because of this – situation our interviewees were very receptive to our questions and willing to relate problems and perspectives of their work reforms to us. The basis for our research was the fact that a large number of individuals, both in management and in the unions, cooperated with us and were willing to provide information. We would like to extend our warmest thanks to all of these people.

At the core of our investigation were changes in work organization and personnel policies. The most interesting question for us was that of the nation and company specific preconditions and their effects on the forms of work, whether they foster or hinder specific solutions, the directions which were pursued by plants at different sites, and what they could learn from each other's experiences with new forms of work. The empirical studies were carried out between 1983 and 1986. They cover automobile companies and their assembly plants in the U.S.A. and Canada, Great Britain and the Federal Republic of Germany. Our final report was published in German in 1989 (Moderne Zeiten in der Automobilfabrik – Strategien der Produktionsmodernisierung im Länder- und Konzernvergleich, Springer Verlag, Berlin etc.). More years have passed until this English version was published and in this time further changes have taken place. Many developments which we could only observe in their early stages have acquired a clearer profile in the meantime. We have attempted to deal with these developments in this version, although we could not update our empirical research in every detail.

The Japanese automobile industry and its production concepts have attained a hegemonic position worldwide in the second half of the 1980s. The most recent and final study of the MIT automobile project "The Machine that Changed the World" reflects this new situation. Our study makes it clear, however, that the established Western manufacturers did not first start to change their traditional concepts for work organization with the discovery of the "lean production system" as the "best practice model." The strategies and concepts we describe still reflect a wide spectrum of nationally and company specific approaches. We show the inertia of outdated structures and mentalities and the difficulties connected with change in existing factories, and thus refer to the preconditions for implementing new forms of work and human resources in general.

With our study we were not attempting to provide recipes for best practice models. Our goal was to present a critical analysis and comparative description of the driving forces, models and forms exhibited by a process of change which obviously affects the central dimensions of work, not only in the automobile industry.

This English version is based on the German version of 1989 which was thoroughly revised and partially updated. This revision was done by Ulrich Jürgens who thus bears the sole responsibility for all deviations from the German text. The English translation was done with great competence and commitment by Jeffrey Butler, an American sociologist and translator residing in Berlin. As the son of a retired automobile worker from Flint, Michigan U.S.A., he also had a special interest in and an affinity for the subject matter of our study.

After all of this is done, we would like to offer our sincerest thanks to all who have contributed to our project with their advice, assistance, and tolerance. But we only can name here a few persons: many thanks to Alan Altshuler and Dan Roos from MIT for the support and the advice they gave us; at the Wissenschaftszentrum Berlin für Sozialforschung, our home base, there are Frieder Naschold, Christian Rabe, Alfred Gutzler, and our secretary Heidi Wintzer who deserve our special thanks. We are deeply saddened by the death of Heidi. Last but not least we want to thank all interviewees in the countries and companies involved in our survey for their warm welcome and the access to information which they kindly granted our project.

Berlin, January 1992

ULRICH JÜRGENS
THOMAS MALSCH
KNUTH DOHSE

Abbreviations

ACTSS	Association of Clerical, Technical, and Supervisory Staffs
AGV	Automated Guided Vehicles
AI	Automotive Industries
AN	Automotive News
ASTMS	Association of Supervisory Technical and Managerial Staffs
AUEW	Amalgamated Union of Engineering Workers
BL	British Leyland
BDE	Betriebsdatenerfassungssystem
BV	Betriebsvereinbarung
CAD	Computer Aided Design
CAM	Computer Aided Manufacturing
CAQ	Computer Aided Quality Control
CIM	Computer Integrated Manufacturing
CKD	Completely Knocked Down Kit
CNC	Computerized Numerical Control
CPRS	Central Policy Review Staff
CQS	Computergestützte Qualitätssteuerung
EETPU	Electrical, Electronic Telecommunication and Plumbing Union
EI	Employee Involvement
EIT	Employee in Training
EITB	Engineering Industry Training Board
EMUG	European Map User Group
EPG	Employee Participation Group
FT	Financial Times
FEBES	integriertes Fertigungsdispositions- und Beschaffungssystem
GM	General Motors
GMAD	General Motors Assembly Division
HB	Handelsblatt
HdA	Humanisierung der Arbeit
IE	Industrial Engineering

IMVP	International Motor Vehicle Program
ILO	International Labour Organization
IMB	Internationaler Metallgewerkschaftsbund
IMF	International Monetary Fund
IPA	Institut für Produktionsautomation (Fraunhofer Gesellschaft)
IuK	Informations- und Kommunikationstechnologien
JAMA	Japan Automobile Manufacturers Association
JIT	Just in Time
JMA	Japan Management Association
MDW	Measured Day Work
MIT	Massachussetts Institute of Technology
MTM	Methods Time Measurement
MVMA	Motor Vehicle Manufacturers Association of the United States, Inc.
NW&M	New Work & Motivation Concepts
OD;OE	Organizational Development, Organisationsentwicklung
OECD	Organization for Economic Cooperation and Development
OSI	Open Systems Interconnection
PPS	Produktionsplanungs- und Steuerungssystem
PVS	Plant Vehicle Scheduling
QDC	Quick Die Change
QUP	Quality Upgrade Program
QWL	"Quality of Work Life"
SMMT	Society of Motor Manufacturers and Traders Limited
SOFI	Soziologisches Forschungsinstitut (Göttingen)
SPC	Statistical Process Control
SPS	Speicherprogrammierbare Steuerung
SYPRO	Systematik der Wirtschafszweige, Fassung für die Statistik im produzierten Gewerbe
TASS	Technical and Supervisory Section der AUEW
TGWU	Transport and General Workers' Union
UAW	United Automobile, Aerospace, and Agricultural Implement Workers of America
VDA	Verband der Automobilindustrie e.V.
WEMR	Welding Equipment Maintenance and Repair
VW	Volkswagen
WF	Work Factor
WZB	Wissenschaftszentrum Berlin für Sozialforschung

1   The restructuring of the world automobile industry: opportunities for new forms of work

1.1 The problem posed and the starting situation in the industry

At the beginning of the 1980s, the automobile industries of Western Europe and the U.S.A. appeared to be following a crisis scenario which was familiar from the steel and shipbuilding industries and had almost become routine: increasing surplus capacity, factory closings, threatening bankruptcies, increasing government subsidies. After the steel industry and the shipyards, the automobile industry appeared to be next in line. The cases of British Leyland in Great Britain and Chrysler in the U.S.A. followed the patterns familiar in other declining industries. It was predicted that the number of independent car companies in the West would shrink from about thirty at the end of the 1970s down to seven or five by the end of the 1980s. One manifestation and a central cause of the plight was the unstoppable loss of market and production shares to Japan.

The prospects for the workers in the automobile industry were bleak: wide-scale reduction in jobs and deteriorating working conditions appeared to be unavoidable. Union demands and reform ideas of the early 1970s, aimed at improving working conditions and introducing new forms of work organization and labor relations, appeared obsolete in view of the changed economic situation. In this situation they appeared unrealistic and no longer achievable. At the same time, the crisis of the industry threatened to become a crisis for the union representation. The time had now come for the employers to win back lost ground in the area of labor policy.

Much was at stake in the decisions coming up. It was clear that more was involved than dealing with temporary economic difficulties. For the participants it was a question of fundamental, strategic reorientation. It was a question of survival and the ability of organizational systems to adjust. But these decisions also concerned the future of an industry crucial to many Western industrial countries. And still more was at stake: the automobile industry and its large companies had, in many respects, shaped

1

central societal institutions and forms of regulation in the Western industrialized countries. The institutions, rationalization strategies, customs, and practices developed in the automobile industry had always had a paradigmatic importance far beyond this one industry. This was and is true for the systems of industrial relations, for vocational training, and labor market management, also for the patterns of technological development, and work organization.

After having proved itself for decades, the historical mode of labor regulation, characterized by "Taylorism" and "Fordism," appeared fundamentally threatened at its core, the automobile industry. Taylorist rationalization, with its strict separation of planning and carrying out work and its extreme division of labor, brought to its culmination with the "Fordist" assembly line, appeared to have reached its limits; the conflicts – between the planning and execution of tasks, between management and workers – had increasingly proved to be counterproductive; the motivational deficits of the dequalified mass worker had caused an explosion in the costs of control and quality; the production structures aligned to a standardized mass product could no longer meet the requirements of the market; and the hierarchical management organization proved to be a massive hindrance to innovation, given the immense challenges. In a word, the Taylorist–Fordist production model was confronted by a deep-reaching destabilization. The automobile industry, up until then a model of a mature industry, had entered a period of "dematurization" (Abernathy 1978).

What were the stimuli which shocked the Western automobile industry out of its "sleep of prosperity" and forced it to seek new strategies and concepts? Many motivations came from external developments: criticism of the automobile and its societal consequences coming from the environmental and consumers' movements, the energy crisis, governmental regulations, and increasing Japanese competition. But it was not only external compulsions which forced the industry to adapt. The internal innovation within the automobile companies had grown considerably in the course of the 1970s. Above all the enormously expanded potential of microelectronics, had opened up new possibilities for differentiating and developing the products offered, for redesigning the production process and making it more flexible, and for consolidating the planning and control capacities of management. The reorganization of inter-company relations and coordination of external suppliers and customers also received a significant impetus from the development of computerized information and communication technologies.

But it was not only new technologies which opened up new dimensions. Added to this were the insights gained from Japan. These were obtained by the Western companies through a hurried study of the causes of the Japanese competitive superiority. The most important result was the insight that technical factors played a secondary role for the Japanese superiority. Factors like personnel management, industrial relations, work organization, and labor deployment were much more important causes. The results of the Japan discussion strengthened the position of those management representatives in the Western companies who were urging that companies develop new forms of labor relations and new methods for dealing with human resources. At the same time the management position was strengthened which held that the Western manufacturers should bring to bear precisely that traditional strength in the area of technological know-how in order to successfully counteract Japanese superiority in other areas, because they were not going to be able to compete with Japan in the area of "people management" anyway.

Management's scope for action also increased with regard to matters concerning labor and industrial relations. The end of the 1970s brought a clear power shift in favor of management which regained much of the "prerogative" to manage it had lost in the decades before. The developments in the labor market, governments' retreat from responsibility for industrial policy, and the indisputable necessity for measures for modernization and rationalization were all causes of this. Management did not let its strengthened position go to waste. Efficiency standards were tightened up again, and, at many sites, the factory management formulated comprehensive "shopping lists" for eliminating regulations and practices of labor deployment which had restricted productivity in the past. Wide ranging union concessions, as in the case of the bail-out of Chrysler in the U.S.A., or the crushing of union positions, as in the rehabilitation of British Leyland, showed clearly in which direction the new wind was blowing. The last big clash over control of the shop floor took place at Fiat in 1980. There was a thirty-five day strike, and finally a pro-company/anti-union demonstration by sections of the work force which marked an end to union "counterforce-policy," not only in Italy.

At the same time, management distinguished itself with reform ideas for labor policy which were amazingly similar to earlier union demands. Traditional models for regulating industrial work, which had previously been considered to be prototypes for automobile production, were now being questioned by management itself. Work reforms, as they were demanded by the unions in the 1970s from the point of view of humanization, were suddenly put on the agenda by management from the perspective of productivity. Management itself appeared to be setting out to tear down the bastions of Taylorist–Fordist production organization. Integrated job descriptions, employee participation offers, reduction of hierarchy, production teams, and wide-scale qualification programs belonged to the arsenal of these work reforms.

The idea of a "New Plant Revolution" (Lawler 1978) had already spread like wildfire in the second half of the 1970s. An assortment of ideas on questions of work motivation, socio-technical system designs for work, and industrial democracy, developed over decades now came to fruition and were brought into textbooks for personnel policy (Milkovich and Glueck 1985) and industrial engineering (Barnes 1980). Titles like "Improving Productivity and the Quality of Worklife" (Cummings and Molloy 1977), "Productivity Gains through Worklife Improvements" (Glaser 1976), and "High Involvement Management" (Lawler III 1986) point in the same direction. In these works it appeared to be a sure thing that a change in the tide in the sense of people-based production concepts had been inaugurated. But couldn't it be that these titles were only an expression of another "fad" in management discussion without having changed the reality of managing a factory and everyday work? Our questions in this book are aimed at the level below the proclamations and promises of new forms of work. We are asking what has really changed in management practice in the areas where they are dealing with the hard reality: the questions of securing efficiency, ensuring quality, and dealing with technology-related demands. Our question is: what is moving management, which gained power and effectivity in the 1980s, to take it upon itself to dismantle traditional forms of control and to demand and support self-regulation and the initiative of the workers. Can such a change in control forms be determined at all in reality in the factory and what are its national and company specific forms and expressions?

1.2 The end of "Modern Times" in the factory?

The criticism of Fordist/Taylorist concepts of work regulation has a long tradition. Protest and criticism had already reached their classic form in Charlie Chaplin's film "Modern Times" which was the inspiration for the title of this section. Countless scientific studies and socially critical discourses dealt with the negative effects of automobile work on the workers: highly repetitive work tasks tied to the speed of the assembly line, physically highly strenuous, but intellectually stupefying for the workers, stifling any initiative and sense of responsibility at the level where work is carried out (Friedman 1964; Widick 1976). In the middle of the 1960s Goldthorpe determined that: "The auto industry is the locus classicus of dissatisfying work; the assembly line its quintessential embodiment" (Goldthorpe 1966, p. 235).

The advantages of Taylorist–Fordist control were also questionable for

Table 1.1 *The Taylorist–Fordist regulatory mode and functional alternatives*

Characteristics of the Taylorist–Fordist regulatory mode	Functional alternatives
Standard product	Product variety
Assembly line	Module production/production islands
Single-purpose mechanization	Flexible mechanization
Unqualified mass worker	Qualified (skilled) worker
Low work motivation (indifference)	High work motivation (identification)
Conflictual labor relations	Cooperative labor relations
Hierarchical management	Participatory management
Vertical division of labor	Vertical job integration
Horizontal division of labor	Horizontal job integration
Workers tied to specific jobs	Job rotation
Machine/assembly line determined work pace	Work pace independent from production cycle
Individual work	Group work
External control of time and motion	Self-control of time and motion

management (see table 1.1). The process yield in utilizing the human and material resources seemed to be much lower than that which was possible. The concept of "X-inefficiency" was coined by Leibenstein in this regard for describing the phenomenon of many strange, little understood causes for inefficiencies in traditionally organized Western mass production factories. (Leibenstein 1987). These inefficiencies were neglected for a long time. The poor quality of worklife and high control costs were treated as inevitable disadvantages of mass production. The study of Japanese practice showed, however, that these disadvantages were definitely avoidable. The "X-inefficiencies" became a real burden in the competition and were by the end no longer a mere problem of theoretical and philanthropic interest.

The old factory regime does not have any open supporters in higher management today. This does not mean that the lower and middle management in the factories themselves do not still practice this system. Declaring a plant to be a team plant does not mean much – there were many merely superficial changes in the 1980s. The omnipresent critique of Taylorism and Fordism has also led increasingly to confusion regarding the basic features of this regime. So what were the basic elements which would have to be removed in order to achieve a new regime? They are, in our opinion, the following two fundamental principles:

1 The separation of planning and control from work execution is constitutive for Taylorism. This implies that the work carried out in mass production is emptied of functions requiring intelligence and degenerates to repetitive partial tasks with minimal qualifications required. Another result of this separation is that various groups of experts outside of production emerge to design technology and jobs for the areas of direct production, set standards for them, and see that they are held to.

2 The principle of standardization is constitutive of Fordism. This implies a standard product, a standardized production process, and the standardization of human labor. The constantly but inexorably moving assembly line is in fact, as Goldthorpe observed "its quintessential embodiment." The production cycle, dictated by the speed of the assembly line, becomes the basis for the regulation of work and performance.

Fordism is more than a production concept, though. Its productivity advantages allowed the companies to pay high wages. Specific forms of social integration and social conflicts emerged. Fordism developed into a system for societal regulation. In the following, however, we will be limiting our account to its character as a production concept.

Although they have a different basis both elements of work regulation grew together in Western factories to the extent that one can speak of a unified form and a specific mode of control over the labor process. In the table 1.1 we have listed what we consider to be the central elements of the Taylorist–Fordist mode of regulation and have paired each of them with functional alternatives which are currently gaining ground in labor deployment and job design practice.

In view of the differing national- and industry-specific developmental paths, one can argue over the coherence and the necessary systemic interdependence of the above-listed characteristics of Taylorism–Fordism. (see Tolliday and Zeitlin 1986 for the automobile industry). But in general it is justified to regard it as the "ideal type" for the regulation of work in Western factories in the 1970s. More difficult to answer is the question of whether the above functional alternatives can be considered as elements of a coherent emerging "post-Taylorist/post-Fordist" type of work regulation. Do the companies have a comprehensive concept in their restructuring measures with regard to the interaction of production and work organization for the future? Are they rather realizing partial solutions in the framework of a search process without clear goals? Are there national- and company-specific approaches and solutions or do the work organizational solutions converge in a "one best way"?

Against the background of this definition of terms we want to formulate our interests in this book. Our questions are thus:

1 What signs can be seen of a turn away from the traditional Taylorist–Fordist paradigm for regulation of work?
2 What are the differences in this respect between different countries, companies, and factories? What conditions support or hinder the establishment of new forms for work regulation?
3 Are there nationally specific approaches toward a new non-Taylorist and non-Fordist work regulation?

1.3 Design of the study

This study is the result of investigations which we carried out from 1982 to 1986. This research was part of MIT's first project dealing with "The Future of the Automobile" (1980–4; cf. Altshuler *et al.* 1984).

Our project[1] was concerned with the effects on workers of the restructuring of the world automobile industry in the 1980s. In view of the decline in demand at the beginning of the 1980s and the enormous rationalization efforts, this question appeared to us at that time to be equivalent to the question of job losses and the deterioration in working conditions in this industry. We did also find, however, three positive implications of the restructuring from the point of view of the workers and the unions:

1 The enormous investment thrust opened up scope for designing new forms of work organization and labor deployment which had previously been obstructed by "hardware restrictions."
2 The analysis of the Japanese competitive advantages revealed countless impulses for a rethinking of the previous Taylorist–Fordist "production philosophy" in Western companies.
3 Not only new design potentials emerged from the technological development in the 1970s, but new concepts were also developed in the course of programs for "Organizational Development" (OD), *"Humanisierung der Arbeit" (HdA)*, "Employee Involvement," and "Quality of Work-life" (QWL).

This raised the following questions: How are degrees of freedom in the determination of new structures being used? To what extent are the critiques of the Taylorist–Fordist production regime and the reform concepts which emerged in the 1970s being dealt with?

In view of the changed competitive constellation and the market related strategies it became apparent that the companies' new objectives necessitated an adaptation in the forms of worker deployment. These objectives were:

the goal of increasing flexibility: the fluctuations in the composition of the production schedule and the frequency of model changes led to cumulating problems with efficiency and quality in production;

the goal of increasing the process yield in the mechanized areas: with the higher capital intensity of production, the costs of machine and installation breakdowns and the technically induced idle time gained importance compared to the classical questions of labor productivity;

the goal of increasing efficiency in the deployment of labor: in view of the enormous lead that the Japanese had in this respect and in view of the rationalization efforts being made by their Western competitors, no company could afford to ignore this competitive parameter.

With these prerequisites in mind we have concentrated on three "classical" fields of responsibility in the factory and the changes taking place there:

(a) labor efficiency and the regulation of performance,

(b) product quality and quality control, and

(c) machine utilization and maintenance.

The focus was thus on questions of production and, in particular, the interface between direct and indirect production tasks if we use the classical division of labor in all Western factories (not those of the Japanese). This concerned both the relations between direct production work and the work of quality inspectors and maintenance personnel, as classical indirect blue-collar jobs, and the relations between direct production work and indirect white-collar work, like that of the industrial engineers and production planners.

Our factory interviews typically included interviews with the following experts:

managers in charge of personnel, industrial relations, employee relations, etc.;

the coordinator for "new forms of work and motivation" activities;

managers in charge of training programs in the factory;

maintenance managers;

managers in charge of production planning/process engineering;

managers of industrial engineering and engineers responsible for the body shop and trim and final assembly;

managers from quality control or quality assurance;

engineers responsible for quality and information systems;

quality engineers responsible for the assembly and body plants;

body plant managers;

managers of the assembly areas;

the plant manager;

union and works council representatives (on the average two works council members, shop stewards/committee men).[2]

In many cases experts on special questions or work areas were consulted on an individual basis (department heads, foremen, etc.). Interviews with production workers took place, but on a case-by-case basis. Our decision not to systematically carry out interviews at the worker level needs an explanation as, after all, our interest is directed at the "challenges and opportunities" of restructuring for the employees. There are three reasons for this decision: first, only a few plants were willing to give us "productive time" for the interviews, like taking workers off the line for a while so that we could interview them; second, the problem of representativeness is posed even more emphatically here than at the expert level. We could not even consider a complete survey, and in the worker interviews we carried out we did not feel competent to judge whether we were dealing with typical or atypical perceptions and interpretations. The simple fact that we carried out the majority of our factory investigations during the day and had contrasting experiences from the few night-shift interviews we carried out led us to be careful in this respect. Third, our questions were not actually aimed at the perception and interpretation of the changes by those affected on the shop floor. These perceptions would not have been very meaningful in many cases as the workers did not have much experience with the new forms of production, the introduction of which was often still to come, and workers' assessments would have come more from rumor than from actual experience.

With regard to the selection of plants for investigation, it was clear that the main focus should be at the production level. The obvious differences which exist in the company-, country- and factory-specific setting, however, led us to expect that significant differences between the units studied would exist, particularly as regards the emphases, concepts, and priorities of their respective programs. We examined the most significant influences: (a) company ties, and (b) their national settings. With company ties, we are more likely to be looking at the element of organizational strategy[3] – the programs, objectives, and methods decided at the company headquarters. The factor of national setting, on the other hand, deals with the institutional prerequisites, like the nationally specific systems of industrial relations, the institutions for regulating the labor market, and vocational training. If we look at the situation in an individual factory it is clear that company and national affiliation overlap as influences. The comparison of factories of differing companies in the same country allows us to examine the influence of company ties, and the comparison of factories of the same company in different countries allows us to examine the influence of national setting.

With the help of this "multilevel approach" we thus attempted to systematically detect variation in the forms of labor deployment
   between different companies,
   between different countries,
   between factories of one company in the same country.

We made the factory selection on the basis of our available information from the standpoint of their being as comparable as possible: in their product (the new type of lower- and middle-class autos, that is with front-wheel drive) and in the degree of modernization of production (larger technical and organizational changes within the period studied). In this manner we attempted to control for the influences of product type and production technology as much as possible so that we could isolate the differences in the comparison which arose from work organization and labor relations. This corresponds to the principles of "most similar design" (see Przeworski and Teune 1970) and of the comparison of "matched" pairs.[4]

The units studied were seventeen assembly plants from three automobile companies in the three countries U.S.A., Great Britain, and the Federal Republic of Germany. We promised the company management that we would keep the factories anonymous and have thus assigned fictitious names to the factories we investigated.

Table 1.2 shows the assignment of the seventeen factories studied to the three countries and the three companies. The selection of the factories proceeded in three steps. In the first selection step we had to decide which automobile companies would be best suited for our questions. In accordance with our question, we focussed directly on the mass manufacturers who have their headquarters in one of our sample countries and have production sites in several countries. The selection thus came down to the type of companies who were most directly confronted by Japanese competition in the 1980s.

The second selection step dealt with the countries to be investigated. In the course of this, the choice boiled down to the three countries: the U.S.A., Great Britain, and the Federal Republic of Germany. This is because these three countries were the only places in which it was possible to connect the company level with the country level in such a manner that at least two of the companies studied would be represented by their own production plants in all three national settings.

The seventeen plants were assembly plants. The selection criterion "assembly plant" resulted from our goal of going into those areas of automobile manufacturing considered to be strongholds of Taylorist–Fordist forms of worker deployment and conflicting labor relations. If substantial changes could be shown in these areas, it would be a stronger

Table 1.2 *The factories studied and their assignment to companies and countries*

Countries	U.S.A./Canada	Great Britain	Federal Republic of Germany
Company A	River City Maple City Motor City	Hartmoor Blackmoor	Weinkirchen Altstadt
Company B	Greentown Indiantown Northtown Steeltown Red Plains	Seaborough Carborough	Mittelort
Company C			Windeck Heidedorf
Totals	8	4	5

indication that a far-reaching restructuring process was taking place. It would be much simpler to introduce such restructuring in plants which produce parts and components, as shown by the multitude of such experiments which had already been carried out in the 1970s (cf. Zager and Rosow 1982). To round off our study we also carried out investigations in assembly plants of other companies and in various stamping and engine plants.

In the following our account concentrates primarily on a sample of seven factories. The selection of this core sample was oriented on the following criteria: first, the factories assembled car models which were mass produced for the lower market segments. We were dealing with front-wheel drive vehicles for the middle class by European standards, or what Americans understand as "compact cars." Second, we have limited the selection to production sites with a minimal depth of production, and did not consider exceptionally large production complexes (like Fiat's Turin complex or Ford's River Rouge plants) for the core sample. Third, the core sample was to be as homogeneous as possible with regard to the line of products. Fourth, we wanted to look at reasonably established structures, that means that large change-overs (model change, large investments) should have taken place some time ago (one year or longer). Table 1.3 with the factory profile of the core sample makes it clear that we could at least partially attain the homogeneity which we sought after with regard to product and production depth. As a matter of fact, three plants from Company A and

Table 1.3 *Factory profile of the core sample*

	B.U.S. Greentown 1983	A.U.S. River City 1981	B.G.B. Seaborough 1985	A.G.B. Hartmoor 1985	B.F.R.G. Mittelort 1985	A.F.R.G. Weinkirchen 1985	C.F.R.G. Windeck 1985
Year of model start	1981	1981	1984	1981	1984	1980	1980
Number of vehicle types (platform/base model)	1	1	1	1	1	1	1[a]
Vertical integration[b]	3	3	3	4	7	4	3
Capacity (units/hr)	85	75	35	72	75	100	54
Hourly output (units/hr)	70	66	21[c]	46	73	93	42
Number of robots[d]	23	15	30	70	170	100	40
	4–6	2–4	4–6	6–8	10+	6–8	8–10
Number of blue-collar employees[e]	4,000–6,000	2,000–4,000	4,000–6,000	6,000–8,000	6,000–10,000	6,000–8,000	8,000–10,000

Notes:

[a] A second model line was produced here until 1985.

[b] On the basis of the following cumulative scale: assembly plants with the plant sections body shop, paint shop, trim and final assembly: 3; also including stamping plant: 4; including engine plant: 5; including parts production (transmissions, axles, etc.): 6; including considerable component parts for other assembly plants (CKD-sets, etc.): 7.

[c] Necessitated by model start.   [d] Rounded off.   [e] In order to keep anonymity only the range is given.

1 The time of the model start is very important for investigations like ours. Although the transition to a new model always means a quantum leap, not only as regards production technology, but also as regard work organization and personnel allocation, the situation generally remains the same afterwards until the next model change. Changes take place more slowly and are marginal in nature. In this phase, the fundamental course of factory operations is fixed.

The change-overs bring the great thrusts of change in the factories. In such plants, conditions are still strongly characterized by the difficulties of the model start for anywhere from six months to one year afterwards. Only a limited comparison can be made with factories where production has just been "broken in." The same is also true for plants in the last months before such a fundamental change-over. Two of the plants studied were still in the phase of the model start at the time of our study – but, because of this, they also gave us the chance to look more closely at some of the problems connected with this period.

This disjointed development mitigated some of the practical investigatory problems of our study. For a number of reasons there was a considerable time lag between the investigations in the U.S. factories and those in the European plants (November 1982/May–June 1983 in the U.S.A.; March 1984/May 1985–January 1986 in Europe). This severely limited the comparability between plants in which model changes took place during this period of time. As one can see in the table, this was the case in three of the plants, which could, however, still be compared in the European context.

2 With regard to the number of "vehicle types" produced in each of the plants, it can be seen that all of the plants only produce one type. We are proceeding here from a distinction between type, model, and options. The same vehicle type (GM's J-car for example) is produced in different models (thus in the U.S.A. as Chevrolet Cavalier, Pontiac 2000, Oldsmobile Firenza, Buick Skyhawk, and Cadillac Cimarron). The option variants are finally the two- or four-door models and the different choices with regard to interiors, engine/ transmission combination, etc.

3 The "number of robots" represents an indicator of the degree of modernization of the production technology – at least in the body area of the respective plants where these robots are concentrated. In the majority of the plants, above all in the U.S. plants, flexible technology had only been introduced to a fairly limited degree at the time of our investigation.

4 The figures for "vertical integration" are based on calculations we made on the basis of our factory investigations. In each case, our studies themselves were concentrated on the body shop and trim and final assembly. The differing degrees of vertical integration of production at different sites naturally has a significant influence on the comparability of the factories. In addition, it was often not possible to make a clear division according to production areas. This problem arose above all with salaried employees and frequently with indirect labor.

We made estimates of the degree of vertical integration on the basis of a scale basically following Abernathy (1978). According to this scale, the "classic" assembly plant, which is the norm for U.S. plants and frequently characterizes "satellite plants" in Europe, has a vertical integration degree of 3. If the factory includes a press works, we give it a value of 4. If major parts production, such as engine production, is included, the value goes up by one again, or, with several parts plants by 2. Locations with several parts plants and with CKD-production have a vertical integration of 7. Factories with the highest vertical integration would be those which include the company's central departments (development departments, etc.).

5 The capacity figures are based on the hourly output which corresponds to the production lay-out of the plants. The figures for the "output per hour" are based on actual average results calculated on the basis of yearly averages. They thus record the actual yearly average capacity usage.

Table 1.4 *Share of female workers on the blue-collar work force in the factories in the core sample (in %)*

Plant	B U.S. Greentown	A U.S. River City	B G.B. Seaborough	A G.B. Hartmoor	B F.R.G. Mittelort	A F.R.G. Weinkirchen	C F.R.G. Windeck
Number of women in production	about 20	about 10	5	172	534	978	668
(%)	0.4	0.3	0.2	2.3	3.3	14.0	8.0

two plants from Company B are parallel plants where, in fact, the same car model is produced. There are, on the other hand, considerable differences between the plants in the level of mechanization (number of robots) and the size of the work forces at the sites. The differences in the number of employees can be explained primarily by the differing degrees of vertical integration.

We would like to make a brief remark as to the gender composition of the work forces. This was not an explicit topic for us. But if we occasionally limit ourselves to the sexist "he" in the following presentation, it has its justification in view of the minimal number of women among the blue collar workers. The share of women was especially small in the British and U.S. plants. This point is clear from table 1.4.

In conclusion we would like to present our explanatory model which describes how we approached our investigation and also helped to determine the structure of the following study. Figure 1.1 shows this model, with the differences in labor deployment at the factory level as the phenomena to be explained, and the explanatory factors which shape and change the forms of labor deployment at different levels. These are first of all the developments in the markets and technology. At the beginning of the 1980s, "learning from Japan" arrives as a separate influence for the automobile industry.

"Markets," "Technology," and "Japan" characterize the starting positions which opened up new options for the company headquarters and, at the same time, compelled them to introduce measures of adjustment. The resultant company strategies influence the factory strategies. Added to this are further factors which independently "filter" these strategies or influence factory strategies: national regulatory systems, the state and the structures of the labor market, the educational system, and finally union policies and the pattern of worker-interest representation in the factory. The combination of these factors shapes labor relations and the forms of deployment of labor in the factory. Changes in the forms and practices of work in the

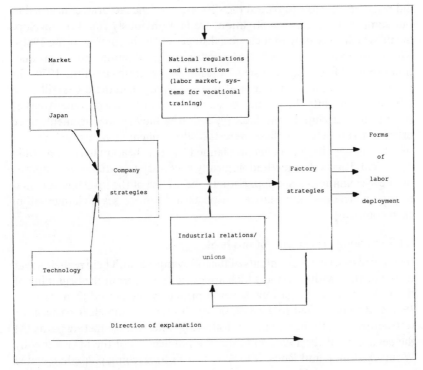

Figure 1.1 Explanatory model

factory have repercussions for the labor market, educational system, and industrial relations which are mediated by the respective factory strategies. The factory strategy is the level at which measures for reorganization and rationalization are planned and carried out. Repercussions for the larger company strategy ensue from the success or failure of these factory measures.

The selection of the factory sample and design of our undertaking were, as we have shown above, strictly geared to a systematic comparison between factories of differing national and company affiliations. In this we proceeded from the assumption that new solutions for problems of labor deployment would already be visible in these modern plants. The new concepts had, in fact, not established themselves in the factories to the extent that we had expected; the change was often still to come or it took place during our investigatory phase. Thus the interviews frequently took place in the shadow of forthcoming measures or at the start of projects for changing the previous practice, without, of course, the interviewees being able to say anything about how they would function. At the same time, it did not seem sensible to record the status quo of the factories concerned in our sample. With our investigation, we had obviously run into developments which were only in their initial stages at the beginning of the 1980s. The decisions about the technical structures of production and the production program had long been set as a result of the strategies of the 1970s. In the question of concrete programs for labor deployment there was still quite a bit of uncertainty. Programs for action were introduced in many cases, but the participants in the factory, even the factory management, were often not sure whether these were transitory phenomena or fashionable trends and whether the goals proclaimed by their headquarters were only rhetorical. It was thus methodologically necessary to reduce our emphasis on the systematic cross-comparison in the course of the investigation, and to give an increased importance to aspects of the processes of change within each company.

1.4 Regarding the contents of this book

If we try to describe the contents of the following we can't help realizing that we are dealing with a period which appeared to be over at the beginning of the 1990s. Our investigations covered primarily the period from 1983 to 1986 and thus applied to a phase in which there was no clear pattern for restructuring, with the companies following different, competing paths. At the beginning of the 1990s and after the publication of the MIT study by Womack, Jones, and Roos, it looked as if this searching phase had ended and a new model had established itself, which the authors call "lean production." The concept of "revolution," which we already saw in discussion at the end of the 1970s, is being used liberally again, but this time we are dealing with a clear, goal-oriented revolution even though the authors admit that it is only beginning. "Yet in the end," they conclude, "we believe, lean production will supplant both mass production and the remaining outposts of craft production in all areas of industrial endeavor to become the standard global production system of the twenty-first century" (Womack, Jones, and Roos 1990, p. 278).

There are many signs at the beginning of the 1990s for a convergence of the company- and country-specific production concepts. In our investigation, the strategy in the spirit of lean production which we call the "after Japan strategy" proved to be by far the most successful in terms of productivity. Our investigation thus describes a process of radical change which was still more in the phase of shaking off an old model than in the strengthening of a new one. On the other hand, on the basis of our investigations we are skeptical of the pronouncement of revolutionary production concepts. Added to this comes the fact that the MIT authors did not give a precise determination of the necessary and sufficient elements of lean production and lean management. In their attempts at realizing this concept the companies see themselves left on their own and it frequently comes to old wine being poured into new bottles. These are observations for Germany in the years 1990/1. In addition, they are faced with the problem of pushing through and modifying the lean concepts in light of nationally and site-specific requirements. Here we believe that the problems of implementing the new production concepts in the different environments we are describing in this study have by no means been overcome.

The leopard cannot change its spots. This is also our principle in the following account. Although development in the industry has proceeded further in many respects since we concluded our investigations, and also since the publication of the German edition of this book, we primarily remain in the developmental phase in which we carried out our investigations. The focus of the account is on describing problem configurations, the processes for introducing new concepts, conflicts over concepts. The book thus reflects the openness and uncertainty in the further development of the process and the clashes over concepts as we found them.

Now to the contents in detail: we begin in the second chapter with the differing patterns of development of the national automobile industries in the countries we compared and – as their most important challenger – Japan. We go back to the 1970s as the expectations, the interpretations of the situation, and the willingness to change of the actors we interviewed in the 1980s were shaped in these years. We combine our account of the Japanese development with the reasons for the Japanese productivity success which can be found in work and social organization. Here we speak of "Toyotism" and its prerequisites. Our investigation did not include any toyotistically organized factories, but the learning from Japan was often the force behind the measures of the companies and factories as we will describe.

In chapter 3 we deal with the strategies of the companies as they were conceived in the 1970s and took effect in the 1980s so as to do justice to the changed sales conditions and competitive relations on the world market. Here we discuss (a) the world car strategy with its implications for site structures and the conditions for realizing central control concepts; (b) the strategy for upgrading the product and its implications for the production sphere and for industrial relations; (3) the technology-oriented strategy for the mechanization and automation of process sequences, and, finally, (d) the people-oriented strategy for tapping new resources in the work force. Our account of these strategies, using examples from different companies on the basis of published material, shows considerable variance between the different companies in prioritizing the strategies as well as in their interpretation of the strategies themselves – variances which can also be found when comparing the companies we studied.

Chapter 4 deals with the role of industrial relations in choosing the concepts for restructuring as well as the changes which industrial relations themselves experience in the course of these restructurings. In the preceding chapter we were primarily dealing with company strategies, here we are looking more at nationally specific characteristics which emerged from the specific history of the union movement and the national labor policy in each case. Corresponding with our focus on the area of direct production, the structures, arrangements, and practices of industrial relations on plant level will be our center of attention here. Here we meet with very different traditions in the countries of our study which, as we will show, more or less correspond to or contradict with the objectives of the new forms of work. For each of the countries we will describe crucial events of the recent past which shaped the way management and especially union representatives in the factories interpreted the situation and which were frequently referred to as experiences in our interviews.

The following two chapters deal with changes in the structuring of work on the shop floor in the division of labor between direct and indirect task areas. Chapter 5 deals with quality control and chapter 6 with the monitoring and maintenance of process technology. Chapter 5 thus begins the report of our empirical findings in the assembly plants we studied.

Chapter 5 centers around three questions: the first concerns the achievement of the goal of increased quality of production in factories with differing company and national affiliations. We see the great influence of the different systems of industrial relations as an especially influential factor here. The second question concerns the emergence of new job descriptions in the course of the growing importance of assuring product quality in the work process against the background of the traditional pattern of the division of labor in the factories. The third question, finally, concerns a choice of directions which the companies are facing with regard to the deployment of computers as opposed to people-oriented strategies.

The modernization of production means naturally also the deployment of new technologies and process automation. In the 1980s this chiefly meant the automation of body-shop operations. Our topic in chapter 6 is the approaches with regard to work organization and labor deployment which were developed in this context in our factories. They apply for one to the work in maintenance, thus to the group of qualified skilled workers. This group is considered to be very capable of pushing through their interests in labor policy in the factory, and thus job demarcation between the "crafts" was considered to be a central problem at many production sites.

In the first section we will be looking more closely at this problem and its significance as a hindrance to the proper adjustment of the management organization to the new technologies. In section 2 we will be dealing with the emergence of different approaches to work organization in the automation areas in the body shops of the assembly plants of our sample. Most of these body shops had been recently automated at the time of our research. The focus here is on the new job descriptions at the interface between production and maintenance tasks. Here we are especially interested in determining the extent to which the new job descriptions represent a tendency toward a reskilling of production jobs in the sense of classical factory work, as the optimistic scenarios expect, or rather a strengthening of polarization tendencies within the production work force.

After we have dealt with the management functions of quality control and maintenance in chapters 5 and 6 we will focus on the function of securing efficiency in chapter 7 and this applies above all to the jobs of the direct production workers. No job is more characteristic for Taylorism–Fordism than that of the industrial engineer, whose job is to prescribe in detail the times and motions which the workers should use when performing their work. We want to determine the extent to which this function is disappearing or changing in the course of more recent developments. Our question is this: if, in view of increased competition from Japan on the world market, labor and cost efficiency in production is a central priority of the companies, why should they weaken the position of their proven rationalization experts and, instead, increase the responsibility and competence of the workers on the shop floor? We will be dealing with problems in connection with the flexibility of production and process mechanization as the most important driving forces for such a change. But it is not only management problems, which are favoring the change in the function of industrial engineering, but also the new possibilities for management control which explain this process. We will show this in our description of benchmarking methods and their increasing importance in the 1980s.

In chapter 8 we will be dealing with the quantitative aspects of development in our sample of assembly plants. At the center there is, first of all, labor productivity. We see great differences in the level and development of productivity in our sample, where the latter can be primarily explained by the differing company strategies for production modernization.

Chapters 9 and 10 will be picking up again two central aspects which clearly attain a greater importance with regard to "modern times": first, the development of human resources and, second, the role of the assembly line and the cycle time, and thus the aspect of technology design, as the basis for new forms of work. The effect of nationally specific influences becomes apparent in both cases: the systems for apprenticeship training and the systems of industrial relations. These have an effect both on the priorities with regard to new forms of work and on technology design.

The focal point of the closing chapter (11) is the question of nationally and company specific influences on the forms of production modernization we observed in the factory sample. In closing, we assess development after the completion of our investigation and attempt to give an outlook for the 1990s. Our question: what will come after the Taylorist–Fordist regime?

2 Changing markets and the rise of Toyotism: the development of the national car industries since the 1970s

The 1970s were a decade of radical change for the automobile industry. The changes at the factory level which we will be investigating in the following chapters were considered and initiated in this period. The differing courses of development in the national automobile industries and the consequences for the working conditions and personnel policies connected with them formed the basis of experience for management, the unions, and the work forces in the companies and factories we studied, and shaped their perceptions of the situation, their expectations, and their willingness to accept change with regard to the established forms for regulating work.

In this chapter we will first depict the most important events of the 1970s which set off the changes. After that we will describe the different trends in production and employment experienced by the national automobile industries in the countries we studied, that is, in the U.S.A., Great Britain, and West Germany. The courses of development proved to be extremely diverse: hectic upward and downward trends in the U.S. automobile industry as well as a far-reaching crisis at the beginning of the 1980s, the dramatic decline of the British automobile industry until about the middle of the 1980s, and a relatively continuous upward trend in West Germany.

We are limiting our description of the courses of development to the period from the beginning of the 1970s until the middle of the 1980s corresponding to the period of our empirical factory case studies. We believe that the essential features of the patterns of development presented here are also valid for the interim period up until the beginning of the 1990s. In this period, however, the influence of the Japanese companies' new plants in the U.S. and Great Britain became increasingly apparent. We will only be touching on this tendency in the following account.

In the second part of the chapter we will be dealing with the rapid growth of the Japanese automobile industry. What are the reasons for the Japanese competitive strength and in what respect can the Western companies "learn from Japan"? To answer this question we will present our concept of

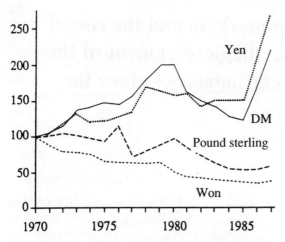

Figure 2.1 The exchange-rate development of selected currencies relative to the U.S. dollar, 1970–86
Source: IMF: International Financial Statistics

Toyotism. This contains, in our opinion, the most important dimensions necessary to explain the competitive strength of Japanese companies to the extent that they can be found in the production organization. At certain points in our account the concept of "Toyotism" will serve us as a point of reference or comparison for the factory practices we studied. We will not be dealing with the question of to what extent "Toyotism" can be an alternative model or the only possible "best practice" model until our final chapter.

2.1 Impulses for change in the 1970s

In the course of the 1970s, there were above all three "events" demanding strategic answers from the companies:

(1) The end of the system of Bretton Woods – set off by Nixon's decision to lift the gold backing of the dollar – initiated a period of often hectic movements of the exchange rates. Figure 2.1 shows the upward or downward movements of selected currencies respective to the U.S. dollar.

As the figure shows, there was hardly a year or even a month in which the relationship between the currencies of these countries did not change. There were longer-term trends of course, but even these were continually interrupted by contrary developments. In any case, increases or decreases in value of 50 percent and more in the relative position of the currency of a country cannot easily be handled, even by the most powerful exporting companies. If they reflect a long-term change, this would have serious effects on the relative advantages or disadvantages of sites in individual countries. But strategies for adjusting to expected long-term currency relations always have to take the uncertainty factor of medium-range developments into account. The greater variability and volatility of the exchange rates necessitated strategic considerations to give the product offering and multinational production structures a higher potential for flexibility. This would allow a switch to other markets or a redistribution of production programs between the company's plants in different countries if necessary.

(2) The energy crisis in 1973 and the shift in buyer behavior in favor of energy-saving vehicles led to a process of innovation in product technology going far beyond the scope of normal model cycles. This had especially far-reaching effects on the model offerings of U.S. companies. Instead of the roomy "gas guzzlers," the buyers now turned to gas-saving compact cars which nevertheless offered luxury features and security, cars that the Big Three did not have in their program. The vacuum created by this supply gap on the U.S. market helped the Japanese importers reach record growth rates. It also helped for instance Volkswagen, whose new model the Golf (or Rabbit) ideally met the changed demands of the market, to rapidly overcome the crisis in 1974 (Brumlop and Jürgens 1986; Streeck 1984). Under pressure from buyer behavior and government regulations, the Big Three had to begin a program of "down-sizing" which was not to have an effect on the market until the 1980s (Altshuler *et al.* 1984; Cray 1980).

The impetus in product technology, which allowed the new concept of front-wheel drive vehicles to achieve a breakthrough, was only the starting point for a phase of product innovation which is still going on and nowhere near its end. If one follows the argument of Abernathy (1978), then this wave of innovation has brought the automobile from the late phase of the product life-cycle back into the innovation phase and allows the automobile industry to become a field of innovation and growth again.

The transition to the new generation of front-wheel drive vehicles also initiated far-reaching changes in other stages of the production chain: the development of new engine types, new transmission types, new systems for axle and wheel suspension, etc. Innovation in product and process technology (deployment of robots, computer aided quality control, etc.) supplement and further stimulate each other.

All this required enormous capital investments in new products and processes. Table 2.1 shows the increase in capital investment for equipment and facilities per vehicle between 1976 and 1985. It must be taken into account that these investments were not only for automobile production.

Table 2.1 *Capital investments of selected manufacturers (in millions of the respective national currencies; adjusted for inflation at the 1980 level)*

	1976	1977	1978	1979	1980	1981	1982	1983	1984	1985
Volkswagen	275	488	921	1,036	1,573	1,284	1,562	1,310	1,065	1,153
Opel	362	502	871	1,064	1,411	1,005	877	809	814	1,321
Ford Germany	199	262	343	477	343	557	670	836	832	648
Ford U.K.	173	132	183	330	249	186	245	169	139	188
Vauxhall	67	20	54	41	22	11	10	15	32	53
GM	3,191	4,736	5,493	5,965	7,761	8,840	5,332	3,344	4,932	7,316
Ford U.S.	1,459	2,289	3,059	3,810	2,724	2,021	2,547	1,947	2,867	2,980

Source: Business reports of the corporations; FT from September 16, 1987; IMF, International Financial Statistics.

According to the companies' reports, however, the wave of modernization in the automobile sector did account for the lion's share of this increase. If the level of capital investments in the middle of the 1970s is compared with that in the middle of the 1980s, then a clearly different profile becomes visible: while the investments of the German companies have almost quadrupled on the average, there was hardly a change in the level of the British companies; the investment level of the U.S. companies was approximately doubled.

(3) The advance of the Japanese competition in the course of the 1970s, not only on the U.S. market but also in Europe and in the developing countries, made it increasingly clear to the traditional Western manufacturers that the changes taking place did not only involve crisis management and innovation in product technology. It was rather a large-scale struggle over redistributing their respective shares of the world market. The fear increasingly spread that the phase of "restructuring" of the existing automobile industry did not only pose the question of adjustment for the traditional manufacturers, but rather the question of whether the traditional production sites and manufacturers could remain competitive and survive at all (Yates 1984; Altschuler *et al.* 1984; Jürgens 1986; Dyer *et al.* 1987).

2.2 The development of the automotive industries of the U.S.A., Great Britain and the Federal Republic of Germany

At the beginning of the 1970s, the world automobile industry was fully dominated by manufacturers in the U.S.A. and Western Europe. It had in

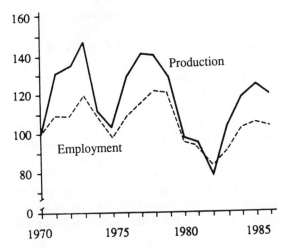

Figure 2.2 Production and employment in the U.S. automobile industry (cars; total employees; index 1970 = 100)
Source: MVMA: Economic Indicators 1986; own calculations.

many cases become a key industry for the national economies of these countries after the Second World War, and it appeared to have good prospects for growth in the future. The worldwide production of automobiles did increase in the years thereafter from ca. 23 million passenger cars in 1970, to 29 million in 1980 and ca. 33 million in 1985. Examining the patterns of development in the individual countries reveals a picture drastically different from this course of growth. In this section, we will be limiting our study to these developments in individual countries. Although the occasionally dramatic differences in the course of development shown here did not necessarily appear at the level of the individual factories, they did shape the different perceptions of the problem and the pressure it exerted in each of the countries in question.

2.2.1 Hectic ups and downs: the development of the U.S. automobile companies

Automobile production in the U.S.A. in 1980 was, looking at the number of units produced, at almost the same level as in 1975 and 1970. The development was by no means a stagnation. The respective five-year periods were marked by frantic upswings and downward trends which raised the production volumes by ca. 50 percent above the level of these three cornerstone years in each case and then allowed them to fall again. Figure 2.2 shows the development in the production volume of passenger cars made "on location" in the U.S.A. and the number of workers employed by the U.S. automakers.[1]

The steep, short-cyclical upswings and downward trends were interrupted at the end of the 1970s by a period of far-reaching recession which did not appear to be overcome until 1985, as the production volumes of the cornerstone years were again achieved.

The up and down movement is reflected, although more weakly, in the employment figures. Employment by the automakers was 21 percent more in 1973 than in 1970, and 25 percent more in 1978 than in 1975. These peak years were marked by an extensive usage of the existing capacities. The periods of excessive overtime and extra work alternated directly with periods of lay-offs and temporary plant closings. The sudden change from over- to underutilization of human labor was seen by all the respondents in our study as one of the main reasons for the deterioration of labor and industrial relations in the 1970s.

The onset of the crisis at the beginning of the 1980s had correspondingly devastating effects on the employment volume. One third of the employees in the auto industry were unemployed in 1982. The big three automakers alone (General Motors, Ford, and Chrysler) reported 264,700 workers unemployed (WAR December 27, 1982, p. 413). The low point of the crisis was reached in 1982, as almost two thirds of the production capacity (63.4 percent) had been temporarily shut down (The Bureau of National Affairs, Daily Labor Report No. 116, July 6, 1986).

The steep decline of the U.S. auto industry cannot only be explained by the economic recession in the United States and falling demand. This is clear to see in figure 2.3. This diagram shows the development in the registration of new cars, the production of the home factories, and the exports out of the U.S.A. Figure 2.3 demonstrates how the corridor between the demand and the production of passenger cars, thus the share of imports on car sales in the U.S.A., widened during the 1970s. The cause is to be seen above all in the increased importation of Japanese vehicles which, after a 4 percent share in 1970, already had a 20 percent share of the market in 1980.

Figure 2.3 also shows that this increase in imports was not compensated for by an increase in exports of U.S. automobiles; the export volume has largely stagnated at a marginal level. The growing import shares chiefly affected the small car market (the sub-compacts) and the middle sized car market (the compacts). Every second "sub-compact" – these include the Ford Escort, the Volkswagen Rabbit, the Toyota Corolla, and the Madza 323 among others – was an import by the middle of the 1980s. This was also the case with every fourth "compact" – the class of Honda Accord, Madza 626, Toyota Camry, etc.

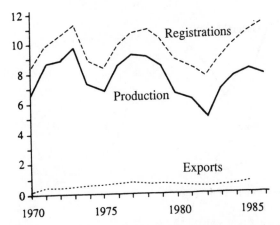

Figure 2.3 U.S. Auto registration/production and export figures of the U.S. automobile industry (in millions of cars)
Source: Consecutive issues of MVMA: Facts and Figures: VDA, Tatsachen und Zahlen.

The U.S. firms also played a part in this import development. In order to fill their product supply gaps in the small car market and to be able to offer cars capable of competitively entering this market, first Chrysler and then General Motors, and later Ford went over to ordering the production of these products outside the U.S.A. and to selling them under their firm name on the home market ("captive imports"). The share of these captive imports on the sales of the Big Three was 2.5 percent (of auto sales) in 1980 and reached a temporary peak with this (MVMA, Economic Indicators 1986, p. 10). This strategy concentrated on Japan at first, but the newly industrialized countries (NIC's) – Taiwan, South Korea, Mexico, and Brazil – have been playing an increasingly important role.

The growth of the captive imports was criticized above all by the automobile workers' union (the United Automobile, Aerospace and Agricultural Implement Workers of America, hereafter referred to as UAW). They not only criticized the direct effects of this measure on employment, but also its long term effect of leading to the destruction of the production potential, and, in the long run, its effect on product and technology development in this sector, thus leading to deindustrialization. The UAW sees the captive imports as an expression of a hollowing out the industrial basis of the corporation (UAW Research Bulletin 1986).

If we disregard the imports, the dominant participants on the U.S. market up to 1985 were still the Big Three – General Motors, Chrysler, and Ford. Figure 2.4 shows the development in their production in the period

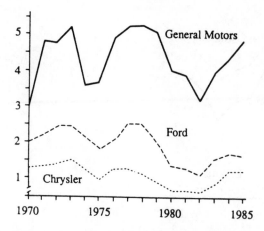

Figure 2.4 Auto production in the U.S. according to manufacturers (in millions of cars)
Source: Ward's Automative Yearbook 1987, pp. 110f.

between 1970 and 1985. It also shows the domination of General Motors, which was still increasing in the 1970s. This corporation had a 46 percent share of the market in 1980, Ford 17 percent and Chrysler 9 percent. (Volkswagen of America and American Motors had a combined market share of 4.6 percent in 1980.) In looking at the production curves, the first five years of the 1980s appeared to follow the usual "up and down" cycles.

"Paradise Lost" was the name of Emma Rothschild's study which described the state of the U.S. automobile industry as early as 1974. The established pattern of development of the 1960s had, with regard to innovation in product and production technology, allowed the auto producers to do highly profitable business with little effort. The after effects of the first oil crisis appeared to put an end to this. Figure 2.5 shows that, except for Chrysler, the actual deep fall in profitability was first seen at the end of the 1970s. In 1980 Chrysler stood on the edge of bankruptcy with a spectacular deficit of 1.8 billion dollars and could only be rescued through a concerted action of the government, the banks, and the union (Chrysler Bail-Out). Ford's deficit was minimally less ($1.5 billion), although it was not so serious as in Chrysler's case when compared with the total sales volume. But Ford was also not very far from a collapse in 1981–2. The developments in profit and loss at General Motors were quite mild in comparison. While Ford and Chrysler experienced existential crises at the beginning of the 1980s, which made the need for a course change apparent to everyone involved, the downturn at General Motors at the beginning of the 1980s was not as profound.

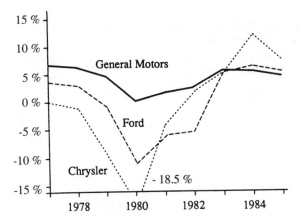

Figure 2.5 Profitability of General Motors, Ford, and Chrysler in the U.S. (net profit as a percentage of turnover)
Source: Fortune, consecutive years.

The development of commercial and production activities proceeded very differently in the two large U.S. automobile companies in the further course of the 1980s. Ford was the more successful company at the middle of the 1980s, its profits were higher than those of General Motors for the first time since the end of the 1920s. Insufficient product differentiation at General Motors and a successful product design at Ford were the causes which were mentioned most often for this differing development. It is also the result of strategic decisions at the beginning of the 1980s. Table 2.2 shows the diverging courses of production activities in the assembly plants of General Motors (GM) and Ford in the U.S.A., comparing 1980 and 1986. While GM even increased the number of its assembly plants in this period, Ford reduced its plants by more than a quarter. The remaining capacity at Ford was now fully utilized – starting at the end of 1984 the average daily production time in many assembly plants was twenty hours, that meant two hours overtime in each shift.

In the assembly plants of GM on the other hand, there was hardly any overtime in the middle of the 1980s. The factory average of twenty four lost production days per year was much higher than the three lost days in the Ford assembly plants. In addition to the high number of production days lost due to declining demand, the large amount of time lost due to technical and organizational change-overs and the difficulties in dealing with new technologies also played a role.

The onset of the crisis of the U.S. automobile industry at the beginning of

Table 2.2 *Production activity at the assembly plants of GM and Ford in the U.S.A., 1980/6 (as an average per plant and year)*

	General Motors		Ford	
	1980	1986	1980	1986
Number of plants[a] out of these, the number in single-	23	25	11	8
shift operation	3	1	3	1
Number of lost production days due to a model change	16	20	12	3
Number of lost production days due to demand	4	4	42	0
Number of overtime days[b]	5	1	1	ca. 90

Notes:
[a] Not including plants which were opened or closed in the same year.
[b] Aggregate of daily overtime and Saturday work.
Source: Own calculations on the basis of the weekly reports: "Automotive Production Activities in the United States – Canada," in WAR Vol. 55 (1980) and Vol. 61 (1986).

the 1980s could be attributed mainly to the general state of the U.S. economy, which found itself in a deep recession. In view of the increasing rate of growth of Japanese imports, even in the recession, the perception of the problem by all concerned at this time was directed at Japan ("Japanese threat"). If the question of Japan at the end of the 1970s was principally one of trade policy and the transfer of Japanese recipes for productivity into the organization of U.S. firms, in the course of the 1980s the confrontation between U.S. and Japanese production organization was extended increasingly to the U.S. production site and thus became blatantly obvious. In addition to further increases in Japanese imports and the U.S. manufacturers' captive imports, the first Japanese production facilities in the U.S. (Honda and Nissan) appeared at the beginning of the 1980s and also the construction of common production facilities – joint ventures – of U.S. and Japanese manufacturers (NUMMI, Diamond Star, CAMJ.). By the middle of the 1980s, all Japanese companies except Daihatsu had either decided to build, or had already realized their own production facilities in the U.S. If

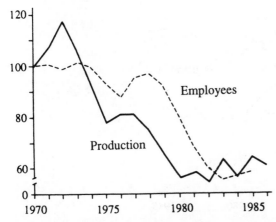

Figure 2.6 Production and employment in the U.K. automobile industry (car production; employees in the automobile industry; index 1970 = 100)
Source: Annual Abstract of Statistics; Employment Gazette; SMMT 1985.

pessimistic U.S. predictions hold true, the Japanese manufacturers could reduce the total Big Three share of the U.S. market for car sales to under 50 percent in the 1990s (UAW Research Bulletin 1986).

2.2.2 Decline and stagnation: the development of the British automobile industry

The automobile industry in Great Britain in the 1960s was also characterized by rapid rates of growth and was, in view of the demise of traditional industry branches like steel and shipbuilding, one of the most important sources of hope for future industrial development. Instead, it came to a dramatic plunge in the 1970s, in the course of which the production volume and employment were cut almost in half at the begin of the 1980s. After that, the first half of the 1980s showed stagnation at a low level (cf. figure 2.6).

The decline in the volume of production could also be seen in the employment figures. Employment by the car makers thus sank from 496,000 to 434,000 in the period between 1970 and 1980, and to 290,000 in 1985.

Three different reasons have to be regarded to explain the plight of the British automobile industry in the 1970s.

The first is the development at British Leyland (now Rover) where they were unable to successfully consolidate the diverse corporate elements which had been thrown together to form a state concern. Despite the

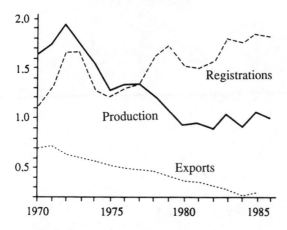

Figure 2.7 Production, registered vehicles, and exports of the U.K. (in millions of cars)
Source: SMMT 1986.

spectacular change of course under Edwardes at the end of the 1970s and despite the privatization of the company they were not able to resist the tendency toward sinking market shares and a loss of importance. The reasons for this and the further development at British Leyland have been often investigated and described (cf. Williams *et al.* 1987; Marsden *et al.* 1985; Willmam and Winch 1985; Edwardes 1983). Only after the company entered a phase of closer cooperation with the Japanese automobile manufacturer Honda does it appear at the end of the 1980s to have consolidated at a modest level (in comparison to its previous size).

The second reason is the policy of the European headquarters of Ford and General Motors to reduce the British shares in their European production consortium and to increasingly supply the British market with "captive imports" from their continental factories. In 1980, the captive imports made up 47 percent of Ford's sales in Great Britain and 38 percent of the sales of General Motors (Vauxhall). As can be seen in figure 2.7, the development of the exchange rates in the 1970s can hardly be held responsible for this. One cause, leading directly into the sphere of production, is the poor quality image of cars built in Great Britain compared to autos built on the Continent. It has often been reported that when British consumers purchase a vehicle type built in both Britain and on the Continent, they take pains to ensure that they get a vehicle made in continental Europe.

The third cause is the loss of British market positions in the developing countries. This took place partly in Commonwealth countries, which had traditionally acquired a good deal of their finished autos and CKD-kits from Great Britain. Some of the reasons for the continual loss of these markets were, to name a few, the dissolution of the Commonwealth, the development in exchange rates, and the offensive of the Japanese manufacturers in the developing countries.

Besides British Leyland, three subsidiaries of foreign parent firms are considered to be traditional British automobile manufacturers: Ford, Vauxhall (GM), and Talbot (Peugeot); the wave of Japanese direct investments, which we will not be dealing with here, did not begin until 1986. In 1968, the corporation British Leyland was formed by a merger and came under state control in 1975. In the course of the privatization of the company in 1986, the passenger car activities were continued by the Rover Group which lost independence in 1988 after being purchased by British Aerospace. In 1985 British Leyland entered into a cooperation with Honda, and in 1990 Honda U.K. became a 20 percent share owner of the Rover group (and vice versa). At the end of the 1960s Ford U.K. became a part of the consortium Ford of Europe whose headquarters was set up in Great Britain. In a similar step, Vauxhall was integrated into a conglomerate of European General Motors concerns which was originally centered at Opel-Rüsselheim. This took place with the modernization of the Kadett-Astra program in 1979. Up until then, Vauxhall had largely functioned as an independent national GM branch. The British branch of Talbot forms the remnants of Chrysler's corporate activity in Great Britain, an activity which was still considerable in 1970. After Chrysler's pullout, production and employment went inexorably downward until it consolidated at a modest level at the end of the 1980s. Figure 2.8 shows the course of production for British Leyland, Ford, and Vauxhall.

Figure 2.8 also shows that there was not such a drastic decline in production at Ford U.K. as at Vauxhall and, above all, at British Leyland. This matches the differing courses of development in the profitability of these corporations in the decade 1975–85. While Ford U.K. returned high profits, above all at the end of the 1970s – also furthered through the policy of captive imports – Vauxhall and, above all, British Leyland found themselves deep in the red (figure 2.9).

2.2.3 A growth and export machine: the development of the automobile industry in the Federal Republic of Germany

The oil price crisis marked a drastic break in German development which was similar to that in Great Britain. Car production fell 22 percent from 1973 to 1974 and the volume of employment by the auto manufacturers[2] went down about 12 percent from 1973 until its low point in 1975. The

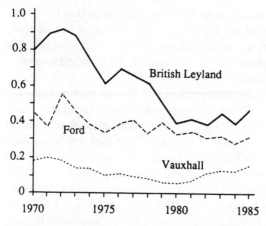

Figure 2.8 Automobile production in Great Britain (in millions of cars)
Source: SMMT 1986.

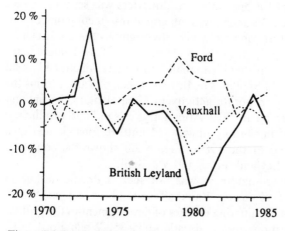

Figure 2.9 Profitability of selected British auto companies (net profit as a
percentage of turnover)
Source: Fortune, consecutive years.

ensuing development was, with exception of the break in 1979–80 and
(because of a strike) 1984, characterized by growth (cf. figure 2.10). The
employment curve also shows a decline as a result of the first oil crisis. This
is considerably weaker than in the U.S. and the employment level was
hardly affected by the decline in production volume in 1979–80.

As opposed to Great Britain, which went from an export-oriented
industrial country to one more oriented to imports in the course of the

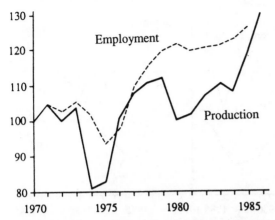

Figure 2.10 Production and employment in the automobile industry in the Federal Republic of Germany (index 1970 = 100)
Source: VDA; Tatsachen und Zahlen; own calculations.

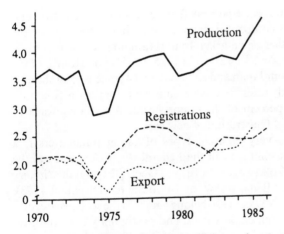

Figure 2.11 Production, registered vehicles, and exports of the Federal Republic of Germany (in million of cars)
Source: See figure 2.10.

1970s, the Federal Republic could expand its role as an "export platform" for the world market. In 1970 55 percent of automobile production was exported, in 1980 53 percent, and in 1985 62 percent (cf. figure 2.11).

In view of this export strength, the phenomenon of "captive imports" was not perceived as a threat in the Federal Republic up to the end of the 1980s, although there are such captive imports at Opel (which belongs to

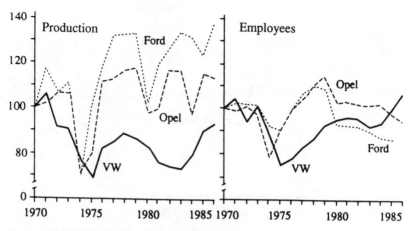

Figure 2.12 Production and employment at the German mass manufacturers
(index 1970 = 100)
Source: Company reports, consecutive years; own calculations.

GM), Ford, and Volkswagen, especially from their factories in Spain and
Belgium. The Japanese competitor has an increasing percentage of the
share of imports on the German market. Imports amounted to 30 percent in
1970, 41 percent in 1980, and 45 percent in 1985. In 1980; one fourth of the
imported autos came from Japan and achieved a 10.4 percent total share of
the market. The growth rates here were cause for concern at the auto
companies: in 1985 30 percent of the imports came from Japan for a 13
percent share of the total registration of new cars.

The existence of two very different types of car manufacturers is a
characteristic of the auto industry in the Federal Republic: these are the
"mass manufacturers" Volkswagen, Ford, and Opel (GM) and the "luxury
manufacturers" Daimler-Benz, BMW, and Porsche (cf. Dieckhoff 1978);
Audi, which is part of the VW concern belongs more to the second category.
The patterns of production, employment, and profitability have traditionally been very different between the two groups. The "luxury manufacturers" have expanded production and employment since 1970, almost
unaffected by the two oil crises. The development at the mass manufacturers proceeded much less favorably. In the following we will be concentrating on this second type of manufacturer.

Figure 2.12 shows that among the three mass manufacturers named
above, Volkswagen (VW) AG (without Audi) shows a course of development different from Ford and Opel: the onset of the crisis in the first half of
the 1970s is just as deep as at Ford and Opel, but the ensuing recovery is
more hesitant and weak. Upswings and downward trends are generally

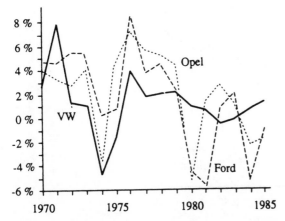

Figure 2.13 Profitability of the German mass producers (net profit as a percentage of turnover)
Source: See figure 2.12.

more weakly developed here. This is also seen when considering the employment levels at the three manufacturers (cf. also Streeck 1984; Düe and Hentrich 1981).

Although Volkswagen lost ground relative to Opel and Ford in the period we examined, it remained the largest West German manufacturer. In 1980 VW produced 1,232,000 cars, as opposed to 787,000 at Opel and 420,000 at Ford. In examining the total development according to production volume and employment, the West German automobile industry shows neither the hectic ups and downs as in the U.S.A. nor the decline and stagnation as in the British case. The consideration of profitability, however (figure 2.13), also reveals increasing problems by the end of the 1970s.

2.3 The "Japan Nightmare": A new power in the world automobile industry

The development of the automobile industry has been characterized since the middle of the 1970s by the advance of Japanese competition in the world market. The "Japanese threat" became a standard term in the auto industry. The Western companies could work it out for themselves: if the trends of the 1970s were continued in the 1980s, the hypothetical Japanese share of world production would grow to almost 40 percent by 1990. In fact, the relative increase in position of Japan on the world market came to a temporary halt and a three way split existed at the end of the 1980s. With

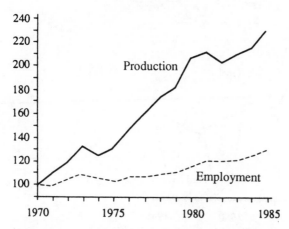

Figure 2.14 Automobile production and employment in Japan (index
1970 = 100)
Source: JAMA 1986.

around 13 million cars produced annually in each of the three regions, the
U.S., Western Europe, and Japan produced almost 84 percent of the cars
made in the world at the end of the decade.

But imbalances become strikingly noticeable when the development of
international trading relations is considered: out of the 4.2 million cars that
went back and forth between Western Europe, the U.S., and Japan in 1985,
almost 80 percent came from Japan, ca. 20 percent from Europe, and only
0.2 percent from the U.S. On the other hand, only 1 percent of this total
volume was imported by Japan, 29 percent went to Europe, and 70 percent
to the U.S. market. This pattern of distribution had already established
itself by the middle of the 1970s – though the total trade volume was only
half as large at that time.

The production capacity of the Japanese automobile industry was
enormously expanded in the 1970s. The four largest Japanese car manufacturers, Toyota, Nissan, Honda, and Mazda thus increased their capacity by
170 percent in this decade (Jürgens 1986; Cusumano 1985). Many new
factory complexes with modern production facilities were established.
Figure 2.14 shows the forward rush of the Japanese automobile industry in
the period from 1970 to 1985 as expressed in the production of autos and in
employment figures.

The differing shapes of the curves of production and employment already
bring our attention to one of the central phenomena of the "Japanese
threat": the employment volume grew to a much smaller extent than the
production volume. The increase in production was achieved through

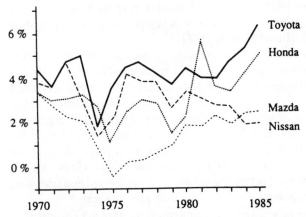

Figure 2.15 Profitability of Japanese auto companies (net profit as a percentage of turnover)
Source: Fortune, consecutive years.

enormous leaps in labor productivity. It is no wonder that the profitability of the Japanese automobile companies developed much more favorably than that of the companies in the countries we studied. In the period from 1970 to 1985, only Mazda once dipped briefly into red ink. Other than this, the Japanese manufacturers made dazzling profits almost without exception. Figure 2.15 shows this for the four leading manufacturers.

By the end of the 1970s, it was already clear that the advance of Japanese competition could not merely be explained by factors such as exchange or trade policy. The traditional Western producing nations and manufacturers saw themselves up against an – apparently – superior system of production organization, to which they either had to adjust or find their own alternatives if they wanted to play a role as manufacturing nations or companies in the future. (Altshuler *et al.* 1984; Womack *et al.* 1990).

Most of the traditional auto producing nations reacted to the threat from Japan with the introduction of protectionist measures in order to hold the Japanese import share at least constant: the U.S. by concluding the "voluntary restraint agreement" limiting Japan to about a 20 percent share of the market and Great Britain to about 10 percent. France and Italy already had import restrictions which only allowed the Japanese minimal export possibilities.

The protectionist measures and the growing political pressure on Japan to introduce measures to reduce its enormous international trade imbalances gave the impetus for the Japanese corporations' internationalization strategies. These consist of establishing their own production facilities outside Japan and of joint ventures with foreign corporations. They will also be one of the distinctive tendencies of development in the automobile industry in the 1990s (Bhaskar *et al.* 1986).

The first big battle over the reallocation of the shares of the world market for car sales was fought in the U.S. The next major conflict will involve the European market. The movement in the exchange rate of the yen compared to the dollar and the restructuring in the U.S. have, in the meantime, led to enormous increases in productivity in the existing plants of the "big three" and to the Japanese companies building highly modern new factories in the U.S. The surplus capacities connected with this reached one third of the entire U.S. production capacity at the beginning of the 1990s. This is roughly the size of the total American car production of Ford and Chrysler. The Japanese export potential will have to seek new horizons.[3]

A discussion of the productivity advantages of the Japanese production organization thus also had to be on the agenda for companies which had previously considered their market position to be safe. What are the exceptional characteristics of the Japanese production organization?

2.4 "Toyotism" and its prerequisites in work and social organization

The Japanese competitive strength, "the Japanese threat," was the dominant topic in the industry at the end of the 1970s. Thus each of our companies had an intensive period in which they studied the challenge posed by Japan. The importance of the topic "Japan" differed greatly in terms of strategic implementation (Jürgens *et al.* 1985a and b; Marsland and Beer 1983). In each case, however, the question of translating the Japan lesson into concrete measures in the companies' different fields of action was very much a matter for the corporate headquarters. It was primarily the experts from the corporate or divisional headquarters who travelled to Japan and were supported there by external consultants who profited significantly from the topic of Japan. The consequences of the Japan reception thus spread "from the top down" in the companies. The central staffs decided what should be done.

The reports of the Japan trips and the diagnoses of the causes for Japanese productivity strength were naturally shaped by the situation of each company and its own strategic considerations. This led to credibility problems. Union representatives were included early in the study trips from the companies but, as in the case of management trips, they could only gain fleeting impressions. They could only speculate as to the causes, extent, and effects of the exceptional features observed in the production organization in Japanese companies. The function of most Japan visits in the first place was to clear away the skepticism that Japanese productivity and competitive strength were only caused by an undervaluing of the yen and low wages.

The "discovery" of and research into the causes of the competitive strength of the Japanese automobile industry at the end of the 1970s met with considerable difficulties. There were hardly any accounts of the production and work organization of Japanese companies in the literature at the beginning of the 1980s to which management could have turned after it had begun to notice Japan.

Both the scientific observation and information systems and the transfer agencies of the different institutions, embassies, and chambers of industry and commerce had largely failed to analyze and convey the extent and dimension of the strengths of the Japanese production system. A leading manager of a European company confessed the following to us in the course of our interview: "This extent of the Japanese competitive superiority totally surprised us. I still ask myself today how that was possible. There are, after all, so many people who observe the development in other countries. This should have been recognized earlier."

In order to close the knowledge gaps which were appearing, management itself took on the task of carrying out "field studies" in Japanese companies. There, they found themselves confronted with countless empirical research problems – the problem of access to the companies, that of finding opportunities for independent observation and also the problem of interpreting procedures without knowledge of historical and cultural contexts. It is no wonder that stereotypes, such as those depicting the "essence" of the Japanese worker as a modern Samurai, frequently play an important role in the company internal reports.

The corporations in the U.S. paid the most attention to Japan. Compared to this, the Japan discussion in the Federal Republic of Germany appears as weak sheet lightning. The U.S.'s interest in Japan was primarily obsessed with examining and quantifying the relative cost advantages of Japanese production. Numerous studies of this have been made – by the companies, by the UAW, and by governmental offices.

In the U.S. discussion the future of the U.S. as a manufacturing site was tied to the question of the causes of the cost advantages of Japanese production. Comparative studies of the production costs of similar automobiles in Japan and the U.S. revealed that the cost prices of the Japanese products at the beginning of the 1980s were, even including the costs of shipping to the U.S.A., up to 40 percent less than those of the U.S. products. Considerable cost differentials were also found in the comparison of Japanese and German products. An internal study of the VW AG thus calculated the cost differential for comparative cars to be approximately 3,000 DM which amounted to 30 percent of the total costs (Handelsblatt,

September 22, 1980). These figures did not raise an alarm at that time in the Federal Republic. There were no public follow-up studies, governmental investigations, etc. as was the case in the U.S. (Goldschmidt Report 1981).

Where does the special proficiency of Japanese management lie? The theories of Ouchi (1981; see also Pascale and Athos 1981) found widespread public interest at the beginning of the 1980s, especially in the U.S.A. They helped focus attention on questions of personnel management and "human resources management." Ouchi's "theory Z" was explicitly tied to the theories of McGregor and the Human Relations School, which had long lectured to the management of the Western world about the necessity of mutual trust, the delegation of responsibility downward, and encouraging the creativity of the workers (cf. Hall and Leidecker 1981). The "theory Z," along with the issue of Japan and the wave of discussion it set off, could have faded just as rapidly as the multitude of other concepts which came from personnel management and organizational development in the tradition of the Human Relations School. This was prevented by the appearance of engineering studies dealing with Japanese production management, process control methods, and the control of quality and efficiency. It became clear that the topic of Japan was no affair of some screwballs in the personnel and organizational development departments of the Western car companies.

The cost differential between the U.S.A. and Japan, according to the findings of a number of U.S. cost analyses, could hardly be accounted for by distorted exchange rates or wage differences. According to a study of the U.S. automobile workers union UAW (actually commissioned in an attempt to weaken the argument of production-caused cost differentials), 38 percent of the cost advantage of Japanese vehicles could be explained by higher efficiency in direct production and assembly, 20 percent by wage differences, 24 percent by the exchange rates at that time, and 18 percent by tax advantages stemming from the Japanese tax system at that time ("Telesis Study" according to Chilton's Automotive Industries 2/1985). But where does the higher efficiency in production and assembly come from?

Abernathy, Clark, and Kantrow (1983b) attempted to quantify the relative influence of a number of factors which could explain the productivity gap between the American and the Japanese auto industry at the beginning of the 1980s. On the basis of management interviews and internal corporate studies they have made a comprehensive list of the most important explanatory factors and their relative importance from the point of view of American automobile managers. According to this, only 10 percent of the Japanese production advantage could be traced back to the degree of automation compared to their own American plants. Seven percent was accounted for by the factor "product design," especially the fact that the Japanese explicitly considered production necessities in the phase of product design. The higher degree of usage of machines and equipment appeared as the most important explanatory factor by far in this listing. Forty percent of the Japanese productivity advantage was attributed to it. Differences in the quality control system explained a further 9 percent. A further 18 percent of the advantage was seen in differences in the division of labor and the higher degree of flexibility of worker deployment in Japanese factories. These were closely tied to the aforementioned factors of production and process control. The authors only attributed 4 percent of the advantage to higher work intensity. Finally, 12 percent of the differences were explained through the lower absenteeism in Japanese plants (Abernathy, Clark, and Kantrow 1983b, pp. 84f.).

This result shows the great importance of the system of process control that makes this high degree of "process yield" possible. Earlier studies had already made reference to the special features of this system of process control, but these mostly anthropologically and sociologically oriented studies scarcely found their way into the management discussions (cf. Abbeglen 1958; Whitehill and Takezawa 1968; Cole 1971; Dore 1973; Clark 1979). In this literature an explanation for the special features of Japanese production organization was generally seen in the historic, cultural, or social structural peculiarities of Japan. These studies usually implicitly or explicitly emphasized the non-transferability of these explanatory factors.

In contrast to this, at the beginning of the 1980s, the studies of Abernathy, Harbour, and Henn (1981), Shingo (1981), Schonberger (1982), Lee and Schwendiman (1982), and Monden (1981, 1983) (these authors were predominantly production engineers and consultants) showed that these characteristic features of process control were the result of management techniques, many of which had been well known in Western literature and practice for some time. They had been further developed in Japan and adjusted to the specific social and cultural prerequisites. This formed a new basis for posing the question of transferability.

Especially for production engineers, the Toyota production system became the model for efficient production management. Taiichi Ohno, who had become vice president of the Toyota Motor Corporation before he left the company in 1978, is considered to be the inventor and promoter of this system. The relevance and growing diffusion of this system make it seem justified to set the name Ohno next to those of Frederick Winslow Taylor and Henry Ford as the founders of systems for mass production organization. Thus Monden (1983) states:

The Toyota production system is a technology of comprehensive production management the Japanese invented a hundred years after opening up to the modern world. More than likely, another such gigantic advance in production methods will not appear for some time to come. (Monden 1983, p. V.)

The principles of production management developed by Ohno have adopted some of Taylor and Ford's objectives and are diametrically opposed to others. Ohno thus follows Ford's idea of assembly line production, but not his preference for product standardization and single-purpose mechanization. In like fashion, Ohno follows Taylor's ideal of the development of optimal time and method control for carrying out the work, but not the goal of reducing work content to create fragmented partial work operations which are as simple as possible.

The supreme principle of the Toyota production system is to minimize "buffers" of people and materials. This is achieved through a control system based on the just-in-time principle. In the Western discussion, this principle is often reduced to a problem of organization, logistics, and coordination with supplier companies. But it has just as far-reaching results as the basic principle for the final manufacturer's production and work organization. In this concept, it is imperative at all levels of production that parts only be produced in the amounts that are actually needed for further processing at the next step of production. In order to ensure this, the operative process control takes place according to the "pull" principle. And, according to the model of supermarket methods, only those parts which were just pulled by the "customers" are produced anew. Interruptions at a later stage of production automatically bring about the interruption of production at earlier levels as the "pulling" does not take place. The regulation of production thus takes place in short-term adjustments to the situation at the next levels, respectively, and with this, ultimately, to the sales situation in the market. This requires short-term adjustments in each previous level's "production program." It means producing lots which are as small as possible for cast parts production, pressing parts, etc. or single-piece production in the machining operations. In order to achieve this frequent tool change, shorter conversion times and high flexibility in the deployment of workers at different machines and installations must be ensured.

Missing or defective parts mean interruptions in the process. Thus the zero-buffer-principle automatically results in the zero-error-principle. It is expected from the workers that they should interrupt the production process themselves before they make mistakes or allow previous mistakes to get through. Convenient devices which each worker can use to stop the line in the assembly areas are an expression of this increased responsibility for quality and self-regulating quality control in production. Beyond this, automatic systems for recognizing defects and interrupting the process are installed wherever possible in order to ensure that the employees do not overtax themselves attempting to compensate, through increased individual effort, for problems stemming from the technical equipment or for understaffing and thereby run the risk of making mistakes. An example of this are contact mats at the boundaries of individual work stations through which the belt is stopped when the workers are carried that far by their work. The workers have, likewise, no opportunity to "work ahead" in order to enjoy informal breaks.

In the case of overload, it is expected that co-workers from adjoining work stations will jump in to avoid or shorten an interruption of the process. To reach the daily production target is the absolute mandate. Lost production has to be made up for by additional work any way. Jumping in to help colleagues is thus in a worker's own interest, just like participating in activities for improvements concerning the course of work in the entire section, not only at the individual work station.

An integral element of the Toyota production system is the pressure for rationalization, also with regard to personnel usage. The zero-buffer-principle serves here to regulate the possibilities as well as the limits of personnel reduction in view of the goal of quality production: if the personnel reduction is so drastic that the operations at a work station can no longer be completed within the allotted time this leads to a stoppage of the assembly line. The endeavors of the supervisors and the group itself are then directed at improving the structuring of work in the section to ensure that it can be performed with the given personnel. Before additional personnel or measures of mechanization are authorized, upper management waits until all possibilities for improvement within the given framework are exhausted. If the reduction of personnel does not have negative effects on the output of the section but rather on the quality, perhaps because the necessary repair tasks can no longer be performed, then the problems will be noticed at once in the subsequent process. The lack of quality leads to a line stoppage there and to the return of the defective parts to the section responsible. This results in efforts at improvement so as to achieve the timely delivery of perfect parts. The system makes high pressure for rationalization possible while keeping to the quality targets through its mechanisms of self-regulation (cf. Monden 1983, pp. 137ff.).

Fixed times and work loads, like those in the system for performance regulation common in Western factories, do not exist in this system. The lower-level supervisors and the group itself endeavor continually to beat the current standards and to raise the performance levels. The industrial engineering experts can limit themselves to advisory activities in questions of optimizing methods. The system of self-regulation has relieved them of the task of pressing for rationalization.

The big advantages of the Toyota production system are found in the way in which the flow of production structures the speed and rhythm of work. Production quality and cost efficiency appear as a quasi automatic result produced by structural constraints. It is apparent, however, that such a system would have to have specific prerequisites for work and social organization in the factory. These are the aspects which are generally discussed in the literature of industrial sociology and labor policy. On the basis of the literature cited above and our own studies (cf. Dohse, Jürgens, and Malsch 1985 and Jürgens and Strömel 1987) we will be especially emphasizing the following factors:

(1) In accordance with the prevailing literature, we see the "basic formula" of the Japanese success in production to be their principle of life-long employment security for part of the work force. On the one hand, it is the prerequisite for the high degree of identification which this part of the work force has with the goals of the company. On the other hand, it explains the great importance which "human resources" have for management. Management has to plan on the basis of these human resources in the long term, and thus cannot develop a throw-away mentality with regard to their employees. This basic formula is, as we know, only true for the leading companies of the Japanese automobile industry and at the "periphery" temporary or part-time employees exist in their factories also.

(2) The lines of segmentation between status and occupational groups within the core work force are, however, perceptibly smaller than in Western factories. This is not only visible in symbolism – executives also wear standard work suits, do not have separate dining rooms, parking lots, etc. and are placed with their desks in open offices. It is also shown in the fewer number of levels in the hierarchy compared to Western companies, and in the smaller income differential between the shop floor and the board of directors.

On the shop floor itself, there are nowhere near as many pronounced demarcation lines between the different job and qualification groups as in Western factories. The skilled worker status does not exist. Career patterns are based on seniority, personnel rating, and additional training, above all "on the job." The boundary lines with respect to the status of the engineer are also less well defined than in Western factories. Engineers are more strongly present on the shop floor and their jobs and career paths overlap with those of the most senior production workers. The reduced distance – spatial, social, organizational – between the tasks of carrying out production, maintenance, and the jobs of engineers makes "face-to-face" communication over problems of production and quality easier.

It is also the case with regard to the entire production organization of the company that organizational dividing lines do not lead to mutual separation and bureaucratic forms of contact in Japan, as is frequently the case in Western factories. This is true also at the level of company management, where it is expected that employees collect experiences in differing areas in the course of their careers – for the top careers, this includes a period of time in the union organization of the company before a position in higher management can be achieved.

(3) An explanation for the absence of lines of demarcation between occupational groups is given by the system of recruiting and qualification. In recruitment, the emphasis is put on a high degree of general education and not on specialized vocational training. The recruitment for blue-collar workers takes place primarily in the general high schools or in vocational high schools. The assignment to the areas of direct production and, for example, maintenance takes place on the basis of entry tests. Although there are different paths for further qualifications for different workers, the high entry qualification forms a prerequisite for communication on the shop floor between technical and production personnel which can be focussed on problem solving.

The entry qualification and the great importance of on-the-job training through rotating tasks in direct production are central prerequisites for this type of work organization. The system of training and life-long employment hardly allow for attitudes like "job control" as in the Anglo-Saxon countries or an understanding of certain work as a "profession" like that in Germany to appear at all.

(4) Direct production has a central importance in the total organization of Japanese production – in its image as well as in its task assignment. In the traditional Western corporate organization, direct production rates as the lowest level of work. The goal of "scientific management" is aimed at simplifying this work as much as possible, at defining the carrying out of work, and the degree of performance as precisely as possible and at reducing the scope of personal disposition. Direct production in the automobile industry in Western companies was a recruiting field for unskilled laborers, frequently for immigrant workers who were often not fluent in the language of the country. In Japan the members of direct production have, as outlined above, the same entry qualification as the workers of the technical departments. Many of the jobs organized as control or support functions in Western plants, like quality control or maintenance, for example, are thus performed by members of direct production in Japan. The indirect activities have neither quantitatively nor qualitatively the same significance that they have in Western factories. This can be seen in the lesser importance of all of the control functions performed by experts in the Japanese plants, e.g., industrial engineering for

setting times and determining work methods, quality control for the product quality and the finance department for cost control. In an interview with us, a leading manager at one of the companies we investigated characterized the situation in this manner: "There are very few 'policemen' in the system."

(5) The group principle plays a central role in the production and social organization in Japanese factories. With this, the emphasis was put directly on using informal aspects of group relations for the goals of productivity and social integration. The group's spectrum of functions for the individual is almost all-encompassing: it is a substitute family and social network, an educational authority (for late risers for example), a place for learning (on-the-job and in its function as quality circle), an organizer of leisure time, a unit for performance regulation (time allocation and efficiency control do not take place in respect to the individual job, but rather in respect to the work area of the entire group) and quality regulation (the production group is responsible for the quality of its area). The great relevance of the group is *not* an expression of democratization in the sense of some Western conceptions where, for example, the groups elect speakers and hierarchical structures are broken down through the use of the group principle. In Japan, the group principle goes along with a multilevel hierarchy structure which gives far-reaching authority to the lower-level production super-visors (cf. Jürgens and Strömel 1987)

(6) Through the establishment of quality circles and other forms of small group activity, the attempt is made to systematically use the production knowledge and experience of the employees to "kaizen," to continuously improve factory operation and performance standards. These group processes outside the direct work situation are, at the same time, processes of socialization and qualification, of transferring experience between older and younger group members, and of acquiring problem-solving skills (methods of statistical process control, presentation techniques, etc.). The participation of group members in enacting solutions which they them-selves developed and the expert role which group members play in such cases is in stark contrast to the extreme estrangement or lack of communi-cation which exists between shop floor workers and staff experts in Western factories.

(7) The central position of the group does not mean that the individual rating of performance and persons is no longer important. It would be unimaginable that a Western factory could have a rating system for workers as ingenious and elaborate in its execution as that which we found in Japanese factories (cf. Tsuda 1974; Demes 1987). The results of the

personnel rating play a major role in remuneration, promotion, and worker deployment, and the role of personnel rating is increasingly growing relative to that of seniority. If the efforts made for personnel rating and the degree of differentiation of the criteria, rating schemes, etc. are considered then the time and effort put into performance appraisal are comparable to what is done in Western factories with respect to time and motion studies. "Human engineering" based on systems for personnel rating in Japan is to some extent a functional equivalent for "industrial engineering" in Western factories.

(8) A final point is with regard to the working hours. This does not only refer to the higher average number of work hours yearly. It also refers to the flexibility which the companies have in accessing their employees' time and the tenuous boundaries between free time and working time. This is expressed in the high number of overtime hours, also those which are not charged to the company (called "service hours" in Japan), the fact that workers do not fully take advantage of their vacation time, that the employees use their free time for small group problem-solving activities in the factory or their own further training. This high "temporal availability" of the employees must, in fact, be regarded as a prerequisite for the smooth functioning of just-in-time production and for the improvement activities described above (cf. Deutschmann 1987).

These eight elements refer to peculiarities of the work and social organization of Japanese factories, and have general validity, at least in the leading companies of the Japanese automobile industry. With regard to their emergence and their consequences, they are obviously closely connected with the system of industrial relations and the system of inter-company relations and government connections with private industry. These are, in turn, shaped by the unique culture and history of Japan. Even though we cannot examine these connections further here, the crucial point in discussing the "Japanese model" is the specific linkage of the systems of process control with the social organization of work. We refer to the system of work regulation resulting from this connection as "Toyotism" (Dohse, Jürgens and Malsch 1985). The acceptance of "Toyotism" by the employees is assured by a certain degree of self-regulation and participation on shop floor matters, tight social controls through peer group pressure within the work groups, and company-organized activities even in the workers' leisure time. This system guarantees a high degree of willingness to make compromises and a high degree of identification with the company's goals on the part of the work force.

An example of the level of integration and control is demonstrated by the systems for union representation. At Toyota, the lower-level supervisors are generally the union representatives for their area and, as we have already mentioned, the managers "rotate" in the course of a successful career for a period of time into the high union positions (Yamamoto 1975). This meant that diverging positions and protest from below could hardly be articulated. There are thus very few reports about the negative sides of Toyotism. The book Kamata wrote about his experiences as a seasonal laborer at Toyota is an exception to this (Kamata 1983), but it does not reflect the experiences and views of the permanent workers. Ohno saw the control which the company exerts over the union organization to be the most important basis for the success of the Toyota production system (Cusumano 1985, p. 306; see also Cusumano 1985 for the differences between the Toyota and Nissan production systems). He admitted that such a system could not have been pushed through at Nissan at the time when it was implemented at Toyota. There the union had a more strongly independent position at that time.

In "Toyotism" we see an independent model for work regulation which, despite countless overlappings, clearly shows a different profile than the Taylorism–Fordism of the Western variety. With this, the main differences from the viewpoint of labor deployment are not only the lack of similarity in process layout and control. Both Taylorism–Fordism and Toyotism are based on assembly line production, and in both cases the structures of the process (line speed, machine cycle, zero-buffer-principle) determine the work rhythm. The main differences are found at the level of work and social organization:

The work organization in Toyotism is based on a higher measure of self-regulation, the task assignments are less horizontally and vertically fragmented than in Taylorism–Fordism.

Its regulation of performance takes place on the basis of extensive use of human resources, including performance reserves which can only be tapped through informal group and communication relations. As opposed to Taylorism–Fordism, which sets the "normal performance" as a goal for the regulation of performance, "Toyotism" aims systematically at attaining extra- and special performances from the workers in all job contexts.

The institutions for the representation of worker interests in Toyotism aim at securing conformity and obedience in cases where they cannot achieve authentic consensus. The idea of adversarial interests between employees and employers and openly dealing with conflicts at the level of industrial relations are foreign to the system; in contrast to this, the institutions and procedures in Taylorism–Fordism assume the possibility or inevitability of conflicting interests in the relations between capital and labor.

"Toyotism" can thus be regarded as an alternative system to Taylorism–Fordism which, at the same time, attains its original objectives in a much more efficient, economical "lean" manner: to attain the maximum use from the resource "human labor" and to realize mass production at the lowest cost and highest efficiency levels. With the exception of selective individual case studies (cf. Jürgens and Strömel 1987) our research project did not perform any research of Taylorism–Fordism in Japan; we also did not carry out research at a Japanese plant in the U.S. either. Therefore, we cannot make comparative observations about the factory reality of Toyotism. Toyotism did not enter the discussion as a comparatively integral concept until the beginning of the 1990s with the study from Womack *et al.* (1990). To consider the Japanese factory and work organization as the "best practice" was a view only held by a minority in management at the time of our investigation, and this was even less the case with the unions. The concept "lean production," which Womack *et al.* propagate as the best management practice on the basis of their studies, clearly has the Toyota production system as its model and it is thus no wonder that the basic features of our Toyotism concept correspond with the lean production system. But Toyotism in our understanding also comprises the forms of social integration and the securing of conformity we describe as necessary system components of a system radically organized with zero-buffer and zero-error objectives, and thus also the negative implications from the point of view of the employees and society.

3 Company strategies for answering the challenges

The radical changes in the 1970s forced all companies to strategically reorient themselves. Previous structures, processes, ways of thinking, and forms of behavior were questioned – more or less radically in the individual companies – and differing focal points and priorities were set. Company strategies were also important for the factories which were not directly affected by the new measures, as they shaped the expectations and considerations with regard to future ways of regulating work – the team concept, for instance. In this chapter we will discuss the strategies which influenced factory expectations or offered solutions to specific problems. Correspondingly, we will be dealing with:

(a) the world car strategy which, as we will see, was very important for the regulation of performance in the factory and the development of industrial relations at individual sites;

(b) the strategy of product upgrading and diversification which, due to its demands on the flexibility of production and personnel deployment, was a fundamental impulse for a new orientation of production and work organization in the factory;

(c) the strategy of flexible automation in view of its clear requirements on the qualifications of the workforce and on the organization of work; and

(d) people related strategies which aim at new forms of work and motivation. General Motors' Quality of Work-Life (QWL) program or Ford's Employee Involvement program are examples of this. When we refer later to such programs at the companies we investigated we will be using the general abbreviation NW&M (new work and motivation) so as to preserve anonymity.

Many further strategy dimensions are not dealt with in this selection: these are the areas of product strategy and marketing, product developments, logistics and supplier relations, management organization and corporate structures, and political strategies as in the question of trade relations. To deal with these in more detail here would go beyond the scope of our investigation.

Our goal in the following is to use selected examples from individual companies to obtain background information about the goals and basic patterns for the strategies that we discovered in the framework of our empirical investigation. We are beginning with the product-related strategies, the world car strategy, and the strategies of product diversification and upgrading.

3.1 The world car strategy

The world car strategy promised to compensate for the enormous costs of the new product generation by reaping the benefits of the economies of scale represented by the worldwide sales volume of the corporations. General Motors and Ford in particular believed that they would have an advantage through their strength as multinational corporations (Dohse and Jürgens 1985; USITC 1985; Whitman 1981). These corporations had maintained independent programs of development and model policies – at least in their European and U.S. areas of operation – up until the 1970s. This had been the basis for their respective production systems having a large degree of technical and organizational independence (cf. for example Denise 1974).

The "world car" strategy meant the simultaneous introduction of a new type of car with a standard basic design at all of the world corporations' production centers. With this, they would achieve prerequisites in product design and process technology which would allow the use of the same components and parts for all regions of the world. The models were to be assembled on location in the most important regional markets. Consumer preference and national regulations could be taken into account through varying the product exterior and adding options. Incidentally, it was assumed that the preferences of U.S. customers after the oil crisis would more closely resemble those of the Europeans.

The world car strategy offered many advantages:

The costs of product development could be spread over a large production series; the same was true for the development of corresponding parts and components "under the hood."

It included the prerequisites for a standardization of central units and components. This would allow the companies to produce them at one or more production sites in lots corresponding to their worldwide sales.

With the parallel production of parts, or of the same or similar car models at different sites, the companies acquire the possibility of flexibly reacting to changes in the exchange rates through expanding or reducing production volumes at individual sites.

A further advantage came with the largely synchronous introduction of the same type of car in differing plants and, with this, the possibility of a unified planning of production structures extending beyond one plant. A much larger degree of comparability between the plants was achieved because the products but also the technical and organizational layout of the plants were the same. With this, the prerequisites were created for initiating mutual learning processes through exchange of experience, and for exerting influence on the situation in individual factories by stimulating competition between the factories.

The Ford corporation developed its world car in the 1970s, code name "Erika." Four sites in the U.S., two in Europe, and one in Latin America were planned as assembly plants for this car line. The "Erika" was also the blueprint for the development of the Mazda 323, which was produced by Mazda and distributed by Ford in Southeast Asia under the name "Laser." The "Escort" became the most well-known model of the Erika program. There was also a worldwide network of supplier relationships in the Escort production system, and Ford's Japanese cooperation partner (Mazda) also played a central role here.

General Motors attempted its first actual world car program with the so-called J-car. This car family was developed from the beginning as an integrated production program. Production began in 1981 in Europe and the U.S. Slightly differing versions of the J-car were being produced at the middle of the 1980s in the U.S.A., the Federal Republic of Germany, Belgium, Great Britain, Australia, Brazil, South Africa, and at Isuzu in Japan. A parallel production of a single vehicle had taken place earlier with the Chevette/Gemini/Kadette series. These cars were also produced at sites around the world, but with very different product generations and levels of production technology.

In the course of the J-car program, engine production in Brazil and Australia was established or expanded. Brazil was to take care of the U.S. and European market, Australia was to deliver to Asia and South Africa. At the same time, GM intensified its links with Isuzu. This Japanese company manufactured the drive train for all J-cars produced outside the U.S. (i.e., transaxles, an assembly module of axles, and gears for front-wheel drive cars). Figure 3.1 shows some of the interconnections within the worldwide J-car production system.

The basic features of the world car strategy, manufacturing a similar product in parallel at different production sites, had already been realized in the U.S. in the 1930s, primarily at General Motors; this was organizationally perfected in the 1960s and 1970s. Experiences with the difficulty in managing huge production complexes, like Ford's River Rouge plant in

Detroit and GM's Buick site in Flint – with regard to technical and organizational considerations, but primarily in regard to industrial relations – had left their mark. Instead, the companies began to build new smaller assembly plants and levelled off at a standard size of about 300,000 vehicles yearly (in two shifts). This plant size did not allow a company to produce large series of the most important models all at one plant. These series often reached magnitudes of more than one million cars yearly. Thus structures of parallel production emerged in plant "families" in which each plant produced nearly similar vehicles with approximately the same equipment. Table 3.1 shows the number of parallel assembly plants at which the most important product lines of GM and Ford were produced in the middle of the 1980s.

In Europe, the emergence of a unified market also created the prerequisites for a strategy of parallel production. Structures of parallel production had existed previously in Europe. These had a totally different character, however, and fulfilled a totally different function. Most companies still have a core site which clearly surpasses the others with regard to production volume and degree of integration and is often the site of the company headquarters. Examples in Germany are Volkswagen's Wolfsburg site, Opel's Rüsselheim site (GM), and Ford's plant in Cologne. The companies' new plants, which were built in the 1960s and 1970s with growing production volumes and a broad product spectrum, often have, on the other hand, even today the character of satellite plants, mere assembly plants. Both management and the union have more bargaining power in the core sites than in the satellite plants and they also know how to use it.

It was in the interest of the core plants to ensure that new model lines were not produced entirely at the newly constructed assembly plants. A part of these lines was also produced at the core works aside from their main production lines. In the wake of worsening employment conditions, increasing surplus capacities, and strongly varying sales figures of the different models, the value of this parallel production for employment security was demonstrated. By increasing the percentage of the more successful model in the product mix, the unemployment risk could be reduced. It was thus the policy of the works councils of German companies that the parallel production of a second model line be continued on a small scale in their core plants even though this capacity would have been available at the satellite plant where this model was primarily produced. This "secondary production" also functioned to hold and secure employment in that it, because of its smaller scale, generally had a lower degree of mechanization.

The U.S. type of parallel production was first established in Europe by

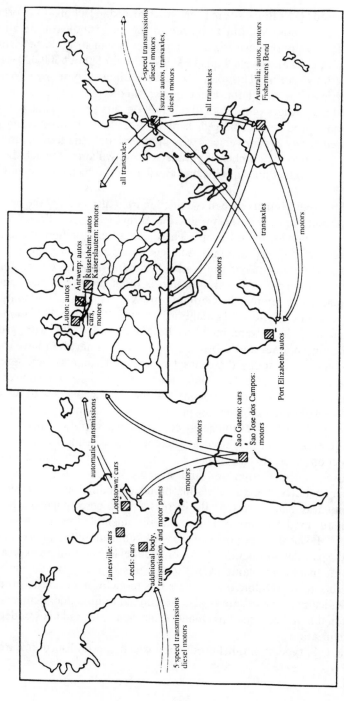

Figure 3.1 Network of General Motors' J-car program, 1983 (engines, transmissions, and assembly plants)

Table 3.1 *Parallel plants* for the production of the same vehicle type for GM and Ford in the U.S. and Europe,** 1983*

General Motors		Ford	
North America	Europe	North America	Europe
J-car: 3 plants	J-car: 3 plants	Erika: 4 plants	Escort: 3 plants
A-car: 4 plants	Kadett: 4 plants	Fox: 2 plants	Sierra: 2 plants
B-car: 4 plants	Omega: 4 plants	Panther: 3 plants	Fiesta: 3 plants
C-car: 2 plants	Corsa: 1 plant	L-Shell: 3 plants	Scorpio: 1 plant
F-car: 2 plants		S-Shell: 2 plants	
G/G special: 5 plants		Topaz: 1 plant	
X-car: 3 plants			
Y-car: 1 plant			
D-car: 1 plant			
E-car: 1 plant			
U-car: 1 plant			
T-car: 1 plant			
Actual number: 21 plants	Actual number: 7 plants	Actual number: 12 plants	Actual number: 6 plants

Notes:
 * Plants were counted double when more than one auto type was produced.
** Without Portugal.
Source: Wards Automotive Yearbooks 1983 and 1984.

the two U.S.-based corporations in the 1970s (or 1980s respectively). European sites of Ford and General Motors thus became part of the world car networks of the Escort and the J-car.

But neither corporation has had the success they had expected with their world car. An internal Ford document from 1981 reckoned with a loss of ca. 400 million dollars per year worldwide or $738 per unit on the Escort program, which was planned for nine and a half years. The source of the losses could be found in the U.S. production (Automotive News, September 17, 1984). At General Motors, the lack of success of the world car in the U.S. also led to losses. Both the J-car and Escort models had been selling like hot cakes since the middle of the 1980s however, also on the U.S.

market, and appeared to be making up ground which they had lost in the course of the disappointing development at the beginning of the 1980s.

After standing on the brink of failure in the early years the hopes of the companies for the world car concept have been significantly dampened. The extent to which a – certainly modified – new edition of the world car concept will come in for cars still under development remains to be seen. Three points will certainly be more carefully considered in the planning of future "world cars":

(1) The possibility of uneven development in different world regions must be taken more strongly into account. Management considerations critical of their own world car concept aim in this direction.

(2) The goal of largely identical equipment "under the hood" with a large variety in product exteriors between the different world regional models would have to be pursued more systematically. From the beginning, the J-cars and Escorts produced in the U.S. and Europe had only a few parts which were actually common (cf. *Business Week*, September 28, 1987). The advantages of producing units and components in large series could thus not be exploited. This was not only for logistical reasons. Due to changes in the product made by the Europeans, in order to improve fits and finishes and the cars' manufacturability, deviations in specifications and fit requirements arose which made a global sourcing of parts for the same types of U.S. and European cars impossible. The goal for the future would be that manufacturing requirements regarding, for instance, the accessibility of the car body, the necessary training measures for the work force, and tooling should be considered as early as possible during the development and testing stages of new models.

(3) A stronger emphasis must be given to actual differentiation between the various models of the same series, above all with respect to the products offered on the U.S. market. The failure of the J-car here can be chiefly traced to the fact that at that time the five GM divisions (Chevrolet, Pontiac, Buick, Oldsmobile, and Cadillac) all offered models which hardly differed from each other. In this case, attempts at achieving a production organization which was as standardized as possible obviously took place at the cost of product differentiation.

In any case the companies' expectations of being able to surpass or even to make up for the advantages of the Japanese production system by exploiting their comparative advantage of multinationality have not been realized in the 1980s. It will be very interesting for future research to see to what extent the Japanese companies on their part are pursuing a world car strategy with their newly established "transplants" in the U.S. and Europe and whether they can successfully implement it.

3.2 The strategy of product diversification and upgrading

The market developments in the 1970s confronted all Western automobile producers with the task of thoroughly reconsidering their model policy and traditional range of vehicles. The increased competition and the shift from a seller's to a buyer's market made reorientation toward product diversification and a high product variety necessary. This signaled the collapse of a basic pillar of the Fordist production philosophy which had aimed at the most complete standardization of the product as possible, and therefore the most extensive use of the cost advantages of large-scale production (economies of scale) (cf. Piore and Sable 1984). The production had to become more market oriented, the product range had to be diversified according to individual customer wishes. The companies had to be able to rapidly cater to changing customer preferences with regard to auto types, models, and equipment variants. For production organization, this meant acquiring the capability to produce a wide spectrum of different models with the same facilities, the ability to quickly switch over to new car types, models, and equipment variations and to be able to adjust the production plan accordingly. The production process became more complex.

The increased unrest tied to this higher flexibility in production boosted production costs. And this was most evident where the structures were still characterized by a Taylorist–Fordist organization. The strategy of product upgrading offered compensation for this increase in costs. Some manufacturers had already begun their strategy of product upgrading in the middle of the 1970s. Figure 3.2 gives an indication of this at four German manufacturers.

The indicator "turnover per vehicle" is of course imprecise because other business areas are also included in the turnover, but the shifting of the product range to more expensive models and accessories made up the main share of this figure at the companies selected. When the price is adjusted for inflation, we see that the turnover per vehicle at Volkswagen had gone up from 6,300 DM in 1971 to 16,900 DM in 1986, a yearly increase of ca. 11 percent compared to the initial year. At BMW the turnover per vehicle had increased from 22,600 DM in 1971 to 48,100 DM in 1985, an average of 20 percent per year.

An enormous increase in comparison to the 1970s can also be seen in the product diversification of the models offered. Table 3.2 shows that the

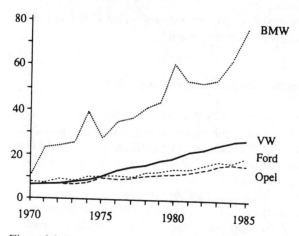

Figure 3.2 Turnover per vehicle at four German manufacturers, 1970–85 (in constant prices from 1970; in 1,000 DM)
Source: Business reports of the companies for consecutive years.

number of models offered by the German manufacturers (except Porsche) in 1985 has increased to up to three times that of 1971.

As table 3.2 shows, there are clear and characteristic differences in the number of models between the different manufacturers. The German subsidiaries of U.S. corporations make up a lesser share of the increase in model variety. Their large number of production sites and parallel plants have made it possible to reduce the number of models produced in one country (and factory). The model variation is naturally most pronounced in companies and factories who supply the entire world market from one production site.

The principle of offering customers the possibility to order individually personalized option packages has brought about greater complexity in production organization at some Western manufacturers than has been customary in the Japanese companies. There, predefined "option packages" are put together at least for vehicles designated for export. These are produced in larger volumes, thereby compensating for the costs of the higher option level.

The strategy of product diversification burdens production organization with enormous complexity problems. The expediency of this high complexity, also from the standpoint of the market, is not undisputed. It was thus established in an internal study of a European company that the vehicle type E was produced with ca. 200,000 options: the number of options of a comparable Japanese model was only 20,000. Many of the options of type E were sold in such small numbers that the question arises as

Table 3.2 *Number of car models offered by six German companies, 1971 and 1985*

Company	1971	1985
Ford	18	25
Opel	18	24
VW	13	44
AUDI	12	34
BMW	11	22
Daimler-Benz	16	34

Note:
Differentiation of models and variations made according to engine size, engine type (diesel, fuel injection, etc.), and drive type (front-wheel drive, etc.) without variations in equipment.
Source: VDA, Tatsachen und Zahlen, table: "Produktion von Kraftwagen and Strassenzugmaschinen" 1971, 1986.

to whether product diversification has not been carried too far, and if the costs of production complexity really pay off. The cost penalty of the diversification strategy, i.e., the demands on the flexibility of production and personnel was named as one of the most serious concerns by all of the managers we interviewed in the course of our study.

The strategy of higher valued products was definitely successful for a number of companies. For the mass manufacturers this was especially true for Volkswagen. Shifting competition to factors like product technology and quality made it possible on the one hand, to use the comparative advantage of the image of quality, conveyed by a label "Made in Germany." Going upscale with the products by introducing expensive product variants could, on the other hand, be seen as a strategy to avoid cost cutting measures as the company would enter market segments where the customers were not so price sensitive. A strategy which made cost considerations secondary was obviously very attractive from a union point of view. The upmarket strategy was seen above all in Germany, with its system of codetermination and its high labor costs, as a chance to jointly develop future-oriented work structures in which a highly qualified and highly paid work force would produce high quality products. "This product and process strategy of an upmarket move within the mass-market segment – with high product variety, flexible specifications and a strong emphasis on quality engineering and manufacturing – brought commercial success in the phase of increased competition and sustained high and growing employment in spite of more efficient production technologies" (Streeck 1989, p. 115).

3.3 Strategies for production automation

On the one hand, the technological development of the 1970s and 1980s was a strong stimulus for a far-reaching reorganization of the production process and work organization. On the other hand, it also appeared to be a chance for Western companies to compensate for the Japanese companies' clear advantage in human resources management, within an area in which they saw their traditional strength – the use of technology. The development of flexible automation technology opened up new possibilities.

Spurred on by Japanese competition and changed market conditions, characterized by increasing numbers of variants and frequent model changes, the companies turned more and more toward equipping their production plants with flexible automation systems. With the help of such systems it was possible to produce different models and vehicle variants on the same line without costly retoolings. Flexible automation thus showed a way out of the dead end of single purpose mechanization, committed to economies of scale.

On the basis of flexible technology it was also possible to push forward mechanization in those areas which could previously not (or at least not profitably) be mechanized. Areas like small lot production, complicated assembly, and joining operations in mass production, which make car production to this day an employment-intensive branch of industry, became capable of being mechanized. The new production automation was also compatible with the classical definition of mechanization, namely, to replace labor, to reduce direct production wage costs, and to increase productivity. General Motors, for example, justified the introduction of robots at the beginning of the 1980s with the fact that wages in the U.S. automobile industry had increased by 200 percent in the 1970s, while the costs for industrial robots had only increased by 40 percent in the same period (*Automotive Industries* 3/1981). Mechanization in the form of flexible production automation, was seen as "company management's most important instrument for increasing productivity and performance and thus improving the competitive situation" (Blick durch die Wirtschaft, August 23, 1982).

The potential for mechanization in car production was distributed quite unevenly between the different production areas though. Table 3.3 from a German company showing the productive labor hours required to build a car makes it clear that the replacement of labor with technology proceeded

Table 3.3 *The total time required to build a car in a German company broken down between the different production areas, 1980 and 1985*

Production area	1980	1985
	%	%
Trim and final assembly	27	35
Body shop	25	20
Plastics/textile	13	10
Mechanical production/foundry	11	9
Component assembly	9	10
Stamping shop	9	12
Paint shop	6	4
Production areas – total	100	100

Source: Koch and Gericke 1986, p. 180.

at different rates in the individual production areas during the first half of the 1980s. It is also a good indication of the changes in the assembly plants we describe.

According to this table, the two areas "trim and final assembly" and "body shop" had the largest share of the total time needed to build a car. This was one of the main reasons why we have selected these two areas for our factory case studies. At the same time, the fact stands out that both areas contrast sharply with respect to the pace at which their mechanization was carried out: while the body plant was at the center of flexible production automation at the beginning of the 1980s, and consequently showed a rapidly shrinking share of the total required time, the share of trim and final assembly had increased considerably – a clear indication of the fact that assembly automation was not in the forefront of the technology strategy up until the middle of the 1980s.

3.3.1 Process automation in the stamping and body welding areas

The specialized transfer line is still the most economical production technology for large series production. Flexible production systems, on the other hand, which can produce different components in "chaotic succession," have only been able to establish themselves in marginal areas (prototypes, small series, spare parts, special components) because of their comparative "slowness."

The disadvantages of conventional transfer lines, especially the way in which they have been used in mechanized parts production and the stamping plant since the 1950s, have become increasingly clear to management, however. There are two main causes for this: first, the fact that rigidly interconnected machine systems are highly susceptible to disruption and, second, the emerging trend towards smaller lot sizes. Reduced lot sizes, because of a growing variety of parts and shorter product life-cycles, reduce the chances for the amortization of capital-intensive transfer lines. This is because these are highly specialized production systems which, for the most part, have to be scrapped as soon as the old model is discontinued and a new one goes into production. The car manufacturers are thus trying to advance flexibility by adapting the traditional transfer line.

While flexible production systems in the strict sense are characterized by the fact that they can handle differing components in any sequence, so-called flexible transfer lines can only produce one component per production run. Their flexibility lies in the possibility of changing over or converting the line from one type of component to another. This flexibility in retooling was previously possible only at the expense of an extensive replacement of equipment. In the course of the development of flexible transfer lines, older dedicated machines were adapted to meet the changed requirements as far as possible by means of modifications and could thus be reused in the new production line. Admittedly, modifications of this type involved an investment expenditure in the millions (cf. the conversion of engine block lines at General Motors: U.S. Department of Transportation (ed.) 1981, *Automobile Manufacturing Processes*, Vol. V, 1978, p. 3).

This investment expenditure is no longer acceptable today. In order to retool the production line without large expenditures of time and money, modern production lines are equipped with stored-program controls (SPC) ("PCs Move into Motion Control," in: *Iron Age*, March 1983). Different from computerized numerical controlled (CNC) technology, these do not control the process itself (position control), but they regulate the sequence of processing steps, setting the tools, and making the necessary adjustments (sequence control). A centrally controlled programmable tool change, taking place in a matter of minutes, thus replaces time-consuming manual retooling at regular preplanned intervals.

The increasing importance of change-over flexibility can be seen in the discussion of the topic "Quick Die Change" (QDC) for stamping lines which manufacture body parts. According to some publications in trade journals, the Japanese had a considerable lead in flexibility here at the beginning of the 1980s. This lead was attained by introducing quick conversion presses which reduced change-over times to a fraction of those customary in the U.S. and Western Europe. Whereas the retooling took six to twelve hours with the traditional technology and organization in the

Western automobile industry, the Japanese car producers claimed to have reduced the change-over times to five to ten minutes. This enormous acceleration could not have been realized without new technological developments. Among these are: better accessibility to the presses, automation of tool and gripper changes, transportation of tools and grippers using sliding and lifting tables, transport devices like automated guided vehicles (AGV) (cf. T. Sakuri 1979, pp. 87ff.).

A more careful analysis of Japanese change-over flexibility shows, though, that their successes come not only through technology, but are based just as much on an improved work organization. The Japanese "QDC secret" is actually based on the consequent organizational separation of direct and indirect times in the course of the change-over." (*Automobil-Industrie* 1/1986). By separating the actual die change from all preceding and subsequent functions the Japanese achieve a considerable reduction in the time spent on the actual die change. When seen in this light, a good part of the Japanese "dream times" for this change which took less than ten minutes rest on a different basis of calculation. The Japanese lead is, however, by no means merely a mathematical trick, because the separation of direct and indirect change-over times has very tangible consequences. It means that all tasks which do not have to be performed on the stamping lines are taken care of outside the line. By materially and temporally separating tool setting and adjustment from the actual tool change, up to 70 percent of the change-over-necessitated down times on a stamping line can already be reduced. A rationalization of the tasks carried out during retooling is thus achieved by transforming a good share of internal direct times into external indirect times (cf. also Shingo 1981).

Thus, it becomes clear that a good deal of change-over flexibility can be achieved by the reorganization of manpower deployment. The task which still took the change-over teams in Western car factories an entire night shift up to the end of the 1970s was performed in fifteen minutes by a Japanese team at Toyota, before the astonished eyes of Western observers – an Olympian achievement, even without the indirect retooling times (*Automotive Industries* 9/1984). Especially astonishing here was the fact that the presses in question were twenty-five years old and thus not equipped with modern quick change-over systems. The Japanese change-over flexibility has found numerous imitators in the West. If "QDC" has not received that much attention in the meantime, however, this is because the JIT-principle underlying the Japanese rationalization strategy has not been driven as far in most Western companies as in Japan. In the case of "synchro-control," for example, it is possible to make longer-term production plans and this shows in the production of larger lots or batches. That is why the stamping lines needed to be changed over every two weeks at

General Motors' stamping plant in Columbus in the middle of the 1980s (*Automotive Industries* 6/1984). Thus mass production is by no means passé and this requires that the quick die change concept be viewed in the proper perspective.

A feature which we will call "process flexibility" makes flexible production systems in the stricter sense different from transfer lines in mechanical production and stamping plants which are made flexible through the use of quick change-over systems. While change-over flexibility characterizes the capability to quickly change dies or transferring and clamping devices which are principally model or component specific, process flexibility refers to running tools or workpieces independent from the model. A change-over process is thus eliminated, as a simple programming command could suffice to initiate a different processing procedure. Components no longer have to be combined into homogeneous lots. They can now be processed in chaotic sequence. In this sense, processing flexibility shows a clearly higher level of flexibility than change-over flexibility.

The most prominent example of the new processing flexibility in automobile production are the industrial robots. This is not only true qualitatively, but also in a quantitative respect. In fact, the automobile industry is by far the largest user of robot technology. In the automobile industry, industrial robots are chiefly used for guiding tools (e.g., welding guns, spray-guns), but to a lesser extent also for handling workpieces (e.g., intermediary transport of stamped parts). Up to the middle of the 1980s, the main area of deployment was spot welding in the body plant. Up to 90 percent of the robots deployed were concentrated here.

Four production stages can be differentiated in the body plant: (1) the stamped parts are welded together to form sub-assemblies. (2) In the second processing stage the sub-assemblies are joined together to major parts (floor, front section, side wall, roof). (3) In the actual body construction the major parts are welded together to form complete bodies at "welding stations." (4) Before the "body in white" leaves the body plant and is transferred to the paint shop, it undergoes a final surface processing (sanding, smoothing) in the body finishing area. Industrial robots come into play mainly in the second and third stages, i.e. in the major part and body assembly. In the first and fourth production stages, the mechanization level had always been lower. It is lowest in body finishing, an extremely labor-intensive area, which occupies up to one third of the total body plant production time (*Zeitschrift für wirtschaftliche Fertigung* 6/1982). A considerable potential for rationalization remains untapped here. Tapping this will only be possible when a new generation of robots is available. These robots would have to be able to perform complex work operations like track welding (arc welding), soldering, smoothing, and sanding. The possibilities for automation are also flourishing there at the beginning of the 1990s.

Major part and body assembly, where the spot welding method (resistance welding) dominates, have been shaken by several waves of mechanization since the beginning of the 1960s. While manual spot welding guns had been used almost exclusively up to then, Fiat had already gone over to using transfer lines with type-specific "multispot welding presses" for its new models at the beginning of the 1960s. VW was a second forerunner, where the manual process was replaced by highly mechanized welding lines at the middle of the 1960s (Hackenberg 1968). The rigid mechanization with multispot welding presses of the 1960s and the 1970s could only be justified, though, in automobile plants with very high production volume. It was not profitable in most plants. The development of flexible welding robots opened up the first significant opportunities for mechanization in this area.

In contrast to type-specific "single-purpose mechanization," robots can handle different models and variants and potentially be reused after a model change. As a flexible technology, welding robots reveal a way out of the classic dilemma which management faces in deciding on a production organization. On the one hand, manual production processes have the advantage of high flexibility, but they are quite costly. On the other hand, rigid single-purpose mechanization has extraordinary cost advantages for large model runs, but high investment risks in the case of fluctuations in demand and short model runs. Industrial robots thus compete simultaneously with highly flexible human labor and specialized single purpose mechanization. They must make up for their lesser flexibility compared to human labor through the greater volume they allow, their reliability, and their increased work speed; compared to type-specific multispot welding presses they have to compensate for their lower productivity through flexibility (Malsch, Dohse, and Jürgens 1984).

Three mechanization levels can be found side by side today: manual and robot-guided welding guns as well as multispot welding presses. Robot deployment was considerably expanded in the first half of the 1980s (see table 3.4) though, at the expense of the manual and conventionally mechanized processes. In the course of this there was a clear predominance of compact deployments of 100–200 and more welding robots per plant. They were typically installed at a model change. This "robotics leap" (Malsch, Dohse, and Jürgens 1984) was the result of capital-intensive investment projects, in which many rationalization concepts interlocked: body design suitable for robotization, new clamping and positioning systems, transfer and transport systems, computer guidance at several hierarchical levels. Thus, with the state of technological development in the

Table 3.4 *Robot focal point "body plant" (number of robots)*

Plant	Year	Body plant	Other	Total
Chrysler-St. Louis (U.S.A.)	1981	64	—	64
Mazda-Hofu (Japan)	1982	130	25	155
Mitsubishi-Okazaki (Japan)	1982	103	—	103
GM-Janesville (U.S.A.)	1983	59	—	59
Ford-Saarlouis (FRG)	1983	102	14	116
Chrysler-Windsor (Canada)	1983	123	12	135
Vauxhall-Ellesmere Port (GB)	1984	52	2	54
GM-Buick City (U.S.A.)	1985	190	32	222
Ford-Cologne (FRG)	1986	210	39	249

Source: Own calculations using data from trade journals.

1980s, robots were no longer devices which stood alone, as was still the case in the 1970s, but were rather components of an integrated production system.

In the course of this, we can differentiate between two characteristic systems which underline the breadth of deployment exhibited by welding robots: flexible production cells for medium sized series and welding transfer lines for large series. In the middle of the 1980s examples of the first type of system, the production cell, could be found at Fiat's famous "Robogate," the "Parcours" for Volkswagen's Polo, the production cells in BMW's Munich plant and the main body welding station at Vauxhall's Ellesmere Port plant (*Industrial Robot* 3/1987). Because these systems worked comparably slowly, with production cycles ranging from 2.4 (Vauxhall) to 4.5 minutes (BMW), two and more parallel stations were deployed in order to produce up to capacity. The flexibility potential had largely remained unused in the cases mentioned (*Industrial Robot* 6/1983, p. 114).

In the second type of system, robots were installed with short cycle times of about sixty seconds in welding transfer lines, frequently combined with multispot welding presses. Most robot deployment in the automobile industry up to the middle of the 1980s could be classified under this second form. The combination of robots with "dedicated" model-dependent process technology and the rigidities of the transfer system with its fixed clamping or positioning devices limited the utilization of the flexibility potential of the robots. Examples were the modernized body lines for the Audi 100 (1982), for the Golf (Rabbit) at VW's Wolfsburg plant (1983), and for Ford-Cologne's Scorpio (1985). These robot systems were designed at the outset to produce one basic model and its derivatives. It must be recalled here that it is no big problem to put together two or three different models on one production line with the current state of technology. Transport and clamping devices are no serious obstacle when there are standardized positioning points for the different body types. Japanese examples verify this. Thus seven variants of three basic models were simultaneously run on the robotized underbody line at Toyota's Tahara plant (*Industrial Robot* 3/ 1982, p. 61); and the body construction line at Mazda's Hofu plant already handled up to nine variants of three basic models in any sequence by the mid 1980s (*Automotive News*, November 29, 1982).

Only when the processing flexibility of robot technology is actually used is it possible to balance out demand fluctuations for the different automobile models, to run a model mix which is flexibly adjusted to the respective market situations, and thus to exhaust the advantages of the new technology. With respect to the flexibility potential, the Japanese manufacturers appear to be ahead of their Western competition, who often use their industrial robots like conventional single-purpose equipment during the run time of a specific model. But even in Japanese factories, the flexibility of robot technology is not optimally used in mass production. If one considers that the robots available at the beginning of the 1980s could perform up to sixty-four different work programs (*Industrial Robot* 12/1982, p. 227) – the current robot generation is much more powerful – so that even with nine programs, as in Mazda's Hofu plant, this flexibility potential would largely lie idle. This was partially due to the fact that the model mix flexibility was not fully utilized in the actual production program. Above all, it was due to the immense engineering difficulties involved in converting basic inventions in process technology into practical system solutions which have to stand up to everyday conditions in the factory. In comparing the robot systems developed today with the preceding conventional equipment generations one can already see that the demands on servicing, monitoring, and maintenance have increased enormously with the growing technological complexity and susceptibility to interference, and that this situation places new demands on manpower utilization. We will be coming back to this problem in more detail in the chapters ahead.

3.3.2 Process technology in the assembly areas

The goal of the assembly line is to increase the productivity of labor by breaking assembly tasks down into extremely short partial operations and then construct "jobs" which fit into the cycle time set for the assembly line. Joining operations, like inserting parts and screwing components together, are considered to be assembly work. With regard to the entirety of assembly operations, we can distinguish between two areas: vehicle assembly and preassembly. Vehicle assembly (encompassing trim assembly and final assembly) includes all of the installation and mounting tasks which are performed on the cars on the main assembly line after the paint shop. In addition to this, there are numerous preassembly areas: for transmission and engine assembly ("engine dress-up"), instrument panel, etc. We will be coming back to the importance of distinguishing between vehicle assembly and preassembly later in the context of assembly automation.

When compared to the other production areas, the mechanization level of the assembly areas has always been lower and had not advanced beyond hand tools (e.g., wrenches for bolting) before the 1980s. At the beginning of the 1980s, this gap became even larger. A tapping of the mechanization potential for vehicle assembly will be dependent on developing "feeling" and "seeing" industrial robots which are capable of localizing workpieces, sorting out defective parts, precisely inserting and bolting components. Despite their extreme reduction and simplification, assembly operations are highly complex and require a complicated hand/eye coordination, which can by no means be dealt with by the first generation of industrial robots. The variety of assembly operations and assembly parts and the large tolerance deviations, even with components which have the same basic design, have set narrow limits on mechanization (cf. Braun *et al.* 1968, pp. 115ff.; Koch and Gericke 1986).

As late as 1981, the robotic study of the *Soziologisches Forschungsinstitut* (SOFI) gave a broader application of industrial robots in the assembly area only minimal chances, even in the foreseeable future (SOFI 1981, p. 594). At that time the Institut für Produktionsautomatisierung (IPA) in Stuttgart, West Germany still considered the industrial usage of "intelligent" robots with visual and tactile sensors to be a vision of the distant future. In 1981, only around 5 percent of all industrial robots in the West German car industry were deployed in the assembly areas ("Handelsblatt," August 10, 1981). This share increased in the 1980s – in comparison to the body plant and paint shop, though, the degree of automation remained low. In fact, of the 2,200 industrial robots deployed by VW in 1988 63 percent were for spot-welding operations and 15 percent for assembly (Lünzmann 1989, p. 68).

It must be emphasized, however, that assembly automation is definitely not foundering on a lack of interest on the part of the companies. The opposite is true: inefficiencies in line balancing, inflexibility of manpower usage, deficient production quality, high fluctuation and absentee rates, and low work motivation have always caused especially high costs in the vehicle assembly areas. Thus the share of those employees in the assembly areas who, as quality controllers and repair workers, deal with quality defects in some way or another amounted to almost 20 percent in most Western companies in the early 1980s. It is higher than in "mechanical processing," in "stamping," and in the "body shop" (own calculation using the figures, SOFI 1981, p. 227). There is indeed no lack of management motivation to eliminate vehicle assembly as a trouble spot and to replace the employees working there with robots.

With the opening of its famous assembly plant *Halle 54* for the then new generation of its bread and butter car, the Golf, at its huge Wolfsburg site in the summer of 1983, VW made the biggest leap in the history of assembly automation up until then (cf. Handelsblatt, August 12/13, 17, 1983; Der Spiegel 37/1983). In the assembly technology for the new Golf, the degree of mechanization was increased from 5 percent in the old assembly plant to 25 percent. The company said that the degree of automation could even be increased to 33 percent in the framework of their concept. Volkswagen was unmatched for quite some time with its leap in high technology in the area of final assembly. Fiat did not follow this strategy until the end of the 1980s in its refurbished car plant in Cassino, Italy which started production in 1989 and was planned to have a 40 percent degree of automation (Johnson 1989, p. 24). The automation concept followed at Fiat's Cassino plan was very similar to that at Volkswagen. A 40 percent degree of automation was never actually achieved there and the figure was scaled down later in light of the enormous problems in coping with the new technology in this plant. The 33 percent target at VW was also abandoned soon as too ambitious.

With its *Halle 54* VW worked on the principle of creating module areas off the main line. With modularization, the complexity of the assembly operations can be reduced and this makes mechanization easier. Fourteen preassembly areas were created in this manner. In addition, a good deal of the automation efforts for the new Golf were concentrated on assembly operations on the main line, for example, on the automatic mounting of wheels, batteries, fuel lines, brake lines, the exhaust system, and for installing the power train. In order to be able to automatically bring in and bolt down the power train – which consisted of subframes, engine, transmission, engine mount, and front axle – it was necessary to design the vehicle in such a manner that the front remained open up till the stage of final assembly. The front piece was then fitted to the car as a complete module. (Schweizer 1986, pp. 521ff.). This example also made clear the close interdependence between product design and technical and organizational change-overs in the production process.

The new Golf was developed from the start with a view to assembly automation. Its design was exactly tuned to the requirements of the new assembly process (Handelsblatt, August 12/13, 1983; *Automotive Industries*

6/1984). This required first of all the utmost of uniformity and adherence to the most exact tolerances for all components. The body must, moreover, be totally free of tension, a requirement which put a special burden on the press and body shop operations. All threaded connections also played a critical role.

In the assembly of the Golf and the Jetta, 300 bolted connections are carried out automatically. A bolt suitable for mechanization had to be developed for this. The bolt received a washer that was rolled on, a grooved shaft and a grooved point. In addition to this, the conditions for delivery were changed to "Delivery in a 5kg. sack, 100% inspected, defective parts not permitted" ... Beyond this, a regulatory device for automatic assembly bolting was developed. The goal was to bring bolting values like torque and angle of rotation exactly into the standards of the tolerance range and to be able to reproducibly document the bolting during the working time. A faulty bolting – due to improper positioning, for example – would be recognized and indicated by the testing device. The transport equipment would be blocked and could only be started again by human hand, so that the vehicle could be brought into a repair station. (Handelsblatt, December 26, 1984)

A characteristic of the assembly automation in *Halle 54* was the fact that it was only partially oriented to flexible production. Structurally, in fact, it was a concept for type-specific automation, although about fifty robots and over 250 flexibly programmable automatons for handling and assembly operations were also deployed in *Halle 54*. VW could only carry out the leap in automation at the beginning of the 1980s because the Golf, its bread and butter car, was a classical mass product with a lengthy model run.

The concept of *Halle 54* was often criticized by interviewees from other companies for its sizeable capital requirements and its high susceptibility to disruption. VW could only take the risk of a type-specific and rigidly linked assembly automation on the main line because of the fact that a single assembly line was not enough for the Golf anyway, with a daily volume of 2,700 vehicles. In addition to the automation area, there was still a parallel manual assembly. Companies with a "more modern" product strategy – that is, a wider range of products, lower production volume per model, and shorter product cycles – could not take such an investment risk. Not least for this reason, a corresponding leap in automation was apparently not on the agenda in the Japanese automobile industry up until the second half of the 1980s. With model cycles of around four years, which were much shorter than those of comparable European products, a massive entry into assembly automation like that of VW would have entailed much greater risks. The situation has now changed at the beginning of the 1990s and the Japanese companies are investing heavily in new automation. We will briefly touch on this aspect in our final chapter.

But the example of VW has shown that a prerequisite for the automation strategy is a change in the course of the assembly process itself. This "detour" over the creation of preassembly areas runs strangely parallel to the humanization ideas with respect to assembly work. Preassembly areas had existed in the traditional assembly plants also, but they had been increasingly reduced, though, in the course of perfecting the assembly line principle. This work was, in part, also outsourced to subcontractors. In any case it is no coincidence that both the humanization and automation considerations are directed at the creation of such module areas separate from the main line again, if possible at stationary work stations. Humanization experiments in these areas have, in fact, often proved to be precursors and preparation for later automation measures.

There is a further rationale, though, for the tendency to draw off operations from the main line into preassembly areas. The growing model mix and the explosion of variants and options for one car model brings increasing difficulties for the classic Fordist assembly line. Modularization is thus especially desirable in the areas where the fluctuations in the work content of the different variants are especially extreme, like in the area of wire harness operations. Modularization thus absorbs the customer oriented flexibility and, at the same time, allows the company to keep the assembly line principle for the remaining operations.

This path can be illustrated by the example of module assembly for Opel and Vauxhall's Kadett (Astra) production in the Bochum, Antwerp, and Ellesmere Port plants. Two separate areas for door and cockpit preassembly were introduced in these plants in 1984 using a new concept (*Production*, January 18, 1984; *Assembly Automation*, 11/1984). Automated guided vehicles, "robomats," which were equipped as assembly platforms, make it possible to assemble the doors and cockpits with all their accessories separately from the main conveyor belt. Even though the assembly operations are still carried out manually, this modular preassembly concept has important advantages over traditional assembly on the main line: first, both units can be completed more efficiently, second, the car interior is better accessible for assembly operations; and, third, the new conception creates prerequisites for a later assembly automation. Design changes in the new Kadett were necessary in order to integrate the cockpit module to form a unified preassembled part, consisting of the instrument panel with all of its cable connections, the steering column, and the pedals. Opel developed this concept further in its refurbished Rüsselheim plant where the new model Omega has been produced since the fall of 1986. Ford also set up off-line module areas for cockpit and door assembly in Cologne for the start of the Scorpio in 1985. They rejected a system for workpiece transport with automated guided vehicles as too costly. Some of the preassembly areas were set up as assembly lines, some as stationary work stations.

It is conspicuous that the new production concepts in the final assembly areas at the beginning of the 1980s, both automation and the establishment of module areas with manual production, were almost exclusively introduced in European plants. Similar production concepts were not introduced in General Motors' U.S. plants until the second half of the 1980s. Although the change-overs in the assembly areas did not take place without problems in Germany, these problems were minor in comparison to those reported in the U.S. plants. The most notorious case is the Hamtramck plant which GM built as a "showcase of its new technology strategy." But instead of a showcase, writes Keller in her book on General Motors in the 1980s, "Hamtramck became a nightmare of technology gone berserk. The stories of robot breakdowns and miscues read like a 1950s B-movie that might have been titled 'Robots from Hell'." Keller continues,

Tales from the dark side of high technology gained momentum as people slowly began to see that this was not the panacea the company had promised it would be. The problems existed, not only at the Hamtramck plant, but in every plant where robots had been installed to perform vital functions. At Hamtramck, what was intended as a high tech solution turned into gross inefficiency. Lines were stopped so frequently for repairs that one observer described car building in the plant as "like viewing a film in slow motion, even when the assembly line is moving, which it isn't." Hamtramck was supposed to produce 60 cars per hour, but after nearly a year of operation it was producing only half that number, and software was still being debugged. (Keller 1989, p. 52)

After this experience, GM returned in part to the conventional solutions of assembly line production. In chapter 10 we will be looking more closely at the new production concepts in the assembly areas and the problems connected with them.

3.3.3 Computer integration as a long-term strategy

The factory of the future will not only consist of robots or a new generation of computer-assisted production technologies. At the core, we are dealing with a synthesis of social integration and computer integration of all company functions. Thus it would not be a continuation of classic production automation with microelectronic means, but a new type of rationalization process using information technology to integrate the company as an entire system. Computer-integrated production does not have the rationalization of individual production and office areas as its goal, it aims rather at optimizing the entire company, a task which would be inconceivable without adequately considering "human resources." In fact, this aim had not been achieved anywhere up to the time of our study. As far as the technological side was concerned, these were only "island solutions" which allowed computer aided design (CAD), computer aided manufacturing (CAM), computerized production planning and control systems (MRP), computer aided quality control (CAQ), and management information systems (MIS) to exist unconnected side by side.

Here we have specified the central criterion for "computer integrated manufacturing" (CIM): all functions must be able to use a common data base in order to allow for the exchange of administrative, technological, and commercial information. Added to this comes an automated system of progress reports which extend much further than the simple recording of processing times and production reports. Furthermore, the data transfers must take place rapidly enough so that the data used in different areas are identical. This is especially important in operations where time is a critical factor. In other words: CIM is not realizable, regardless of its form, without a common logistical data base for the entire company.

These prerequisites were only partially fulfilled in the car industry – at the time of our study and up to today. Due to the heterogeneity of their production processes and the use of countless special machines from differing manufacturers the companies employed many different computer systems at the time of our study, mixed together and side by side. They either could not communicate with each other at all or the point-to-point connections between them were unclear and confusing. In order to come closer to the goal of an interconnection between different areas, the automobile companies were making considerable efforts to reduce the variety of management and communication systems through standardization. The forerunner here was General Motors with its "manufacturing automation protocol" (MAP) since 1985.

In looking more closely at the CIM concepts being discussed at the time of our study, we can distinguish between two different directions of integration in the companies. In the "vertical" direction, integration refers to that line which leads from the strategic product planning over research and development, product design, process control, production, and quality control up to the finished product. The second direction of integration refers to the business management/commercial flow of material and information on the "horizontal" level. Here we are dealing with the logistic chain, which runs from the parts suppliers, to material disposition and filling orders, wholesaling, and delivery – right down to the customer. Production planning and control is at the interface of the two directions of integration.

An example of vertical integration was that the car manufacturers had already begun to install CAD dialogue systems in their mainframe computers at the beginning of the 1970s. In the 1980s, they had gone over to equipping entire production sections with complete CAM systems, especially in the body and paint plants. At the same time, the logistic chain at the horizontal integration level was becoming a focal point for rationalization interest. The decisive impulse for this came from the JIT ("just-in-time") principle of the Japanese automobile producers which, while extensively eliminating parts supplies and intermediary buffers, made a drastic decrease in inventory and a shortening of delivery times possible.

The pilot projects of integrated production logistics in the West German automobile industry had already achieved remarkable economic results in a short two- to three-year period. According to Olle (1986), the time required for a product to pass through production could be shortened by 60–90 percent, parts inventories could be reduced from 50 percent to 70 percent and overhead costs from 20 percent to 50 percent, while labor productivity was increased from 20 percent to 50 percent (Olle 1986, p. 315). In order to support this development and reduce investments and depreciation, the companies were trying to achieve an inter-company standardization of data transmission networks. Thus, in 1985, the association of the British automobile industry took a first step toward standardizing sales and purchasing activities with its "Motornet" project. This system was accessible for all manufacturers, suppliers, and dealers in the British automobile industry. The possibilities for the direct exchange of information between the participants were improved by a data processing network. Similar systems were developed in the U.S. and in Germany.

The "Association of the German Automobile Industry" (*Verband der deutschen Automobilindustrie* – VDA) had also initiated a standardization project which should alleviate data transmission between automobile manufacturers and suppliers. Daimler-Benz played a forerunner role with its logistic system FORS, which was developed following the VDA guidelines. Daimler-Benz was planning to link itself with between 100 and 1,500 suppliers over a standardized data transmission network in the coming four to five years (*Computerwoche*, September 13, 1985). As table 3.5 shows, Daimler-Benz, Opel, and VW were about equal in their development, while Ford was about a year behind with its installations in 1986.

VW has been developing its logistics system FEBES (integrated production disposition and procurement system) since 1984. It was to be implemented in several stages by 1988 (*Handelsblatt*, October 11, 1983). In the first stage of implementation, to last until the middle of 1984, an organizational linkage of supply and process control would be introduced in the individual plants; in the second stage, the installation of a logistics headquarters was planned; and the full realization of FEBES, with the connection of all suppliers, was to take place by 1988. The advantages that the company was expecting to achieve with its new logistics concept was in

Table 3.5 *Computer linkage of companies and suppliers*

	Number of suppliers connected over a computer network		
Automobile manufacturer	1984	1985	1986
VW/Audi	30	40	250
Opel	20	40	—
Daimler-Benz	10	30	250
Ford	—	10	—

Source: Computerwoche, September 13, 1985, p. 26.

their expectation that the average run time for the entire range of models could be reduced from an average of thirty-three days in 1983 to fifteen days.

The implementation of FEBES made it clear that the computerized linkage begins at the intersection of both integration levels. At the same time, a shift in focus from production automation (beginning of assembly automation, 1983) to total optimization through computer integration (starting in 1983) became visible. Volkswagen worked closely with Siemens in this respect and, compared to the difficulties of other companies, it can be said that the use of hard and software systems from a single manufacturer could make the transition to CIM considerably easier.

In contrast to VW, General Motors' CIM strategy faced a proliferation of many different information and control technologies. GM's strategic approach was to overcome the incompatibility of the different systems using its newly conceived network standard, the "manufacturing automation protocol" (MAP). As a building block of GM's CIM conception, MAP was a so-called backbone network, a data transmitting system which runs through the factory and to which all production systems could be connected, regardless of manufacturer. The idea of this backbone network was to collect all relevant information and distribute it throughout the factory. In this sense, MAP was a central component of CIM. (Yet the MAP conception by no means excluded the coexistence of differing technological solutions. These would no longer have the character of island solution, as they would then be linked with each other over the MAP system.)

General Motors first introduced MAP to the public in 1984. The model which was introduced, partially meeting the expectations of other users as it follows the trend toward "Open Systems Interconnection" (OSI), is since on its way to becoming an industry standard worldwide. The technological persuasiveness of this conception alone would not be sufficient to explain this diffusion. Added to this came the market clout of General Motors, which drew countless companies into the suction of the initiative started by the industry giant. Renowned electronic firms like Digital Equipment, Alan Bradley, IBM, and General Electric supported the initiative; car companies like Ford, Peugeot, and BMW joined in; and the European MAP User Group (EMUG) was formed at the end of 1985. Even though MAP was by no means mature – the versions 1.0 to 3.0 came in rapid succession since 1987 – its triumphal march could no longer be stopped (*Computerwoche*, July 25, 1986). MAP's final configuration was still open, though. Not all problems had been solved satisfactorily. Here was a chance for other companies to create their own network concepts and simultaneously remain open for MAP compatibility (*Hard and Soft* 6/1986; Weißbach 1988).

General Motors has already established networks in several plants in the U.S.A. using the MAP standard. (The new conception was more advantageous than old solutions because of reduced expenditures for hard- and software.) The company developed a five stage implementation plan to establish this network conception. This implementation would extend over a five-year period (*Hard and Soft* 6/1986). General Motors' automobile activities provide favorable prerequisites for this "migration strategy." As they built new factories, they had the opportunity to establish and test MAP with all of its consequences in totally new facilities.

Due to the fact that the MAP strategy was connected with enormous investment risks which only few users could handle, experts see difficulties for the adoption of MAP in Europe. Added to this came the fact that a change of course, even for firms which like Ford were participating in the MAP initiative, could not take place overnight. Ford, with its Plant Vehicle Scheduling (PVS), developed a similar communications system in its eight European plants. As the MAP conception was not yet available in 1983/4, when the system was to be introduced in the Cologne and Saarlouis plants, Ford had no alternative but to "develop its own software and communication protocols for point-to-point interconnection" (*Handelsblatt*, February 18, 1987). These insecurities and the lack of tested and inexpensive software meant that other companies, despite a great deal of interest, had only used MAP on a small scale up until the end of the decade.

The breakthrough of MAP presupposes, though, that the doubts experts have raised about MAP's reliability in such a critical environment as car production (*Handelsblatt*, February 18, 1987) could be refuted in practice. In the long run, however, the strategy of a decisive leap into the age of high technology could prove its superiority as it offers a chance to build up a stock of technological experience which the competition could not simply acquire or obtain with their wait-and-imitate strategy. That is still quite far in the future, though.

3.3.4 Company-specific differences in technology policies

As can be seen in pertinent articles in the trade journals, the factor "production technology" played quite a different role in company restructuring strategies. We will show this using the examples of Volkswagen, General Motors, and Ford.

VW is often named as a forerunner in technological development in the automobile industry. In its main plant it was one of the first companies to mechanize most body shop operations at the beginning of the 1970s. Here, manual welding work was replaced by highly modern type-specific welding transfer lines. Modern robotized welding systems were by no means an entirely new technology in the mid 1980s. They were, rather, the result of the development of transfer line technology since the 1970s. In the course of this, the company could continually build up and develop its stockpile of experience.

At the peak of Beetle production in the early 1970s, VW had already reached a level of mechanization far exceeding that of the competition. That changed with the differentiation of the product range at the middle of the 1970s. Rigid single-purpose mechanization had reached its limits, mechanization efforts now had to be oriented more closely to the demands of flexibilization. VW's marked fixation on mass production technology, more intense than that of other big companies like GM or Ford, could be the reason for the fact that VW deployed its first industrial robots later than the Japanese automobile manufacturers, and also later than General Motors and Fiat. Starting with the first compact deployment of welding robots in its Hannover plant in 1979, VW proceeded all the more resolutely, and robotized its small car (Polo) production (1981), the Audi production (1982), and production of the Golf (1983) in rapid succession. In the course of this, different concepts of robot deployment were tested to open up options for the future.

What distinguished VW was its policy of technological self-sufficiency regarding robot deployment. VW management had set the course early for a self-sufficient entry into robotic technology by tenaciously building up its own robot production since the beginning of the 1970s. At the time of our study, VW and Audi almost exclusively used robots from their own production, and VW was the largest robot producer in West Germany. With this self-sufficiency strategy, VW did not undergo a transformation, it rather tied on to and built upon its traditional competence in mechanical engineering. Because of the close personnel and organizational interconnection between their expertise as manufacturer and their expertise as user, the development and use of new technologies for production could be accomplished relatively smoothly.

If we had labelled VW's technology policy a self-sufficiency strategy, this was only true in the strictest sense for its mechanical engineering capacities. In the area of information and control technologies VW had formed a liaison with the German company Siemens. This close manufacturing connection was expensive for VW, but it offered the advantage that each side could accumulate much experience regarding the actual application of its products and could deal with developmental problems more specifically and over a longer period of time.

The technology strategies of General Motors in the 1980s were clearly different from VW. Up until the end of the 1970s, General Motors had understood itself as a company whose goal was to build automobiles, not to develop and manufacture new production technologies. To this extent, GM's management had always considered itself as a user, not a manufacturer of production technology. This was furthered by the circumstance that GM owed its historic success over Ford, its main competitor on the U.S. market, to a model policy which stressed diversification and frequent "face lifts." This model policy was dependent from the beginning on a high degree of production flexibility which, as long as flexible automation was not yet available, could only be secured by employee and organizational flexibility. In order to avoid high conversion costs with the yearly face lift on the U.S. market, manual production dominated in GM's body and assembly plants. Consequently, an extremely high level of mechanization, like that at VW, was never reached and mechanization never had the decisive role which it had at VW. General Motors was, though, one of the first companies which already had some experience with industrial robots at the beginning of the 1970s (Lordstown). But they had difficulties with the not yet mature robot generation. The experiment was not systematically evaluated and robotization stagnated at GM until the end of the 1970s.

At the beginning of the 1980s, when top management became convinced that the decisive battles over shares of the world market would be fought out in the area of technology, the corporation then took radical countermeasures. General Motors' first answer to the competition on the world market in 1980 was a forced technology strategy. Roger B. Smith, then president of General Motors, was quoted in this connection: "This worldwide technology race is a race to survive. The best advice I can give in regard to our technological future until the year 2000 is to put on your seat belt, and be ready for the ride of your life." General Motors has since staged its change in strategy with a large journalistic effort. Thus, a planning concept for the deployment of robots until 1990 was published in 1981 which at that time far overshadowed the announced and actual deployment of the other large automobile companies.

In contrast to VW and GM, technology only had a secondary importance in Ford's company strategy. European firms like Fiat and VW, with their technology tradition and historically evolved technological know-how, the Japanese, with their strategy of forced modernization of the 1970s, and General Motors with its high-tech acquisition policy all had experience with the compact introduction of fifty industrial robots and more at a time when Ford-Europe only had twenty experimental robots deployed (*Automotive Industries* 9/1985). Ford had a starting position structurally similar to that of General Motors, but it had a much weaker economic situation and could not afford an external acquisition of technological know-how for the time being.

The first large thrust of automation at Ford-Europe started in 1983 with the new Sierra model at the plants in Genk and Dagenham (with 130 robots each). The most important investment and modernization project, however, was the Scorpio, as the successor to the Granada, whose development and new production systems cost $1 billion. The plant Cologne-Niehl, where the Scorpio has been produced since 1985, was equipped with 249 industrial robots, and was among the most modern automobile factories in the world at the middle of the 1980s. In the production of the Scorpio, 91 percent of the point welds were performed by robots, whereby they only performed 25 percent of the welds for its predecessor (*Blick durch die Wirtschaft*, August 20, 1985).

Ford U.S.A.'s most important technology project was the twin model Taurus/Sable. This model was manufactured in the modernized assembly plants in Atlanta and Chicago. The Atlanta plant had to handle six model changes between 1978 and 1985 and was equipped with an automated body plant and a modular assembly concept for the production of the Taurus/Sable. The parallel plant in Chicago had 117 industrial robots with approximately the same technological level (*Ward's Automotive Yearbook* 1986, p. 206). These were, however, quantities which could at best be considered average for assembly plants with a yearly output of about 250,000 cars in 1985.

In comparison to General Motors', Ford's U.S. automation projects could by no means be characterized as ambitious as GM's with its "factory of the future" projects at Saturn and Saginaw. A decisive aspect of the Alpha project for Ford management was to consolidate and further develop the technology lessons which the company had learned in the preceding years. In the course of this, results of the Alpha project were already being gradually applied in the new Chicago and Atlanta plants. Alpha has therefore become the code word for an organic technology strategy which was satisfied with a solid second place and did not strive for the forerunner role.

Ford thus decided to concentrate on improving its management methods and to set the emphasis in its rationalization on the organization of work and the management style in the factory. Ford management had examined the technological planning and system solutions of its competitors at the beginning of the 1980s and came to the conclusion that no big break-throughs in technology could be expected in the foreseeable future. With this strategy, Ford obviously learned a lesson from the Japan reception that the factor "technology" had a relatively marginal importance for explaining the productivity advantages of Japanese factories (Abernathy, Clark, Kantrow 1983b, pp. 84f.).

In summary, we have seen that there were clear focal points for the utilization of new production technology in the framework of the investment programs of the 1980s; on the other hand, there were clear differences in the weighting of the factor "technology" as a problem solving strategy for the companies – differences which were also clearly expressed in the sample we studied, as we will see later.

3.4 People-related strategies

In concluding this chapter we will be dealing with the people-related strategies. The fact that this comes last, behind questions of market strategy and the use of technology, corresponds to an old tradition in Western industrial practice which was, however, beginning to change at the time of our research. The improvement of cooperation and communication has been recognized as a central strategic question by individual companies. The Japan example had given these strategies a decided thrust at the end of the 1970s, although there were many other points of reference – models and forerunners. Especially important in this regard were the new production concepts that had been developed in the Swedish companies, primarily through the initiative of Volvo (Berggren 1991). In the framework of our study it was primarily the new work and motivation (NW&M) concepts of the worldwide corporations General Motors and Ford which influenced the processes of change observable at the factory level. In the following, we will briefly describe the basic features of these programs – at GM they are called Quality of Work-Life (QWL), at Ford Employe Involvement (EI).

Both GM's and Ford's programs were developed in their respective U.S. corporate headquarters and diffused, supported, and evaluated from there. The common sponsorship by the companies and the UAW helped the programs spread rapidly in North American factories. In 1984 there were ca. eighty-six EI programs in the U.S. Ford factories and QWL was established in each of the 151 GM factories. The participation programs at GM covered individual sections with 50 to 200 workers, but in some cases went much further (Serrin 1984, p. 136).

While Ford's EI program was apparently touched off to a great extent by the lessons learned from Japan at the end of the 1970s, the QWL program at General Motors already had a longer tradition. It had its beginnings in the 1960s, in Organizational Development (OD) projects for salaried employees and management. Irving Bluestone, as director of the GM's division of the UAW, gave the QWL process at GM strong impulses. The OD staff at General Motors, under the leadership of "Dutch" Landen (until 1982), worked out systematic goal conceptions and strategies for the QWL process which, in their long range perspectives and in their comprehensive demands for a change in the traditional type of management and organization of production, extended far beyond the EI program at Ford.

3.4.1 The QWL program at General Motors

A presentation of the essence and objectives of the QWL program can be found in Landen and Carlson (1982). In this work, the authors defined QWL as an evolutionary, holistic process, which begins with the relationship of the individual to his work and leads, finally, to a changed relation between the company and society. The essential element in the QWL process was, according to Landen and Carlson, the redistribution of the positions of power and influence within the organization. It dealt chiefly with the reduction of hierarchy and a greater degree of self-regulation in the jobs carried out. In this, the group principle was central to all considerations. The process of group formation made up the core of the QWL process. The goal was to establish semi-autonomous work groups as the heart of work and social organization in the factory of the future.

From the point of view of redistributing power, an important intermediate stage of this process would be reached with the establishment of quality circles. The difference between this and establishing discussion forums, committees, and project groups – stages which must first be gone through – is "that a quality circle is not only intended to be permanent but its members are *empowered* to meet regularly; receive problem-solving training; have access to information, data, and people; and either recommend actions to be taken or implement their own decisions. Therefore, a quality circle represents a significant shift in organizational decision-making. Moreover, it is an ongoing and self-adjusting, decision-making system that is freer than task forces or committees from the influence of external whims or capricious contracts." (Landon and Carlson 1982, pp. 306ff.).

As soon as the quality circle system was firmly established, Landen and Carlson expected that tasks which were traditionally supervisory responsibilities, such as work planning, job assignment, breaking-in new workers and on-the-job training, structuring the process layout and sequences of operations, and ordering tools and material, would be taken over by circle members. With this, the role of the supervisors would have to change. In order to further the process of shifting responsibility downward, new supervisory roles would have to be encouraged and supported. The supervisors would then have a helping and supporting function for the newly emerging semi-autonomous quality circle. General Motors used the term "Employee Participation Group" (EPG) for these upgraded quality circles (Landon and Carlson 1982, p. 307).

The prerequisites for a larger organizational restructuring would have been reached as soon as the EPG reached a stage of development where the group could form its own leadership structure: the role of the lower-level supervisor could be removed from the vertical structure and be brought into a cooperatively organized supervisory team. A fundamental transformation of the system would have taken place when supervisory work had been shifted downward in this manner and new support systems had been created. In these systems, former supervisors would take on new responsibilities such as planning, plant-wide problem-solving, coordination between different functions, and, generally, "trouble shooting."

The organization at this stage has reached a high level of sophistication and the overall structure has been transformed from a quite traditional one to one beginning to approximate a high-level socio-technical system. (Landen and Carlson 1982, p. 303)

To what extent this theoretical model for the development and transformation of organizations had actually influenced decisions about corresponding programs in individual GM plants is not known. It is hard to imagine that the time frame which Landen and Carlson's model for the QWL process would require due to its complex preconditions in learning and organizational theory could have been adequately taken into account in plant-level considerations of new work structures. But it is obvious that the company headquarters had allowed the process of organizational development a considerable period of time and a broad scope for experimentation. The large domain of GM offered many possibilities for testing the various NW&M concepts in different plants. Primarily plants for parts and components were selected for this. The most risky experiment, transforming an assembly plant for one of the company's "bread and butter" products into a team plant was left to Japanese management. This was the case in GM's joint venture with Toyota in California, the New

United Motor Manufacturing Incorporated, NUMMI. The production and work organization at NUMMI and the performance levels thus attained are now considered as a prime example and model for the success of the team concept in GM's worldwide corporate organization. NUMMI thus contributed considerably to the spreading of the team concept in the second half of the 1980s.

Of greater importance for our research were experiments with new forms of work which GM had in part already introduced in individual plants in the 1970s. An example of this was the Livonia Cadillac Motor Plant, which became a "team plant" in 1979 and whose organizational principles were also used as a model for the new General Motors' engine plant in Europe, in Aspern near Vienna (Scheinecker 1988; Bayer 1982; Haas 1985). Approximately four years were allowed for the process of the delegation of responsibility to the teams in the Aspern plant (cf. table 3.6).

In this period of time the members of the team would have gone through three stages. These extended from the acquisition of work-related qualifications, over tasks of work coordination within the team and organizational tasks extending beyond the team, up to administrative tasks of budgeting in the final stage.

Special features of the team organization in Aspern are:
the integration of direct and indirect production tasks into the job spectrum of the team;
a change in the leadership organization through appointing team speakers, and especially a changed role for the first line supervisor ("Meister");
establishing "team meetings" as work related discussions within the team after working hours;
the introduction of a new wage principle, "pay for knowledge" or flexibility wage.

The developments that took place on this basis – in the Aspern plant, in the plants of Cadillac Livonia, at NUMMI and elsewhere – were links in a large-scale chain of "laboratories" for experiments in work organization. Added to this came the experiences at GM's new production sites in the U.S. which were to start production in the middle of the eighties, one example of this being "Buick City." The orientation on Japanese production systems went so far here that even the energy-saving tight spatial conditions of Japanese factories were to be taken over, and the principle of zero-error-production would be forced by the closeness: there would be no room for cars to be taken out of the flow of production for repairs (*Automotive News*, December 31, 1984). In contrast to the concept of functionally specialized, spatially dispersed scattered plants of the 1960s and 1970s, Buick City was again planned as an integrated production

Table 3.6 *Delegation of responsibility in the course of the QWL process*

Phase					
I	Safety training Machine servicing Tool change Small repairs Hygiene/cleaning Flow of information				
II		Breaking in new co-workers Monitoring of materials Program planning Production reports			
III			Monitoring of material circulation Preventative maintenance Calculation of productivity figures Setting up of work place Budget monitoring Continuing training		
IV				Preventive maintenance of machine installations Diagnosis of mistakes Personel budgeting Lending workers, assessment Preparation of and holding to budget	
Begin Aug. 82	1 1983	2 1984	3 1985	4 1986	Year
Degree of difficulty of the qualification					
Basic qualification	Coordination	Organization		Administration	

Source: Haas 1983.

complex with a stamping plant and component plants on site and a network of supplier plants close by – just like the model of Toyota City. This should allow the realization of just-in-time delivery concepts.

The Saturn Project, which was proclaimed at the beginning of the 1980s, was an even longer term and more comprehensive approach for realizing new production concepts which should allow the company to again build compact cars competitive with Japan, but under U.S. management and using U.S. workers. It was only natural that the experiences from other plants flowed into this project, those in the area of production technology as well as those concerning work and social organization. The most spectacular element of this project was to be the close cooperation of GM and the UAW in this project. The trade journals characterized it as virtually a "joint venture" of GM and the UAW (FT, September 23, 1986; *Automotive News*, July 15, 1985, p. 2; *Automotive News*, January 14, 1985, p. 1; Saturn – UAW Agreement 1985; Fisher 1985).

Summed up, the QWL process at General Motors appeared as a part of a comprehensive transformation strategy. This process was above all geared to the activation of "the group" as a resource to be developed. The QWL process had, with semi-autonomous groups, a concrete objective for work organization and the regulation of performance in the factory of the future.

3.4.2 The EI process at Ford

At Ford, the "Employe Involvement"[1] (EI) program served the purpose that the QWL program did at GM. This program was brought into being in 1979 as a "joint program" of the company and the UAW. The objectives followed out of a "Policy Letter" from Ford president Caldwell which also became the official guideline of Ford of Europe in 1981.

Subject: Employe Involvement
It is the policy of the Company to encourage and enable all employes to become involved in and contribute to the success of the Company. A work climate should be created and maintained in which employes at all levels can achieve individual goals and work satisfaction by directing their talents and energies toward clearly defined Company goals.

To the extent practicable, management is expected to operate within the following guidelines:

Management systems, procedures, and practices should take into account that human resources are among the Company's most important assets and that imagination, ingenuity and creativity are widely distributed throughout the entire work force, as are dedication and the desire to contribute.

Methods of managing should encourage employe participation in identifying and solving work-related problems.

Communication programs and procedures should be implemented that encourage frequent, timely and constructive two-way communication with employes concerning work-related problems. Employe work suggestions and ideas should be solicited, and employe questions should be answered as completely as possible.

There is no simple or universal prescription associated with human resources management. All members of management should identify and evaluate available methods and employ those most suited to their particular set of circumstances.

This declaration of intent contained definite measures supporting worker participation in identifying and solving work-related problems. Other measures aimed at improving the information policy and at supporting communicative relationships between management and workers over work-related problems. In addition, it rejected the idea of simple or universally valid concepts and it was left up to local management to develop methods and forms which corresponded to their local conditions most closely.

The EI strategy sought after an increased employee identification with the company through increased input in solving factory problems, but not the creation of new forms for organizing the work itself. The formation of semi-autonomous production teams was not a direct goal of the EI program as was the case in the QWL strategy at General Motors.

Employe Involvement formed only one cog in the wheel embodying the interests of the company in the diagram of the system of interconnecting gears which represented cooperation between the company and the union and the interlocking of interests and measures for securing the success of the company. Despite this, the system of gears has become one of the most widely known emblems for EI (figure 3.3).

In this system of interlocking gears Employe Involvement was put into the framework of the Mutual Growth Program. A policy letter of the UAW–Ford National Joint Committee on Employe Involvement stated that the factory consultation forums established in the course of the common program (Mutual Growth Program, Employe Training and Development, as well as EI) were closely connected. The strengthening of the elements of "jointness" between management and the union was itself seen to be a result of the EI process. Savoie, one of the protagonists of the EI process at Ford and a representative of the company on the national steering committee explained it like this:

while local Employe Involvement Programs are directed by a joint union-management steering committee, the focus of EI is on making work a more satisfying and stimulating experience by providing employes the opportunity to participate in decisions that affect their work and work environment. The focus of the local Mutual Growth Forum is on promoting better union-management relations through constructive discussion by the parties of significant issues of mutual concern. These "programs" and the new Employe Development and Training Program share, however, the characteristic of being mutually supportive. Better communications, understanding and relations are important common features and objectives. (Letter No. 13, April 20, 1983)

The effects of EI on industrial relations were obviously not seen as merely incidental in the eyes of the protagonists. Savoie notes: "When it is at its best, EI (and QWL) is simply a strategy of reciprocity, a process in which

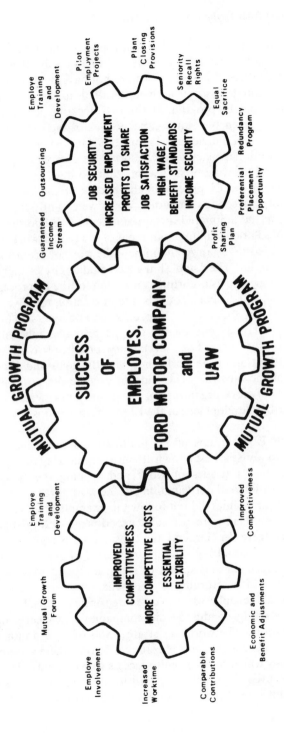

Figure 3.3 The emblem for the "Mutual Growth Program" of Ford and the UAW

both management and the union take initiatives in bringing their problems to each other, and then taking cooperative action to resolve them" (Letter No. 13, April 20, 1983). Although Ford did not have its own conceptual development and predecessor projects in the 1970s to the same degree as General Motors, the EI program at the U.S. location was carried out organization-wide from the start – and not, as in the case of General Motors, in the form of individual pilot projects. One driving force for the more rapid institutional enactment was surely the company's poor economic situation and the widespread fear of plant closings.

At the center of the EI process in the middle of the 1980s was the establishment of EI steering committees which were jointly supported by management and the union and the appointment of EI coordinators for both the area of salaried employees and that of blue collar workers. These coordinators served to organize and initiate the work of problem-solving groups/quality circles. The establishment of quality circles or problem-solving groups appeared as a starting conception for the EI process which was comprehensible for all and could be put into action rapidly.

To summarize, the focus of the EI process was on a change in factory communication relations and on the use the resources inherent in the participation of the work force in factory problem-solving and the increased identification of the work force with the goals and operational requirements of the factories. This did not exclude the possibility that certain concepts of work organization, like group work, would be advocated in the further development of the EI program; the possibilities were open here.

The QWL or EI programs of the multinational companies General Motors and Ford were the best known attempts at changing the traditional social relations and attitudes of work and tapping the productivity resources "motivation and participation" of the work force. The majority of the European companies did not follow this example at the time of our study, even though there were also some experiments with quality circles and group work there. In Germany the considerations regarding human resources were – one could say – totally dominated by questions of skilled labor, the reinforcement and spread of skills needed to work with new technologies. We will be returning to this in chapter 9.

At the close of this chapter we can make three observations. First, due to their differing starting conditions the companies had clearly different strategic orientations. The world car strategy was only an option for the largest multinational companies, for example. Second, there was no "ideal way" in a strategy which could promise success with certainty. There were certain risks involved, especially in regard to the strategy of automation and computer integrated manufacturing. Third, recognizing the importance of the people-related strategy was, in many cases, first a question of the learning processes and experiences with the problems of the high technology strategy.

All of these strategies required far-reaching restructurings in the companies. A radical break from previous practice came at best in cases of a consequent enactment of the people-related strategy. "Revolutionary" concepts with an integral attempt at making a change in the sense of the discussion of "lean production" at the beginning of the 1990s were not on the agenda at the beginning of the 1980s. This does not mean, however, that against the background of the previous structures and practices of industrial relations, the above discussed strategies were not perceived as far-reaching and revolutionary by those involved. We will bring more about this in the next chapter.

4 Industrial relations in the process of change

Industrial relations, the arrangements, forms of conflict, and behaviors typical for them, are, to an extent, "intervening variables" for the achievement of corporate strategies with regard to new forms of work. At the same time, however, industrial relations themselves were involved in the restructuring process and changed also. The goal of this chapter is to depict these interrelations more closely.

We will not be spending a lot of time describing the institutions and arrangements of the national systems of industrial relations. In the first section, rather, we will be dealing with the differing "logics" of the rules and regulations concerning the workers' interest representation in the area of plant-level labor regulation. These differing logics explain the importance of, for example, job demarcations, seniority arrangements, or restrictive practices, or the codeterminants in the three countries studied.

In the second section we will describe events and impulses for the change in the traditional practices in the period from the early 1970s up until the beginning of the 1980s in each country. In this we are referring to such historical episodes which clearly left their mark on the attitudes and assessments of the actors with regard to the transformation process. In the course of this we will be referring to some of our actual factory studies.

4.1 The different "logics" of regulation in the traditional industrial relations systems

We found strong, functioning unions representing the workers in all of the factories studied. Despite the differences in the structures of union organization in the U.S.A., Great Britain, and West Germany there were great similarities in the institutions for representation of worker interests. In all factories there was a central body for interest representation (shop committee/joint committee/works council) whose members were elected by the work force and in which the unions were represented. This made unified collective bargaining with the factory management possible.

New work and motivation policies could not be implemented against the will of these interest representations and that of the dominant unions. These were in the U.S.A. the "UAW," in West Germany the "IG Metall," and in Great Britain the "Transport and General Workers Union" (TGWU) for non- and semi-skilled workers, the "Amalgamated and General Workers Union" (AUEW) for both skilled and non-skilled workers and the "Electric, Electronic, Telecommunication and Plumbing Union" (EETPU) as an important skilled workers union (further unions had only insignificant membership figures in the British factories studied and played only a marginal role in factory policy).

In all of the different national contexts, it was necessary to make a more or less far-reaching break with the previous forms and demands of the worker representation in order to achieve the required level of cooperation or toleration. This was because the strategies for change were frequently aimed directly at the heart of traditional interest representation in the factories: the seniority system, the demarcation rules, the principle of direct interest representation.

The seniority rules were the traditional core of grass roots union work in the American automobile industry (Jürgens and Dohse 1982; Köhler 1981). They were primarily used for personnel selection in the context of various different personnel policy measures: seniority determines the order of employees to be laid off, the selection of personnel in the event of job openings and transfers inside the company, decisions about shift preferences, sometimes even the assignment of the most convenient parking lots.

Although it was fought for and secured by the unions, seniority in the U.S.A. was a criterion of selection which, in the case of an individual personnel action, was also independent of union preferences. The fact that the individual workers "possess" seniority was independent of their conformity and performance in the work process. Seniority rules were objectively valid and their validity did not require any further action from the participants. They thus offered protection against discrimination or favoritism in management's personnel selection as well as against possible discrimination by or preferences of the unions. Because of the fixed rank order for selection, personnel matters were therefore generally not an occasion for negotiation. Supposed violations of the rules were dealt with in established grievance procedures.

The system of seniority rules has a far-reaching importance for labor deployment and work organization. On the basis of this system, expectations and behavioral patterns emerged, not only on the part of management, which were diametrically opposed to the principles of

NW&M concepts. The principle of carrying out personnel measures "without respect to person" justifies a disinterest in the personal situation, problems, and individual potential of the workers. There is a clear advantage for management connected with seniority. Decisions must or could – depending on the perspective – simply be made without respect for person. Thus, management is relieved of personal or social considerations which could, in individual cases, speak for or against the person affected. But the tremendous fluctuation in jobs which took place through the domino effect of the seniority principle were connected with substantial costs. When the jobs of senior workers are eliminated, they can use their seniority rights to take the jobs of those workers who were next on the seniority list, and these could, in turn, "bump" those below them, and so on.

All the U.S. factories compared exhibited highly differentiated systems of seniority (cf. Köhler and Sengenberger 1983; Dohse *et al.* 1982; Jürgens and Dohse 1983). The negative consequences of these systems were a central concern of management in many cases. In one factory out of our sample, which had a total of about 5,000 employees, management made a study of the costs that arose through "seniority bumping" between the van and car plants at the same site. According to the study, there was a yearly average of 1,500 "moves" between 1976 and 1983, 260 of these were skilled workers; the weekly average was five skilled workers and twenty-five non-skilled workers. The majority of these moves were not caused by reduction of personnel, but resulted from workers using their seniority rights to apply for positions which had opened up in other areas. In another factory with about 2,200 workers, there were 2,500 requests for transfers into other work areas in June of 1982. Because seniority considerations for the jobs to be filled only included those who had filed a request, the workers had obviously reacted with "just-in-case" behavior and had filed several such requests. In the first half of 1982 there were about 735 transfers involving seniority. A good part of them were, according to management, results of the bumping effect. This was not only regarded as a problem because of the massive costs required to administrate this process, but also due to the retraining which became necessary time and again. The plant's personnel manager stated in an interview: "The double break-in and sometimes more than double, create a great training inefficiency throughout the plant."

The advantages of the high flexibility for adjustments in the amount of personnel found in the framework of the "hire-and-fire" personnel policy were more than made up for by the disadvantages they brought about in the factory – which, however, generally did not show up in the calculation of costs: training costs, quality costs, motivational costs. Added to this came the seniority system's close connection with the system of demarcation rules and the number of job classifications. The latter were job groups defined in the local contracts. Each classification marked a position within a certain mobility chain in the "flow charts." The more levels and chains that existed, the less a worker with high seniority would descend when it came to a personnel reduction in his or her job group. A great number of finely differentiated "job classifications" would thus be in the interests of the workers in the seniority system. As long as the division of job groups corresponds to the technological and organizational demands, then it does not necessarily entail disadvantages for management, even from the viewpoint of efficiency. Inefficiencies arose when the contractually established division of labor in the factory no longer corresponded to the demands of production. The dissolution of demarcations was thus a central goal of restructuring in the U.S. factories and was packaged in QWL and EI (NW&M) programs. Thus in the new "team factories" there were generally no longer job classifications for the non-skilled area; and in the skilled worker area, the number of job classifications had been reduced from around thirty to four or five. It becomes clear to what extent this was a far-reaching break from previous structures for regulating labor deployment in the factory when the above account is considered.

In the U.S.A. the union leadership decided to undertake the development of fundamental new forms of labor regulation together with the companies and to support and initiate the corresponding processes of transformation in the factory. In the British context, agreement on such a pact at the central contractual level was not possible. The workers' distrust of management's motives was too great and management itself was not willing to give in to union demands in a kind of "productivity deal" in order to achieve NW&M goals. The mistrust was in many cases even greater at the factory and shop floor level; the shop steward organization saw the NW&M concepts as a direct attack on *their* system for the self-regulation of work.

In the British plants we investigated we did not find detailed and formal rules for deploying labor as they existed with respect to seniority in U.S. local contracts. Even the General Agreements between the company and the unions were, in comparison to those in the U.S.A. and West Germany, comparatively thin pamphlets with few concrete rules and many statements of intent by the bargaining parties. There were, on the other hand, a multitude of locally specific rules – at the factory level and even at the department or section level within factories. But these were, as it seems, nowhere systematically collected and documented. Their existence was often a matter of "collective memory", and enforcing individual regulations was dependent on the power constellation existing in each case.

The problem with the validity of norms, the possibility of reviewing norms whose validity is claimed by one of the parties, was a central labor policy problem in the British context. This problem was deeply rooted in the British conception of law as it had developed in the course of history. On the basis of this legal framework, it was exactly the – from a German perspective – "soft norms," based on customs and practices, which seemed most legitimate in the British context. In an attempt to avoid written sets of rules, existing formal regulations were often of questionable validity (see, e.g., Armstrong *et al.* 1981; Brown 1972).

This did not mean that norms and rules had a lesser importance in the British context. In view of the frequently uncertain grounds for the validity of such norms and regulations, the collective memory, the threshold of sensibility for customary rights and principles of fairness among the employees, was more highly developed than, for example, in West Germany. The great importance of informal rules also had another origin here: it was based on the tradition of negotiations with lower- and middle-ranking supervisors at the work place, to settle problems in their own context and on a basis of mutuality. It was quite frequently the case that such a practice was precisely in the interests of local management (Ogden 1982; Willman and Winch 1985).

Decentralized agreements were often unfamiliar at the upper levels of management and the practice was strongly criticized there. There was a widespread assessment at the corporate headquarters level that many problems of industrial relations were caused by this decentralized form of conflict management and that more attention should be given to exerting more influence over the behavior, recruitment, and qualification of lower-level supervisors (Willman and Winch 1985, pp. 129ff.; Child and Partridge 1982; Daniel and Millward 1983, pp. 105ff.).

In addition to the situation of multiple unions and the informality of many arrangements, the principle of direct interest representation was a further characteristic element of the British system of industrial relations which we found at work in the factories we studied. In many agreements, the shop stewards were seen as the most important representatives of this system. In representing the interests of their section, they frequently defied being restricted by higher principles and procedures, even those of their own union. The system of direct interest representation also had its roots, however, in the employees themselves, who often enough autonomously defined their interests and attempted to push them through (Batstone 1984, pp. 129ff.; Batstone *et al.* 1977; Marchington and Armstrong 1983; Terry 1983; Tolliday and Zeitland 1986; Willman 1986a).

The differences in the form of interest representation became clear in such everyday events as the choice of personnel in situations where employees were temporarily lent from one work area to another. In the U.S. context, the traditional criterion for selection would be seniority. Because of this it would be clear from the beginning who would have to go. It would generally always be the same people – with the result that they would feel discriminated against. In the British factories we investigated, the solution of this problem was often voted upon at the level of the foremen groups. A vote was taken in the group to decide if they would lend a worker according to the rotation principle, according to the "last in–first out" principle, or according to another method. Each group supervised the adherence to this itself. In the West German companies the selection of personnel would be carried out by the lower level supervisors, frequently with the approval of the steward ("Vertrauensfrau/mann") or the works council representative of the area (see also Dohse and Jürgens 1982).

Thus, in the British plants, the patterns of action and the arrangements which had developed on the basis of this form of interest representation did possess an element of independent work structuring "from below" – not as a result of an orderly process but of "unorganized" action on the shop floor. Organized action and an orderly process defined "from above" formed the characteristic pattern for representing worker interests in West German factories – a sharp contrast to the British situation.

In West German factories, the Works Constitution Act is the basis which gives the works council – depending on the issue – legal rights to information, cooperation, or codetermination. Measures in the factory generally go through an ordered process of negotiation with the institutions for representing workers' interests which – in view of the legal codetermination rights and the ban on strikes as a means of carrying out factory conflicts – are under significant pressure to reach an agreement. This system of factory interest regulation has contributed to the fact that forms of informal self-regulation on the shop floor, like we found in the U.S. and British factories, had attained no great importance in West Germany. The basis of this system was thus also a specific conception of law and the role of the law in disputes within the company. Simple customary rights or the marking of precedents are not enough in the German context. The basis upon which a practice is considered "normal" has to be a formal and written one, with orderly procedures in the case of a conflict. In such a case the collective agreements either call for arbitration or a hearing before an industrial court (see also Dombois 1982a). It would, however, be incorrect to assume from this that this legal regulation leads to disputes in the factory generally being settled by external authorities. An internal factory agreement in the course of negotiations between the two sides is much more common. The inclusion of external authorities for regulating cases of disputes within the company occur very rarely in most factories. In only one factory of our German factory sample had several such procedures been dealt with "externally" in the past.

As in the factories which we studied in other countries, negotiation and minor agreements between lower level supervisors and union representatives also take place on the "shop floor" in the German factories. Characteristic differences exist, however, in the orientation of their actions: in the U.S.A. traditionally, the central position of the seniority principle cannot be violated by such agreements, in Great Britain it is the principle of customary rights and precedents, and in West Germany the agreements cannot violate legally binding factory agreements. The negotiation of these agreements is at the center of interest representation in the German factory. Particular interest positions are therefore forced to seek formulations capable of being universalized and to accept a process in which interests are balanced by central negotiations in the factory and between the factories of the company. "Restrictive practices," for example, which are not covered by such specifically negotiated arrangements are thus not protected by the works council.

The rules and demands oriented toward "protection" are, in the German context, not so much aimed at the effects of personnel selection, as in the case of the U.S.A., but at the effects on personnel volume. In the case of dismissing personnel, the works council is required by law to ensure that the selection is made according to socially oriented considerations (taking criteria such as age, number of children, family, and financial situation into account). Above and beyond this, works council policy attempts to avoid the necessity of such a selection through measures aimed at protecting both income levels and the overall employment level (see also Dombois 1976; Schulz-Wild 1978; Dombois 1979).

A further peculiarity of the German system is the traditional works council policy of allowing problems to be compensated for monetarily. According to our observations this explains the smoother achievement of technological and organizational measures in West Germany in many cases. The possibility for negotiating wage incentives for individual groups of workers gives the works councils more flexibility for compromise. Added to this comes the wage system in the German context which – in comparison – can deal more flexibly with differences in work requirements than the system of job classifications in the Anglo-Saxon countries. The works councils also have more flexibility to bring up wage considerations by measures of "job design."

The wage negotiations in the U.S. and British companies aim at defining wage rates for job categories which have been previously established or contractually negotiated. For the individual employee, the wage is determined by the job classification into which he or she was hired or transferred. The worker could only achieve a wage increase by being transferred to another job classification. The master agreements in Germany only establish the general structure of wage levels. Each job is assigned ("grouped in") to a certain wage level on the basis of certain "analytic" criteria. But this assignment of individual jobs to the wage levels is not merely derived from these criteria, it is rather the result of a decision-making process at the factory level. In this framework there is considerable leeway for bargaining between the local works council and management in the factory wage commission. Reference to the assigned wage level of similar jobs as well as reference to the assigned wage level of the same jobs at the company's other plants do play an important role. But they only form the starting point for plant-level negotiations.

Because the assignment of jobs to wage levels is specific to each individual job and not to the job category, the possibility arises for wage increases by means of "job design," i.e., by structuring the tasks in the section in such a way that more demanding tasks are added to this job. In contrast, there was no wage-related incentive in the U.S. or British context to entice the unions or the workers affected to consider job design. When the works councils in Germany are speculating how to raise the pay level of a job they always consider changes in the job's demands, its degree of difficulty, and the qualifications required. A restructuring of tasks in the sense of new work concepts is fully in line with traditional wage-related practices when it can promise higher wage levels.

As long as the status boundary of the skilled workers, or especially of the salaried employees, is not crossed in German factories, the worker's job classification, such as spot-welder, assembler, and material handler is secondary and, from the point of view of the workers, unimportant. We found only few job demarcation conflicts, where non-skilled blue-collar workers protested the loss of occupational titles due to the redesign of jobs. Because the employees in semi-skilled jobs hardly identified themselves with their job classification, their interests in regard to technological and organizational changes were directed above all at improving their level of income – their only fear is of being downgraded. If fears are allayed in this respect, then they will not cling to the existing job descriptions. We found this attitude time and again in our investigations. Thus a works council member of Ford's Weinkirchen plant gave two reasons for the work force's acceptance of measures which would entrust production jobs with additional tasks from the indirect area:

1. Production has an interest in taking over such additional tasks from the indirect area in order to maintain the wage group 3 to 4. The current danger that the wage groups 3 and 4 in the direct area will erode is tied in with the fact that, because of the improved quality, less and less repair work is needed and the repair jobs are

traditionally the better paid jobs in direct production. 2. The maintenance workers are in favor of giving up lesser qualified maintenance tasks on production because they tend to strive for the more highly rated tasks in wage groups 6, 7 and 8.

As the integration measures were planned we were afraid that revolt would take place here. That was not the case. In the wage area the colleagues didn't care which job they would have to do as long as they would keep the same wage. Problems arose in the area of salaried workers. In this case the people weren't so concerned about the income security, but also about the status. (Works council member at the Weinkirchen plant)

There are no clear status barriers with regard to wage differentiation. Semi-skilled workers can indeed receive higher hourly wages than qualified skilled workers (*Facharbeiter*). This brings us to the last central point for distinguishing between the three systems which we will be dealing with here: the gap in status and pay between skilled and non-skilled workers.

We found the distinct status of "skilled worker" in all three countries studied (in contrast to Japan), someone who had gone through some sort of an apprenticeship and had acquired the certification as a craftsman. In chapter 9 we will deal more specifically with differences in the training systems between the counties, which are indeed quite considerable. Because of such differences, the use of a general category like "craftsman" is indeed questionable in certain circumstances. In such cases we will thus also be using the German term "*Facharbeiter*."

There were also far-reaching differences in the deployment of skilled workers and in the breadth of the gap between skilled and non-skilled work in the three countries studied. The interfaces between skilled and non-skilled jobs are, however, of particular importance for the establishment of new forms of work organization and labor deployment.

The status gap was wider in the British and U.S. factories. The skilled workers in the British automobile plants traditionally have their trade-specific union organizations (with the exception of the AUEW, which represents skilled and non-skilled workers). Even in union organizations like the EETPU, which represented several trades, conflicts between the trades of "electrician" and "mechanic" arose time and again.

The UAW in the U.S. factories organizes skilled and non-skilled workers. There is, however, a deep split in the way these two groups perceive their interests – on the local and on the central level. In some factories, the skilled and non-skilled workers vote separately on the ratification of new contracts. The skilled workers have in some cases waived their right to send delegates to the shop committee of their factory. In the course of our interviews, we frequently found hostile or contemptuous relationships between the representatives of skilled and non-skilled workers. This relationship reflected the situation in the U.S. factories: skilled workers and non-skilled workers were two different worlds with regard to the arrangements and practices of labor deployment, and with regard to their interest orientations and demands.

The IG Metall in the German factories also organizes skilled and non-skilled workers, and representatives of both status groups sit in the works councils. Although the relationship between the two groups is not without tension here either, this does not have the central importance that it had in the U.S. and British situations. One expression of the differences is the wage differentiation and the gap in pay between skilled and semi-skilled workers.

The German wage structure clearly contrasts to the British and U.S. structures in this respect: on the one hand, the wage structure of skilled workers is more differentiated within itself, and, on the other hand, there is a zone of overlap between the semi-skilled and skilled workers' wages. The skilled worker status thus does not guarantee higher pay than that of the non-skilled workers.

Figure 4.1 shows the hourly wage rate for selected job groups which can be considered as representative for the job spectrum in the area of hourly workers in assembly plants at the time of our investigation. We have included the lowest paid non-skilled jobs and the highest paid qualified skilled workers in the respective factories. In the German factories the job of electronics mechanic exists in addition to that of electrician, a distinction which does not exist in British and U.S. factories. The figure shows the distance between the hourly wage rates of these job groups with reference to the average hourly wage of this job spectrum.

For U.S. companies, a graduated wage hierarchy can be seen from the floor cleaner up to the dingman, who removes dings and dents in the body in white and is traditionally the highest qualified and highest paid non-skilled worker in U.S. factories. The deep status gap between skilled-workers and non-skilled workers can also be clearly seen. The wage differences within the skilled worker categories are minimal, though, with toolmakers and electricians being the highest paid skilled workers.

Greater differences between the companies can be seen in British plants. In the British plants of Company B, there are practically only two different wage levels, one for non-skilled jobs and one for skilled workers. The gap in pay between non-skilled workers and skilled workers in the British plants is indeed small, but it does exist and that is the essential fact.

In the two German plants selected, the "Weinkirchen" plant has a far greater wage differentiation in its skilled worker department than the U.S. and British plants, but the skilled-worker wages are without exception clearly above those of the non- and semi-skilled workers; in the case of Mittelort, on the other hand, the wage rates of skilled workers overlap

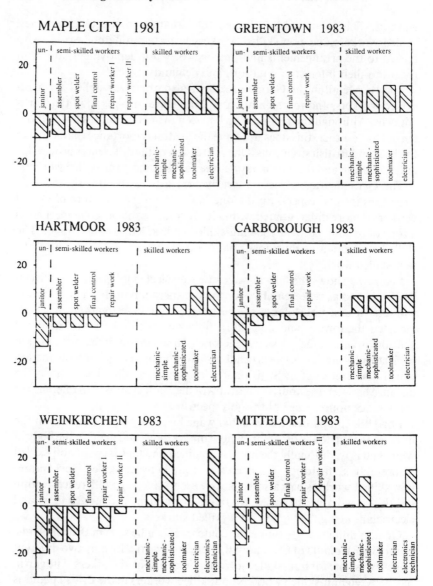

Figure 4.1   Wage differentiation for selected job groups in a comparison between American, British, and German assembly plants
Source: Company contracts and the IG Metall 1983.

considerably with those of qualified semi-skilled workers. Company C's Windeck and Heidedorf plants show a picture similar to Mittelort.

The greater equality between the British and U.S. plants, on the one hand, and the German, on the other, should not obscure this difference. Another point which we would like to call attention to is the stronger pay differentiation in the skilled worker categories themselves. We will be returning to this in chapter 6.

To summarize we can conclude that the traditional systems of industrial relations in the countries investigated offered differing prerequisites for the adoption of new work forms. In the U.S.A. they presupposed a break with the previous regulatory structures, which were largely codified in the local contracts at the plant level. The transition to a "team plant" meant a totally new situation for labor policy in the plant and it could be expected that local factory unions would not accept this easily. But, at the same time, management's new production concepts did not mean a questioning of union interest representation in the factories as such. In Great Britain, with the shop steward system a form of decentralized self-regulation on the shop floor already existed in which a certain type of "participatory management" was already being practiced. That was the reason that the British shop stewards felt so threatened by the NW & M concepts. It seemed that these concepts could only be introduced if the traditional system were removed all together. In Germany, the works council's legally vested right to codetermination or involvement as well as the previously established regulatory forms allowed, in principle, an easier transition to new forms of work, as long as this took place with the consent of the works council.

4.2 Events and impetuses which led to a change from the traditional practices in the industrial relations arena

Each country has its own "milestones" in its change process toward new forms of work and, in some cases, also new forms of industrial relations. The events or impulses of the following account were, in fact, often referred to by interviewees in the plants when it came to explaining the reason why this transformation process was necessary and the dangers involved in it. We will begin our account in the U.S.A.

4.2.1 The U.S.A.

Three events were characteristic for the development of industrial relations in the U.S. automobile industry of the 1970s: (1) the conflicts over the working conditions in automobile production at the beginning of the 1970s, (2) the "Southern strategy," and (3) the entry into the phase of "new industrial relations" in the 1979 bargaining round between the UAW and the "Big Three." We will begin with the conflicts over better working conditions in which the General Motors Lordstown plant played a key role.

(1) Lordstown

Inspired by the enormous fluctuations in production and employment, but also by the problems in integrating the Vietnam generation and the racial conflicts, the production facilities of the U.S. automakers often became a battlefield for conflicts in the early 1970s. Conflicts in the companies escalated quickly (see, e.g., Rothschild 1973; Aronowitz 1973; Widick 1976; *Work in America* 1973). The relations between management and union representatives were based on opposition. The employees and the lower-level supervisors had, from time to time, their fingers close to the triggers of their pistols – not only figuratively. This was not true for all factories, of course. The picture at the beginning of the 1970s, however, is dominated by the "wild plants." One of these was Lordstown.

At Lordstown, it's one hundred cars an hour, every hour, for eight hours a day ... so if the foreman gives you the jaws, you cut a gasline here, some upholstery there ... General Motors can afford it. (Norman 1972, p. 104).

The labor conflicts at Lordstown became a worldwide symbol for the protest of the production workers against Taylorized forms of work organization, against speed-up, machine pacing, the pressure of rationalization, against the conditions of work in mass production as a whole.

The description of the situation cited above comes from an article in "Playboy" recommended to us by participants in the conflict at Lordstown as a more realistic account than much that was written elsewhere. Lordstown was considered at the beginning of the 1970s to be one of the most modern assembly plants in the world and the most powerful U.S. company's answer to the growing pressure of imports coming from Germany and Japan. As management proceeded to increase the line speed to achieve the planned production efficiency after the start-up period of the new plant, the workers revolted.

The cries of speed-up resulted from the changes in work assignments. There were people who were not working anyplace near a full hour on the job. Lets say you have three people working 35 minutes each. You consolidate that job. It is a total of 105 minutes of work, so you can have two people working $52\frac{1}{2}$ apiece. You save an employee. The speed-up gripe came from that man who was working 35 minutes and now has to work almost the full hour. – "Look," says the production manager to this same argument, "in my section there are a third less guys on the line doing the same job in the same amount of time. We sure as shit have to work faster. That's what I call speed-up." (Norman 1972, p. 104).

De Lorean, at that time the head of the Chevrolet Division, later concurred with this assessment in his biography (Wright 1979, p. 199).

The union called for the workers to continue working but to follow the old time standards; at the shop floor level, however, the workers took up more radical means of protesting:

Oh, man, you should have seen some of those cars. No way that wasn't sabotage. Things were cut and scratched – you know brake lines, gas lines, upholstery, windshields. Dashboards were smashed up. Some engines had bolts driven through the block. They were just tearing those cars up. (Norman 1972, p. 250).

Such forms of protest went together with high absenteeism and a larger number of voluntary quits – forms of passive resistance supplementing active resistance. The high degree of attention which these received from among the general public, the parallels with similar events in other countries, companies, and factories gave the impression that this was the beginning of a general phenomenon. Some heralded the rise of a new type of worker, the end of the era of the "affluent worker" who was only concerned with his paycheck (Goldthorpe *et al.* 1969).

Although the interpretation of the Lordstown episode as a workers' rebellion against Fordist–Taylorist working conditions can be questioned[1] it was not any less influential. Lordstown became a symbol of the worldwide protest movement against working conditions in mass production, specifically against the assembly line. But this protest seems to have met deaf ears in the American companies in the 1970s. It was largely ignored by the planners of the new or refurbished plants that followed, up into the 1980s. We will come back to this point in chapter 10.

(2) The "Southern strategy"

The Southern strategy characterized the attempts of U.S. car manufacturers to escape the sphere of influence of the union, which traditionally had its strongholds in the North and East, by establishing new plants in the South of the U.S.A. The conflict over this strategy reached its peak in the dispute over General Motors' establishment of a new assembly plant in Oklahoma City. It was waged by the UAW nationwide and marked a turning point in industrial relations, not only at General Motors. We visited the Oklahoma City plant as part of our background studies for the interviews with our research sample.

The building of the Oklahoma City plant was announced in 1973, its construction was delayed, however, by the decline in sales during the first oil crisis. Construction started in 1977 and the plant started operations in 1979. With a production volume of 300,000 cars per year, the company proclaimed the Indiantown plant at the beginning of the 1980s to be "the nation's newest and largest passenger car plant" and the world's "most modern automotive facility (Company Brochure). The plant was given a modern layout but was equipped with "low technology," so that the technological leap was not too large for workers who did not even have experience in industrial production, to say nothing of automotive production. The first robots were introduced with the start of a new model line in 1982.

Instead, the plant was to be the state of the art from an OD (organizational design) perspective. To this end, QWL objectives were tied to the goal of operating without a union. The team was the basic unit of work regulation, the offer of participation was aimed at individuals as team members – not as union members. In a booklet handed out to the employees in place of a local contract, management sought out a personal touch: "Each of you is encouraged to be a participating member of your team as your contribution to the team is necessary to help (the plant) build a quality product. We want you to be involved in decisions that affect your work life."

This participation was to extend to questions of work planning, cleaning at the work place, continuous training, quality inspection, conduct of team members in the factory, formulating team goals, ensuring health and safety, and selecting a team leader. The supervisory hierarchy above the elected team leaders were termed "advisors." The lower supervisory level was introduced in an especially mild manner in the booklet: "You have a friend in your Area Advisor. This person understands the problems facing a new employee, is anxious to help you to adjust to the new work environment, and will do everything reasonably possible to assist you. Your success is necessary to the success of the team."

The introduction of the team concept without and against the union was seen by the management we interviewed as a serious mistake in retrospect. The concept of a "team" and everything that was connected with it received a negative, anti-union image. It was seen with regret by management that the union supported the concept in the new plants built after this, while it was difficult to free the concepts of "team" and "quality circle" from their anti-union stigma in their own plant.

The expansion southward took place at the same time as plants in other regions were shut down. Besides the question of union organization, the question of employment security in the General Motors' system extending beyond the individual factory was up for discussion. The demand to have re-employment rights apply to the entire corporation, and not only to one specific plant, came up and was put into the contract after hard struggles. The "preferential hiring agreement" only meant that applicants from other GM plants must be considered when recruiting workers for a new plant. In the case of the Oklahoma City plant, there was for the first time – in contrast to hiring practices of the 1960s and 1970s – an extensive screening process. This was combined with a "job awareness" program which prepared the selected applicants for the working conditions that awaited them in an assembly plant. The program also made it possible to carry out a selection based on the individual qualities of the potential employee, something which had not been possible with the traditional system. The traditional "hire and fire" system had allowed management to simply lay off excess personnel, but this did not sever the individual worker's employment relationship with the plant. When the factory wanted to hire personnel again, the workers laid off would have to be rehired in the order of their seniority. With the new arrangement, unexcused absences, disciplinary actions, and union activity became important criteria for employment in the new plant. Applicants who were active in the union in their previous plant had little chance to be hired again.

The criticism of these hiring practices by the union grew to a nationwide campaign during the 1979 bargaining round. Under this pressure, the hiring practices in the new plant were finally changed and the resistance to the union organization of the new site abandoned. With the corresponding agreements, the end of the Southern strategy simultaneously marked the beginning of GM's strategy of "new industrial relations" (Katz 1985).

Except for Lordstown, the Oklahoma City plant was General Motors' only *new* assembly plant built in the U.S.A. in the 1970s.[2] It was the first of their chain of assembly plants on "greenfield sites" which followed in the 1980s. At subsequent sites, the UAW was brought in on the planning from the beginning. The fact should not be ignored, however, that the policy of establishing new sites also aimed at a process of personnel selection on a large scale. Even if the applicants from closed down GM plants in other parts of the country were successful, they would have had to undergo careful screening. In this manner, around one quarter of the work force of GM's U.S. assembly plants went through such a phase of critical entry selection in the course of the 1980s; and the work forces of the other plants, over which the Damocles' sword of a possible closing was looming, had to reckon on the possibility of having to undergo such a recruiting procedure some day.

(3) The strategy of new industrial relations

The strategy began with the Chrysler "bail-out" in 1979. This was a concerted action of banks, the government, and the union to rescue the corporation, and is the largest financial transaction dealing with industrial policy in the history of the U.S.A. The UAW contributed considerably to the rescue of Chrysler through contractual concessions to reduce the wage and wage-related costs adding up to an average of $5,000 per worker

(*Ward's Automotive Yearbook* 1981, p. 207). The institutional arrangement of the Chrysler bail-out remained an exception (union president Fraser became a member of the Chrysler board of directors), but union concessions in the negotiation of contracts remained a central issue in the period that followed (see BNA No. 955, January 7, 1982; Katz 1984 and 1985).

In 1982, the UAW also made contractual concessions with Ford and General Motors. This was the low point of the recession in the U.S. automobile industry – a point in time where 215,000 of the 1.5 million UAW members were permanently laid off and 123,000 temporarily laid off and thus unemployed. Among other things, the union had to give up automatic wage increases to match the rate of inflation (COLA) and accepted the elimination of nine personal vacation days per worker yearly (see also Cappelli 1985; Craft *et al.* 1985; Mitchell 1986). For the duration of the contract (1982–4) these concessions allowed Ford to save $1 billion in labor costs which they would have incurred if they had simply continued the pattern of the old contract (see BNA No. 959, March 4, 1982 and No. 961, April 1, 1982). Added to this came the introduction of a second decentralized bargaining round at the plant level over local work practices. This gave local management and the union a chance to check over the local contracts from the standpoint of productivity, and, if need be, to negotiate new agreements. Even though the negotiations at the local level were usually broken off without reaching an outcome, and thus the previous local contracts were automatically extended, local management now had concrete "shopping lists" of demands to achieve changes in rules which they considered to be obstructions to productivity. (Kochan and McKersie 1983; Craft *et al.* 1985; Katz and Sabel 1985).

In the negotiations over the concessions contract of 1982, the union also made it clear from the beginning that concessions in wages and benefits could only be agreed to if they were tied to further measures to increase job security. The UAW expressed its interest in projects which aimed at transferring Japanese conceptions for lifelong employment security for the permanent work force into the U.S. context (see Katz and Sabel 1985, Katz 1985, p. 55ff. and p. 67ff.). In the end, both sides agreed that pilot projects would be carried out in four General Motors plants and three Ford plants, where 80 percent of the work force would receive the Permanent Employment Guarantee (PEG). This was, however, not achieved without concessions in these plants' local contracts concerning rules with regard to working practices. The corresponding agreements on this point were to be worked out between the union and local management in these plants in the course of renegotiating the local contracts.

A further element of the 1982 concessions contract was the establishment of a joint committee of union and management representatives for mutual information and consultation over the situation in the plant and for problem-solving measures. We have mentioned these in the previous chapter. In practice, these committees – at Ford the "Mutual Growth Forums," at GM the "Competitive Edge Committees" – served as an institutionalized opportunity for a dialogue between management and the union in the plant (or the representatives of the contractual parties at lower levels). There were no arrangements going beyond this, like in West Germany where the union has the right to be informed about pending moves of management and, in turn, respected the confidentiality of information received. These institutions did, however, form a starting point for the creation of a system of joint committees like those already existing in some plants in Britain and West Germany. In the U.S. context this meant a lot. In the traditional militant plants in the 1970s, it was almost a tabu for union and management representatives to have contact at all – even privately.

To summarize: the outlines of a new system of work and industrial relations emerged in the U.S. at the beginning of the 1980s. Negotiated at the highest levels, these measures were then sent forcefully down both management and union communication channels to the lower echelons; the factories received a package of offers which they were forced to deal with, as follows:

cooperative relationships between the bargaining partners in the plant, the establishment of joint committees, involvement of the union representatives in planning and increased information for the union in the framework of these committees;

participation of the work force in questions regarding regulating and structuring work through their participation in the QWL and EI programs;

elimination of the traditional work practices, seniority and job classification systems on the plant level.

This elimination of traditional regulation structures was not a direct condition for entry into cooperation or participation, but it was an expectation apparent to both sides. The goal was clear: increasing productivity. Incidentally, the elimination of traditional regulation structures was not only a result of the new productivity arrangement. The new structures for securing employment also had their effects. Thus, seniority rules were often suspended with the consent of both sides in lay-offs in the 1980s. "Inverse seniority" was created in these cases, and the workers with high seniority were laid off first because their income was more or less insured through SUB (supplemental unemployment benefit) pay.

The offer of the new productivity arrangements was highly controversial within the union at the factory level. This is also shown in the results of the ratification vote for the 1982 contracts: 52 percent of the union members voted for the contract at General Motors – at Ford it was 75 percent. The opposition was especially strong in the assembly plants. The attitudes in these plants were – as we found out in our study – still largely dominated by the traditional patterns of industrial relations. The demands put forward by the unions in the local bargaining rounds often reflected this.[3]

4.2.2 Great Britain

Here, two topics of the 1970s are especially important from our perspective: the debates in connection with the government's studies exploring the future of the British car industry and the initiatives of the companies and management to win back the prerogative for action on the "shop floor."

(1) The debate over the future of the British car industry

The debate in the 1970s about the future direction of the car industry was carried out more bitterly and intensely in the British public and political arena than in any other Western industrial country. In view of the precarious situation of British Leyland, the nationalized flagship of the British car industry and at that time the last truly British car company, and in view of the European strategies of the two U.S. corporations, it was clear that the entire future of the British automobile industry was being discussed in this context.

At the center of the discussion were several reports prepared at the request of the British government over the situation of the British automobile industry. The question of the causes of the British productivity problems was in the foreground in these reports: what was responsible for this dreadful situation, was it a special feature of British industrial relations, or was it the companies' reticence to make investments? In 1975, two different reports came to contrary conclusions with regard to this question.

The central statement of the Central Policy Review Staff (CPRS) in its report over "The Future of the British Car Industry" (CPRS 1975) was that the reason for the low productivity of the British automobile industry could be such factors as personnel overstaffing, low work intensity, and poor work relations:

There is not the slightest chance of Britain retaining a volume automobile industry at anything like its present size if present shop floor attitudes persist. Present "trench warfare" attitudes of management and labour will not serve in the assembly lines of 20th century Western Europe. The British car industry's approach to quality of workmanship, to new working practices, to continuity of production and manning levels is so out of date that it cannot survive. Workers and management must see the danger and adapt rapidly or go under: They must not be pressured by politically motivated militants. (CPRS 1975, p. XIV)

On the basis of productivity comparisons with other plants in Western Europe the report determined that:

With the same power at his elbow and doing the same job as his continental counterparts, the British car assembly worker produces only half as much output per shift. (CPRS 1975, p. XIV)

In contrast to this, the report of the "Expenditure Committee" (1975) concluded:

Inadequate investment and the lower productivity of the old plants have been the greatest contributors to poor productivity of the mass-production car side of the industry. ("Expenditure committee" 1975, p. 39)

Bhaskar summarized the most important problems of the British automobile industry in his investigation of "The Future of the UK Motor Industry" (Bhaskar 1979, p. 390) with reference to both reports:
1 Excess capacity;
2 Too many (out-dated) models;
3 Too many plants;
4 Over-manning;
5 Low productivity;
6 Inadequate capital investment;
7 Poor product quality, durability and reliability;
8 Some evidence of poor distribution and inept marketing[4]

In view of the poor state of work and industrial relations, the CPRS report, like the Donovan report (1968), referred to the climate of mistrust, the lack of communication and information in the relationships between management, unions, shop stewards, and work forces. It determined that:

Management is unable to communicate clearly and convincingly with its work force the true competitive state of the British industry. Consequently, the work force does not accept the urgency and the scale of improvements required, but rather sees management's efforts, for example, to reduce manning levels, as an attempt to boost profits at the expense of the work force. (CPRS 1975, p. 102f.)

In its recommendations for improving the shop stewards' level of information, the CPRS pointed out the possibility of making visits to continental plants in order to personally study personnel policy and work practices there (CPRS 1975, p. 131f.) (In chapter 9 we will show that this advice was followed and even ordinary workers were given a chance to make such visits.)

British Leyland was generally at the center of the debate: it became especially clear here that a Gordian knot would have to be severed in order to carry out both the modernization of the factories and a fundamental change in labor and industrial relations (see Bhaskar 1980; Edwardes 1983; Willman and Winch 1985; Marsden *et al.* 1985). As hard and as drastic as management's policies in dealing with the unions or individual occupational groups actually were, the basic attitude remained unchanged until the end of the 1970s – namely that the company expected to receive support from and an intervention by the state in difficult times. This was especially true with regard to securing the necessary funds for modernization measures. This intervention was plainly also expected with respect to bringing about fundamental changes in industrial relations, as this topic had been a focus for government legislation since the end of the 1960s. For quite some time the company and unions had obviously found it expedient to first wait for the results of governmental labor policy before taking steps in the area of industrial relations (Dunnett 1980).

At the beginning of the 1980s it became clear to all parties in the industry that, in view of the policies of the conservative Thatcher government, the idea of the government being the last, and actual, authority for problem-solving was no longer justified. Edwardes, the chairman of British Leyland, described the increasing difficulty in receiving support from the government in his autobiography. (Edwardes 1983).

(2) "We will manage" – struggle over the prerogative of management

The second important chain of events shaping attitudes and behavior were the struggles over control of the shop floor and management's scope for action. As we have already described above, the corresponding political debates over the reforms of industrial relations also affected the behavior of the unions and management in the companies and factories.

At the end of the 1970s, it came to a showdown in the struggle for control of the shop floor at British Leyland. This was in 1979, in the course of the conflicts over the "Edwardes Plan" (see, e.g., Willman 1986a; Willman and Winch 1985; Marsden *et al.* 1985). Nevertheless, similar conflicts over the question of management control at the factory level also took place earlier in other companies. We refer to our own research in the following account.

In Company A's Hartmoor plant, for example, management terminated the existing form of labor relations exactly on November 15, 1976. At the plant they told us: "This is the date we declared war." On this day, the members of the work force received a letter from management announcing the change and the line supervisors received instructions not to tolerate certain practices any more. These instructions were aimed, above all, at "restrictive practices" which were widespread up until then. An example of this was "welt working," often called "doubling up" in the U.S., in which the workers at a work place divide up their work so that individual workers can take informal breaks while others do their work for them (see Hyman and Elger 1982 and Batstone *et al.* 1977 who deal with "restrictive practices" in general). The line supervisors at Hartmoor were instructed not to tolerate this any more. They were ordered to:

Ensure that all your employees know when they should be on the job and when they can take their relief. If any operator leaves the job without permission, do not allow it to pass without doing something about it. While a man is on the job, i.e. not on relief, he is expected to remain on the line. Do not permit any non-work pursuits, i.e. card playing, darts, table tennis, billiards beside the line. (...) If operators apply other methods of work restriction which are less obvious, i.e. broken tools, process problems, alleged safety problems etc., be patient, but call on support from your general foreman, the Industrial Engineering Dept., Safety, Maintenance etc. If it is clear that bad quality work is being produced deliberately, this must be dealt with in accordance with the attached guidelines. (Supervisors Bulletin/Project Records).

In this way, management attempted to regain control over the shop floor which it had largely lost at the middle of the 1970s. Thus the plant director we interviewed remembers this time:

The labor situation was really volatile. There was complete anarchy in the plant. Discipline had completely gone. Management was not in charge any more of the things happening in the plant. (A G.B. 1)

One expression of this situation was the fact that portable time-clocks were used in order to end the repeated destruction of time-clocks. The foremen had to carry these clocks around at the beginning and end of each shift in order for workers to check in and out. The "declaration of war" by management did not remain without consequences:

The unions did not really declare war in retaliation, but the workers did. It turned into a nightmare. We enforced discipline, they would walk out. We would again enforce discipline, win some battles, lose others, we would take discipline, they would walk out. It was hell to work here. Nobody wanted to come to work in the morning, because everyone knew we would move right into a battle. (A G.B. 1)

This conflict was bitterly waged for two or three years. Then, the preparations for the change-over to a new model line began. This created a new situation for both sides. Neither management nor the union wanted to endanger central management's decision to produce this model at their site and make the necessary investments for modernization. The conflicts receded. The local conflict was also eclipsed in 1978, however, by the big strike in the course of the national contract dispute. A break in the conflicts

Table 4.1 *Lost time due to strikes in the Hartmoor assembly plant, 1976–85*

Year	Number of work conflicts[a]	Hours lost because of strikes	Hours lost because of lock-outs	Lost production in pieces
1976	310	341,000	504,000	16,122
1977	264	930,378	545,708	25,475
1978	116	3,912,225	1,592,696	78,273
1979	69	14,949	9,600	7,500
1980	116	89,931	178,332	18,218
1981	52	700,341	256,653	26,892
1982	73	650,312	355,610	28,098
1983	34	892,778	834,065	27,758
1984	31	21,304	956,380	28,838
5/85	8	3,203	—	2,517

Note:
[a] Work conflicts are defined as walk-outs by three or more employees lasting at least fifteen minutes.

can be clearly seen in 1979. After this, the struggle erupted violently again. The reason for this was the company's determination to finally eliminate the use of strikes and walk-outs as a means for enforcing decentralized demands of individual employee groups or shop stewards. A new set of work rules set off a spiral of conflicts at that time. These foresaw in the case of a walk-out a lock-out for the balance of the shift, not only of the production area affected but also for those indirectly affected. Conflicts arose, for example, when "innocent" indirect participants were punished through no fault of their own and were also radicalized. It was a policy for enforcing principal questions of industrial relations, frequently referred to by management as the "four times four" policy. Thus management time and again locked out the entire work force of the plant in retaliation for a walk-out of a few workers somewhere in the plant. The development shown in table 4.1 speaks for itself.

At Company B's Seaborough plant, management attempted to regain control of the shop floor in 1979. There was a twelve-week strike in that year which was generally considered to be a turning point in labor relations in the plant. The cause of the strike – the walk-out of one occupational group over questions of classification – would probably not have led to such a bitter work struggle in other circumstances. But in this case management decided to set an example. The pent up emotions over the situation in the 1970s came to the surface, especially by the lower-level supervisors and middle management. According to one of our interviewees, they were thoroughly fed up with the methods of blackmail, sabotage, etc. (Personnel manager, B G.B. 1).

Management thus used the break in production to put together its demands and to specify them according to departments. The position paper "We Will Manage" was issued. "Customs and practices," procedures which had evolved through customary right, were terminated unilaterally by management, and those who could not accept this – this was told to the work force at the end of the work struggle – should not bother to come back to work again. This position was firmly held to on the first work day, and was retained in the following negotiation process. "So we did the opposite of Quality of Worklife. We became very autocratic. More autocratic than in normal circumstances" (Personnel manager, B G.B. 1).

During the time of the strike the management had cleaned up. They collected the dart boards, for example, which had hung in some work areas and burned them, televisions were also not tolerated any longer. A bar, which had existed in the factory up until then and had been well visited during working hours, was closed.

The contents of "We Will Manage" were mailed to the employees as the "Conditions of a Return to Work." "We Will Manage" was aimed, above all, at questions of punctuality and attendance in the factory, it was aimed at the practices mentioned above, like "welt working," being late for work, leaving early and games and entertainment at the work place (darts, radio etc.). The lower level supervisors were asked above all to show firmness and not to let themselves become involved in local bargaining and reciprocity clauses:

show a resolute management attitude
insist on time keeping and attendance
do not permit extended rest breaks
accept full responsibility at all levels
show by example
do not deviate from the line set because others deviate
set a standard that is fair and stick to it
all members of management must be fully committed.

The target group of "We Will Manage" was not only, perhaps not even primarily, the workers on the shop floor, but rather the lower-level supervisors themselves. One goal was, above all, to do away with decentralized agreements and arrangements: "We Will Manage" did not contain any offers, no considerations of perspectives about the possible structuring of labor relations, work organization, or work practices. "We Will Manage" was a final stroke, not a program of perspectives.

If we compare the development in Great Britain with that in the U.S.A., then a fundamental difference is that no "joint strategy" between the companies and the union headquarters emerged in Great Britain. The reorganization was carried out unilaterally by management. It aimed primarily at practices of "job control" or autonomous actions of workers or their shop stewards, over which the formal union organization had little influence. As management set out to "clean up" these practices, it even accommodated certain interests of the formal union organization. Management's drastic action, though, also forced the formal union organization into making repeated pronouncements against and clashing with management. In addition, these actions repeatedly destroyed approaches which attempted to reach a common understanding regarding the problems of the British automobile industry and discuss programs of action to solve them.

4.2.3 The Federal Republic of Germany

Important events and developments which prepared the ground for new forms of work in Germany were (1) the campaign to protect workers against the effects of rationalization due to the technological and organizational restructuring measures at the beginning of the 1980s, accompanied by (2) the demand for the humanization of work, and (3) the training of skilled workers beyond the level actually needed in the plants, a practice which was primarily motivated by the social policy of reducing youth unemployment since the end of the 1970s.

(1) The collapse in production and employment in 1974/5 represented a deep break for the three "mass producers" among the German automobile companies. Employment as a whole at Volkswagen (VW) was reduced by 26 percent. The majority of the almost 33,000 affected workers left within a period of several months (see Streeck 1984, p.56ff.). In spite of the enormous pressure to release personnel at Volkswagen and the other companies, it was possible to achieve the reduction of personnel by means of so-called "bloodless" measures: voluntary pay-offs, early retirements, "natural fluctuation," and a hiring freeze (cf. Schultz-Wild 1978; Streeck 1984; Dombois 1982b, Brumlop and Jürgens 1986). Thus, the reduction of personnel at VW could be carried out without dismissals.

Foreign workers functioned to a certain extent as a crisis buffer when these measures were carried out. In the case of VW, they were released in much higher proportions than were German workers. Since then, the percentage of foreign workers employed has not been significantly increased (Brumlop and Jürgens 1986). Although the percentage was still high in certain production areas, it was clear that from then on measures of personnel reduction would increasingly affect the German permanent work force. Also with regard to the design of work and new technology the replacement of the "Gastarbeiter" by German workers had consequences (with which we will deal later).

It was a part of the crisis experience of 1974/5 that the rapid upswing which immediately followed in 1975 brought about renewed hirings while severance pay programs were still being carried out. Workers who had left their plants with large pay-offs were already being hired again a few months later – to the great displeasure of their fellow workers who had remained at their jobs. Work sometimes alternated between short time on the one hand and overtime accompanied by extra shifts on the other. This experience led to a demand for a longer term orientation of personnel policy in order to keep the employment level stable, not just at VW (see also Streeck 1984, p. 66f.). The works council declared it would use its right to veto overtime and extra shifts (by using its codetermination right on these issues) if necessary and began to check more thoroughly the medium-range effects on employment and capacity before allowing overtime.

With regard to the goal of stabilizing employment, VW proclaimed the "personnel policy of the middle line" (1975). In order to protect personnel levels from short-term fluctuations in demand, the production program would no longer directly follow all peaks in demand by rehiring employees who had become redundant when demand was low. The production program would be aligned to the medium-range prognosis with respect to sales developments. This personnel policy principle was often violated in the years that followed – to the chagrin of many managers. According to a manager of the personnel department we interviewed this principle had become practically meaningless at the beginning of the 1980s.[5]

Nevertheless, employment security remained a primary goal of the works councils in the following years and due to the success of this policy the German workforce in companies like VW factually had employment guarantees similar to those of the core workforce of Japanese companies. This policy did have its exceptions and the share of atypical employment contracts (temporary employment, for example) increased, but not to the extent found in Japanese companies.

The guarantee of employment security was put to the test at the beginning of the 1980s in view of the German automobile manufacturers' big projects for technological and organizational restructuring. The most important experience resulting from these projects was that the dismissals and downgrading measures which had been feared did not actually take place. The restructuring became, rather, an occasion for quite far-reaching agreements for securing the jobs of those threatened by rationalization. The following case gives an example from our research.

In March of 1984, an agreement dealing with personnel measures in connection with the investment program for the years 1984–8 was reached for Company B's German branch, and thus also covered the change-over at the Mittelort plant. This agreement contained the following points:

Company necessitated dismissals were formally waived for the first-time.

Wage and salary safeguards were agreed to for older workers (fifty years of age with fifteen years service, or fifty-five years of age with ten years service) without a time limitation. (The average age of Mittelort's work force was forty-one.)

The wage safeguards for all other workers were extended and limited to four years.

Downgraded employees received preference rights for taking over suitable positions that became vacant.

It was guaranteed that workers transferred into new departments would not be downgraded.

Finally, firm management promised that:

the appropriate committees of the works council would continually be informed regarding the current stage of planning and would be instructed about effects on production technology, organization and personnel in a timely manner – that is, when they could still influence the planning and when the final decisions had not been made. (Local agreements Nr. 86, Nr. 2).

Wage safeguards of this kind were practically non-existent in the U.S.A. In Great Britain, they were realized only after the German affiliate made the first steps.[6]

(2) The second characteristic topic and sequence of events in the German context was tied to the headings "humanization of work life" and "qualitative contract policy." As in other countries (e.g., the U.S.A. with the establishment of the Work in America Institute) (Auer *et al.* 1983) the discussion of these questions started in Germany at the beginning of the 1970s. The most important impulses and concepts came out of the corresponding Swedish discussion.

Yet West Germany developed differently from countries like the U.S.A., where such projects were initiated chiefly at the corporate level, or Sweden where the employers' associations played a central role. Here the development was primarily characterized by the governmental program for "humanization of work life" and the fact that the unions, especially the IG Metall, along with the works councils in the factories actively advocated the objectives of a more humane organization of work. A further characteristic is that in West Germany, of the two theoretical positions at the heart of the discussion of "new forms of work" – the socio-technological approach and the human relations approach (see also Strauss-Fehlberg 1978; Schäuble 1979) – only the socio-technological approach could establish itself. The consequence was that, in contrast to the U.S.A., the discussion in Germany was oriented more toward job design than organizational design, and as a result, more oriented toward technological solutions.[7]

The two central topics of the different "humanization of work life" programs and initiatives could be summed up under the headings of "stress and strain," and "participation." Each of them had important implications for the introduction of new technology and new forms of work organization.

In Germany the topic "stress and strain" received the most attention and corresponding ergonomic measures were more rapidly and comprehensively implemented. In fact, the reduction of stress and strain became a terrain of common interest between management and the work council in connection with the introduction of new technology. This was because of the possibilities opened up by new technologies for ergonomically improving the working conditions. These measures coincided with demands for preventing work related illnesses and planning new technology. A finding of our comparative study was that ergonomic considerations received by far the most attention in German companies, from management as well as from the works councils. Many members of the works councils have taken courses and have acquired the corresponding training in ergonomics. Ergonomic factors also play a very important role in the review of projects for technological change. According to codetermination legislation, works councils have the right to intervene in management measures of technological and organizational change, especially when the works council can refer to "generally accepted findings of ergonomic science" (Plant Constitution Act 90/91).

The emphasis on ergonomics and on technical answers to reduce work-related stress and strain also reflects the greater problem of illness-related absences and disability. The number of illness-related absences and the percentage of disabled workers is considerably higher in the factories of all three West German companies compared to the British and U.S. plants (see table 4.2).

If we do not want to assert that contractual and governmental regulations have led to an increase in disabled workers in Germany without this being based on actual health limitations, then the question of why there was such a small number of disabled workers in the U.S. and British plants has to be posed. What is it then that prevents a potential problem from being recognized and dealt with in the U.S.A. and the U.K.? Actually we would expect that the actual problems with health-related performance restrictions should at least be as great as those in the German factories. The average age in these plants was even greater than in the West German plants, as we can see in table 4.3.

Table 4.2 *Illness and disability, 1985*

	Illness-necessitated absences[a]	Disabled workers[b]
Maple City	4.8%	5.9%
Northtown	3.5%	1.6%
Hartmoor[c]	4.6%	3.0%
Weinkirchen[c]	8.9%	11.6%
Mittelort[c]	9.2%	14.9%
Windeck	8.3%	14.9%

Notes:
[a] In percentage of the workforce as a whole.
[b] In percentage of the workers.
[c] 1984.

Table 4.3 *Average age of the work force[a] in selected assembly plants, 1985 levels*

Plant	Greentown	River City	Hartmoor	Seaborough	Weinkirchen	Mittelort	Windeck
Average age	40	41	46	42[b]	37[b]	41	37

Notes:
[a] For U.S. plants only the workers
[b] 1984 level.
Source: Company data.

Demands for compensating occupational stress and strain and preventing work-related illnesses through reducing the intensity of work provided the justification for introducing personal relief time allowances and lengthening breaks in many German companies in the 1970s (Sperling 1983). This issue also provided an important argument for expanding individual vacation rights in the 1970s and for reducing weekly working time in the 1980s. The objective of humanizing work thus contributed significantly to the great variation between the countries studied in the temporal availability of the individual worker, i.e., the time his or her labor power can actually be utilized by the employer.

It can be seen from the comparison in table 4.4 that the average "utilization time" per worker in the blue-collar area at Company C's Windeck plant was 16% less than in the U.S. plant compared. In this

Table 4.4 *Differences in the temporal availability of the workers in a comparison between a German and a U.S. assembly plant, 1985*

	River City	Windeck
Paid breaks per shift	48 min.	64 min.
Regular weekly working time	40 hours	38.5 hours[a]
Holidays which do not fall on Saturday or Sunday	13 days	10 days
Contractual vacation days	20 days[b]	30 days
Illness-necessitated absences	6 days	18 days[c]
Available working hours per year[d]	1,590 hours	1,340 hours

Notes:
[a] Number for 1984.
[b] With an average seniority of fifteen years; the vacation entitlements vary between two weeks for one to three years of seniority and five weeks for twenty years seniority and more.
[c] Average for the entire factory including salaried employees.
[d] Calculations proceed from a theoretical maximum number of 260 weekdays per year.
Source: Own surveys and estimates; VDA-Pressedienst No. 20a, December 20, 1984.

comparison, the time off granted for education or training was not included. The difference becomes more drastic when the availability for overtime was considered. At one of Company A's plants in the U.S., the company did pay a small "penalty" per hour of overtime worked into a training fund, as provided for in the general contract, but was not limited in setting overtime hours. After demand had picked up, the amount of overtime hours soared up to 30 percent of regular working. On the basis of the codetermination rights concerning overtime work and on a corresponding contractual agreement, the works councils at the German plant Windeck insisted that overtime essentially be made up for by additional free time ("free shifts"). This policy widened the "utilization time" gap to about 50 percent between the two plants.

The temporal availability of the individual worker will be further reduced in the course of shortening the work week. At the time of our research, the standard working week had already been reduced from forty to thirty-eight and a half hours. The agreement between the IG Metall and the employers' federation calls for a gradual further reduction to thirty-five hours a week in 1995 in West Germany (1998 in East Germany). This policy in respect of the working time will of course create problems for an efficient usage of the capacities in the German factories.[8]

(3) A third line of development which had important consequences for the emergence of new forms of work in Germany was the policy of training more apprentices to become qualified skilled workers (*Facharbeiter*) than were needed in the plants. The background for this were the high unemployment figures which had become a structural problem in the West German economy since the end of the 1970s and could not be significantly reduced by the beginning of the 1990s. With unemployment rates of 7–9 percent in the 1980s, the danger existed that this rate could be much greater for young people just starting to work. To prevent this a general consensus emerged early between the political parties and in the relationship between union and management that every secondary school graduate who wanted to begin an apprenticeship should be able to find a slot in a training program. Thus the works councils in the automobile companies also called for an increase in the number of apprenticeship positions. The staffing requirements of the skilled-worker departments (above all maintenance) were no longer the determining factor for the companies' intake of apprentices. In order not to have to dismiss the young skilled workers who were trained in this manner the company had to find other jobs for them. In this manner, an increasing number of qualified skilled workers with skills relevant to the automobile industry was deployed in direct production. This development was totally supported by the union and works councils.

Since the end of the 1970s an exchange of personnel in direct production with a growing share of skilled workers coming from the plant's own apprenticeship program could be seen. As the trend is still continuing at the end of the 1980s it could be foreseen that this share will increase to reach about two thirds to three quarters of the direct production work force of the assembly plants in the 1990s. While the share of skilled workers employed in the indirect departments (mainly maintenance) was about 10 percent of the total number of blue collar workers in the German, British and U.S. plants, an additional number of skilled workers were employed in direct production in Germany. If we only count those with industry-relevant qualifications (mechanical and electrical trades) their share was between 25 and 50 percent of direct production workers in our German plant sample.

This exchange of personnel was not motivated by technological or organizational necessities, but rather induced by the labor market. NW&M concepts did not initially play a role in this. But, once initiated, the exchange of personnel soon developed its own logic: the advance of the skilled workers into direct production increased both the necessity and the possibility for the creation of "more intelligent" work structures here.

Pressure for action came from two sources: on the one hand, there was the danger of growing fluctuation rates as the skilled workers who were deployed below their qualifications started to look for work elsewhere as soon as the general labor market situation improved. On the other hand, the factory and the worker affected had the common interest in using the acquired qualifications, and thus preserving them. In the opinion of several management experts, unused skilled qualifications had an extremely short "half-life," or deterioration time, after which they can no longer be called upon in practice. According to this opinion, so much would have been forgotten or unlearned again after the passage of three to four years of underqualified work, that the worker affected could not easily be deployed in the skilled-worker sections. From this an increasing pressure arose to enrich production jobs with qualified work requirements.

The special situation linked with the high availability of skilled workers in the German plants has led to the question of how to use the available skilled-worker potential, particularly when considering job integration and group work. Problems concerning job integration resulted not so much from status questions as from the wage systems. Here again the works councils held a strategic position. The following comments of a management representative at Company B's "Mittelort" plant makes this clear:

People who are highly graded, like electricians and electronic specialists for example, also have to be willing to do things which they currently do not do. We also need a new wage system for this. Or, look at the combination of quality control and repair. These people can not presently be integrated. The works council refuses to allow hourly wage work be changed to piece rate work. We cannot change the type of wages without the works council. The works council has full codetermination here. (Personnel manager, "Mittelort")

Here the manager is referring to the works council's right to codetermination in all matters related to incentive wages (methods, system change, etc.) under the Works Constitution Act (§87 BVG). Measures of work reorganization which bridge the dividing line between the hourly wage and the incentive wage therefore need the approval of the works council. This does indeed hinder such considerations of integrating job descriptions or forming production groups which are principally aimed at the increased deployment of skilled workers – e.g., through their taking over of "lower" tasks. However, it was just this right to codetermination, the balancing of interests, and participation of the works council in creating new work structures which it necessitated, that has furthered rather than hindered the movement toward job integration and the formation of production groups in West Germany.

In the following chapters we will deal more closely with measures of job integration. Industrial relations will also remain a central topic there. This corresponds to their importance as an influence on the solutions that were chosen at the different sites.

In this chapter we have seen that the turn toward new forms of work took very differing courses in the different systems, in part conflictual and against the resistance of the unions, in part consentual and with the participation of the unions. With regard to the inclusion of the unions in this process we will summarize our observations in the three countries as follows.

In the British plants we investigated, shop floor rules and union policy did not hinder traditional measures of rationalization once the resistance of the militants had been broken. But the situation there has not been conducive to the introduction of new concepts of work organization and participation. The unions generally took on a purely blocking role in response to corresponding measures of management. The labor market situation and the growing dependence of the British plants on the decisions of the Europe-wide organizations have undercut the bargaining power of the British work force and increased the pressure for the change in plant level industrial relations.

The greatest change compared to traditional practices in plant level industrial relations was found in the U.S. Most of these changes had been introduced and arranged jointly by headquarters staffs of the companies and the UAW. The thrust of these initiatives went toward a more NW&M-oriented way of running the operations at the plant level. This joint policy was more a matter of a (temporary) consensus and of "new thinking" than of formal or even legally stipulated institutions, such as those provided by codetermination in West Germany. These changes had taken root already at the plant and shop floor level in some cases. A process had been started which was obviously not easily reversible. But there were few impulses and concepts arising "from below" which would have given the change process depth and variation. Even the union central staff had largely abstained from developing its own ideas in the framework of the jointly supported participation programs (or refrained from making them public). This was even more true for the local unions, which in most cases were rather indifferent, in some cases even opposed, to the joint union–management programs.

In West Germany, the introduction of new technology and work organization has not caused pressures for changing factory-level industrial relations as it has in the U.S. and Great Britain. Organizational changes and job design are negotiated both centrally and locally, brought up by the company as well as by the union. This corresponds to an orientation of union policy, which, in the course of the 1970s, developed demands increasingly oriented toward preventing health and safety risks. The statutory rights of the works council to information, participation and even codetermination have led to the practice of cooperative problem-solving patterns at the factory level in West Germany. At the same time, the works council members and union representatives were able to develop their own concepts and alternatives for designing the forms of labor deployment, not least because of the institutions of codetermination. We did not find such an independent union policy for job design in either of the other countries studied.

5 Reorganizing quality control – between pressure for efficiency and a job enrichment orientation

As we pointed out in chapter 2, the importance of product quality for the marketing success of a car model increased considerably in the 1980s. Competition, not only with regard to price, but also with regard to quality intensified enormously. Quality standards were noticeably tightened in all Western companies after the Japanese manufacturers had mercilessly exposed the proverbial quality weaknesses of many an old-established automobile producer. The companies set out rigorously to put a stop to the 1970s ideology which emphasized quantity. A new customer-oriented quality policy was proclaimed. "Quality is number one!" became the new slogan; and an appeal was made to the workers: "Produce it as if you are buying it!"

The orientation toward customer preferences was the most striking feature of the new quality strategy. It indicated the change from the seller's market of the 1960s to the buyer's market of the 1980s, which can be characterized by three developments: first, the burden of proof in warranty cases was increasingly transferred from the buyer to the seller and even became, to an extent, a producer's liability; second, because the markets were increasingly expanded most of the customers were not buying their first cars any longer and thus knew what to look for when making such a purchase. Third, an increased emphasis on the so-called delivery quality, which meant that it does not matter if there is a scratch on the car or not, the question is whether the customer would actually recognize it. All this increased the importance of the production process, above all in the last labor-intensive stages of the assembly. Thus concurring expert estimates concluded that only about 20 percent of the overall quality defects of a car could be attributed to mistakes by the production workers in manufacturing. If, however, only the problems in delivery quality are used as a basis, then more than two thirds of these quality defects can be traced back to faulty human work. This is why the companies were directing special attention to reorganizing manpower utilization in order to increase quality responsibility and work motivation in production. The most important concept for this reorganization was the integration of the previously indirect task of quality control into the task area of direct production.

"Integration" was the central slogan for the work reforms in the 1980s anyway, and it also concerned other indirect jobs. In the next chapter, where we deal with the reorganization of maintenance, we will again be dealing with this topic. The "integration" of direct and indirect tasks has often been described in the literature as "job enrichment." Connected with this were often great hopes with regard to the humanization of work, but there were also skeptical assessments. Thus Altmann *et al.* (1981) reported on the basis of such new forms of work at the end of the 1970s in Germany that job integration meant increased responsibility and, at the same time, additional stress and strain for the workers, while the increase in skill requirements generally tended to remain within quite modest limits. A goal of this chapter will be to deal more closely with the question of to what extent does the reorganization of quality control bring about new job profiles which diverge from the Taylorist patterns.

A new feature of the reorganization of quality control in the 1980s compared to previous reorganization attempts was that from the beginning it pursued the goal of improving product quality while at the same time increasing efficiency in production work. Thus, a central goal of job integration was to carry the "efficiency drive" beyond direct production into the areas of indirect labor as well. We will be looking more closely at this using the example of strategies for integrating quality control with direct production. These indirect areas had played a subordinate role in the traditional rationalization strategy – efficiency was traditionally measured by the number of direct production hours per car. The Taylorist fixation on direct labor efficiency went along with a compensatory inflation of supervisory and control functions: the more stressful, monotonous, and intensive the work on the line was, the more rebellious or apathetic the line workers. This then necessitated tighter measures for supervision and control and more personnel to enforce them. A vicious circle arose: the less the direct workers were responsible for quality, the more elaborate the policing apparatus of quality control had to be, the more narrowly the tasks in direct production were defined so as to achieve the highest possible efficiency there, the more the inherently unproductive area of quality control grew. The new strategy of job integration promised to put an end to this circle. With this, job integration aimed at comprehensive manpower savings.

The relations between indirect quality control workers and direct production workers varied quite considerably between the individual companies we studied (see table 5.1). This can be explained by the companies' differing strategic priorities, but also by differing implementation

Table 5.1 *Inspection workers as a percentage of direct production workers*

Plant	1979	1980	1981	1982	1983	1984	1985
Greentown	8.8	9.5	9.3	8.8	8.6	—	—
Northtown	—	10.0	10.1	11.4	11.4	—	—
River City	13.0	13.2	13.3	13.3	12.6	10.8	10.0
Maple City	11.3	12.8	14.8	13.4	11.0	8.0	8.1
Hartmoor	11.7	11.9	12.0	11.6	12.0	11.5	11.1
Weinkirchen	12.9	11.0	10.2	8.6	7.4	6.8	6.8
Windeck	8.7	8.2	7.4	8.7	8.2	7.6	7.6

Note:
We have no comparable figures for the Mittelort and Seaborough plants.

conditions at the national sites. At the center of this chapter are thus the strategies of the three companies we studied and their implementation conditions in each of the three countries we studied. We will be dealing with this question in the first section of this chapter. The reorganization of quality control, with its reallocation of traditional task structures and the targeted rationalization effect, inevitably became an object of contention in the sphere of industrial relations.

Another question which we will be pursuing in the second section of this chapter deals with the use of computer-assisted methods for quality control, which had only been introduced in some factories at the time of our research, but obviously spread rapidly. These systems served primarily to communicate and feed-back error messages to the shop floor. This poses the question of the extent to which the development of new forms of work is promoted or hindered by such technological systems and how these systems must be designed to promote the development of new forms of work.

5.1 Company strategies for reorganizing quality control and their implementation in different industrial relations environments

5.1.1 Company A in the U.S.A.

The efficiency goal was propagated more emphatically at Company A U.S. in the 1980s than at the other two companies and it was clearly the indirect areas which were the target of its efficiency campaign. Efficiency comparisons with Japanese automobile plants had led to shattering results (we will give an example for such a comparison in chapter 7). As a consequence, the rationalization targets ("tasks") set for the assembly plants by the divisional headquarters were drastically increased. In order to reach the target, the central staffs concentrated on the areas and activities with the greatest potential for rationalization. It had previously been customary to just add a uniform two and a half hours for inspection and repair to the direct production time required to make a compact car in order to determine the required manpower in this area at assembly plants. This figure which had almost become a standard was questioned by the company after the Japan shock. As a consequence, Company A's North American assembly division changed its planning procedure.

They did away with the system of yearly planning and the extrapolation of experiential values like the two and a half hours mentioned above. According to the 1983 planning data, more than 40 percent of the repair and maintenance personnel were to be reduced in the planning period from 1981 to 1985. At the time of this study, the objectives for the first two planning years had already been overachieved. Given this high speed of rationalization, it is no wonder that for everyone we interviewed, the reduction of inspection and repair work was a "highly sensitive" topic in terms of labor policy. When we investigated Company A's North American plants in the summer of 1983, we got the impression that the process was being carried out relatively peacefully due to management's more open information policy and the UAW's willingness to make concessions. Our interviewees traced this expressly back to the efforts of management at establishing a trusting cooperation with the workers' representatives. According to managers, the fact that the union received early information was especially effective. They then virtually took over the work from management in implementing the reduction of quality inspection and repair:

The more the union representation knows, the better it is for us in management. Through this, the union saves us a lot of work. If we tell them that we will have to reduce twenty-five inspectors in the next months, then the "committee men" already prepare the work force for this, discuss the reasons, and talk to the workers. (Department management, Company A/River City)

At the core of the personnel reduction was a purposeful reduction of simple checking operations. The first priority was the repetitive full controls, or 100 percent inspections. They were analyzed to determine whether they were necessary or unnecessary from the point of view of customer satisfaction. A consequence in one case was that only six especially critical points were to be exhaustively measured on one specific body part, the remaining twelve points were to be monitored by means of random visual checks and sample measurements. Doing away with 100 percent controls was, according to experts, rather easy to realize because full controls were in reality only 75 percent controls, as the concentration and vigilance of the inspector diminishes over time anyway.

The speed of the personnel reduction in the American plant River City was so great at times, though, that quality defects increased considerably after several inspection stations were closed in rapid succession. Divisional management then instructed the plant management to order the inspectors back to their work stations. This characterizes a process of rationalization where management must proceed according to trial and error as it cannot control the most crucial factor: the quality responsibility of the production workers.

Trial and error did not mean, however, that management was advancing without a plan. They systematically calculated the risks involved in reducing inspection through an exact functional analysis of each individual check. The result of this analysis were "candidates for reduction" which were spread out over four types of inspections:

double or triple inspections of the same source of defects;

inspection for defects which seldom appear;

inspection for defects which have no consequences (no customer complaints);

inspection aimed at solving production problems.

In one plant we heard that 60 percent of all quality inspections in the past fell under these four categories.

At the beginning of our research in the U.S.A. in the summer of 1983, Company A's American car plants exhibited very little of what was being sought after under the catchwords "integration" and "quality responsibility." The following three measures were being discussed:

motivational measures to increase the quality responsibility of direct production workers;

self-inspection by the line workers through defect cards ("stickers");

integration of inspection and repair.

Individual experiments had been only carried out surreptitiously and they were subject to revocation up to then. River City had some individual cases of self-inspection in the body shop; in the Maple City plant, some repair workers operated according to the "seek and repair" principle, i.e., they looked for and repaired defects in one integrated operation without involving an inspector, as was normal practice. The dashboard was given to us as an example. This had been previously checked over by three inspectors for proper wiring, after which the repair people undertook the appropriate corrections. It was shown here that the inspectors could be dispensed with without a loss of quality.

Management particularly emphasized that a prerequisite for the strategy of reducing inspection was the willingness of production and repair workers to take over inspection work. We found local unions, which generally supported the company strategy of upgrading product quality and reorganizing work, to be in a dilemma. This explains the distinction which a union representative in Maple City made with regard to production taking over quality responsibility: first, formalized quality responsibility through self-inspection, which was opposed by the union; and second, the non-formalized quality responsibility, which was supported by the union. In practice both components were, admittedly, fused together which enabled the union to cryptically be both for and against the "integration." The fact that this game was not fooling anyone can be seen in the following remark by a union representative:

Doesn't each worker somehow inspect his own work? Lets assume that a co-worker on the line determines that a component or a fitting is not in order. He then corrects the thing naturally, thus doing repair work. And he had naturally also inspected before he started with that. (Union representative, Maple City)

Different from this "natural" but obviously not self-evident quality responsibility were those formalized forms of additional responsibility where the production worker took over clear visible task elements from inspection work. These latter included the inspection of the dashboard by repair workers and the line workers' "self-certification" in which they either used a sticker to confirm that they had completed their tasks according to specifications, or on the other hand, filled out a defect card to point out the need for their operation to be corrected. These defect cards, which the workers used to make others aware of the fact that they had been unable to complete their tasks, existed for about eight to ten operations in the plant in Maple City at the time of our study.

Such experiments were a very sensitive subject in the summer of 1983 and had led to considerable uneasiness among the quality inspectors. Some of them had filed formal grievances. This reaction of the inspection workers has to be seen against the background of the massive reduction of inspection jobs which the union was attempting to stem by defending the existing job demarcations in each case. Company A's response to this was the "quality upgrade operator."

With the "quality upgrade program" (QUP) in its North American factories, Company A created a new category of worker which made it possible to avoid the arduous negotiation problems between each of the existing classification groups when job elements were combined or fused. The introduction of the quality upgrade operators as a separate personnel category made the company's new emphasis on quality very clear and, at the same time, allowed for the continuity of the old patterns of work organization in production. The QUP was introduced as a direct answer to the Japanese competition. It was therefore first introduced in the plants whose models were most intensely in competition with the Japanese imports. In 1980 a new model was introduced in this market segment for which the company had high hopes. We will be dealing primarily with the developments in the assembly plants for this model in the following.

In order to attain both goals as soon as possible with the new car, Company A's North American body and assembly division allocated more than 400 "quality reliefmen" in addition to the budgeted QC personnel to its River City and Maple City factories: the "Quality Upgrade Program" was born. The program was started in the River City and Maple City plants in the summer of 1980 to deal with the start-up problems of the new model line more easily and more rapidly, especially in terms of product quality. Because it involved additional jobs, the program met with great interest by the union locals in view of the desolate economic situation and increasing unemployment in these areas.

The job of the QUP workers in the turbulent time of the model start was to ensure that the workers on the line brought about the planned production quality. They were required to intervene in the production process in order to correct mistakes and help the direct production worker if necessary, e.g., to ease problems with defective materials or tools. The QUP workers performed their jobs in close cooperation with the line foreman. Similar to reliefmen and repair workers, the QUP worker belonged to a higher wage group ("utility classification"). During the 1980 model start, there was one QUP worker for every seven to nine direct production workers in the River City and Maple City plants. Before the model start, the QUP workers went through a special training program which made them familiar with the product design and production process of the new model, as well as with participative management methods. It proved to be advantageous that not only the foremen, but also the "hand picked" QUP workers, were more thoroughly trained than usual. Thus the start phase was considerably shortened and it was much easier to break in the entire work force.

The increase in quality and output in the first six months after the model start was aided by management's intention of not using the QUP program in the spirit of the old philosophy of sanctions and control, but instead to appeal to the positive motivation of the line workers:

They tell their co-workers: You are not going to be disciplined if you don't complete the entire operation at once or if you make a mistake. You only have to point it out to us. We can only do something about it and remove the cause of the mistake if the foreman or the QUP man has been notified. (Staff engineer, Company A U.S. divisional headquarters)

Table 5.2 *QUP workers in the factory personnel structure, 1983*

Employment classification	River City entire plant	Maple City trim department
Indirect inspectors	292	16
Direct workers, of these	2,312	160
reliefmen	228	16
repair workers	130	19
QUP workers	140	13

The success of the QUP program can also be seen in the considerable personnel reductions which could be realized later. The QUP program was conceived from the start to complement the planned reduction in inspection and repair work. On balance, the rationalization planning amounted to the savings of one inspection worker and one repair worker for each newly created QUP position.

A form of budgeting in the framework of the QUP program was called self-financing. Those assembly plants which were not confronted quite as severely by the Japanese competition had to pay for the QUP people, one per foreman, out of their own resources, through the reduction of quality inspectors and repair people. Those plants which had to fight on the forefront with the Japanese competition, like the River City and Maple City plants which we studied, received a higher contingent of QUP workers – two QUP per foreman – as a "grant" from the division with no immediate reduction of regular quality inspection and repair workers.

The QUP program created conflicts when the unions recognized it as a plan for indirect rationalization. The program definitely did not serve to increase personnel. It was rather designed to kill two birds with one stone. First, it would make the model start easier, and, second, it would flank the planned reduction of inspection and repair personnel.

As table 5.2 shows, there were about as many QUP workers at the plant level (River City) or at the departmental level (Maple City) as repair workers or inspectors. QUP workers, inspectors, and repair workers were reduced by comparable amounts starting in 1981. This fact becomes clear in table 5.3.

The development led to some concern among the work force of the Maple City plant. The union representation too had voiced its misgivings early, but had been reassured by management:

As an answer to our question of what would happen to the inspectors and repair people, the management representative said that it would not take away any jobs.

Table 5.3 *Reduction of QUP workers, inspectors, and repair workers at plant Maple City from 1981 to 1983*

Classification	1981	1982	1983
QUP workers	220	180	140
Inspectors	360	309	219
Repair workers	195	193	161

But then it became apparent that these QUP people did repair work for up to 60 percent of their working time. As management then went about reducing the repair workers, we then demanded that management withdraw the QUP program. Management said last week that it would talk with us about that and that it is willing to bring this group back to its originally intended functions. (Union representative, Maple City)

The reduction of the QUP workers as such was not a point of conflict because it followed the old pattern of experience that additional workers were always reduced after the first phase of the model cycle. The conflict was rather concentrated on the question: what tasks should the QUP people be allowed to perform? And the union answer was: no inspection and repair work.

What was the job description and what were the actual functions of the QUP workers? First of all, the QUP workers had no special task in the production process. Their work was "free effort," so to speak. When a line worker did not complete his or her operation in a satisfactory manner or was unable to complete it, then the QUP worker should make the correction. They should specifically look for the reason why the worker was unable to perform his work correctly and eliminate it. The QUP workers were mobile, they had no fixed work station, and were even allowed to leave their area if necessary. This was because one of their tasks was also to check and see if mistakes had come from earlier production sections. In the case of complicated tasks, they checked over the quality of execution and corrected or completed the work performed when necessary. Work operations of a complicated nature, the so-called "critical jobs" (like the wiring of the dashboard) were assigned in bundles of three to four individual jobs to a QUP worker who checked out the work quality and eliminated defects. The strain on the foremen was relieved and they had more time for administrative tasks. In all, the job description of the QUP workers contained the following tasks:

supporting the foreman;

filling in for absent workers at the beginning of the shift;

breaking in production workers;
monitoring product quality;
bridging bottlenecks in material supply;
working as reliefmen during disciplinary talks
reading and understanding the process sheet in the production section of
the foreman's area.

This demand profile did, in fact, infringe on the tasks of other employee groups and literally provoked "boundary violations." From the point of view of the union, management had the right to create such "bastard classifications" as long as they paid the appropriate wage and kept to the agreed to demarcations. The union representatives raised the objection, however, that the work of the QUP personnel was more demanding than their classification in the wage structure allowed for and that the demarcations were constantly violated. Thus the union representatives cited the QUP worker's performing work of reliefmen and repairmen as a violation of rules. Supporting the line workers, on the other hand, conformed to the goal of making sure that quality is built in from the start.

A grey area in factory practice had emerged here, which led to continuous friction and to grievances from inspection and repair workers. This held true all the more considering that many QUP workers had apparently developed an expanded understanding of their role:

The company had glorified the QUP workers much too much. These people should simply be called workers for special tasks ("utility classification"). Now they consider themselves to be a type of deputy foreman, and the workers on the line naturally don't like to take orders from their fellow workers. (Union representative, River City)

Remarkably enough, however, this conflict did not smoulder any less at River City than at Maple City, even though there was a formal "letter of understanding" on the question of QUP workers at River City and no such agreement at Maple City.

Without a doubt, the conflict over "delimitations" and "boundary violations" only became virulent with the massive personnel reductions in inspection and repair. The union representatives were especially upset by the fact that they had trusted management's assurances that no disadvantages would arise for inspection and repair people, and had thus advised the repair people with high seniority not to apply for the newly created QUP positions. Because the recruitment also went according to strict seniority rules at Maple City, the fact that the repair people did not apply for the positions, offered openings to workers with less seniority. In reality, however, the reduction plans and efficiency goals had already been decided on, so that the drastic personnel reduction in the areas of quality inspection and repair which then started caused additional tension in the work force. One of the union representatives summed it up with resignation:

This is a big topic. It gives us continual headaches and can keep a union functionary in suspense almost around the clock. We will probably bring it up at the bargaining table again in the wage round next year. (Union representative, Maple City)

We were not able to follow this conflict further to see what came of it.

5.1.2 Company A in Great Britain

In Britain, the concept of job integration met with greater union resistance. In North America the UAW headquarters had tolerated the integration strategy from the beginning, so that the resistance could only be articulated at the local level. In Britain, on the other hand, the new strategy immediately met with massive union opposition, from the leadership to the grass roots. Thus management's announcement that they were going to cut down on inspection jobs through integration measures was seen by the union as a declaration of war.

Management at A's Hartmoor plant was first able to achieve a major breakthrough in the area of job integration in 1985. With regard to the contents of these measures, we have to differentiate here between the integration of inspection and repair work ("seek and repair") and self-inspection ("self-certification").

In the body shop, management had suggested the concept "seek and repair" time and again to the shop stewards and the workers affected. The finishing line of the body shop led the way. This was the only section in the body shop where the shop stewards tolerated "seek and repair" on a trial basis. Here, the repair workers checked over the completeness and correct placement of the spot welds and made appropriate repairs. Management hoped that the example of the finishing line would serve as a lesson and dispel the reservations of the work force in other parts of the plant.

The concept of "self-inspection" meant that the production workers used blue stickers to confirm that they have carried out their operation according to specifications. This practice of positive certification was gradually introduced since 1981. At the middle of the 1980s, there were about 140 jobs in assembly where the quality was confirmed by the direct workers with blue stickers. In the body shop, the system of self-inspection had even been extended to 250 jobs. Up to the time of our study self-inspection had, according to a QC manager we interviewed, not functioned satisfactorily because quality responsibility had not become sufficiently rooted in the behavior of the workers. The traditional "job protection" attitude appeared still to be in force, as the production workers refused to extend the system of self-inspection to marking mistakes occurring at work stations other than their own. So as not to set a precedent, this was also applied to their own work: so-called "negative certification," i.e., marking mistakes instead of certifying one's own work, was tabu. Management had been unsuccessful in its attempt at introducing red stickers for marking quality errors up until the time of our study.

The introduction of self-inspection was flanked by measures for furthering the sense of responsibility for quality among the workers in the Hartmoor plant. The "black ball" system was also one of these measures: if the workers believed that a particular vehicle could be used to demonstrate a particular problem which came up again and again at their work station, then they were asked to place a black ball on this car. It was then brought into the inspection area where an evaluation took place with inspectors, foremen, and workers from other areas. The worker who placed the black ball could present the problem personally here. The black ball system was restricted to two days a week and to the day shift.

In the course of our investigation we were able to observe a case when the "black ball" was actually used and participate in the problem solving discussion which emerged in this case. Nevertheless, during our interviews with experts at Hartmoor we were repeatedly warned not to confuse management's intentions with actual practice, even where the integration was accepted or tacitly tolerated by the shop stewards. There were also doubts in management about the integration strategy because the lack of motivation in the work force:

Somehow we still have the feeling that it could have been a mistake to integrate quality inspection into production work. We still hear remarks like this from the workers: "If you want it cheap, then you'll get it cheap". That means if we take the inspectors out, then it is our responsibility if we don't get quality work. (Personnel manager, Hartmoor)

But there could be no doubt that union opposition gradually softened up, mainly due to two reasons: first, the change from uncompromising opposition to grudging toleration went together with an increased willingness of the shop stewards to attempt a trade-off of manpower savings for compensatory measures: in the form of severance pay for workers who left voluntarily and in wage increases. In this manner, extra time allowances were used to sell self-inspection to the workers in seat production (sewing, upholstering), a traditional weak point in production quality. Statistical process control (SPC) was gradually being introduced in a similar fashion. The shop stewards themselves were taking courses so as not to lose control over this process and to be able to negotiate wage improvements when SPC was implemented. The production workers in the paint shop had also been compensated for their taking over the role of quality inspectors with a higher classification. Here, it was apparent that the hard line of British unions on "job control" was turning into a "continental" type of worker's representation where the emphasis is put on compensatory measures. We could not even see the outlines of a comparable compensation deal in Company A's North American plants in 1983. There, management expected to be able to push through the integration without wage compensation.

The second factor was management's strategy of including the shop stewards in cooperative decision-making. Management did not let the lines of communication be broken down and tried to involve the shop stewards instead of excluding them. As with the introduction of SPC, management tried to bring the shop stewards "on board" when aiming at innovations, offering training courses, having discussions, and in measures for additional training. After a long dry spell this strategy finally showed some effects. Thus union representatives also took part in some problem-solving groups at the time of our study. These groups dealt with quality problems and quality responsibility. One of the interviewees commented:

The union representatives helped us quite a bit in this. For one, they have more time for such things than management. And then they began to develop a deeper interest in this. Thus it was much easier for us to awaken the interest of the workers and receive positive feedback. (Personnel manager, Hartmoor)

One thing cannot be emphasized strongly enough: it was not the workers, but only the shop stewards who had taken part in the problem solving groups up to the time of our study. Quality circles involving the "rank and file" were still being blocked by the unions, at least in the blue collar sector. They were not willing to allow NW & M measures which would lead to direct communication between management and the work force. They saw this as undermining the actual source of union strength in the factories.

5.1.3 Company A in the Federal Republic of Germany

At the German Weinkirchen plant we were dealing with established practices of self-inspection and job integration at the intersection of quality control and repair work already. Plant management at Weinkirchen had set out in 1981 to convert top management's concepts into decentralized action while other plants were only gradually starting to consider the "how" and "when." If we come to the conclusion that Weinkirchen was ahead of its European and North American sister plants with regard to job integration then this was primarily for the following reason: the West German system of industrial relations had shown itself more open to change.

Table 5.4 *Inspection workers in the area press/body shop at Weinkirchen, 1985*

Year	Inspection workers (absolute)
1980	86
1985	101
1988	40 (planned)

What management in the U.S.A. and Great Britain first had to learn with difficulty, namely to involve the representatives of the work force, could already be presupposed at the beginning of the strategic change in West Germany. While the reorganization of production work, quality control, and repair was still in the trial stage in the U.S. plants in 1983 and had been blocked by the union "ban" in the British plants, reorganization measures had already been largely realized at Weinkirchen.

Table 5.4 gives the figures for 1980 and 1985 in the press and body shop.

Management hoped to be able to absorb the planned personnel reduction largely through normal fluctuations. With this, however, transfers and reassignments in production would be unavoidable. They did not reckon with any great resistance from the works councils and the work force. When asked whether the harshness of the reduction process for the people involved troubled him personally, a manager responsible for the reduction answered:

No. I had two advantages when I took this position three years ago. My first advantage is that I come from toolmaking, and thus have not worked in quality control for years and years. And I have personally experienced how life for a production man can be made difficult through quality control. My second advantage is that I did not know anyone here but rather came new into the plant. Thus I did not have to make any personal considerations. And that is only possible if you don't let down the people who you have worked with for years. Because of this I don't feel uncomfortable. (Quality control manager, Weinkirchen)

The active toleration by the works council was assured by management primarily through the argument that the reorganization would help to maintain or increase the plant's competitive advantage over its sister plants. This argument was coupled with an employment guarantee for those who would lose their present job through the integration. The strategic goal of the personnel reduction was to be cushioned in a "socially acceptable" manner – that meant using early retirement to avoid dismissals.

From the beginning, management made it perfectly clear that the reorganization of quality control would have a dual function: the reduction of inspection personnel and an improvement in quality through increased responsibility of the direct production workers. The directive was to achieve manpower savings through task integration. According to this, integration measures were only to be carried out when a rationalization effect could be demonstrated. The directive prescribed that a savings of at least 30 percent must be attained through an integration measure.

In order not to endanger the dual goal, plant management at Weinkirchen proceeded carefully and gradually. One of the quality managers described this process as follows:

The entire process of reduction and integration of quality inspectors was very thoroughly prepared with the involvement of the works council. This did not take place all at once, the course of integration was rather tackled very carefully. Thus, for example, in body finishing, where the inspectors still stood by at the beginning as the finishers (= repair workers) took over applying the I.O. stamp (I.O. = in order). After fourteen days we allowed the inspectors to "disappear." Then there was a trial phase without the inspectors, and at the end one could even see an improvement in quality at the final inspection after three months. (Quality manager, Weinkirchen)

The redundant inspectors were transferred back to production in the course of the reorganization, where they generally remained in their area:

In principle, the quality inspectors were always transferred back into those production areas where they had previously been assigned as controllers, e.g., a controller in the area of the welding line was generally assigned to the welding line, in the area of body finishing on the finishing line, etc. They thus remained predominantly in these areas. This was thoroughly discussed with the works council in each case, whereby it came to quite a few personnel discussions. (Quality manager, Weinkirchen)

The works council confirmed this description of a conflict-free reorganization and emphasized the "humanization aspect" of integration measures: it was expected that the integration would mean "job enrichment" for the direct workers. The most important reason for the works councils not to oppose the reorganization was management's assurance that it would not lead to a loss of employment if carried out smoothly, but rather to a strengthening of Weinkirchen in the competition between the plants of Company A's European network. The reduction of personnel in quality inspection was, in fact, accompanied by increasing production volumes at Weinkirchen. As a consequence, the introduction of a "self-certification system" and job integration, which met so many hindrances in the British and U.S. plants, was carried out smoothly here.

The "self-certification system" was introduced and accepted by the works council and work force in the form of positive *and* negative self-inspection in all areas of the factory. They also introduced the "negative"

Table 5.5 *Categories of production and repair workers in final assembly*

Category	Number
Direct workers	1,846
Repair workers of these	243
inspection-finishers	88
group leaders[a]	20

Note:

[a] The position of group leader ("Kolonnenführer") refers to a leadership function below the first line supervisory level ("*Meister*"). The group leader has no authority over personnel and is assigned to normal production work. The function existed traditionally in some areas of the plant and was redefined in 1985. We will be dealing more closely with this in chapter 6, page 204.

certification of errors here, a feature which could not be introduced in the British sister plant up until then. The workers used error cards, chalk markings, stickers, or tags applied to the car body. In contrast to the U.K. plants, the "self-certification system" was widely used in practice. According to a production supervisor ("Meister") in assembly, about 60 percent of the repair work was recorded through the "error card system." These cards were collected by the inspection finisher and hung on a bulletin board. Here, it could be determined which line workers had made error reports most frequently. Management stressed the fact that this was not interpreted by the supervisor as poor work, but rather as a sign of the worker's extra attentiveness and responsibility.

The job integration policy created a new job classification of "inspection-finisher" which combined the task of the former quality inspector and the repair worker. This new job classification was introduced in Company A's German assembly plants in 1982–3. As table 5.5 shows, about one third of the repair workers in the trim and final assembly areas at Weinkirchen had become inspection-finishers by 1985.

The job description of the inspection-finisher required additional training. For the assembly area it amounted to four weeks. Even the deployment profile for the "normal" repair workers required that they be the "top people" in their work area and be able to master all of the operations. Beyond this, the inspection-finishers were also responsible for statistical process control within their section of the line. At the same time, they took over the function of looking after their production group and alerting co-workers to mistakes. This responsibility was aimed at creating a better feedback of information and stopping errors at the place where they were committed.

There was also a more restrictive interpretation of the job profile of the inspection-finisher, which was found especially in the body shop. With closer examination, it was apparent that this was designed to appease the demands of the union and works council for reviewing wages with a higher job classification. We are mentioning this detail because it gives an example of the level of intervention which the German workers' interest representation has in the construction of new job profiles. The point of conflict was obviously in the actual difference between the old finisher and the new inspection-finisher. This difference is played down in the following remark of the body shop manager:

We don't call these people inspection-finishers. We simply say finisher, even though the people who do repair work at the end of the finishing line naturally control and repair. Actually we could call them controlling finishers, but we simply say finishers. Incidentally, we have hardly any new finishers. The old finishers have actually only received the additional assignment of looking for the repair cases without having to depend on inspectors and their markings. (Production manager, body shop, Weinkirchen)

Behind these terminological ambiguities was the question of who was entitled to the so-called "integration allowance." According to this, management had agreed to pay those direct workers whose work included more than 20 percent indirect additional tasks an integration allowance of 40 Pfennig per hour. "Full" inspection-finishers were in principle entitled to this allowance provided that the inspection work exceeded 20 percent of their work. This was similarly true for other indirect tasks such as line feeding and set-up tasks. The argument above referred indirectly to this 20 percent and to the fact that the works council and management could not agree on the question of how to determine the additional amount of work required by the finishers' new task of inspecting their own work. There was no controversy over the principle of integrating the task of the formerly separate job classifications.

5.1.4 Company B in the U.S.A.

Management at Company B in the U.S. also tried to tap the rationalization potential of indirect functions. In an internal company study, it was calculated that in the company's North American assembly plants alone, with an average work force of 4,700 workers, 500 quality inspectors and repair workers could be saved if, as in the Japanese plants, the production workers would take over the responsibility for quality. These figures were published in a trade journal in the spring of 1983. Different from Company A, Company B's assembly plants had up until then no concrete objectives for the reduction of inspection, nor had a comparable "integration campaign" been started up. The image of a more leisurely change in strategy was also confirmed in the European branch of the company. Company B only followed the integration strategy in 1985 with a two-year (Great Britain) or four-year (West Germany) time lag compared to Company A.

When compared with the changes at Company A in the U.S.A., routine reigned in Company B's U.S. assembly plants in the summer of 1983. This was true for personnel reduction as well as for the organizational design in quality control. A multitude of organizational patterns could be found in the plants, most of which had already emerged in the 1970s. They were heterogeneous, now and then contradictory, and a consistent strategy outline could not be perceived. Among these, though, were some interesting approaches for bringing back quality responsibility into production which we will address later.

While Company A tied their reorganization measures together into a campaign, no strategic design could be seen at Company B. In response to a question about the possibility of integrating production work and inspection, we received this answer at the divisional headquarters:

We are in the process of organizing that. There is nothing wrong with giving the workers the responsibility for quality, in the end they are paid to do it right. But it is the decision of the plant manager as to how that is to be done at the plant level. The divisional headquarters does not issue any special suggestions to the individual plants as to whether they should give the inspection work to inspectors or to the production workers. (Quality engineer, divisional headquarters, Company B U.S.)

This information was generally confirmed at the factory level. When we visited the Greentown and Northtown plants, the idea of self-inspection had only been discussed recently in management. At Northtown, management had started thinking about introducing stickers for self-inspection. The first practical testing of self-inspection was planned for the engine dressing line. This line is especially critical for quality everywhere because the assembly errors made here are covered by the subsequent components and thus not easy to identify afterwards. Here it is particularly expedient for the line assemblers to use stickers to confirm that they have completed their work correctly. In addition, the management of Northtown was looking at possibilities for reducing the number of inspection workers. In order to sort this out, representatives of plant management and the local union jointly visited another plant in the assembly division where the reduction of inspectors had already been accomplished to a large extent.

A further difference to Company A was that a certain amount of reduction in inspection had already taken place in Company B's U.S. plants in the late 1970s as a reaction to a temporary surplus of quality controls. At the beginning of the 1970s, conflicts had arisen in the plants, dissatisfaction with work increased, and product quality deteriorated dramatically. Management responded to this development with increased and intensified quality controls. Final inspection was bloated. A management representative from Greentown commented on this:

In 1971, we were overloaded with "buyers" who checked out repairs and corrective measures. In the meantime, we have got rid of most of them. The repair worker stamps his work himself and there is no re-inspection any more. (Quality manager, Greentown)

In some production areas the practice had become established by 1979 that the repair workers mark their repairs or corrections with a personal stamp. The repairman carried a rubber stamp with his individual combination of letters. This had replaced the practice that each repair carried out be stamped by a quality inspector. The responsibility of the repair worker came especially into play in tasks where quality was critical: axles, motors, brakes, air conditioner, shock absorbers, fitting of the hood, etc. The repair worker's taking over of final inspection did not, however, lead to an increase in the wage level.

In addition to this, we found numerous examples at Company B in the U.S. where simple line inspectors, the so-called "direct inspectors," took over typical production tasks on the assembly line. This was possible because they were classified as direct workers, and thus had the same status as the production workers. As a result of the uniform status, the flexibility between the classifications was higher than at Company A which classified inspection in general as "indirect" labor. Because the direct inspectors, like the line operators, worked under time standards, it was possible to assign the inspectors production work with improved pay:

The union said that this is a way to reduce the inspectors, but there wasn't any real resistance to this because these inspectors can earn more money through adding work elements. It must be said, though, that the number of inspectors who actually take over production work in this sense is very small and hardly adds up to more than 1 percent: (Quality control manager, Northtown)

Quality control workers at Northtown, for instance, had already taken over production tasks in some areas in the 1970s. For example, those who were responsible for radio inspection were also temporarily entrusted with installing the aerials. At Greentown there were also individual line inspectors who had additional assembly tasks (interior lighting, dip stick, glove compartment).

There was no consistent "integration policy" to be perceived at Company B's North American plants. Integration approaches peacefully coexisted rather, with intensified approaches for disintegrating production and inspection. When asked about the most far-reaching measures in the area of quality control in the last years, an expert at Northtown said:

The most important reorganization of quality control took place in the painting process in 1981/2. Because the paint shop is a special sub-area of production with its special problems, the production people there had already taken over the responsibility for quality a long time ago. And this quality responsibility was transferred back to our quality control department. Up until 1981 there was no special quality inspection for the paint shop. The impetus for the reorganization came with pronounced quality problems with the paint jobs. The inspection tasks were given back to quality control one and a half years ago and, at the same time, the quality control department received a considerable instrument for exerting pressure on those responsible for production. Although the manager of the paint shop is still responsible for changes in its production process, for reorganizations and changeovers, we in quality control now have a decisive influence on the layout of the process, on corrections and changes. This is expressly established in the new inspection directive. (Quality control manager, Northtown)

Management was proceeding pragmatically, and even took the opposite path in the case described above: an increased separation of quality control and the responsibility for production, returned to or strengthened the old policing function.

5.1.5 Company B in Great Britain

In the fall of 1983 Company B's management in the U.K., like that of the U.S. parent company, had not yet developed a clear policy for job integration. This did not come until one year later and led to a massive confrontation with the work force at the end of 1984. We can reconstruct the development from 1983 to 1985 fairly well, as we carried out our empirical studies at three different points in time and could successively deepen them. First of all, it was emphasized in all of our expert interviews, both by management and the unions, that the question of changing work practices was a recurring issue. Since the beginning of the 1980s there had been a clause in the yearly wage contracts which called for self-inspection and strengthened the quality responsibility of the production workers. In the 1982 wage round, management attempted to make the introduction of self-inspection mandatory, a move which was not accepted by the unions at that time.

In 1983, management achieved a success when a sub-committee of the

JNC ("Joint National Council") for work practices was established to consider a changed distribution of tasks between quality inspection and line work. This sub-committee still did not agree to formal changes in the forms of manpower utilization, though. Doubts grew in management as to whether an integration of production and inspection could be realized by means of wage contracts at all. Thus a personnel manager said that it was a big mistake to link changes in work practices with wage bargaining. This was because a wage agreement was always an "emotionally charged affair," as the workers' standard of life was at stake. Wage negotiations were thus an extremely disadvantageous place to push through changes in work practices.

Also, in the 1983 wage negotiations management was only able to get a general clause into the agreement. The unions' rejection of the demand for integration was summed up by a union representative of the TGWU:

This is a big danger. When the production workers even start to inspect their own work, then the danger of losing the entire inspection department exists. (Union representative of the TGWU)

The union representative was by no means sure that management would not be able to get around the unions and convince the workers to adopt new work forms. All the same, he implied that the union would be willing to negotiate this question if this were linked to wage increases, a safeguard for the status of the inspectors, and employment security.

Management had, in fact, frequently attempted to introduce similar reorganization measures. At the Carborough assembly plant, management had withdrawn some paint shop and body shop inspectors from the line and assigned production workers to carry out the quality checks. In the paint shop, this went together with the offer of being reclassified from the wage group of production workers into the higher wage group enjoyed by the inspectors. These changes, introduced unilaterally by management, were stopped immediately by the shop stewards. That was not always possible, though. Proper information did not always come from the work force, that is, changes were occasionally tolerated tacitly by those affected without being passed on to the "convenors" (chairmen of the factory union organization). This was especially a problem in the case of new work practices. When these had been practiced for a longer period of time, it was almost impossible to return to the previous condition because they would have already become "established" work practices through customary right.

For management, this union position was incomprehensible, especially since it only concerned a minor change, namely the repairman's self-inspection after a completed repair. The procedure valid at the time of our research was that a quality defect which had been discovered was passed on by the inspector to the repairman who then carried out the correction or repair. After this, an additional inspector checked to see that the repair was performed properly. This reinspection was now to be taken over by the repairmen themselves. They would have to vouch for the elimination of the defect with their signature, according to the model in the U.S. sister plants. With regard to wages and qualifications, this would be no problem at all from the point of view of management, as the repair workers were generally more competent than the quality inspectors and were better paid anyway.

An obvious difference between this and our investigation at B, U.S. was that the quality objective in the U.S.A. was always associated with the idea of integration in terms of NW&M goals. The "integration debate" in both of the two British car companies did not, however, conceal the fact that its goal was personnel reduction. An interviewee stated very bluntly that the combination of inspection and production is not a strategy for improving product quality, but rather a strategy for reducing personnel:

As far as product quality is concerned, an integration will not change much there. The integration would neither improve nor impair the product quality. There are, however, personnel savings possible. Plans have already been made here in which a number of inspectors in the paint shop and the body shop were especially earmarked for such measures. This has not been attempted up to now, though, and a decision to proceed in this direction has not yet been made. The main problem in this regard has been less the union opposition than in the changes in the personnel structure, whereby the loss of inspection functions would cut off a chance for advancement for the line workers. Inspection tasks are regarded as preferred jobs here. Such possibilities for advancement are important for the people, and they would definitely not like it if these advancement jobs were to disappear. (Production manager, Seaborough)

These remarks also make it clear that the company was proceeding hesitantly on the question of integration and had not yet developed a clear strategy by 1983. But the British management was under the pressure of a Europe-wide policy. A Belgian parallel plant, where far-reaching changes had already been achieved in the relation between production work, inspection, and repair work, set standards for comparison here. In 1984, management had decided on a strategy. They were now convinced that they could not get anything from the unions with "soft" negotiation. They had presented their reorganization ideas at the bargaining table during the 1984 wage round, but were unable to reach an agreement this time either. In contrast to 1983, management were willing to carry out what they saw to be a trade-off of integration measures for a wage increase. The corresponding contract clause read that the production workers would generally declare themselves willing to look for errors and to correct or eliminate them. This declaration of their willingness, which was established under the formula "detect and correct," was described by a quality control manager interviewed at Seaborough's British sister plant as "the biggest manpower saving clause we got."

"Integration" or "self-inspection" was to be introduced in a systematic sequence: in the first step, the repair workers should mark their work after corrections or repairs themselves and the "reinspectors" be taken out; in the second step, the regular line workers would take over responsibility for inspecting work done at stations prior to their own; in the third step, the regular line workers would inspect their own work by themselves and attest to the quality.

These measures were the beginning of a far-reaching reorganization which, in its emphasis, dealt with the entire task spectrum of repair work and inspection. The prerequisites for this were created in the 1984 wage agreement as the repair workers were classified in a higher wage group. It was then expected of the repair workers (rectifiers) that they become more flexible and be able to perform a wider range of repair tasks, and also work in the "rectification bays" (repair areas independent from the line), not only on the line. A week of training in the "rectification bays" was foreseen for this. The flexibility of repair workers between the line and off-line work stations which was thus achieved would be organizationally safeguarded by forming a "pool" of rectifiers, out of which workers could be drawn to be deployed at different work stations and in different foreman areas.

At the same time, one "rectification man" per foreman area would be made redundant through the reorganization. Beyond this, it was planned to create a closer linkage between the inspectors and rectifiers who were already cooperating as "pairs" in the old structure. Management intended to intensify their cooperation and interchangeability and thus to increase the possibility of reducing personnel.

As to the direct line workers' self-inspection, a system largely similar to that in Company A's British plants was planned. The headword for this is "line identification of defects." A special form which replaced the old vehicle identification sheet was to be introduced for each section with its specific inspection operations. Each line worker who had problems with his work should circle a corresponding marking on this form. The errors which were marked would be corrected and the form would be signed by a repairman or an inspector. At the end of the foreman's area, the form would be taken out and preserved by the foreman, who checked, evaluated, and analyzed the information contained every two hours.

Management had introduced this catalogue of measures against union resistance in 1984 and, in doing this, calculated on an open test of strength. In this, management had underestimated the readiness of the work force to fight. On the first working day after the measure was introduced workers at the Carborough plant laid down their work to protest against it. Management saw itself forced to withdraw the integration measures and, for the time being, to reinstate the about twenty inspectors who had already been transferred to other work stations.

The clashes over the reorganization measures and the corresponding wage classifications have also led to conflicts and walk-outs at Seaborough. From the point of view of management, the changes still were not functioning satisfactorily in 1985, even though they had finally been tolerated by the union representatives, and, even worse, the quality had suffered under the clashes. A personnel manager had the following comments:

The quality has suffered since the new wage structure has been in effect. The shop stewards had declared at a meeting that the relationship between inspectors and repairmen is extremely tense. The inspectors do not help with repair work, and the production foremen go around and threaten the inspectors: we'll soon be rid of you any way. Sooner or later you will be working for me on the line again. (Personnel manager, Seaborough)

Self-inspection by the line workers also had its problems. The markings and the error information of the self-inspecting line workers were often very incomplete and inconsistent, which was frustrating for the inspectors. The work force had not accepted the reorganization by 1985 and the union representatives still spoke of the one-sided measures of management which they refused to consent to.

5.1.6 Company B in the Federal Republic of Germany

The goals of the reorganization in the F.R.G. were not fundamentally different than those in Britain. As in the British case studies, the measures to reduce personnel and improve productivity in the operations at the interface of quality inspection and direct production were not considered directly related to the question of new task descriptions and new forms of work organization at Company B's West German plants. Up until early 1986, the relationship between direct production and quality inspection remained organizationally unchanged. On the one hand, management concepts had been rejected by the works council. On the other hand, management had not attached great importance to a reorganization. But, nevertheless, about 10 percent of the inspection personnel had been reduced between 1983 and 1985 and further reductions were planned.

Of great importance was the fact that a transfer of "indirect" quality inspectors to "direct" production work could not be achieved by management without the consent of the works council. This was due to the clause in the Works Constitution Act giving the works council full codetermination in all decisions concerning the principles of wage determination. On this basis, the regional master wage agreement stated clearly that management could not unilaterally allocate direct work to indirect workers or vice versa. But allocating indirect work to direct workers, like giving inspection work to production workers, would meet less opposition from the work councils as it meant shifting work into the realm of incentive wages where the works council's codetermination rights are much stronger than in the straight hourly wage area. In fact, in the body finish area of the plant, flexibility in this direction was practiced on a daily basis. But this had nothing to do with job integration, as the workers in this case would just perform quality inspection and no direct production work. As soon as they were dealing with fundamental questions of integration, though, the works council blocked. Management complained that the logical continuation of this path, i.e., the integration of inspection and repair work on the line, was foundering on the objection of the works council. The following statement of the plant manager made it very clear, though, that management was determined to achieve this flexibility and that it saw the corresponding manpower savings as a question of the survival of the plant:

Take the combination of quality control and repair work. At the present time, I cannot integrate these people. The works council refuses to allow hourly wage tasks to go over to the incentive wage area. There are examples here which are totally incomprehensible. For example, we had material handling people who were performing machine-paced work, and we offered to pay them an incentive wage, where they would have got even more money. But the works council said that this could not be done. I cannot change the wage without the works council. They have complete codetermination here. And this question has really become very urgent for us in connection with increasing efficiency. It is no secret that we do not look good in comparisons within our worldwide corporate organization, and that we are especially compared with the other European plants. Changing the wage system has become so urgent for us in the meantime that one would have to say that the plant could go under because of it. Take the wage intensive areas like assembly. Looking at costs, Great Britain is clearly better than we are. Or take Company A: we recently studied the German plant, Weinkirchen, and they are 20 percent better than we are in the assembly areas. (Factory manager, Mittelort)

While the works council's objection to integration measures was depicted as the main obstacle in our management interviews, this was rated far lower by the works council members themselves. According to our interviews, there was no firm position of the central works council on the question of integration. The integration measures in final assembly were treated by the works council on a case-by-case basis. At the time of our interviews, one of the works council members was working on a planned case of self-inspection, where the job of one inspector would be eliminated. "I am going to talk with the people to see whether or not that can be done. And we will desperately look for arguments to prevent it" (Works council member, Mittelort).

According to the works council interviewee, this situation came up quite frequently. The most important case here was management's intention to introduce the self-marking of errors in the body finishing area. Through this measure, all of the inspectors in the final section of the body shop would be eliminated. This section had thirty-five production workers and eight inspectors at that time. Our interviews showed that the works council did not take a position of basic rejection. This was also because of management's cautious implementation strategy, which was clearly different from the conflict strategy of British management: "That is coming to us little by little, and we now have to see what we should do" (Works council member, Mittelort).

With this, it becomes clear that in the codetermined process of implementing new forms of manpower utilization management was attempting to avoid a conflict. In contrast to the U.S.A. and Britain, the question of integration in the German plant Mittelort was treated on a "case by case" basis by the plant's work council and was not handed over to the works council at the company level (*"Gesamtbetriebsrat"*) to formulate a general policy. As just one issue among many others crossing the desk of a works council member in his daily work, the individual measure was dealt with in detail and rendered harmless. In general, the works council concentrated on securing an adequate wage level for the workers in the new jobs. We have already become acquainted with this "German" pattern of a primarily compensation-oriented works council strategy at the German division of Company A. The national pattern of industrial relations plays a dominant role here.

5.1.6 Company C in West Germany

The words "self-inspection" or "integration of inspection and repair work," which were emotionally charged at Companies A and B, did not have an aggressive tone at Company C at the time of our investigation. On looking more carefully, however, the situation was quite complicated. The findings also point toward a gradual dismantling of the separate quality control function and toward a strengthening of the quality responsibility of production at Company C's factories. The weakening of the formal quality control organization – called "quality assurance" in this company – became apparent above all by the fact that it had more and more been forced to give up one of its most important control mechanisms in the production process, line inspection, and turn over this responsibility to the production department. This transfer of the repetitive full controls (100 percent line inspection) to production had been at the core of a strategy which Company C had pursued since 1980.

This strategy shows clear parallels but also clear differences to Company A's and Company B's strategies of reorganization and rationalization. The "transfer" strategy was also linked with a sizeable personnel reduction and to the elimination of inspection functions in large numbers. A strengthening of the production workers' quality responsibility was also considered to be appropriate at Company C. At the same time, however, the quality control management insisted energetically on keeping its policing role, which it believed to be indispensable – a clear contrast to the quality policy of Company A. The inspection tasks given over to production remained strictly separated from production work in most cases and a systematic integration of these tasks with direct production tasks, as in Company A's integration program, was not sought.

The transfer of inspection work from indirect to direct work created a potential for integration measures and job enrichment in production which, so to speak, was begging to be utilized. But this had been effectively blocked up to the time of our research by the quality department (not the works council!) which still controlled the execution of its inspection schedules. Thus a stock of options for job design existed, but was not being used, in fact, almost up to the end of the decade. We will now be looking more closely at the reduction of inspection and then come back to this odd state of suspense.

As a whole, the number of inspection employees at Company C was reduced by about 27 percent between 1979 and 1984 (from 9,500 to around 7,500). In order to better specify the strategy for reduction, we looked at the Heidedorf plant more closely, especially the areas "assembly" and "stamping/body shop."

At the Heidedorf plant, quality control was sub-divided into two large areas and two smaller organizational units with analysis and service functions. While the two smaller departments "quality analysis" and "testing lab" recorded no, or only minimal, personnel cuts, the major burden of the personnel reduction fell on the two large inspection departments. The 1984 plans intended to further reduce the number of inspection workers. The focus of this reduction was to be placed on line inspection, especially in the assembly area and in the body and component assembly areas because the full controls were concentrated here. These were predominantly unqualified sorting or repetitive visual inspections on the assembly line. Over 60 percent of the inspection tasks of this main department were still ordinary full controls, which were at the center of the planned personnel reduction. In the course of the strategy, which had been pursued since 1982, the majority of the so-called sorting inspections had been handed over to production. A considerable reduction of jobs had already been realized in the paint shop. Most of visual inspections could be eliminated due to the improved quality of the paint work following the introduction of spraying robots. The production workers looked for their paint mistakes themselves in the meantime, while the quality control personnel had largely withdrawn to auditing functions.

The quality control department, with responsibility for the production areas "press shop," "body shop," and "mechanical production," showed a continuous reduction in employees by about 24 percent between 1974 and 1981 and then a constant employment level until 1984. As was the case at Companies A and B, the reduction of the simple repetitive inspection work meant the loss of promotion opportunities in production and the loss of jobs which could be filled by older and disabled workers. Traditionally, there were two criteria for the recruitment or promotion of workers to the position of "inspector": first, the length of service in the company and, second, a good record of quality performance as a production worker. The path of promotion ran from the incentive wage workers on the production line, to the "rectifiers" (repair workers), then to the straight hourly wage inspection workers. The promotion to inspector was also linked with a clearly higher wage level. Traditionally, inspection also functioned as a gathering place for older and disabled workers. This was changing in the course of the new strategy. The average age in inspection of Company C in 1981 was still fifty. In 1984, it was down to forty-two – it was, however, still clearly above the average age of the incentive wage workers.

The new strategy consisted of a package of measures which was based on separating full controls or sorting inspections, which were classified as direct work, from the inspections relevant from the customer's point of view, which were considered to be indirect work. The latter inspections remained organizationally under the roof of quality control, while sorting inspections were given to the production department. Thus the quality control organization retained the more sophisticated, analytical, safety-relevant, and complicated tasks; the less qualified inspection tasks and those using technical testing equipment were delegated to production.

The observed transfer of quality inspection work into production was not an integration of tasks in the sense of "job enrichment," but rather an integration of different spheres of management organizations. As the line inspectors were placed under production supervision they lost their independence from production management. In the case of conflicts, they would be more subject to pressure from production and perhaps be more ready to put aside "quality interests" in favor of "production interests." The fear that this might happen was often expressed by quality managers we talked to at Company C. They watched all the more closely to see that demarcations between production and inspection tasks were held to meticulously. Although it was obvious that inspection and production workers had to cooperate and the trend was towards job integration, quality management resolutely blocked this until the end of the 1980s, however. At that time production management had clearly won the upper hand in the power games between the departments and the company proceeded resolutely to use the stock of options which it had built up.

Management's persistence in holding on to the strict division of labor between direct production and quality control can be shown from reactions to any mention of "self-inspection" and "integration of inspection and repair work." The general opinion of management in our interviews became evident in the following comments: self-inspection is "not a topic here," stickers and chalk markings for work performed incompletely or improperly would be "fully unthinkable here."

We have not yet reached the point at which we could introduce self-inspection. First, we cannot assume that the worker would perform his work properly and correctly right away. And, second, we also cannot assume that they would immediately report to repair or to the next production station if they are not able to complete their work or make a mistake. (Quality engineer, Windeck)

But there are exceptions to the rule. These refer to exactly defined checks of the functioning of parts critical for safety. Such safety inspections, like the proper insertion of the steering, which cannot be controlled after the steering column is subsequently covered, must be signed for by the worker involved. In response to our question whether there are certain tasks where self-inspection virtually imposes itself, like surface treatment in the body finishing area, for example, a preferred field for job integration at the other companies, we received this answer:

The finishers can do this and naturally should also do it, especially here. How could they work on mistakes otherwise, if they did not inspect before and after. Strangely enough, though, we cannot do without strict quality control especially in body finishing. If quality control would pull out, then the mistakes would shoot up. Especially here one would think that a self-inspection would cause relatively few problems. From our experience this is not the case. (Quality engineer, Windeck)

Management also strictly refused to approach the integration idea more closely in respect to the interface between inspection and repair work. There had been a binding job description since 1980 which stated that "rectifiers should seek, identify and rectify mistakes." In practice, however, the inspectors still sought and identified mistakes, whereby the "rectifiers" limited themselves to correcting them. The quality inspector went around the car and pointed out quality defects by marking them on the vehicle's inspection card. In a separate operation, the repair worker looked at the mistake marked on the card, eliminated it, and stamped the correction work on the card. This had to be countersigned again by the inspection worker after a concluding reinspection.

It has happened that a mistake was not corrected, but also not written down. For this reason, we pay strict attention to insure that the inspectors write down all of the mistakes, and are skeptical of a fraternization. (Quality manager, Heidedorf)

The quality management thus attached great importance to the quality inspectors keeping a close eye on the repair workers and propagated the concept of "pair formation" so that the repair worker could not "retreat into anonymity." In order to insure that the mistake was immediately corrected, directly under the eyes of the inspector, the concept of "pair formation" intended that the inspectors and rectifiers went around together looking for mistakes. This concept was tried out in 1984 in one of the assembly shops. But even the principle of working in pairs was looked at skeptically by traditionally minded quality managers. Such close cooperative relations had developed between the members of some pairs that the boundary lines of who did the inspection and who the rectification work became blurred. The management at Heidedorf therefore propagated all the more vocally the dogma of a strict separation of inspection and repair work.

The conservative attitude of quality management at Company C with regard to transferring quality responsibility to production did not mean that they were in principle opposed to this worldwide trend. We had the impression that they were trying to win time until their own strategy, which aimed at professionalization, could be brought to bear. An expression of this was the creation of a "quality monitor" (*Güteprüfer*) as a new qualified skilled-worker (*Facharbeiter*) category. The quality monitor was planned to be the pillar of the quality assurance organization of the future.

In creating the "quality monitor," Company C was as a consequence making use of its skilled-worker oriented strategy of work reorganization. Skilled workers had already played a prominent role in the QC organization in the past. Table 5.6 shows that half of the salaried QC employees had gone through a *Facharbeiter* training at Company C in 1984. Additional *Facharbeiter* could be found under the blue collar workers. The "professionalization" of quality control was only beginning in 1984. Table 5.7 shows the different types of quality inspectors in the Heidedorf plant. Around 20

Table 5.6 *Personnel structure of quality control at Company C, 1984*

Inspection workers		6,000	86%
Salaried employees in QC, out of these		1,000	14%
skilled workers	500 (50%)		
engineers	300 (30%)		
Quality control (total)		7,000	100%

percent of the inspection workers are qualified skilled workers, namely those working in the measuring room and audit, or as quality monitors and group leaders.

The negotiation of new job descriptions for qualified inspectors which started in 1982 was complicated by the intertwined interest positions within management and between management and the works council. This concerned not only the "quality monitor," but also the task descriptions for "rectifiers" and mobile inspectors (random sample testers). According to quality management interviewees, mobile inspectors should be qualified skilled workers. Personnel management had reservations here, as this would be a further impetus to move the wage structure upwards. This upward movement, on the other hand, corresponded to the work council's negotiating line, which in itself was not totally without contradictions, as they attempted to simultaneously keep more highly graded jobs (e.g., automated systems controllers, setters) open for workers without skilled worker's certificates. And this was only possible when the corresponding job description was not fixed at the qualified skilled-worker level.

The job description of the quality monitor (*"Güteprüfer"*) was a compromise. An important reason for this was the embarrassment that the then existing semi-official category of group leader in quality control could not be dealt with anywhere in the 1982 wage agreement. A lower classification for those affected, however, did not come into consideration. A second reason for establishing a qualified category of inspectors at the skilled worker level came from the major priority which quality control work was to receive in the future. The solution of transforming the group leaders into quality monitors was also supported by the works council.

Thus the department "Assembly II" had 120 inspection workers, of which fourteen were quality monitors. These quality monitors were all former group leaders.

Each of the deputy first line supervisors (*"Vizemeister"*) in our area had two group leaders. This was questioned by the works council because the group leaders were officially nothing other than inspectors according to the wage commission,

Table 5.7 *Inspection personnel in selected areas at Heidedorf*

Worker group	Share in %
Line inspector (full control)	30
Random sample tester	25
Line controller	25
Measuring room/audit inspector	10
Quality monitor/group leader	10
Total inspection workers	100

although they actually had a leading position in their group. The group leaders had actually performed all types of work, but generally not the normal inspection work which their colleagues had. This was one of the reasons to make them quality monitors. (Quality manager, Heidedorf)

The quality monitor had thus functioned as an advancement job for semi-skilled workers here. When compared to their previous work, the group leaders who were brought into the position of quality monitor would no longer be in charge of personnel. It was, however, doubtful as to whether they would be able to support the professionalization sought after by management. In the assembly areas, it appeared as though the new employee category had primarily served the purpose of job protection. The quality management in the press and body shop areas however practiced a restrictive recruiting policy which was definitely oriented toward the skilled-worker (*Facharbeiter*) status. The thirty-five inspectors which had up to then been deployed as quality monitors in the press and body shop were not former group leaders, but were qualified skilled workers.

According to the job description at the time of our study, the quality monitors must either have had apprenticeship training as a skilled worker or equivalent previous training. Some segments of management would surely prefer to recruit more young apprenticed skilled workers to the position of quality monitor. But a plant agreement prescribed that young skilled workers must first work on the line in production. If the term "equivalent previous training" were to be interpreted more strictly, then it would be impossible to get around bringing in skilled workers (and especially young skilled workers) for these tasks and training them further. The official works council position was, on the other hand, that the possibility should also remain open for non-skilled workers to be able to enter the quality monitor positions. In reality, however, the demanding additional training would be an effective deterrent with regard to older and non- or semi-skilled workers. In view of the competition, few non-skilled workers have the nerve to take part in the additional training courses. Thus the new job of "quality monitor" can be used to support the thesis of a "reprofessionalization of production work," as it is used by the German industrial sociologists Kern and Schumann in their influential book "Das Ende der Arbeitsteilung?" (Kern and Schumann 1984). But it becomes clear that this shift generally does not take place in the course of an individual worker's career, but is connected with a generation change, whereby the non-skilled workers and their qualifications become largely obsolete.

With this we come to the end of this section. A fundamental difference in our account could be found at the level of company policies: Company A pushed forward the integration strategy very rigorously worldwide. As we can see in table 5.1 and as we will show in chapter 8, this company was able to realize by far the greatest personnel reduction in our comparison sample. The large increases in productivity which can be observed in its factories are probably based primarily on the manner in which the reorganization of quality control was carried out.

At Company B, the area of quality control was obviously not at the center of the restructuring strategy. There were, as we have seen, experiments and suggestions in this direction, but without emphasis or consistency. An explanation for this could be that the considerations here were based on the more highly aimed goal of self-regulation based on group work with integrated quality responsibility. With regard to this ambitious objective though, the 1980s were allowed to slip by in large areas of Company B without the emergence of new work forms in the area of quality control.

The possibilities for an integration strategy were created early at Company C. They were, however, hardly tapped and used to create new forms of work in the course of the 1980s.

As a whole, relatively few new job descriptions were defined in the course of the reorganization of quality control. We had the quality upgrade operator at Company A in the U.S.A. and the inspection-finisher at the same company's German branch and the quality monitor at Company C. The inspection-finisher, as a hybrid job between inspection and repair work would probably also correspond most closely to Company A's objectives in the U.S.A.; at the time of our research, though, it could not be pushed through there. The job description of the quality upgrade operator as a "utility man" was, in contrast, more an unstable provisional solution. The new job category of quality monitor, finally, corresponded to a pattern of skilled worker based new production concepts which are widespread in Germany.

In looking at the steps taken to reintegrate quality inspection and production work we do see a departure from the Fordist–Taylorist principles for organizing production. The separation of those who execute work and those who control it has been diminished. A certain degree of external control is being reintegrated as self-control into the work carried out. Possibilities for an enrichment of direct production jobs have been created, although only used very hesitantly – and this is also true for the German plants where demarcation problems do not play quite such a large a role as in the other countries.

There was more resistance to the transfer of quality responsibility to the production workers in the American and British plants caused by the system of industrial relations than in the German plants. This could be demonstrated in the case of the use of stickers or defect cards. The example of Company C, however, where such measures met hardly any resistance from the union, but where instead management blocked moves in this direction, shows that the diffusion of this concept is not only a question of industrial relations.

If in the British plants resistance was primarily based in the traditional system of industrial relations, in the case of Company C's German plants the most noticeable resistance came from the management organization and the interests in retaining the power which was rooted in it. We have up to now not dealt with another aspect of Fordist–Taylorist production management. This refers to the forms of production organization, and here we are primarily referring to the conditions of assembly line work. We will be coming back to this point in more detail in chapter 10. At this point we only want to point out that, in practice, the criticism of the assembly line with its short-cyclic, pace-bound, repetitive, and mindless work hardly had an effect on the reorganization of quality control. Especially in the American plants, where we saw the unbroken influence of the assembly line organization, there was no contradiction seen between this and the proclaimed goal "quality is number one." Although the German management interviewees frequently saw a negative connection between short-cyclic assembly line work and the resulting quality, the American managers interviewed tended to hold the contrary position.

Also in the Japanese plant, the strong emphasis on quality work goes together with conditions of short-cyclic repetitive assembly line work. The strong receptivity of American management for the Japanese production organization, which we will be discussing in the final chapter could perhaps be due in part to the largely unbroken tradition of assembly line organization in the U.S.A. and Japan.

5.2 Computer-aided quality control and its limits

The following is a digression dealing with a process which had only established itself in a few plants in our sample: the introduction of computers to communicate quality-related feedback to production workers. We want to depict the experiences with these systems in Company A's Weinkirchen and Windeck plants and Company C's Heidedorf plant. Our question in this respect is to what extent did these systems have a conducive or impeding effect on the establishment of quality responsibility in production and new forms of work based on this.

5.2.1 Computer-aided quality control (CQS) at Company A

The computer-aided information system at the European branch of Company A was developed at the end of the 1970s and had been introduced in most of the European plants in the following years. The goal of CQS was to provide a systematic record of quality defects and product repair in the production process. Defect and repair information was fed into the computer at input stations. The on-line input took the place of hourly written defect notices on the tally boards. In this manner information should be available more rapidly and effectively, and it was possible to enact faster and appropriate correction measures in production. Specific information over the current defect priorities was given in the hourly defect alarm report. CQS assigned each defect to the production supervisor ("*Meister*") who was responsible for the area and automatically printed out a separate alarm report for each area. Special reports to analyze and localize specific defects could also be printed out on request. An effective feedback of information with regard to the respective defect situations in the individual departments was thus provided. This made it possible to increasingly avoid defects, and thus contribute to a reduction of defects in production and to an improvement in product quality.

The forerunners of CQS were clearly more awkward. The error messages were previously analyzed in several manual intermediate stages before they made it into the computer. A feedback of information only came twelve to twenty-four hours later. This meant that the data were practically useless for monitoring and correcting current production events. They served rather as management reports, but not as a direct aid for production personnel on the shop floor.

Data input was the critical point of CQS. Quality defects were fed in manually and the data quality was accordingly dependent on the reliability and objectivity of the quality inspectors who fed in the data. The work sequence "inspection – defect detection – data input" was largely identical with that of the manual information system which CQS had replaced. In the former, most basic information was obtained through visual controls. Aids like transportable measuring devices ("datamyte," "unimet") for checking out the car's electrical system or hammer and chisel for testing weld quality were exceptions. If defects appeared during the quality inspection, then they were written down by the inspector on tally sheets or cards which accompany the car body.

In the manual information system, the tally sheets were collected in the department's quality control office. There they were copied and passed on to the separate areas. Plant management only obtained them in a condensed form, after the individual defect cards had been combined to form a shift report. It contained the delivery quality ("first run capability") for each production section. If the origin of a defect was questionable, then the production supervisors and the departmental manager would determine the possible causes, perhaps together with the process engineer and the quality engineer.

CQS differed from manual data collection and processing in two ways. First, it was more selective as it covered only a part of the quality inspections, while all other inspections still had to be manually ascertained and processed. Limited by the memory capacity of the computer, CQS had a processing program for 1,000 components and 100 defect cards. This was the second difference from the manual system. The respective component/ defect combination which had been manually marked on the vehicle card was fed in at the terminal. A vehicle inspection card specially tailored to CQS was developed for generating basic information. The correct and reliable use of the vehicle cards and terminals involved an increased responsibility for the inspection personnel. Corresponding training measures were carried out with about 150 workers in quality assurance before putting the system into operation.

While the data input was more selective and systematic with CQS, it was performed in much the same way as in the manual system. The actual difference in the new system was reflected in the processing of the information collected. CQS was considerably more efficient and reliable. The system provided four types of information, some were printed out automatically and some by request: the hourly defect alarm, reports over defect trends, defect concentrations ("top repairs"), and condensed management reports. We will be looking more closely at the defect alarm and management reports, as they often contradicted each other when they were actually used in practice. Both were printed out automatically, whereas the trend analyses and "top repairs" reports were only printed out on request. This is an indication of the greater importance given to the alarm and condensed reports by management.

The hourly defect alarms consisted of separate print-outs for each section. They contained information pinpointing the major types of defects for the previous hour and the place the inputs were made. The production supervisors ("*Meister*") affected were obliged to study the hourly alarm carefully and to take necessary corrective measures. To confirm this, the supervisors had to countersign the hourly alarm report. The report thus functioned as a source of information close to production, and only became legitimate when actively and intelligently used at the implementation level of the production process.

The condensed management reports ("summary reports") covered a two week period and itemized the quality performance per day and per shift. These were brought together to form monthly reports and had the function of giving plant management and the central staff highly aggregated indicators to evaluate trends in production quality. The most important of these indicators were "defects per vehicle," "first run capability," and "system performance review." These data were not connected with the direct quality control on the shop floor, but served rather as management instruments.

It has been shown in practice that these two main functions of the CQS stood in conflict with each other. After the system was introduced, it soon became clear that it was hardly possible to use the CQS data as a central instrument for monitoring and sanctioning following the traditional control philosophy and simultaneously motivate the production supervisors and workers to use the system actively and creatively to improve the delivery quality.

The conflict was that quality assurance took over this system, even though it was originally designed for use by production. In this, quality assurance not only looked after the data, but also the *system*. Production did not take part in this and defended itself against the system. (Quality engineer, Weinkirchen)

At the same time, quality assurance's responsibility for CQS should not be interpreted as a cause, but as a symptom of the problem. It is the symptom of a quality policy which put its money on a centralized reporting system and considered it unrealistic to expect that individual responsibility for quality on the part of the production personnel could be activated. This traditional company policy became a "self-fulfilling prophesy." It either quashed the mobilization of quality responsibility under the production supervisors in its initial stages or, as with CQS, did not even let it emerge. One of the quality managers characterized the contradictory double function of the system as follows:

Abuse was made of this system. In addition, it became much too inflated. Management wanted to have the infos and the corresponding statistics much too detailed. Management wanted to make comparisons. CQS was used at the beginning primarily as a quality reporting system. The actual conflicts between production and quality assurance first really started to come up here. Then, the following problem arose in its application. The data were used directly for control purposes, and it was said that even top management was informed about the actual

CQS data. Then production made the counterdemand on the line inspectors not to record so many defects and not to inspect so rigorously. (Quality manager, Weinkirchen)

A production manager described this conflict situation in a rather veiled manner:

At first, I didn't think much of the system. It didn't even bring any savings. Perhaps it did lead to more information than before, but the tally boards also did the job. CQS is a treat for management because they now get the information fast. I also let myself get caught up in that for a while. But that is actually not important. It is important that the work unit, the production group, receives the information rapidly. If the system is run properly, it is the best, fastest and most exact information system. The man can see what is going on with his trend and problems. On this basis, the quality engineers can then be put to work solving the problem. It is a question of training and management for the system to run properly. (Production manager, Weinkirchen)

The works council also emphasized the fact that management was inadequate in this area. Problems arose not only due to the lack of objectivity of the quality information, but also due to the pressure which, in the end, rested with the production departments. As soon as the defects registered on the terminal became a matter for negotiation between production and quality assurance, the indicator "first run capability" became totally worthless, repair work within the department was not even recorded any more and taken care of informally. Therefore, the pressure for control inherent in the system had the side effect that

half of the repairs were done under hand by the people in production. High I.O. figures meant that the people down there were sweating blood and water just to achieve the success goals of the quality statistics. (Works council member, Weinkirchen)

These examples explain why there was little inclination in the production departments to constructively work with CQS. Added to this came the fact that with the old vehicle inspection cards, the old tally board system, was in fact retained. True to the old control philosophy, management wanted to ensure that the quality inspector actually did pass his instructions on to the repairman. Thus CQS remained an alien element in the direct information sub-system of quality assurance at the level of direct production.

This only changed when the "Japan effect" began to weaken the traditional control philosophy and bring CQS out of its dead end. Specialists from a Japanese automobile company who had seen the system had even characterized it as unnecessary and the emphasis should rather be on attacking the roots of quality defects directly. Beginning in 1983, this rethinking also had consequences for the work organization in quality control and for CQS. The system was put into the hands of production. There it could be used as a production–internal management instrument and its second function as an information system for upper management was largely eliminated. But it remained potentially available in the double function described above. Highly aggregated management reports were still being drawn up, although our interviewees maintained that these were not being read in the spirit of the old control philosophy. It is thus all the more important to assess the corporate culture and the work policy context and how they changed. The importance of this becomes quite clear in looking at the "history" of CQS in England. In Company A's British plants, it did not prove possible to free the quality information system from its political dead end and to change its function as was the case at Weinkirchen. The system was introduced at Hartmoor in 1982. There, management had later attempted vainly to transfer the system responsibility to production and convince the production workers to take over the input of data. For reasons of "job control," however, the union stewards at Hartmoor insisted that the input of quality data did not correspond to the work obligations of production workers. In our management interviews, though, the British management emphasized that "these attitudes are being broken down."

In Company A's American factories, the introduction of the system was still imminent during our studies in the summer of 1983. The introduction, for which a two year implementation period was planned, was intended from the start to be brought into line with the new policy of decentralized quality responsibility. CQS was to be installed on local mini-computers. It was to serve exclusively as a instrument for monitoring the direct production quality ("in-process-control"), thus as an aid for the production departments, but not for drawing up central quality reports. The experts emphasized, though, that an interconnection of the plant computers via the divisional headquarters was being considered for the future.

In contrast to this system, the situation in the 1970s had been characterized by a highly centralized control system which sought complete control. The ensuing flood of information could neither be dealt with, nor was it suitable for a complete control of the quality performance. It also did not contribute to improved quality. The computer system dominant at that time (using the batch procedure) could do nothing to counteract these deficiencies. It added to the deluge of information: the factories prepared monstrous masses of data which were processed by the central computer into batches of paper. These mammoth reports were only used inadequately and were doomed to extinction as management followed the new participation philosophy and retreated from the old policing principles. In this situation of upheaval, top management decided in 1981 that the plant internal quality data and reports should only serve as instruments for quality assurance there and no longer as information for central management.

Our investigations at the Maple City plant confirmed the picture of a transition phase which allowed the individual factory broad possibilities for self-regulation in the framework of specific quality goals. Up until about 1981, daily quality reports were sent from the plant to the divisional headquarters (reports on critical items like bumper height, water test, etc.). Now, such specific information from the plants was only sent to the divisional office in exceptional cases. The company had learned that daily monitoring by the upper hierarchy levels did not help to improve product quality. In this, the highly touted turn away from traditional control thinking was also carried out in practice. A welcome side effect of the new strategy was the fact that the strain on the quality department at the divisional headquarters was eased, especially since the central office had to cope with a considerable personnel cut which started in 1981.

The quality manager at Maple City was, in principle, positively inclined toward a computerized interconnection of quality information in the future:

If a unified computerized quality information system would be worked out for all plants, then the quality data from the individual plants would be centrally summarized and processed. Such an interconnection would also have advantages: if, for example, our dimension measurement engineer had a specific problem and would want to find out how this problem was solved at River City, then he could simply call up the corresponding information over the computer. If it should turn out to be a material defect, then we could call up the supplier quality on the monitor as a next step, etc. (Quality manager, Maple City)

These were still visions for the distant future, though, and "island solutions" will probably dominate in the foreseeable future, until the extraordinarily difficult problems of a company-wide computer network have been solved. When this is achieved, however, controversies stemming from the "double function" of computer networks as a means for central control and self-regulation, could break out anew. Perhaps the decentral use of quality information systems will someday be interpreted retrospectively as a pendulum movement running the gamut from the ponderous, centralized control of the 1970s to the decentral growing and learning processes of the 1980s, up to recentralized information and communication networks of the late 1990s.

5.2.2 Computer-aided quality control and people-based "quality feedback units" at Company C

The example of Company A makes clear what a central role the labor policy context has for the utilization of the new information and communication technologies in the factories. The viability of computer-aided information systems is extremely dependent on the willingness of the workers to actively work with them. For this reason, we can speak of a functional complementarity between an organizational culture open to communication and the productive usage of computer-aided information systems. But this complementarity is threatened from the labor relations side through conflict and mistrust and from the new technologies side through their immanent control potential which can develop considerable explosiveness, not only in the case of conflictive labor relations.

Management's NW&M objective of opening up work-related communication with the shop floor and relieving it of hierarchical constraints, which went together with new participation programs, fits in well structurally with an intensive usage of computer-aided information systems – even though this effect was not explicitly intended by management. We will now demonstrate this connection of participative work communication and computer-aided communication systems with the example of quality control and team-like "quality feedback units" (Qualitätsregelkreise). Here, it becomes clear that fostering the use of verbal communication must by no means contradict the usage of communication systems in the form of machines, as common prejudices would suggest. We can rather speak of a differentiation of two types of communication which are related to each other in a variety of ways. In the following, we will first deal with the computer aided systems for quality control and then turn to the "quality feedback units."

The planning for the computer aided information and monitoring system for quality assurance at Company C began in 1979. The goal of the project was to develop an on-line information system to shorten reaction time in the case of quality defects, to identify concentrations of defects, and to meet them with a flexible inspection program and immediate repair measures. This was based on improving customer-oriented delivery quality and, at the same time, reducing the cost- and personnel-intensive full controls. With this, the new quality system moved totally in line with the traditional control philosophy. Control was not supposed to be reduced, but to be changed from personal to technical control and, at the same time, its effectiveness and intensity was to be increased. As a result, the responsibility for the system rested with the quality assurance department from the beginning. A transfer of the system to production's responsibility was not considered at any time. The unbroken continuance of the control philosophy was, however, accompanied by management's open information policy towards the works council and the work force. This was no different with respect to the new quality system. The works council was thoroughly informed from the beginning and had an advisory role in the multistage introduction of the system.

Despite the fact that it corresponded to many of the objectives of Company A's quality system, Company C's projected system went one decisive technological step further, however. The intervention in the evolved social organization was, accordingly, also more profound. This could already be seen in the technological configuration of the system. On the one hand, the system functioned as a "dynamic inspection plan," which means that inspection instructions were given automatically and rapidly conveyed, whereas the information feedback in Company A's CQS system was considerably slower. On the other hand, an integrated computer network had already been realized at Company C: the quality system drew on the same set of data as the system for process control, which was introduced at the same time. It was originally planned to couple the process control and quality control systems even more closely, but this plan had to be abandoned due to technological difficulties.

As far as the course of the inspection and the corresponding data processing were concerned, the data about quality defects were fed into the system in coded form by the inspection worker by means of a portable infrared transmitter. This device was similar to the familiar remote control devices for televisions. These portable terminals allowed for the fact that the quality inspectors had to be able to move freely and communicate with the computer at the same time. Instead of recording the observed defects by hand on the vehicle inspection card, the inspector types the numerical code of the detected defects into the portable terminal and, after completing the inspection process, transmits the defect data to the receiver.[1] Three digits of this code were reserved for the identification of the cause of the defect. But the quality inspector was also being controlled, as he had to sign on and off with the system using his identity number at the beginning and end of the shift.

After the data were fed into the system, the computer program went into action: it drew up instructions for the following inspection work stations in a matter of seconds; it used basic data and all defect messages which had come in during the shift and took the shift's schedule of car variants into account. A dynamic inspection plan came into being which allowed a flexible change between full controls and random sample tests and adjusted the scope of the inspection to the individual vehicle: to equipment variants as well as to the current defect trends. The fundamental improvement compared to CQS, which we described in the previous section, was that this dynamic inspection plan's program was capable of supplying the individual inspection sections with specific instructions for each vehicle in an on-line procedure. In this manner, the items to be inspected could be adjusted rapidly to the continually changing circumstances. The system therefore made an automatic "inspector guidance" possible, that is, the instructions were given out at each inspection site as standards for the subsequent areas and printed out on a specially developed machine readable vehicle inspection card which replaced the old manual vehicle inspection card and the old inflexible inspection plan.

The new card accompanied the car after it left the paint shop. Quality inspectors and rectifiers worked with it in the following manner: the inspectors took the card from the car, read the inspection instructions, and worked through them. They transmitted the defects which turned up at the computer using their portable terminals. After the transmission was confirmed, the inspector stuck the card in the slot of the protocol card printer located at the end of each inspection site which printed out the repair instructions for the rectifiers and the instructions for the subsequent inspectors. The automatic printing of the repair and inspection instructions on the card only took a few seconds, then the card was returned to the car.[2]

Besides ensuring a reliable identification and control of the individual inspector and repair worker, the system of computer-aided inspector guidance brought considerable changes in the job profile of quality inspection. The dynamic inspection plan, with its specific inspection instructions, made the standardized, repetitive full controls unnecessary and increased the variety and task spectrum at the individual inspection work station. Increased qualification requirements for the quality inspectors also arose as the inspectors had to be capable of mastering the more complex data code and be able to mentally go back and forth between the code system and the instructions in plain language. A gradual overcoming of the dequalified Taylorized manpower utilization was also becoming apparent in the area of simple line inspection. A "professionalism" was emerging even more clearly in those areas of quality assurance where the analytical use of the quality control system predominates: the evaluation of warning messages, shift protocols, and consultative feedback.

Such more demanding analytical tasks were primarily a concern of the "large" information feedback loop, which extended beyond the "small" information loop between direct line inspection and immediate actualization of the inspection plan. The quality information provided by the large loop was evaluated according to the cause of the defect and then fed back to the areas beyond assembly: research and development, design, purchasing, component production, stamping, body shop, and the paint shop operations. The differing analytical and evaluative competence of the system users were taken into account in differentiating the types of output for quality information: the first type was the warning message, aiming at immediately showing short term, sporadic defects and pursuing them further for a limited period of time. Warning messages were always set off when the pre-set defect limit for a certain quality item had been exceeded. The situation would then be observed for a predefined number of cars. The second type of information were the so-called defect protocols, which were routinely given out to the supervisory sections in a two to eight hour rhythm. These were, like the first type, automatically issued by the system. Thirdly, the system made it possible for the users to call up certain information in a dialogue communication. Starting out from warning or trend messages, this on-line procedure allowed users to isolate suspected causes of defects more exactly, to call up additional combinations of characteristics and to relate defect development to particular vehicle equipment.

It is obvious that, with the introduction of the new system, quality assurance's competence for control and intervention in the area of information technology grew in comparison to that of the production staff. At the same time, however, the traditional control and intervention authority was changing from a supervisory and disciplinary function to an advisory one. The latter required increased specialized competence and project-like organizational forms which would include quality assurance, product development, and production as equal partners. This was because analyzing defects and eliminating the causes could only be successfully carried out by quality assurance personnel when they had exact knowledge of the overall process, from design to production. This knowledge was not as comprehensive as that of the production and technical departments, but an increasing degree of professionalism was required for the quality personnel to communicate competently with these departments about the causes of quality defects and their elimination. It made sense for this communication process to take place in the form of projects, so that the production supervisors and engineers from the production departments could also make use of the system for quality control. They received their own terminals and printers for communication with the system. As the system provided information on the defects which had slipped through line inspection, and thus on line inspection itself, it allowed for a certain degree of counter control of production over quality control. The quality control system thus opened new fields for control conflicts, but also for new forms of cooperation and communication beyond the departmental borders. In the course of this, conflicts typically did not only take the form of the conflict between departmental goals (e.g., quality versus output), but dealt also with the usefulness of the information system itself.

For example, conflicts came up over the limits in the number of defects before warning messages would be sent. Production criticized that the limits were set too low, warnings therefore came unnecessarily often, and the warning message thus lost its effectiveness. More problematic than this was the fact that the introduction of the system was drawn out over several years due to its technology. Thus severe system breakdowns arose again and again, for instance because a vehicle inspection card would be inserted crookedly into the printer and stick; that vehicles would be brought into production outside of the scheduled production plan and travel as "Ufos"; or that a programming mistake, an improper data input, or an incorrect defect assignment slipped in and set off hopeless confusion in the system. These and similar problems have led to the fact that, although the system was installed on all assembly lines at Heidedorf between 1980 and the time of our study in 1984, the old manual system for quality control still remained in force in parallel to this.

We know from our interviewees that problems of worker acceptance were also behind the implementation problems with the quality system. Such acceptance problems were an expression of control conflicts and unwanted social side effects of the new information and communication technologies. They could become stumbling blocks in the implementation period if they were not specifically taken into consideration in the planning phase. In the concrete case of the computerized quality control, such problems with acceptance were not articulated along the traditional line of conflict between the interests of management and those of the work force. The consultation with the works council was limited to conventional ergonomic questions., e.g., the weight of the new portable terminal.

More fundamental criticism came from production management, however, who cast doubt on the usefulness of the system. This criticism was based on a largely similar constellation as at Company A: both companies had a control system using information technology, which, on the one hand, was under the control of the quality management, but, on the other hand, should also be used by production personnel. This was all supervised by a production management which set out to take over the responsibility for production quality itself with participatory organizational forms. At Company C production management of the assembly areas actually did start an initiative to form so-called "quality feedback units" parallel to the introduction of the computerized quality system. These units served to directly feed back information, to specifically eliminate defects, and to increase the quality responsibility of the assembly workers in a given production section. With this purpose, they were simultaneously in a competitive and complementary relation to the computerized feedback of information.

Quality feedback units were only introduced in the assembly areas, at Heidedorf in 1982 and in 1984 also at Windeck. They were made up of sections in the assembly line with twelve to fifteen work stations. In management organization, this corresponded to the lowest supervisory area ("Vizemeister") with about thirty-five workers. They formed the basis of an organizational system consisting of three levels: two quality feedback units made up a quality feedback section with twenty-five to thirty work stations and two quality feedback sections comprised a quality feedback block. These "blocks" were required to fulfill a particular quality standard and compete with the other blocks in final assembly with regard to this standard. The delivery quality was inspected at the end of the respective blocks and compared with the objective. A central means for fulfilling the objective was a verbal reporting of quality information on the basis of team spirit and improved communication relations. In the course of this, the task of the quality feedback unit was to achieve as high a level of quality as possible in their own line section and, by any means, not to allow a vehicle to leave the section if its defects had not been corrected. The computerized system messages should also be used in this process. But the principle of quality feedback units had also proved itself without the computer. A good many production supervisors even considered the feedback units to be much more effective than the computer system which was always breaking down.

The first pilot attempt with quality feedback units was carried out in a problem area in assembly which exhibited extremely great shortcomings. The performance could be noticeably improved in a very short time. The existence of a parallel line with a largely similar model mix whose work organization was left unchanged ensured an objective comparison. It was emphasized by interviewees that the quality feedback units had not only contributed considerably to improving quality, but also that the cooperation and mutual support of the line workers in the section and the common interest in a perfect product have increased.

The motivation has improved to the extent that the Vizemeister begins to run immediately when one of his workers shouts that his parts are running out, even though this is not formally his job. The Vizemeister thus voluntarily goes beyond his prescribed task area by bridging material bottlenecks and contributing to the motivation of his workers in other ways. (Quality manager, Windeck)

One or two rectifiers worked in each quality feedback unit. Their primary responsibility was to ensure that only flawless vehicles leave the quality control unit. According to our findings, they were moving more and more into the role of informal supervisors and were especially active in the common discussion, analysis and solving of quality problems in the line section. In the course of this, the "Japanese" disciplinary function of the group idea appeared conspicuously:

It also comes to a self-disciplining in the individual units. It happens occasionally that a rectifier even gives the people from his own unit a dressing down. The danger exists to an extent that the system of quality feed-back units could be overextended and that the rectifiers could ruin the whole project if they act too brashly. From the point of view of management, one almost has to fear that it will go too far. But if the rectifiers have the proper tact and feeling, then the production workers are more likely to accept it than when we intervene as management. We could not afford something like that. Then there would be trouble. (Quality manager, Windeck)

This quote makes both the ambivalence and the disciplinary function of the quality feedback units evident. Beyond this, a point with further-reaching implications becomes visible: to simply consider work communication in dialogue form as suitable for people, pro-employee and humane, and communication with information technology as anti-employee and alienating would not do justice to the empirical reality. In order to analyze and understand the complicated interplay between computerized information systems and the communication culture in the factory, it is necessary to simultaneously take the differences and mutual supplementing of both communication forms into account. A theory which understands the new information and communication technologies as a simple expansion of the Taylorist access to labor and, on the other hand, the introduction of team concepts as overcoming alienated working conditions, does not help us further here.

6 Coping with new technology: skilled workers between specialization and flexibilization

The task of dealing with technology in production in Western companies belongs traditionally to the realm of the distinct status group of qualified skilled workers, the craftsmen or *"Facharbeiter."* The deployment pattern of these skilled workers, the skill formation systems, and the interfaces between skilled and non-skilled work are among the most critical and controversial subject areas in company policies for modernizing production.

In the first section of this chapter we will be dealing with the influence of the arrangements and practices of industrial relations which affect the production organization and the deployment of skilled workers. We are concentrating particularly on the arrangements and practices with regard to the question of job demarcations. It was our impression that job demarcations played an important role in structuring work and often brought disadvantages for coping with the problems arising from the new technologies. But we believe that the underlying shortcomings in training and the training systems are often overlooked in the discussion, also by the factory practicians in the U.S.A. and Great Britain.

In the second section we will investigate the new job profiles in the automation areas. Here we will be concentrating on the body shop operations. As we have shown in chapter 3, body shops of the assembly plants were at the center of production automation in the 1980s. Here, manual labor, especially that of semi-skilled spot welders, was displaced on a large scale by robots in all Western mass producing companies. Three factors were characteristic of the technological change-overs: first, they led to a fundamental change in the job requirements which were previously typical of this area – welding qualifications were no longer called for – second, the change-over did not only affect individual work stations, but an entire production area with hundreds of work stations. Finally, the change-over did not take place gradually, but all at once. It was our impression that no company and no factory was sufficiently prepared for reorganization

173

and retraining of the work force which were connected with such a change-over – though there were considerable differences between the companies in this respect.

With the introduction of the highly automated welding systems, the line-paced jobs of the semi-skilled spot welders were being eliminated in the body shop. On the one hand, the new robot welding transfer lines which replaced the old manual welding lines led to a greater need for qualified monitoring and maintenance work due to their complicated technology. On the other hand, they required new jobs at an unskilled qualification level, the so-called "stopgap functions" or "residual jobs" like feeding parts into machines, stacking magazines, doing simple handling jobs. In Germany, this class of jobs is often referred to as a "feeder" ("Einleger"). Thus the automation of the body shop was leading to a polarization of qualification requirements, whereas the body shop was previously dominated by a rather homogeneous work force of spot welders. At the same time, however, it is obvious that there would be less and less need for feeder work due to more sophisticated technical systems in the future. Automatic parts feeding, handling equipment, and inventory systems were increasingly filling up the mechanization gaps, thus eliminating the residual jobs.

It is important to differentiate precisely between the tasks and functional requirements of the new technology and the job profiles and work organization which were geared to it. In view of the functional requirements of the technology two paths were possible, a strategy of job enrichment and a polarization between "residual workers" and "high-tech workers." In the first case there was no specialization for certain tasks and thus no workers were tied to "residual jobs" without a perspective for development. In the second case, the polarization of the qualification requirements would also lead to a polarization of winners and losers with regard to the new technology. The winners would get the better paid and higher valued jobs, the losers would perform the "feeder jobs." This could mean that qualified skilled workers would be admitted to the upgraded production jobs in the plants of the future and the semi-skilled workers, who were previously dominant in the body areas, would have to make do with the non-skilled residual jobs.

The topics to be addressed in this chapter are at the center of the German discussion of the "new production concepts." The question is whether there will be a reprofessionalization and upgrading of production work due to the increase in automation. The main question in the discussion about new production concepts is: do the simple production workers still have a chance or will they be pushed aside as the "rationalization losers" (Kern and Schumann 1984, 1989) in the course of the modernization of car production?

6.1 Demarcation rules and skilled labor in production

In all the companies and countries we investigated the unions had a basically positive attitude toward the modernization and the introduction of technology in the production processes. But this was accompanied by a large degree of uncertainty with regard to the thrusts in the introduction of technology which were actually taking place. From what was largely a defensive stance the unions were trying – with different degrees of success or failure depending on the country and the economic situation – to cushion as much as possible the negative consequences of technological developments for the employees, especially redundancies and downgrading. As to the question of replacing work with technology there was no basic union counter-position. Indeed, the substitution effect was accepted in principle, although the unions tried to attenuate the redundancy and reassignment effects with agreements for wage and employment security. In this respect they were quite successful in West Germany, but the pressure on employees and their representatives was much, much greater in the U.S.A. and Great Britain – if only because of the economic situation. In these countries, the unions were putting up greater resistance to the management's concepts to reorganize the utilization of skilled labor. This applied not only to the question of manning but also to the question of flexibilization or demarcation between different categories of skilled workers. Thus, "manning levels" and "demarcations" were terms that marked the contested zones in Great Britain and the U.S.A.

6.1.1 Formalized demarcation rules in the U.S.A.

To achieve staff cuts management of the American plants were primarily attempting to expand the range of usage for skilled workers and combine different groups of workers. They called this policy the "consolidation" of skilled labor. Reduction of the skilled trades classifications and flexibilization in the deployment of skilled labor were among the primary demands of management as documented in the "shopping lists" put forward to the unions in the course of "concession bargaining" at the beginning of the 1980s. What was striking was that these shopping lists were mostly compiled without regard to the qualification structure of the skilled workers and the existing functional division of labor. The fact that consolidation policies were in many cases confronted by genuine qualification barriers – which could only be cleared away by extensive training – seemed to have disappeared from management's field of view. Its paradigm culminated in a maintenance organization reduced to two trades: electricians and mechanics.

These demands were addressed to the UAW locals. They used demarcation rules to protect against work intensification and staff reduction. These demarcation rules were traditionally highly formalized in the American automobile industry and the result of bargaining between union and management at the plant level. At this time management was aiming at flexible manpower utilization and an erosion of job demarcations, especially regarding "incidental work." This refers to operations which have a peripheral character with respect to the main task and, in principle, belong to another trade. For example, the installation and removal of protective enclosures was usually the responsibility of the plant fitters. If, however, an electrical malfunction had to be repaired and this could only be done with the protective enclosures open, their removal was, from the point of view of the electrician, incidental work which did not fall into his area of responsibility. The same applied if a mechanic could only eliminate mechanical malfunction when the facility's electrical system was first disconnected by the electricians or the pneumatic hoses by the pipefitters.

In many cases where task areas overlapped there were good objective reasons for the management's demand that demarcations be eliminated. Classical demarcation rules played only a marginal role in everyday plant life, though, especially in trouble-shooting cases when, according to the managers we interviewed, incidental work was hardly ever refused. There were, however, also cases of incidental work which for safety reasons could not be performed by just any trade. This was particularly true with regard to the electrical systems. In addition, there were surely numerous tasks in overlapping areas that could only be dealt with by a qualified expert. But such arguments about barriers formed by qualification and industrial safety were overshadowed by a conflict rhetoric which often prevented an objective discussion of the problems at the time of our research in the U.S.A.

Demarcation rules were originally merely job descriptions and functional demarcations introduced by management. The following example of the maintenance of electrodes, i.e., the replacement or resharpening of welding electrodes (tips) shows a division of labor which was functional from management's point of view at the outset and became inefficient after being generalized and codified in labor-policy rules. The functional complex of electrode maintenance can be assigned differently to individual workers or work stations. Three typical patterns can be observed. The first is the creation of a separate category for electrode maintenance at a semi-skilled level, second, the integration of electrode maintenance into the task package of a skilled-worker category like the electricians, or third, the non-skilled spot welders assumption of responsibility for electrode maintenance in the sense of an "enrichment" of direct production labor. Neither of these patterns of organization would be efficient or inefficient per se. Instead they can be very functional or also very dysfunctional, depending on the organizational and technical arrangement.

At River City, there was a special category of maintenance employee for the task area of electrode maintenance, the welding-gun repairmen. They were not only responsible for electrode maintenance but also for the mechanical functioning of the welding gun. This separate classification had proved to be quite functional in a production arrangement of short-cycle, repetitive, spot-welding work. The cycle-bound work of spot welders on the welding line was very labor-intensive, the work load was high, and the cycle-loss times were low. Because the electrodes hardly cooled off between the operation cycles, each lasting about one minute, they wore out very quickly. These conditions existed to a great extent on the conventional circular (carousel) line in the plant for side panels, for instance, where a preventive routine replacement of welding tips was practiced. These tips were replaced every twenty minutes by the welding-gun repairman, who spent about twenty seconds on this job. In this arrangement it was nearly impossible to entrust the direct production worker with the resharpening ("tip dressing") or replacement of electrodes (a task which could have been easily learned and which does not require high dexterity) since there would be no time left over for this task due to the high intensity of their work and the strict time regime of the moving belt. At the same time, this way the welding-gun repairman had enough work to be fully loaded-up with his own particular tasks.

The efficiency advantages did not apply though for work by spot welders at stationary work stations which were off the assembly line. The electrode wear was much less at those work stations. Here the welding electrodes had time to cool off, since the workers themselves had to place the sheet-metal parts in a clamping fixture before carrying out the welding operation. In addition, different welding guns were used at the same work stations so that one or two welding guns were at rest at any point in time. To arrive at a relatively high utilization of their work capacity the welding-gun repairmen were employed in a large working area, and considerable walking time was required to cover it. Due to this and the uneven wear of electrodes in these areas, management at River City had an interest in transferring the work of the welding-gun repairman to the production worker and redistributing and recombining the entire bundle of tasks performed by the welding-gun repairmen. This ran contrary to the established demarcation rules in the plant, however.

Typical of the demarcation rules in the American automobile industry is their local character. Demarcation rules had evolved over time on a case-by-case basis. For this reason there were hardly any patterns of manpower

Table 6.1 *Skilled-labor demarcations in welding-electrode maintenance in the body shop*

Task	River City	Maple City	Greentown
Transformer/ param. adjust.	Electricians (37)	Electricians (36)	Welding equipment maintenance & repair (WEMR) (63)
Electrode changes	Welding-gun repairmen (26)	Welding-tip maintenance (12)	
Electrode sharpening			
Welding-gun mechanism		Millwrights (63)	
Pneumatic and water hoses	Pipefitters (25)	Pipefitters (36)	

utilization that extended to other plants or throughout one company. Thus, for example, River City's parallel plant Maple City had the semi-skilled job of welding-gun maintenance man who, unlike the welding-gun repairman at River City, was not responsible for changing electrodes or for the welding-gun mechanism, but exclusively for the resharpening of the electrodes, the "tip dressing," and was also only paid as a semi-skilled worker in keeping with his lower qualifications. At Maple City, the electrician was responsible for changing electrodes and the millwrights for the welding-gun mechanism. The above overview (table 6.1) shows that three categories of employees were required for the task of welding-gun maintenance at River City and four categories of employees at Maple City.

The overview also shows that instead of the three or four classifications in the two plants of Company A in the U.S.A., there was only one classification at Company B's Greentown plant: the skilled-worker classification of "welding equipment maintenance and repair" (WEMR). This group of skilled workers responsible for all maintenance work on the welding machines was also found at two other assembly plants of Company B outside the core sample of our investigation (Steeltown and Red Plains). The WEMR category did not exist, however, at other Company B plants like Northtown and Indiantown. There, the job structuring with regard to welding guns or, in a broader sense, welding systems was similar to that in the two Company A plants of our core sample.

Although it had surely proved its worth as a consolidation of technical responsibilities which were involved in dealing with welding devices, the

WEMR had by no means led to a reduced number of skilled-worker classifications. Instead, the WEMR became a special classification alongside the existing skilled trades like electricians, pipefitters, millwrights, toolmakers, and others. In comparing the number of skilled-worker classifications with other American automobile plants we studied, Greentown, despite the WEMR classification, did not have fewer skilled worker classifications. Paradoxically, the introduction of the integrated WEMR category had led to an expansion of the classification spectrum in the skilled-worker sector.

The WEMR category certainly represents a consolidation of skilled-worker functions with respect to a certain technology. At the same time, however, it did not prevent the union from continuing its policy of job protection, although in a slightly modified way. In this case, the point of departure was no longer the work content belonging to a certain skilled trade, but rather the specific area of employment and the characteristics of the machinery. Occupational specialization was replaced by machine specialization. This change in perspective became especially obvious in the British car plants.

6.1.2 Informal restrictive practices and craft unions in Great Britain

While demarcations displayed an extraordinarily high degree of formalized regulation in American plants, there were rarely such detailed rules of demarcation in the British car industry. That did not mean that demarcations between trades were less prevalent than in the U.S.A. We would like to illustrate the role of informal demarcations with the example of Company B in the U.K. But, according to our findings, it also applied just as much to the British plants of Company A.

At B U.K., no binding classification system for skilled workers had been negotiated. It is true that in the mid 1970s, in connection with the development of the wage structure, a so-called "job title" book was prepared in which the categories of skilled workers were listed and their job specifications described. But both the trade unions and companies agreed that they did not want to be bound to this document. While in the past the unions in particular had always stressed that they had never signed the "job titles," management was also conspicuously interested in playing down the importance of the job title book at the time of our investigation. This book, which was mentioned a number of times in our interviews, was the only written document over demarcation. The document was only mentioned confidentially, though it was quite paradoxical that it became a "state secret" precisely when its contents had apparently become obsolete.

This is explained by management's fear of being tied down to old job descriptions by the unions. At the time of our investigation, as the deployment of skilled manpower in Company B's factories in the U.K. was being profoundly restructured, management was endeavoring to avoid written plant agreements.

> As of late, management has not signed any more local agreements. This is done to remain flexible. Otherwise, we as management could be nailed down if we wanted to change the written agreement. The same is probably true of the unions. If we wanted to change something for which at some time or another there was a written agreement, a union representative could come and say, "You signed it, it's sacrosanct! No change!" Without a signature we have more flexibility. That is why I cannot remember a local agreement ever being signed in this plant. (Personnel manager, Company B U.K.)

Most work rules also had an informal character at Company A U.K. In contrast to the highly formalized demarcation rules in the U.S. plants, this informality meant that changes in the balance of power between management and the unions directly affected actual practice. This explains the fact that, since management had been gaining back its prerogative to manage since the late 1980s, it became more interested in keeping this system of informality.

But that did not mean that management already had a clear prerogative on the question of work structuring. Although demarcation rules in the skilled-labor sector were not codified, they were nevertheless effective. They were part of the repertory of "customs and practices" which were never clearly outlined. They tied on to the established patterns of the division of labor in the plant. The same observation applies in this respect in both the British and American plants: union demarcation rules were forms of a division of labor originally laid down by management.

The demarcation problem in British plants was more accentuated than in the U.S.A., though, because the skilled workers did not belong to a single industrial union but were organized and represented by different craft unions. The variety of British craft unions formed the structural basis for changing coalitions, whereby management's encroachments against one group of skilled workers were often supported by another skilled-worker group. The central dividing line between the unions ran between the mechanical maintenance occupations organized by the TGWU and the electricians and plumbers organized by the EETPU. We will come back to this in connection with the introduction of new technologies at Seaborough. But the craft unions were not the only reason for the differences from the U.S.A. The British conflicts surrounding the flexibilization of skilled-manpower utilization displayed a wide variety of features that had little to do with occupational demarcations. After all, a job is not only characterized by the skills required, but also by its time regime, its process layout, and its deployment pattern. Skilled workers in the British car industry made use of all these dimensions in a highly flexible way to protect their jobs when it came to a conflict.

The secondary importance of craft demarcations by themselves can be seen from the fact that, in contrast to the practice in American plants, such boundaries were generally not observed in the day-to-day routine work in the plant. One example of this was the routine replacement of welding electrodes. Under formal American demarcation rules it would be necessary to have a plumber or pipefitter remove the water and pneumatic hoses, an electrician disconnect the electrical system, and, finally, a mechanic remove and repair the socket. In practice, a mechanic performed all of these partial operations at Hartmoor in the U.K. Problems would not crop up until management started reducing the manning of one skilled trade. Only then would the mechanic "demonstrate" that he required a plumber, electrician, etc. to change the socket.

This flexibility did not help though when B U.K. made the attempt to transfer the tip-dressing to the production workers. This management demand could not be implemented, although this work had originally belonged to the task area of production workers. In the interest of a more efficient balancing of the spot-welding line and in the course of the introduction of multi-spot-welding equipment, which made direct production workers in these areas redundant anyway, the task of maintaining the electrodes was transferred from production to maintenance where it became a semi-skilled maintenance occupation. The function of the electrode maintenance worker was later upgraded in the interest of both parties and the wages were adjusted to those of the other maintenance trades by entrusting the electrode maintenance workers with the additional tasks of replacing the electrodes and hoses. This led to the craft category of welding fitter.

One last example that points out the differences between U.S. and British skilled-worker deployment concerns "dedicated" maintenance at Blackmoor. There, mixed occupational groups of maintenance personnel were permanently stationed at the large, complex facilities in the body shop. The classical occupational demarcations did not play a role any longer there.

In American car plants, on the other hand, the management would have no trouble in, for instance, changing the number of people stationed at welding machines in a WEMR group at its discretion. On the question of "manning levels" it clearly had the prerogative. For the unions in North America, demarcation rules had only a very indirect protective function against a cutback in employment. It is a different case in British plants where the cardinal question was always the manning levels. In the case of a test of strength, the restrictive practices were highly variable and the opponents were accordingly inventive in discovering new rigidification and flexibilization practices.

6.1.3 Skilled-worker flexibility and its preconditions in Germany

There are no union demarcation rules or equivalent barriers to the flexible utilization of skilled manpower for maintenance tasks in the West German automobile industry. This was supported by the German managers we interviewed as well:

There is no question of demarcations. The crew on the site provides mutual help. In simple things like unscrewing guard screens, etc. we do not have any demarcation problems. There are no waiting times due to senseless demarcation disputes between skilled workers. Real skilled workers, who live their professional description, don't do that. (Maintenance manager, Heidedorf)

Germany's automobile managers are envied by their American and British colleagues for the absence of restrictive regulations, like demarcations. Demarcations between skilled "trades" have no tradition in West German industrial relations. The flexibility and breadth of skilled-manpower utilization are furthered by the training of German skilled workers. We referred above to the fact that, in the U.S.A., in contrast, the union's demarcation rules enter the picture primarily as a problem of industrial relations and less as a problem of qualification barriers. The real barriers in qualification there are hardly discussed since their role in labor policy is completely obscured by the well-known conflict scenarios.

Before the background of a prospering automobile industry there was obviously no functional need for job protection in the eyes of the union in West Germany. The German companies pursue a policy which gives the skilled workers additional employment security in times of crisis. The companies always try to keep their skilled workers, if necessary they try to deploy them at underqualified production jobs while laying off the non-skilled workers. All this produces a bond of loyalty and assures the opportunity for a broad and flexible usage of skilled manpower.

This does not mean that demarcation lines cannot also be found in factory practice there – we can see examples of this in the next section. This is, however, not an important topic for the works councils. How is the utilization of skilled manpower then structured by a management free of union restrictions and how does skilled-manpower utilization in Germany differ from the American and British plants? Surprisingly enough the patterns of the division of labor are quite similar to those in the British and American car plants. There is the usual range of occupations which we have also seen in the two other countries, and it is possible that the classification spectrum is even broader. Normally it is the case that the electrician is responsible for the electrical system, the electronics specialists for computer control units, hydraulics fitters for the hydraulic system, pipefitters for the supply of water and air, etc. Integrated job descriptions at the intersection of electricians' and fitters' qualifications are the exception.

At Company C's German plants particularly the maintenance organization was based on the principle of the separation of skilled-worker responsibility up to the 1980s. These separate lines of responsibility were thoroughly structured, as in the American automobile industry, right down to the individual equipment in production. The millwrights were responsible for protective enclosures, the pipefitters for the supply of energy and fluid materials, the machine fitter for the system mechanics, lubrication and hydraulic systems, the electrical maintenance workers for the electrical and control systems, the toolmakers for fixtures and the pneumatic system. This structure proved to be complicated and clumsy. Even without demarcations the availability of maintenance personnel from the respective trades obviously left much to be desired. The problem was partly solved by assigning the responsibility for certain types of equipment to one of the respective mechanical maintenance groups. Thus hydraulically driven robots went to the machine fitters, robots with servomotors, on the other hand, to the fixture makers. But since the old boundaries of the separate lines of responsibility were still in existence, the maintenance system became even more complicated and the confusion of lines of authority increased. This situation was aggravated even more by the massive introduction of new technologies, so that management had to look for a new solution which we will describe in the next section.

Is the whole idea of consolidating skilled-worker groups a suitable means for inducing skilled labor to become more flexible, and thus achieving a greater efficiency? Our findings give cause to doubt this. Thus there are no demarcation rules of the kind characteristic in the American automobile industry in West Germany. Nevertheless, the statistics on skilled workers at the Windeck plant show a degree of differentiation which, with twenty-four skilled-worker categories, far exceeds that in American plants as table 6.2 shows. Therefore, German management could afford to have an extensive differentiation of special categories without having to fear a rigidity in manpower deployment. On the other hand, we know that the demarcation problem in the British automobile industry was at least as virulent as in the U.S.A. This also applied to the British plant Blackmoor. There, however, we found only seven classifications of skilled workers, although the demarcation problems had by no means been cleared up with this "consolidation." Table 6.2 shows that there is no direct relationship between the

Table 6.2 *Number of skilled-worker classifications in the plant*

Plant	Number
Greentown	14
Northtown	12
River City	12
Maple City	14
Seaborough	22
Windeck	24

number of skilled-worker classifications and the severity of the demarcation problem. In the countries we studied, the U.S. plants generally had the lowest number of skilled-worker classifications.

In looking again at the demarcation rules in the U.S.A. and the flexibility demands of management there, the conflicts appear to a certain extent to be "symbolic policy." If the American automobile management could wheel and deal as it pleased in the case of skilled-manpower utilization, it would realize only a fraction of its flexibility demands, because excessive flexibility can be poison for the utilization of skilled labor. Efficient maintenance can only be realized if the respective skilled workers can familiarize themselves with a reasonable number of different facilities; if they can establish stable cooperative relationships with the production staff; if they can make themselves experts on specific maintenance problems; if they are familiar with the local conditions, etc. All this presupposes specialization in temporal, material, and spatial dimensions, and thus gives the structuring patterns of skilled-manpower utilization a high degree of stability, even under the conditions of extensive management prerogatives.

There is a certain tension between flexibility and specialization for which, in our opinion, industrial relations and restrictive practices cannot be held responsible. This tension can be reduced by increasing the intensity and quality of the training policy. We will return to this point in chapter 9 and show the differences between the countries studied in this respect.

6.2 New job profiles in the automation areas

In the following we have to take into account the fact that the plants we investigated were at very differing levels with regard to the technology leap. In the American plants we studied we found old, time-proven, conventional technology and process layout characterized by a rather low level of mechanization and dominated by manual labor. To a certain extent it was the quiet before the storm of robotization. Only one of the plants which we investigated (Northtown) had already undergone an appreciable modernization of its body shop in 1980/1.

We experienced quite a different state of affairs during our empirical studies in European plants in 1984 and 1985. Here, the introduction of new technologies had already become a dominant topic. How to cope with the use of technology, the starting-up of new facilities and the difficulties of trouble-free production were becoming more and more central topics for management.

At Company C, technological innovation in the production sector has had the highest priority for quite some time. The European branches of Companies A and B differed, as the modernization of A's plants in the U.K. and the Federal Republic began earlier than those of B. In the Weinkirchen and Hartmoor plants, the model change and the corresponding robotization had already taken place three years before our field studies. At Company B, on the other hand, the introduction of technology was going at full speed in the Seaborough and Mittelort plants at the time of our study.

There were also differences between the organizational concepts which the corporations were using when trying to cope with the new technologies. Company A had already created the prerequisites for dealing with the coming technological development with its reorganization of the maintenance function in Europe at the end of the 1970s. In contrast, we found traditional patterns of organization in the U.S.A. that were still completely untouched by the impending waves of automation. The situation at Company C and the European division of Company B were quite different: there the waves of mechanization had obviously evoked pressure to adjust which had led to the questioning of old organizational models but not to the definitive formation of new ones.

6.2.1 The American assembly plants on the eve of the "robotics invasion"

It is by no means an accident that the discussion of job integration concentrated on quality inspection work in the American companies, and that in this respect considerable changes could be achieved, whereas there was almost no movement with respect to enriching direct production with minor maintenance tasks.

This finding can partially be explained by the fact that for the most part the plants we studied in the U.S. were still manufacturing with a conventional process layout. With the exception of Northtown the American plants we investigated were on the verge of a wave of automation, apparently without being fully aware of it. New technology seemed not to be of pressing importance to plant management and their union partners, but an abstract idea which did not demand immediate attention. For management, dealing with skilled labor in this scenario did not mean preparation for the impending waves of technology introduction, but rather shedding personnel and struggling against union demarcation rules. It was a scenario which gave little consideration to future production automation. And, when the problems of technology did intrude, management seemed primarily concerned with achieving "skilled trade consolidation."

The American plants we studied all had small stocks of robots for quite some time – ten to twenty units, most of which were used on the final welding lines in the body shop. But up until the time of our study they had not had large compact installations – with the sole exception of Northtown; but even in this case, the old organizational patterns had managed to remain unchanged, despite professedly major problems with the new technology. In every case, we observed an unbroken continuation of the old demarcation lines with regard to robot technology. The established areas of responsibility were simply transferred to the new robot technology. As a result of this continuation, the demarcations had become more complicated.

Robot maintenance was even more fragmented than the maintenance of the manual welding guns. The areas of responsibility for the maintenance of welding guns on the robots, including the electrodes, hose packages, and transformers, were taken over unchanged. Additional system components were electronic control units, hydraulic drives, etc. Accordingly, at River City the electricians were responsible for electronics and electrical systems, robot programming, and sequence correction as well as for the initial diagnoses of malfunctions; the pipefitters' responsibility encompassed the robots' hydraulic system and the hoses of the welding guns; the machine repairmen were responsible for mechanical components like gears, shafts, etc.; and, finally, there was the semi-skilled maintenance group for welding-electrode repairs with its responsibility for replacing and servicing electrodes and for the welding-gun mechanism. For the installation, assembly, and dismantling of the robots, it was also necessary to enlist the services of millwrights. The "general welders" were necessary for any type of maintenance welding work.

At Northtown, where the skilled workers had received no preparation to deal with the more than fifty spot-welding robots all installed at once, there were particular tensions between the skilled trades due to frequent malfunctions. The greatest friction involving robot technology was between the pipefitters and electricians. But even between the electricians and toolmakers, who were responsible for gears and mechanical components, there

Table 6.3 *Maintenance work according to occupational groups for hydraulically driven ("old") and electrically driven ("new") industrial robots at River City*

Skilled trade	Old robots	New robots
Electricians	60%	85%
Machine repair	20%	5%
Pipefitters	15%	5%
Welding-gun repairmen	5%	5%

had been problems with cooperation and demarcation. As one jig-and-fixture engineer put it:

The toolmakers are not permitted to perform any electrical functions, toolmakers and jig-and-fixture makers are not allowed to turn the machine on or off. Nor may they make any adjustments, e.g., with the help of the "teach gun." An electrician is required for both. Nor may they run the robot back to the zero position to make repairs. During day shifts that does not create any problems, but the problems come in the third shift when there are no electricians. We try to have the preventive maintenance tasks of the toolmakers and electricians carried out parallel to each other on the respective robot installations, but the toolmakers normally need longer for their maintenance work, so that the electricians are already gone again. The toolmakers did take a course on robots at the manufacturer's to obtain the qualifications to handle the teach gun, but they still don't have permission to do so because of the demarcations. (Engineer in the tool and die shop, Northtown)

At Greentown, a new machine for the application of urethane on windshields was equipped with a hydraulic control system instead of an electrical one because the urethane facility was within the pipefitters' scope of responsibility, some of whom had a good knowledge of hydraulics. In this way it was possible for the equipment to remain in the hands of one skilled trade, while in the case of an electronic control system, the electricians would also have had to deal with the system.

Another example where existing demarcation lines "structured" the new work organization was the replacement of the old hydraulically driven robots with a new generation of robots equipped with servo-motors at River City (table 6.3) which were faster and more flexible than the former robot generation. In addition, this new generation also had the advantage for management that hydraulic specialists from the pipefitting shop were no longer required. This task area was being transferred to the electricians. Already responsible for some 60 percent of robot maintenance in the old generation, the electricians were thus becoming the predominant maintenance figures, their share of robot maintenance rising to about 85 percent. The remaining 15 percent was divided in equal parts among three other trades: machine fitters, pipefitters, and welding-gun repairmen.

But the demarcation problem found in robot maintenance was not diminished by the fact that the percentage of maintenance done by the mechanical trades was declining. The electricians had rather to rely on the functionally necessary "incidental work" of the other trades when they want to make repairs.

In fact, the electricians' occupation was viewed as the key skill for coping with the new technologies. This appears to be a universal pattern which we encountered in more or less all of the locations compared. It was always the electricians, preferably those with a certified qualification in electronics, who were responsible for the first diagnosis on the new robot lines and who were stationed close to the equipment in order to intervene quickly in the case of malfunctions. The mechanical maintenance trades, on the other hand, did not take action until later.

At Company B U.S., the hybrid job classification of WEMR seemed to have the ideal prerequisites for comprehensively dealing with robot technology. The WEMR was in many B U.S. plants a recognized skilled trade with an integrated electrical and mechanical training and thus seemed to provide the necessary overlap of skill qualifications. Their deployment area in the past was the servicing and maintenance of welding guns. At this point we will leave open the question of the extent to which they helped to reduce demarcation problems in that area; here the question is whether they could assure the smoothest possible introduction and optimum utilization of the sophisticated robot technology. Even though, for instance, the robotized final welding line at Greentown was supervised and maintained by four WEMR specialists stationed directly at the installation, production management had some doubts about whether this stationing pattern would be the optimal solution.

There were two arguments against the WEMR solution. The first was that the WEMR category was limited to deployment on welding equipment, so that their dual qualification for mechanical and electrical maintenance was confined to the welding technology. Spot-welding robots were interpreted as welding technology in the sense of the WEMR responsibility. Because spot-welding robots were the only type of robot found at Greentown, the WEMRs were the only ones who had been able to gain experience with robot technology. That means that if robots were introduced in other non-welding production areas, i.e., in the paint shop or the assembly areas, there would be no experienced group of specialists to maintain the robots. Instead, in keeping with the traditional demarcation rules, new robots outside the body shop would have to be assigned into several specialized skilled-worker classifications. For this reason the plant's management was looking forward to the introduction of robots in the areas outside the body shop with highly mixed feelings.

The second argument concerned the technical qualifications of the WEMR. Although the robotized final welding line at Greentown had already been in existence for more than ten years at the time of our study, only some twenty of the total of sixty-five WEMR workers were regarded as capable of attending to the robot system by the plant maintenance manager. The others lacked the fundamental qualifications according to management's assessment. On a closer look it could be seen that the dual qualification was largely a fiction, a label which concealed individual electronics specialists and a lot of mechanics who did nothing but repair and maintain welding guns. At the same time, the new technologies required the development of special qualifications at a high level, which the WEMR group could not provide.[1]

These observations made from the example of WEMR can be generalized. In the American automobile industry there was a definite training deficit at the skilled-worker level. This training deficit was still largely latent in most of the American plants we studied, with their low degree of mechanization and conventional manufacturing technologies. It would only fully appear when the new technologies were introduced to a greater extent in the plants. But the signs were alarming enough. Thus, at Northtown, the only American plant we studied which had already undergone its first wave of robotization, only five out of sixty-one electricians in the body shop were considered by management to be truly competent to maintain the complicated Robogate systems.

Although our empirical findings show that management's awareness of the training deficit was not at all pronounced, there were numerous concepts and ideas, however, which indicated that something had to be done to avert a disaster when the high-tech leap was made. Thus at Maple City, management was considering a differentiation of the wage system for skilled workers in order to create an independent category of electronics specialists and thus increase the incentive for further training in the electrical trade. Company B launched massive training programs in the U.S.A. to prepare for the impending start of production in the new high-tech assembly plants. We will be dealing with these programs in more detail in chapter 10. As a whole, however, the efforts were too little and too late. The demands for training and work organization in the new high-tech areas could not be dealt with in this manner. At the Northtown plant, breakdowns occurred time after time even a year after the start up of the new equipment and the process yield in the high-tech areas was hardly 50 percent. In view of the massive difficulties in building up skilled-worker potential capable of dealing with the new technologies in the U.S., the question of the continued existence of or the opportunities for the non-skilled production workers in the technology areas was not the focus of debate at the time of our investigation.

6.2.2 Differences between twins: conflicts over the introduction of technology in a British and a German plant

The British plant Seaborough and the German plant Mittelort of Company B's European organization were twin plants producing the same product, but at quite different volumes. The body shop was modernized in both plants in 1983/4 and the concepts pursued were largely similar.

For Seaborough, this investment helped secure the core functions of assembly operations at the location. At the same time, the stamping plant and the mechanical production areas were closed down. This affected in particular the skilled workers from the mechanical trades, who had comprised the major share of the employees in the machining areas. In this situation, the new production technology in the body shop and final assembly seemed to offer qualified skilled workers a chance to avoid the impending loss of jobs. A minimal chance as it were, for in addition to the long-established maintenance groups from the body shop and assembly there were also skilled workers from closed-down parts production areas on site.

On the question of which skilled-worker group should be entrusted with the care and maintenance of the new robot systems, management chose the path of least resistance. Conflict avoidance with regard to demarcation problems was given first priority. Questions concerning the qualification requirements played a secondary role in management's decision. This explains why the machine fitters and electricians laid off due to the closing of the parts machining departments were not taken into account although they had more experience with computer controlled process technology. Instead, management decided to transfer the responsibility for robot technology to welding-machine maintenance. This decision allowed the modernization train to hurtle headlong into that zone of conflict which it had originally intended to circumvent.

The skilled group of welding-machine maintenance personnel had already been formed in the British plants in the 1960s, apparently following the American example of WEMR. Like WEMR, the group consisted of electricians and fitters. Unlike the WEMR concept, however, it was not an independent skilled trade in the British plants. Worthy of note is also the fact that the welding-machine maintenance staff, though integrated in a uniform specialized group, were organized and represented by different craft unions depending on the trade they learned, namely the electricians by the EEPTU and the fitters by the AUEW. Accordingly, there were constant skirmishes between the two integrated occupational groups. They were finally settled in a written demarcation agreement according to which a job disputed by the two occupation groups could be performed by both. Thus management's goal of creating a maintenance group of overlapping trades was attained. There were two factors which made the consolidation easier. For one, no electrical safety problems stood in the way of integration since the welding technology worked with low voltages of 9 to 12 volts: "In the low-voltage areas nobody cares who takes the cables off." For another, the qualification requirements for maintenance of the conventional manual welding guns were not especially high.

Thus the welding-machine maintenance department appeared to be the most appropriate group to master the leap in modernization without demarcation conflicts. Here management saw a chance to carry traditional organizational structures over into the high-technology phase, and thereby avoid reorganization conflicts. These considerations failed, however, to recognize the limited qualifications of the welding-machine maintenance personnel, who were not yet up to the demands of the new robot technology.

When the new manufacturing equipment was started up in the summer of 1984, it was no longer possible to overlook the training deficit of the welding-machine maintenance men. Just one year earlier, when the under-body line was equipped with spot-welding robots in an early modernization phase, the management realized that it was in for trouble. The maintenance department could not get a grip on the new manufacturing system. Instead of producing forty units per hour it was only possible to achieve ten units per hour for many months. Almost a year after starting, the underbody area had begun to function more or less properly, but by this time the robot systems in the side-panel production, which were even more complicated, were now giving the engineers nightmares: "I sometimes feel as if the planners are sticking knives into me. Our plant manager is under a lot of pressure. How can he justify the machine downtime? I think he would have jumped out of the window already and killed himself if the building had been high enough" (Maintenance manager, Seaborough).

This complaint provides a clear impression of how management was forced to rethink its strategy for the introduction of technology in a painful learning process. In hindsight, it appears to have been a serious mistake to entrust the maintenance of the most complicated machinery to that occupational group who were disparagingly referred to in plant jargon as "roof dancers" because of their poor qualifications. Management therefore decided to station only the most qualified experts from the welding-machine maintenance department on the new robots systems, mainly the electrical tradesmen. The new policy aimed at creating a new group of electronics specialists for the high-tech areas, for which a special wage group above the uniform wage level of the skilled workers was to be created. But the AUEW, which represented the skilled mechanical trades among others, turned down such a differentiation.

The conflict flamed up again over the question of additional training. Management only wanted to include those welding-machine maintenance workers who had the best qualifications in the training courses, while the shop stewards insisted on proceeding according to seniority. In this situation management saw no way to push through its ideas on selection and had to agree to a compromise that could have been avoided had it used more cautious tactics:

We handled the selection process very badly, to tell the truth. If we had suggested a mixture of people to the unions, with the ones we wanted and maybe a few others, we could have gone ahead. But to just take the best people and hand pick them ... I guess we did not have enough sensitivity on these issues. (Personnel manager, Seaborough)

Thus the chain of events closed to form a vicious circle, which contributed significantly to aggravate the difficulties of dealing with the new technology: to avoid demarcation conflicts, a skilled-worker category with a qualification level which was clearly below average was entrusted with the maintenance of the robots. Management tried to make up for this deficit by hand-picking personnel who would take part in additional training programs. But this in turn provoked the union into demanding that seniority criteria be applied when selecting the participants. This necessitated the inclusion of older workers (over forty years of age), who often comprised the less qualified welding-machine maintenance staff. To obtain the candidates for training which it actually wanted, management now had to include much more personnel in the additional training programs than originally planned. That, in turn, led to compromises in the intensity of the training due to the limited training budget. This led to a shortening and, in the end, a deterioration of the advanced-training courses. As a result, the new manufacturing systems were put into operation by a badly prepared team that was overloaded in a wide variety of respects.

A second conflict flared up over the question of who should be in charge of running the system. The task of monitoring highly automated robot lines in the body shop comprises primarily turning the system on and off, overseeing the equipment, making the first diagnosis in the event of malfunctions, and performing minor maintenance work. How these individual functions are bundled or split up at the intersection between production and maintenance is not only a technical/organizational question, but also one of labor policy. As we mentioned already, in addition to the task complex of controlling the system there are the so-called residual functions like feeding and unloading parts. We want to take a closer look at the structuring of work functions and the conflicts going along with this, using the example of side-panel production in the body shop of the Seaborough plant.

Prior to modernization, the side-panels were welded on a carrousel line with seventeen spot welders. With the new technology, provided it was functioning trouble-free, only four parts feeders were needed for loading and unloading the equipment on the side-panel line. These four non-skilled workers were the only production workers directly employed on the equipment. As non-skilled workers, they had no idea of how the side-panel line functioned and, due to their own work and their location at the loading stations, they also hardly had a chance to pick up technical knowledge. When the facility was shut down because of a malfunction they took a break:

They are not expected to help. They just sit down and relax. Maintenance work is so complicated that even maintenance men do not fully understand it. We do not presently know whether the production worker could at some time help do some maintenance. (Maintenance engineer, Seaborough)

The production foreman also did not have any knowledge of the system, even though he traditionally was responsible for starting and stopping the equipment at the beginning and end of shifts and for the shift output. The new system was therefore run by the welding-machine maintenance men, which drastically changed their role. The maintenance experts now assumed direct responsibility for production:

A fundamental change is going on, which has up to now been hardly understood: skilled personnel is becoming responsible for operating equipment. The foremen have not comprehended this, management is only starting to, but the unions have not realized this at all. If maintenance becomes responsible for operating equipment, then a new situation arises. Every competent person can operate equipment, whether he is an electrician or a mechanic. You only need specialist skills if you have to repair complex machinery. An intelligent mechanic might not be able to repair everything, but he can certainly diagnose if something goes wrong. (Maintenance engineer, Seaborough)

The new bundle of tasks which were given to the maintenance organiza-tion in Seaborough, included not only responsibility for maintenance but also starting and stopping the system, checking the control panels, and thus constantly monitoring the production process. For this purpose a mainten-ance team was stationed directly on the side-panel line. They had nothing to do with the feeding of parts. This was reserved for non-skilled production workers who, for their part, had no responsibility with regard to the tasks of system monitoring.

After the old demarcation conflicts between electricians and mechanics in the welding-machine maintenance department had been opened up again by the dispute over additional training, the new task description led directly to a new type of demarcation conflict. Management, dissatisfied with the strategy of technology introduction based on the welding-machine main-tenance staff, wanted to strengthen the role of the electricians and hand over the whole task to the electricians' trade as a basic qualification. The electricians' union, the EEPTU, therefore saw a chance to reserve the new jobs for its members. In 1983, the plant management concluded an agreement with the electricians' union without having let the other unions in on the secret, let alone consulting with them. Only after the electricians boasted of their shop stewards' coup did the AUEW, responsible for fitters and mechanics in the body shop, take action. A representative of the electricians' union reported on the conflict as follows:

The electricians decided to take over the entire job. I am not talking of taking over all the mechanical repairs, but about taking over the production responsibility for the robot lines. At that time the AUEW was sleeping, they were just not paying enough attention. So we got what we wanted. But our electricians made a very big mistake. Instead of keeping quiet about what they got, they went up and challenged the fitters. They were boasting that they will be running the new automation and the fitters would become a second-class trade. And the fitters took action, they fought back. (Union representative, Seaborough)

The welding-machine fitters laid down their work and paralyzed the whole plant by shutting down the body shop. The separate agreement between the management and electricians was revoked. They returned to the old basis of mixed maintenance of the welding machines: "Any job in dispute is done by both grades." Consequently, monitoring the system was organized accord-ing to the principle of "two-trade-responsibility," with an electrician and a fitter stationed as "pairs" at the facility.

We can see from these episodes that in the British case the question of who gets access to the qualified jobs in the automation areas was very much a question to be fought out among the skilled trades. The non-skilled workers obviously did not play a role in this fight. They remained clearly confined to the area of residual jobs.

At the German plant Mittelort the skilled maintenance workers were also assigned the system monitoring function in production. As a consequence, the non-skilled "residual workers" (loading, feeding) were completely excluded from this job, although a team-like organizational model, with the

Table 6.4 *Deployment patterns on the welding
line with fifty industrial robots at Mittelort*

Employee classification	Number
Skilled maintenance workers	16
Spot welders	8
Reliefmen	1
Material handler	1
Quality inspector	1

inclusion of the feeders, had been proposed by the works council. We thus found at Mittelort an expansion of the maintenance department's responsibility to include production tasks and a limitation of production workers to the "old jobs." As an example we can take the manning and division of tasks on one of the robotized body shop lines at Mittelort (table 6.4).

The table confirms the findings for a "German" division of labor only displaying minimal formalized demarcations in the deployment of skilled manpower. The job of the "automated system controllor" (*Anlagenführer*) on the robot lines was given to two crews of skilled workers (*Facharbeiter*) stationed directly at the equipment. As we can see from the table, a few non-skilled jobs remained in the automation area but, in contrast to the previous situation, skilled labor now clearly dominated. This gave German management cause to consider how flexibility of skilled workers could be achieved so that they could take on non-skilled jobs – we did not find a similar emphasis in the British twin plant. The skilled workers were to take over the tasks of quality inspection, material handling, and parts feeding at their facility.

We have made the proposal that production and inspection be taken over by the maintenance department in the course of an experiment. The aim is, naturally, to reduce downtimes. At present it is the case that the production and inspection people do nothing when the system is not running. And when the system is running, then the skilled maintenance workers do nothing. Whether or not such an experiment will take place depends on the demands the works council makes with regard to the manning. The experiment naturally also depends on whether the maintenance people are willing to do productive feeding work. That is, after all, a question of professional pride. It is also this professional pride that prevents the skilled workers from taking over these production jobs. (Maintenance manager, Mittelort)

Here, we can see a reversal of the theme of job integration in the case of structuring work in the automation areas. Integration in this case would not mean job enrichment in the sense of adding more qualified work tasks to direct production work. Now, it would mean adding less qualified work tasks to skilled workers' work. From the point of view of the maintenance worker who has taken over production responsibility, the integration of low qualification tasks would surely be seen as a "deskilling." It is obvious that the practicability of such ideas, their failure or realization, were to be determined mainly in the arena of industrial relations. The technological structure determines nothing in this question.

As an alternative in this case, the works council had suggested the formation of mixed teams encompassing the functions of systems control and feeding work, between which the workers in the group would rotate. This would help achieve an enrichment of production jobs. Because of the complicated system technology, this suggestion would have required a considerable training effort to retrain the former spot welders. Management shied away from these costs. As a result, there arose the much more modest concept of groups, which included only non-skilled workers' jobs, excluding even the more qualified jobs within the non-skilled category.

The feeders form one group. Not included in the group are the repair workers and spot welders. There is probably no other way to do it, for not everyone can weld, not everyone can do the repair work. That presupposes a certain multiplicity of skills that not everyone has and not everyone wants to develop. The group members work at different feeder positions in accordance with the rotation principle. (Works council member, Mittelort)

The agreement which was finally reached stated that group members rotating between different work stations perform a more demanding job, as they have to handle different parts at different places, even though all jobs were feeding jobs. They should therefore receive a higher wage than feeders at stationary work stations. The statement above makes it clear that in hindsight the works council looked skeptically at its own team concept, which would have included a broader qualification spectrum. The works council's concept obviously exerted some pressure on management which led to the compromise of a pay upgrade for the feeders. The rejection of the works council's concept, finally, avoided a conflict feared both by management and the union. Even under German conditions the attempt to merge the skilled trade of automated system controlling and non-skilled feeding work would have mobilized the resistance of the skilled maintenance workers and their union shop stewards ("*Vertrauensleute*"). But many interviewees in the plant feared that such a conflict would have to be fought out in the near future anyway. In this respect the situation is still open at the plant at the end of the 1980s.

6.2.3 New jobs of controlling automated systems: a comparison of Company A's British and German twin plants

In contrast to Company B's European system, Company A's European branch can be described as a system with rather uniform organizational concepts and rationalization strategies. During the process of introducing technology between 1980 and 1985, approaches were developed which had two organizational principles: first the principle of monitoring the system by two trades ("two trade responsibility") and second the principle of assigning permanently stationed automated systems controllers (*Anlagenführer*) to the production departments.

At the two assembly plants Hartmoor and Weinkirchen, the first phase of body shop modernization began in 1980 with the introduction of a new generation of models. These two plants were thus the pioneers on the path to flexible automation in Company A's European organization. The experience gained with robot technology and new manpower-utilization concepts at the model start was developed further in 1982 during the modernization of Blackmoor and the Belgian parallel plant and led in the end to the concept of group leader (called "*Kolonnenführer*" in the German plants of Company A), which was first put into practice with the modernization of the Altstadt plant in 1985. But at first everything stayed pretty much the same after 1980 at the two plants Hartmoor and Weinkirchen. The organization of manpower utilization in the maintenance area was adopted fairly unchanged in order to at least have peace and quiet on the work organizational front in view of the turbulence caused by the technological conversion.

This relative quiet was helped along by two factors. For one, the robotization of the body shop was stretched over a three-year period from 1980 to 1983. The leap in robotization, i.e., the abrupt, compact use of robotized welding systems, with their immense conversion problems, was spread out, so to speak, over a number of small leaps. Thus the maintenance and production workers had an easier time familiarizing themselves with the new technology than at other plants in which the number of robots suddenly grew from zero to one hundred. The engineers and skilled workers were able to gradually "grow" into the robot technology. The policy of a "soft" introduction of technology in British plants turned out to be disadvantageous from the point of view of efficiency, though. Due to the much lower work efficiency compared with parallel German plants and the much higher manning, both in direct and indirect areas, massive employment cutbacks would have been the order of the day for management at British plants. These large-scale lay-offs were postponed at Hartmoor, however, so as not to jeopardize industrial peace during the introduction of the new technology:

We did not link new technology and the redundancy programs. If we had said we are bringing in this new technology and it makes 600 people redundant, the new technology would not have been accepted to the extent it has been. Because of this policy, the technology was not regarded as a threat. (Personnel manager, Hartmoor)

Thus Hartmoor retained its relatively high level of employment for one or two years longer than management had considered necessary and, at the same time, preserved its established organizational structures in the modernized body shop areas. For the robotized body shop lines this meant that four different craft groups were responsible for attending to them: electricians, millwrights, toolmakers, and pipefitters. This divided responsibility must not, of course, be thought of as strict segmentation in the sense of the American demarcation rules. Close cooperation and flexible intermeshing between the four special groups was already practiced in the European division of Company A on the basis of the principle of a mixed trade responsibility for area maintenance. According to this principle, some twelve to seventeen skilled workers from the different trades were under a maintenance foreman and together bore the responsibility for maintenance of the production equipment in their area.

Under normal circumstances everybody does everybody else's work. Demarcations really do not play a role in day-to-day operations. The workers do in fact work very flexibly. You only get resistance if you want to formalize it. Through the flexibility they make their work easier. Therefore, under normal circumstances they would not wait for another trade to come in if they can easily do this work themselves. But if you move into a dispute situation, demarcations come up immediately. (Maintenance manager, Hartmoor)

A more flexible assignment of area maintenance to include quality inspection and direct production work became a tempting rationalization potential. The direct production workers, who were primarily employed as feeders and occasionally as spot welders at residual jobs on the automated welding lines, had not the least to do with monitoring and maintenance work. Although management would be happy to see the direct production workers help the maintenance specialists in the event of malfunctions or during routine servicing, this would be absolutely unrealistic. In the case of break downs caused by malfunctions, the spot welders and feeders were idle and waited until the production equipment was started up again. It was not even possible for management to reassign these workers to other production jobs during the time required for repairs. They could only be reassigned when there was an official "back-up" production line, where the operations continue manually in case the automated equipment breaks down, and when it could be foreseen that the repairs would take a whole shift. But reassignments with subsequent return to the regular job in the case of short shutdowns lasting only a few minutes or an hour were rejected by the union as "excessive mobility."

On the other hand, the traditional work rules for maintenance workers were still valid. According to these, the maintenance group permanently stationed at the production system was idle in the case of trouble-free production and did not take over any tasks to support production, let alone direct production work. What was especially critical from an efficiency point of view was the fact that the relatively large number of permanently stationed maintenance men, who had been indispensable during the starting-up of complex machinery with their numerous malfunctions, had become superfluous after the starting problems had been settled. In this phase it was not necessary for the whole maintenance group to be constantly present at the equipment any longer. Rationalization of skilled-manpower utilization through a more flexible assignment, including preventive maintenance and quality inspection, would be a way out under these circumstances if management did not want to reduce personnel. A maintenance engineer estimated that about one-fourth of the maintenance crew would suffice for controlling the high-tech area, while the other specialists could be used for repair work outside the production lines in the workshops. What happened, however, was that the old pattern of personnel allocation from the introduction phase still remained in force, even three years after starting-up the new robot systems. According to this pattern, the maintenance crew had to spend about three quarters of its time on controlling the equipment and trouble-shooting. The resulting underutilization of the maintenance personnel was a thorn in the eye of management. Nevertheless, as we have already mentioned, management had thus far not made any major changes so as not to mobilize the potential resistance on the part of the maintenance workers: "If I would send a fitter away for other work, we would miraculously find out that we are suddenly in need of a fitter. The maintenance workers would immediately demonstrate to you that the manpower is actually required on the spot" (Maintenance manager, Hartmoor). In fact, the Hartmoor management had relatively little success in introducing more efficient methods of manpower utilization and reducing the number of skilled workers in the years 1982 to 1985. Compared with the groups of direct and indirect production workers, whose numbers were reduced by about one-third in the period in question, the share of skilled workers employed dropped by less than 10 percent (see table 8.9).

This is also clearly expressed in a comparison of the stationing patterns

Table 6.5 *Skilled-worker utilization on the robotized side panel line – a comparison between the British plant Hartmoor and the German plant Weinkirchen*

		Weinkirchen			Hartmoor		
		shift			shift		
		1	2	3	1	2	3
Side panel line	electricians	4	4		5	5	4
	fitters				2	2	2
	toolmakers			4	2	2	2
	pipefitters				1	1	1
Side panel sub-group	electricians	2	2		2	2	2
	fitters				1		
	toolmakers				1	1	1
Central workshop			12				
		Weinkirchen total 28			Hartmoor total 39		

and manning levels of the maintenance staff on the automatic body-shop lines at Hartmoor and Weinkirchen. Table 6.5 shows that in the two identical, robotized manufacturing systems, thirty-nine skilled workers were needed at Hartmoor and twenty-eight at Weinkirchen. This difference was explained partially by the British practices of demarcation which we have described. But it was surely also due to the better qualifications of skilled workers at the plant at Weinkirchen and the stationing pattern practiced in the high-tech area there, which was significantly different from that of the Hartmoor plant.

In the phase of introducing technology, the German parallel plant at Weinkirchen also continued the existing organizational patterns. As the practices of "job control" are largely unknown in German plants, management actually was able to realize its plans for a cutback in maintenance staff. This took place to such an extent that some of the managers we interviewed feared that the staff cutbacks were achieved at the expense of preventive maintenance and that the risk of avoidable technical malfunctions was growing. Although it had been possible to increase the machine up-time ratio to more than 90 percent in the five years since starting-up the new body-shop technologies, the ever smaller number of personnel was leading to the risk of endangering the goal of improving this ratio. The goal of reducing personnel still had absolute priority, however, and the pressure to justify this practice was extraordinarily high: "You have to know: once or twice in the case of technical problems and malfunctions you can argue there's a shortage of staff. But the third time nobody's listening any more. Then you have to see how you get along yourself" (Maintenance manager Weinkirchen).

The maintenance organization had so far been able to cope with this rationalization pressure only because it could rely on a highly qualified core group of skilled workers. Aided by the regional labor market, the Weinkirchen plant also had an extraordinarily high percentage of employees (even by German standards) who had gone through an industry-relevant skilled-worker apprenticeship and were momentarily working in direct production jobs, waiting for a chance to advance to the skilled-labor positions. Moreover, the personnel structure of the skilled work force at Weinkirchen was basically different from that at Hartmoor and Altstadt. While the electricians/electronics mechanics accounted for about 25 percent of the skilled workers in the maintenance department at Altstadt and Hartmoor, the share was 55 percent at the Weinkirchen plant. (We will be dealing more closely with the special skilled-worker job description of "electronics mechanic" in chapter 9.)

Against this exceptional background it is not surprising that the considerations about how to organize work in the automation area were centering on these qualified skilled-worker resources. At Weinkirchen, therefore, the automated systems controllers (*Anlagenführer*) were recruited from among the electricians from the maintenance department who remained members of this department despite their new assignment. There were top-rate workers involved, some of whom were classified in the highest pay group depending on the system complexity and degree of difficulty of the tasks involved. The maintenance electricians responsible for the side-panel line usually had not only a certification in electronics, but had also received additional training in digital technology. They were fully responsible for the technical functioning of the entire equipment and it was their task to make sure that the scheduled output was achieved. They would start up and turn off this system and make sure that it ran according to the preplanned parameters of the production schedule. The task of the "Anlagenführer" also included mechanic's work such as replacing hoses, repairing valves, and maintaining electrodes. In addition, they were responsible for readjusting the transfer mechanism, where an improper setting could often lead to dents in the sensitive sheet-metal parts. In the case of more time-consuming and complicated work, they enlisted the services of additional personnel from the maintenance workshops. This would apply to changing a welding gun, for instance, which was a task for the fitters.

According to management, the willingness of the electricians to take over mechanical maintenance work was extraordinarily high. At times, the superiors even saw themselves forced to put a brake on the electricians' spirit and willingness to learn. The limit was reached, for instance, when an electrician wanted to repair a manual welding unit and, in so doing, caused a fire, or when an area electrician tried out of curiosity to take apart a five-way valve without the help of an expert fitter.

Compared with this wide radius of action for the electricians, the limits on the mechanics' work were much tighter. What is remarkable is that the skilled trades groups in the mechanical trades had allowed themselves to be excluded precisely from these functions which were specific for this new technology and potentially growing in the future. At the beginning, during the starting-up of the new robot systems, the mechanics who had attended the training courses at the robot manufacturer also took over tasks like robot programming. But it seemed more expedient for management to first concentrate programming, program correction, and program back-ups in one place, i.e., with the electricians/electronics mechanics, in order to keep this area under control and assure proper processing. The mechanical maintenance work on the new systems was, no doubt, still extensive, but nevertheless, it is obvious that the flexibilization of manpower had been settled one-sidedly in favor of the electricians (and electronics mechanics) who were able to expand their task area at the expense of the fitters.

This conquest of terrain by the electricians in the automation only stopped at less demanding tasks. Thus the replacement of welding tips in the high-tech area became the task of the night-shift mechanic. Experience had shown that the welding electrodes in the robot lines normally held up for two full shifts so that an electrode change was not required until the night shift. If there was, nevertheless, premature electrode wear in the first two shifts during regular operation, the automated systems controller was the man responsible for maintaining the electrodes.

Due to negative experience, management very soon departed from the practice of having electrodes changed by non-skilled "feeders," as was tried out at the beginning. The direct production workers did more harm than good in this work. When replacing welding tips, they sometimes damaged limit switches and copper pipes. This would surely have been avoidable if the production workers had been trained and familiarized more thoroughly with the equipment. The fact that this was not done could be interpreted as a sign of a management strategy which did not really attempt to couple ordinary production work to modernization. Job enrichment by means of task integration remained accordingly restricted to the manual production areas without opening up substantial opportunities in the high-tech areas for those concerned.

When the Blackmoor and Altstadt plans were modernized in the mid 1980s, Company A's European branch could build on their experience with the concepts described above. The new concepts introduced uniformly in the British and German plants were not more promising for the non-skilled production workers, though. But now, the two principles of work organization in high-tech areas became clearly visible: the principle of two-trade responsibility and the principle of assigning automated systems control to the production department. These two principles shall be investigated in more detail below, beginning with the principle of two-trade responsibility.

Whereas four skilled groups were responsible for direct equipment monitoring at Hartmoor, and at Weinkirchen it was the electricians/ electronics mechanics, the principle of two-trade responsibility applied at Blackmoor and Altstadt, both of which were modernized later. At Blackmoor, whose body shop was thoroughly modernized for the model change in 1982, there were twelve maintenance men in the production section for the side-panel line, half of them electricians and half of them mechanics. The mechanics' group was composed of different skilled trades like millwrights, toolmakers, and pipefitters. From management's point of view, this composition represented progress over the parcelled-out use of skilled mechanics at the Hartmoor plant, an advance that was pushed through against the old rules by means of personnel selection during the introduction of the new technologies. Whoever wanted to be employed as a skilled worker in the high-tech area had to declare that he or she was also willing to perform work outside the customary field of his trade group. This also included minor maintenance work like electrode maintenance, changing of hoses, etc. According to management, one important factor for gaining the skilled workers' willingness was "the pride of being involved in the new technologies." But the new regulation did not apply outside of the high-tech area. Elsewhere, for example, electrode maintenance was still the responsibility of the repairmen.

In the dual concept of skilled-manpower utilization, the electricians also played the most important role at Blackmoor, for it was above all their job profile that had changed drastically in the course of the introduction of new technologies, shifting from the task area of electromechanics, with its fixed wired circuits, to electronics. When asked why system controlling was not transferred exclusively to the electricians, our interviewees in management replied that the change in the job specifications of the electricians was already so profound that it was unrealistic to demand that they also familiarize themselves with the tasks of mechanical maintenance, which had also become more complicated. The best solution was therefore to fuse the electricians and mechanics into a team tied to the system. This guaranteed that the two special groups learned from each other in a cooperative fashion and familiarized themselves more and more with the technical fields of the other respective "faculty."

For us this posed the question of whether the principle of giving system responsibility solely to the electrical trade was at all realistic in the British automobile industry, if only in view of the experience at Hartmoor and, even more, at Seaborough. The argument that a transfer of system responsibility to the electricians would have provoked massive demarcation conflicts cannot be simply shrugged off. Nevertheless, the advantage of specialization at a higher level, as pointed out to us at Blackmoor, is also important. This was underlined by the dual concept of manpower utilization also being implemented at the Altstadt plant in 1985. There, management would have had a free hand to follow the example of the Weinkirchen plant without having to deal with restrictive demarcation rules and rigidity practices.

We see three reasons why the concept of monistic electricians' responsibility could not be generalized in Company A's European division. The first was the increasing qualification required, especially in mechanics, but also in hydraulics and pneumatics, which was leading to a new type of specialization at a high level. There were various possibilities for the ensuing redistribution of responsibilities in the relationship between direct system responsibility and central maintenance. Tying electronics specialists to the equipment, as at the Weinkirchen plant, was only one of many reasonable solutions. It is unrealistic, however, to expect that these workers could master not only the electronic control technology but also the complicated mechanical systems of the large facility.

Second, from the viewpoint of labor policy it is highly risky to uncouple the mechanical trades from the new technologies. It is true that the demand for electricians and electronics specialists is growing more rapidly than that for the mechanical trades, yet the latter will retain their numerical supremacy for some time and thus cannot be neglected. That the protest potential of the mechanical trades is less clearly articulated in the West German automobile industry than in Great Britain does not by any means imply that the electricians' "conquest" could be implemented everywhere as smoothly as at Weinkirchen. This will become very clear in the next section with the example of Company C.

Third, fixation on a certain occupational skill was not in line with the ideas management was now pursuing with regard to the automated systems controllers. They should also play a key role in a more team-oriented organization of production. In this model of a group leader ("*Kolonnenführer*"), complex technical and social competence were to be united in a job description which only partially coincided with that of the electronics specialist.

The new position of group leader was first established with the model start at Altstadt in 1985. At the time of our investigations, there were twenty group leaders at this plant, employed as automated systems controllers on the highly automated body shop lines. Half of the new group leaders were mechanics and half electricians. As they had completed advanced training courses, the mechanics were also able to diagnose malfunctions in the control electronics and eliminate them in some cases. One electrician and one mechanic worked as a pair on each system. The group leaders were responsible for the more sophisticated technical aspects of systems control. Since they were subordinate to the production organization, they also bore direct responsibility for product quality and output. They were also responsible for the supply of material and could give orders to the other workers in the production system, the feeders. They did not do feeding work themselves.

The group leader became the key figure in a new work organization with an integrative function between production and maintenance. Nevertheless, what we were looking at here was quite clearly the integration of work from the top down, and it was more than questionable whether the non-skilled "residual workers" would be given a genuine chance – above and beyond a symbolic participation – to gain access to the new technologies and thereby attain job enrichment and further training. In fact, this was not mentioned at all in the concept of the group leader. An upgrading of simple production work was just not a topic. The disadvantages of the new concept were seen more in the fears of the skilled maintenance workers that they would suffer a status loss as future group leaders in production.

These fears, which were raised particularly by the interviewees at Weinkirchen, were quite real. It was the fear of being employed in an underqualified position and at a lower wage when more and more non-skilled work in the automation area was taken over. Personnel management argued quite unambiguously: an electrician in production should earn less than an electrician in the technical departments as he loses his versatility when tied to the system. At the time of this study there were also concrete plans to introduce the group leader at Blackmoor. Here, too, one could already foresee that the maintenance workers would put up resistance to the feared loss in status, especially since the management's plans aimed at a distinct reduction in the number of skilled workers in connection with the introduction of the group leader. That meant reducing the manning level of the skilled worker departments through the transfer of skilled maintenance workers to the production departments.

6.2.4 The "Anlagenführer" at Company C: a German production concept

The automated systems controller at Company C was established as early as the 1960s when highly modern welding transfer lines were introduced. The early automated systems controller belonged to the production department. This also applies to the new type of automated systems controller created in 1983 at Heidedorf: a reinforcement and expansion of the historically evolved concept of the 1960s which followed from the pressure to reorganize and was triggered by the massive introduction of flexible manufacturing systems.

The faults of the old maintenance organization, with its extreme centralism and inflexible principle of separate lines of skilled-worker responsibility, were making themselves felt increasingly negatively at Heidedorf in the early 1980s, yet the development of a new type of work organization proceeded very laboriously. The process of achieving consensus in management took a great deal of time, and, even after a general outline of the new concept had emerged, no attempt whatsoever was made to quickly push through the new principles at the plant level. Thus for quite some time management still had to work with the old, fragmented organization of trades both during and after the introduction of the new robot systems in the body shop. The traditional trade boundaries were simply applied to the robot technology. The electrical connections leading to the transformer remained in the hands of the supply department; the robot technology was the responsibility of the jig-and-fixture people; in the case of hydraulic robots, on the other hand, the mechanisms were completely within the millwrights' department; the control technology, including the programming of the robots, remained the exclusive field of the electrical trades, the exclusivity went so far that jig-and-fixture makers and millwrights were not even able to return the robots to the starting position for maintenance or repair purposes. Corresponding training programs for the mechanical trades were not planned until later.

For example, a malfunction was detected, and the electrician was called. It naturally took a while for the electrician to get there. The electrician looked at the equipment and said it was not in his scope of responsibility, that it was the millwright's. So the millwright was called, and that also took a while. Now it might happen that the millwright also determined the malfunction is not in his scope of responsibility but in that of the pipefitter. This has reached such dimensions that the company has said we have to get away from it. (Production manager, Heidedorf)

Through the job description of automated systems controller, maintenance was relieved of the pressure to reorganize, and production management was given a tool to cope better with the urgent problems of facilities uptime, without having to wait out the tedious harmonizing process between the production and maintenance management.

The function of the automated systems controller has expanded gradually since the 1960s. At the beginning of this development was the production staff's task of turning the production equipment on and off at the beginning and end of shifts – in the 1960s these were trestles for body welding and multi-spot welding presses. But it did not end with simply switching on and off – which was, after all, already part of the spot welder's work in operating a welding gun. The installations had to be readied for operation before being started, material had to be supplied, safety devices examined, and water, air, gas, and oil checked. The task of starting, stopping, and monitoring the machinery had grown out of its preliminary stage of simple operating work at the latest when the first type-specific and rigidly coupled welding transfer lines moved into the body shop. The coordinated start-up of the integrated complex, opening valves, setting specified welding parameters, and activating the control units were entrusted to the supervisors ("*Vizemeister*"), who were supported by the maintenance staff. With the ever larger number of machines and systems, it could soon no longer be expected that the maintenance workers be involved in production to such an extent. Instead, the Vizemeister brought in certain production workers who had already had experience in dealing with automated process equipment. This was the birth of the automated systems controller, the way in which this position emerged in one form or another in almost all production areas in the course of the automation process.

The decisive difference between our findings at Company C and the other German companies is, however, that the function of automated systems controller emerged earlier here and continued to grow in the course of time. Without a formal codification at first, the *Anlagenführer* gradually took over jobs involving quality inspection and routine servicing, like the resharpening and replacement of electrode tips. They took care of various minor malfunctions, corrected the position of lop-sided or incorrectly placed parts, eliminated snags, and, with the "benevolent permission" of maintenance, familiarized themselves with the functional relationships of their respective systems:

Clever automated systems controllers noticed they could master a few maintenance jobs themselves. They watched the maintenance men, and when their equipment stopped, took out screws, did simple repairs and made their system run again. The skilled workers were happy that they did not have to do work that was an annoyance to them. For the maintenance men it was a relief, for 80 percent of malfunction-related downtimes are accounted for by simple, brief disturbances. (Works council member, Heidedorf)

Thus, the automated systems controller at Company C was able to firmly establish itself and it became a sought-after career position in the years of expansion. For the new position was in principle open to non-skilled workers, who were able to "work their way up step by step to become automated systems controllers." As this job profile came into the spotlight of reorganization with the introduction of flexible robot systems, the furtive shift in competence at the interface of maintenance/production in favor of the production organization could no longer be reversed. On the contrary, there were strong motives to further expand the technical competence of the automated systems controller. The employees had come to take for granted the fact that promising jobs and paths for advancement would also be kept open to direct production workers and production management had long demanded a direct access to skilled maintenance workers. Thus the expanded job specifications of the new automated systems controller were supported by broad consensus and could be quickly enacted and put into force by 1983.

Compared with the automated systems controller of the old type, the new concept entailed first of all the formalization of tasks which were hitherto only informally in the jurisdiction of this job. This included changing welding tips, air and water pipes, and performing supply checks and lubrication jobs of all kinds. Second, new tasks were added, like attending to unmanned transport systems, bringing robots back to the zero position, running them free and restarting them as well as making small corrections to the robot programs. Third, however, the limits of the automated systems controller's work were set: direct interventions in the electrical equipment, the switchboxes, the control and drive systems were forbidden. In contrast to Company A's group leaders Company C's *Anlagenführer* were not given any supervisory tasks regarding personnel, although they were of course "primus inter pares" compared with the "residual workers" on their system. Two aspects in the context of the newly conceived automated systems controller are especially important with regard to our question dealing with the prospects of ordinary production workers and we must now take a closer look at these topics: the problem of feeding work and recruiting problems.

The automated systems controller at Company C is, so to speak, our last test case for the question of whether and how non-skilled production work can be coupled to the modernization strategies. To come to the point: this test also had negative results. Although the 1983 job specifications for the automated systems controller contained the formulation "feeding and removing parts if necessary," neither this passage nor something similar appeared in Windeck's corresponding job specifications from 1985. The line of segregation from the feeders had become more sharply drawn; the position of *Anlagenführer* was on its way to professionalization, which means it received a formalized job description, higher qualification requirements, and systematic training with a prepared curriculum and set criteria for its successful completion.

This "professionalization" was increasingly cutting off the traditional lines of advancement. The automated systems controllers of the old type came from their respective production areas; in many cases they had no vocational training whatsoever. Some of them were already skilled workers fully trained in the relevant crafts, but deployed in machinery production jobs. Their share gradually grew with increased system complexity and expanded training of apprentices, but still accounted for only one-third at the end of the 1970s. With the institutionalization of the new type of automated systems controller, the selection criteria had become drastically tougher. Although the new position was formally open to non-skilled workers as well, the skilled worker's certificate had become the *de facto* precondition for access to more demanding advanced training courses for automated systems controllers. Here advanced training proved to be a reliable deterrent to keep non-skilled production workers from applying for advancement positions.

While management wanted a free posting of automated systems controller positions, the works council still insisted on the channel of advancement being kept open to non-skilled workers as well. In the meantime, a recruiting mechanism had emerged by which those who completed training courses in the company's own training workshops first had to work for two or three years as a production worker on the line in an underqualified position before they could apply for *Anlagenführer* positions. The same principle also applied, by the way, to job openings in maintenance, toolmaking, and pattern making. This circuitous procedure could not change the fact that the non-skilled production workers hardly had a chance to advance to the automated systems controller jobs.

Looked at soberly, this circuitous procedure was an attempt to provide for a more just distribution of automated systems controller positions among the *skilled* workers. With the steady expansion of training capacity, this process served the purpose of defusing the competition for appropriate jobs between the skilled workers in underqualified positions on the line and the young skilled workers graduating from training pushing up from behind. We often heard from our interviewees that as a general rule a worker who successfully finishes his apprenticeship but is not given the chance to use and develop his skills will lose them quickly, and after a few years of work on the line could less and less be considered for work as a *Anlagenführer*. The competition for the small number of such jobs, was therefore concentrated on those skilled workers who had finished their training no more than three years before. Thus, the "older" skilled workers, i.e., those over twenty-five years of age, hardly had a chance, let alone the non-skilled workers.

What was striking was how little the special interests of skilled workers had been brought forward by this group itself in Germany. A shift in responsibility from maintenance to production, as in the case of the *Anlagenführer*, would, if it were feasible at all, be accompanied by massive conflicts in the American and British automobile industry. We saw no conflicts of interest between the different trades in our investigation in Germany, although, of course, the electrical trades were structurally favored. The corresponding potential for conflict was already defused in the system of industrial relations prior to the rationalization measures. Thus management and the works council at Company C agreed on a quota system according to which some of the newly created automated systems controller positions were filled by skilled workers deployed in underqualified positions on the assembly lines, some by electronics specialists from other departments. Through this quota-based recruitment, management also secured that skilled workers were willing to leave the maintenance section and join the production organization.

While the institutionalization of the new automated systems controller proceeded relatively smoothly at Heidedorf, the new concept met with strong reservations from the works council at Windeck. Especially the skilled workers' works council members, tended to assign the entire task of automated systems control to the maintenance department. But this attitude did not stand a chance in view of the dominance which the concepts developed at Heidedorf had in the whole organization of Company C. A second reason was to be found in the ambivalent attitude of the skilled maintenance workers affected who feared a loss of status and dequalification if they went into production as automated systems controllers:

System control is a pseudo area, because it's only half knowledge that is needed there. The automated systems controllers are not taken seriously by the maintenance workers. They are not really considered competent discussion partners by maintenance. That is naturally due to the automated systems controllers' lack of qualifications, even if they are trained skilled workers, because they have no idea of control technology. (Maintenance manager, Windeck)

It is not surprising therefore, that the young automated systems controllers who had received the best training were among the first to apply for vacant positions in the maintenance department and thus to give up their *Anlagenführer* job. The position of *Anlagenführer*, in the 1960s a chance for non-skilled workers to advance, had become stuck with the odium of dequalification and downgrading to the same extent that predominantly skilled workers were recruited.

Although the skilled maintenance workers themselves would not want to work as automated systems controllers in production, they naturally and justifiably feared that an assignment of genuine maintenance tasks to production could take place at the expense of established positions in maintenance. To this extent there was thus a certain interest in not closing access to systems control, keeping a sharp eye on the field of work done by automated systems controllers and, when necessary, rebuffing transgressions. As a skilled workers' works council representative put it: "Due to the repercussions for the skilled-labor areas we also have to have control over the position of automated systems controller" (Works council member, Windeck). As a whole, a quite dismal picture of the opportunities for non-skilled workers to get access to the jobs in the newly created automation areas is also emerging at Company C. This problem was taken up more and more vigorously by the union in the 1980s and had been shifted to the center of the union's "training offensive." Thus, in the case of factory restructuring, the works councils and the union at Company C demanded the same right for skilled and non-skilled workers to take part in the training courses, leading for instance to the position of automated systems controller, so that both could apply for the corresponding positions. As a result, a number of non-skilled workers qualified for the position of automated systems controller in the second half of the 1980s. This improvement in the job opportunities for non-skilled production workers in the automation areas contrasts with a reform of the vocational training system which has created new job descriptions for skilled workers who are to be deployed in production. Many of our interviewees saw these "skilled production workers" as a pool out of which future automated systems controllers could be recruited. The result of training strategies and union demands for the opening of this position to non-skilled workers is that the "competitive advantage" of the skilled workers remains, although the union could avert a formal closing of the more qualified work in automation areas for non-skilled workers.

We thus come to the end of this section.

On the question of winners and losers in the course of rationalization, we did see the non-skilled production workers being uncoupled from work on the automated process equipment in the high-tech area in all of the units we investigated. This tended also to hold true at Company C where this advancement position was formally held open for non-skilled workers. In our observations in the factories we studied we could not find evidence of a general trend toward an upgrading of production work due to the increase in automation as, e.g., Kern and Schumann hypothesized (1984).

Will this picture change with the establishment of team work structures in the high technology areas? Team work was only an idea about the direction of future development in most plants we investigated. We did not find concrete forms in which it had been realized and at the beginning of the 1990s the development in this direction was still proceeding much slower than the "new management" proponents often realized.

With a closing reference to a plant not in our sample we will show that the integration of skilled and non-skilled workers is often hard to realize even in the framework of team work conceptions which are aimed explicitly at such an integration. In a plant of the German automobile company AUDI the body shop was modernized in 1982 and about 140 welding robots were installed. In this context the work was reorganized according to the team principle.

In this modern body shop almost all welding operations had been taken over by an army of robots and some dedicated machinery. The body assembly line had been divided up into three sections (floor pan welding, underbody assembly, and body assembly), which were decoupled by means of buffers. There was one team in each section which was thus clearly technically and spatially separate from the others. The production of parts modules (for instance the side and rear panels, roofs, frame, etc.) was also decoupled and allotted to separate production teams. Each team was responsible for production and, in part, also for maintenance and quality inspection in its section. The interesting new feature of this set-up was the transfer of maintenance and inspection tasks to a production team. Direct and indirect work had been redivided. Of course, there were still separate departments for quality assurance and maintenance/repair, but several more or less routine tasks of these departments had been transferred to production. Incidentally, not only the tasks, but also several dozen workers (inspectors) had moved out of quality into production, i.e., they had become more direct "productive" workers. The more noticeable aspect of the new set-up, however, was the increase in the responsibility of production workers, which had been made possible by an extended training program.

The teams were not homogeneous in terms of qualification and pay levels. Each team consists of one system controller called a *Straßenführer*, one or more robot/equipment-attendants (*Anlagenbediener*), one or more quality inspectors, several feeders, and usually some other personnel if required. In the context of the discussion of new production concepts, the tasks of the feeders (parts loaders) are of special interest. A management representative described them as follows:

The feeders' tasks basically involves keeping the parts supply silos for the automatic welding system filled and placing small parts in the magazines and fixtures. In addition, they have a monitoring function to perform in the section of the plant which they can see, with a view toward identifying malfunctions as soon as possible or initiating preventive action before they occur. Furthermore, they perform minor repair and maintenance tasks in their areas, for example the replacement of electrode-caps and assisting the system controller and the robot/equipment attendant or skilled repair staff if more extensive repairs have to be carried out. (Heizmann 1984, p. 111)

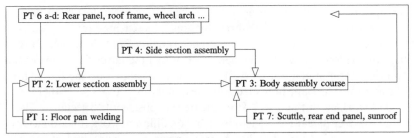

Layout of production teams in a bodyshell assembly shop

- Loading parts from bins and conveyors into magazines and fixtures
- Loading silos of parts-feeding fixture
- Controlling part supply
- Cleaning the installations
- Monitoring the production equipment
- Rectifying malfunctions in parts-feeding fixtures

- Changing robot welding tongs and checking zero/datum points
- Checking for wear, renewing and setting up of welding electrodes
- Maintaining, repairing and renewing water/air hoses of machinery
- Maintaining and renewing secondary wiring incl. insulation
- Monitoring and refilling air supply oilers

Summary of functions in production team

Figure 6.1 Production teams in a body assembly shop
Source: J. Heizmann 1984, p.114.

The system controllers ("*Straßenführer*") and the robot/equipment attendants are obviously the more qualified persons on the team. Long before the new production line started up, about forty skilled workers (*Facharbeiter*) of the old body shop were selected for these functions. They received about twenty-five to thirty weeks training. Apart from their responsibilities for production, it was also their task to teach the feeders and encourage them to assist in maintenance and repair activities. Management's expressed aim was eventually to bring all feeders to the level of robot/equipment attendants. All robot/equipment attendants would then be expected to carry out maintenance work as well as feeding tasks. Moreover, team members were expected to assist in specialized repair and maintenance work, which was currently carried out by the separate maintenance department, in order to make a further transfer of tasks to direct workers possible. Figure 6.1 provides a summary of the functions of one production team.

Management's motive for the new set-up was clear: skilled work is generally needed when there are problems and production comes to a stand-still. Non-skilled work (feeding) takes place when the line is running without problems. If both kinds of work are carried out by the same person, it can be expected that the presence of many qualified workers will increase the uptime of the installations, which is becoming an important consideration where capital intensity of production is increasing rapidly.

There is a steep qualification difference ranging from the skilled jobs to the non-skilled jobs of the "feeders." Although the latter do receive some additional training, it is not possible for them to rotate into the skilled jobs of the team. The same holds true for the quality inspectors and other semi-skilled workers of the team. Thus, the team consists of "specialists" who share the overall team responsibilities but do different work functions. Only in the long run is it expected that, by learning on the job within the team and by further training, job rotation between all team members might become feasible. In the meantime, job rotation on a more limited scope takes place between the jobs of the more skilled workers, on the one hand, and those of the semi- and non-skilled workers, on the other.

As shown in the research which we carried out in 1987 this extensive task rotation could not be realized in practice. It was thwarted from the very beginning by the segmentation between the some forty automated systems controllers and robot attendants with skilled-worker qualifications, on the one hand, and the unqualified quality inspectors and feeders, on the other. This segmentation was aggravated by the fact that this "core team" of forty skilled workers, with many years of experience in the body shop, went through an eighteen-month training program before starting-up the new facilities while the rest of the team only had a gradual process of "on the job" training. Nevertheless, this concept was trend-setting in the sense that the integrated overall responsibility of the team was strengthened to secure a fast elimination of malfunctions and high systems availability, output, and product quality.

The case of AUDI's production teams only confirms our general finding that there is definitely a limit to the new production concepts of a holistic-reprofessionalized manpower utilization and the upgrading of simple production work.

7 Regulating work performance and plant efficiency: changes in control structures of work

In view of the intensified competitive situation and the cost and productivity advantages of the Japanese competition, the goal of rationalization had to be a top priority of all measures which were introduced in the Western companies at the beginning of the 1980s. At this time no company could afford to pursue any fancy ideas for new forms of work if their effects were uncertain from the standpoint of cost efficiency. It appeared rather to be a time for the companies to reassert the proven forms of control. After all, every plant had a staff of industrial engineers in their functions as classical efficiency experts. The most obvious thought was thus to remember this function and these experts and to bring them to bear emphatically.

The following statement in the professional journal "Industrial Engineering" exhorted the companies in this vein:

During tough and competitive times, increased attention is given to productivity improvement and work measurement. Work measurement as one of the basic tools for productivity improvement, quite logically varies in popularity according to need. . . . There will always be sociologists, psychologists and consultants who declare the time study to be unnecessary, un-American and antisocial. Thus "new insights about human nature" come every ten years on whose basis time studies are supposedly unnecessary. (Sellie 1984, p. 82)

According to this author, it was high time to revive the classical functions of the industrial engineers.

Such a demand did not seem to be entirely in keeping with the times, though. After all, the industrial engineers were the actual core troop of F.W. Taylor's system of work regulation. As experts in the "times and motions" of work processes, they had become the guardians of the Fordist–Taylorist system of control over work which developed in the U.S.A. in the 1920s and was introduced in Europe in the 1950s. In any case they represented the old system of control from above and the degradation of direct production workers to employees who were ordered around.

This totally contradicted everything connected with the concepts of new forms of work and motivation. As we saw in chapter 3, some companies saw such NW&M concepts as a strategic focus for their restructuring at the beginning of the 1980s. Under these conditions it could be expected that the representatives of Industrial Engineering (IE) must have seen themselves threatened by the objectives and concepts propagated in this framework. The concepts for participation assigned a new role to the "clients" of IE. They were no longer merely to be organs for carrying out work assignments prescribed by the experts. This seemed to indicate an inherent contradiction between IE (Industrial Engineering) and EI (Employee Involvement). What chances could be ascribed to NW&M under these conditions? After all, the established control structures were supported by powerful institutions and interests. What would induce their agents to surrender control and wither away? Did they realize that the new problems posed by production cannot be coped with in the traditional way?

These questions are the central focus of this chapter. Their main addressee is the staff function of Industrial Engineering (IE). We will be looking into these questions in the following three sections. In the first section we are dealing with the changes in the tasks and procedures of industrial engineers in the areas of work measurement and performance regulation on the shop floor. Here, we will be comparing the companies and countries to look at the differences in the practice of work measurement and the changes which became visible against the background of the comprehensive restructuring. One point in this context is the question of the changed role of the stop watch which, like the assembly line, is one of the most criticized symbols of the Fordist–Taylorist system (see Friedman 1964).

In the second section we will be looking at the reasons behind the change we observed in the responsibility of IE. This initiated a change in the forms of control over work and performance which in our opinion definitely opens up opportunities for NW&M concepts. The reasons for the change in IE tasks were:

1 Increased demands for an improvement in work methods in order to reduce work-related stress and strain and to make work more attractive. Behind this is a change in the composition of the production work force. The share of older and disabled workers was increasing, but also the share of more highly qualified workers.
2 Increased demands for flexibility in production were a second reason. Problems of process control in the production of an ever-increasing range of products on the same line lead to the fact that the traditional instruments of "line balancing" are less and less effective.
3 The tendency toward mechanization and automation removes large

shares of the work force from IE's classical field of action and also requires new approaches for regulating performance.

The third section deals with a new form of performance regulation which is carried out directly through external competition. In fact, it is a carefully organized and staged competition on the basis of systematic factory comparisons and bench marking with "best practices" factories. This is a totally different form of performance regulation when compared to the past. An integral element of this strategy is comprehensive information for all factory personnel as to where their factory stands in relation to the competition. The goal is an internalization of performance goals by the workers themselves. This allows the regulation of performance to be compatible with participative management.

We first want to investigate whether a change in the roles and functions of IE can be seen in practice and what differences exist between the factories in our sample. We will begin with a description of the organization and traditional task areas of IE.

7.1 Industrial engineering – a change in the role of the guardians of Taylorism

7.1.1 Task areas of industrial engineering

In the traditional plant organization, the function of IE was an independent organizational area – just like process engineering, quality control, and maintenance. As a rule it is a department (called, e.g., the Industrial Engineering or Work Measurement Department) which reports directly to the plant manager. In the division of labor in the plant, IE is one of the production-related staff functions whose task is to plan and control the processes of production and to be available for support functions. Whereas the staff groups of quality control and plant technology itself have extended arms into production via the indirect labor functions like quality inspectors, maintenance personnel, IE in Western factories is purely an expert function. In Japanese factories there is seldom a separate IE department. The range of functions of industrial engineering is integrated here with the tasks of production planning and lower-level production supervisors.

In comparison with the other staff units, the industrial engineers form only a small group of around fifteen to twenty people for an assembly plant with around 3,000 employees. In a comparison of the number of IE personnel with that of production workers, their main clientele, there was a relation of one industrial engineer to between 150 and 180 workers in the factories of Companies A and B at the time of our study. In this respect there were only minimal differences between the national locations or the company affiliation. Company C's factories, with around one industrial engineer per 400 workers, exhibited a significantly lower IE density. With regard to jobs in direct production, the domain of an industrial engineer extended from seventy-five up to 200 work stations in the factories studied.[1] To judge from the staffing figures, it can be concluded that Company C attached a much lesser importance to the IE function than the other two companies studied. Here we have a first indication of considerable differences in the systems for performance regulation.

The main task areas of the IE departments in the companies we studied were:

1 Working on the production plans for a new or modified production set-up in the event of technological and organizational change-overs; IE will set the price in terms of time required for each of the job elements planned by the process engineers;
2 performing "work measurement," i.e., checking over and improving on work methods and times in production;
3 balancing the line on the basis of production programs and determining the amount of personnel required to run production;
4 preparing efficiency reports and inter-factory efficiency comparisons;
5 calculating and evaluating the costs and benefits of proposed technical and organizational changes.

In addition to the above list, in many companies the IE function was traditionally linked closely to matters of wages and performance pay. The search for an objective basis for determining the fair or appropriate wage, or, conversely, the appropriate level of performance with regard to the given wage was, in fact, the force behind the birth of the IE-function. The car industry in particular was very anxious to introduce incentive wage systems by differentiating individual wages according to the effort exerted by each individual worker. Only the Ford corporation has always kept a distance from these attempts. Henry Ford I, the founder of the company, was a strict opponent of all piece rate systems. He favored standard wages for employees with the same work. This quota-wage or measured day work system became a firm component of the "corporate culture" ("5 dollars a day") (Meyer III 1981).

The opponents of this system advocated piece rate systems. Tolliday reports that in the 1930s the larger British automobile manufacturers rejected the Fordist system of regulating performance using the machine pace and a standard wage as not applicable in the British circumstances (Tolliday and Zeitlin 1986, p. 39). This was because this system was necessarily tied to the principle of mass production and that the market conditions for this did not exist in Britain. Under British conditions, they argued, the wage system had to take over the task of regulating performance. Earnings would have to be, according to a British manager of this period, "calculated literally on a scale based on the amount of sweat given off by the workers to produce one unit. Nothing else is real" (quoted according to Tolliday and Zeitlin 1986, p. 39).

As long as management were able to retain a tight control over the wage rates, manning levels and job standards the piece rate was an ideal system to drive labour. (...) Once unions became entrenched in the motor industry in the 1960s, they demonstrated how piecework systems could be "captured" by the unions and used to great bargaining advantage. (ibid)

In the U.S. automobile industry, the attempt to use wage incentives as a means for performance regulation was given up in the 1950s. The experience was that the performance standards became increasingly "looser" through this coupling. In order to legitimize wage increases, the performance standards were raised also, but often only on paper. This was especially the case in the U.S.A. in the framework of the war economy. The attempt of some companies to correct this after the war led to hard confrontations in the factories. The collapse of Studebaker-Packard can be traced back to the fact that the attempt to tighten standards was unsuccessful (Hutchinson 1961, pp. 30ff.). Since then, the system of a "fair day's work" or "measured day's work" has established itself firmly in the Big Three factories: the workers who fulfil the daily quota receive the contractual wages. For this they are expected to give a "normal performance." To determine what this means in the concrete case is the task of the industrial engineers.

In the REFA methods manual, the "Bible" of the German industrial engineers, "normal performance" is understood as:

the carrying out of a movement which appears to the observer as especially harmonious, natural and balanced in regard to the single movement, the succession of movements and their coordination. According to experience it can be reproduced at length and in the middle of the shift by each worker who is suitable for the task, has had sufficient practice and has been fully broken-in insofar as he has received the allotted time for personal needs and for recovery, and that nothing is hindering the free development of his competence.[2]

Regulating performance according to the principle of the "normal performance" and the contractually fixed wage was increasingly also accepted in Great Britain and the German automobile industry in the 1960s and 1970s. In Germany the automobile companies, with the exception of the German branch of Company A, continued to use the measured day's work system as an incentive wage by attempting to obtain performance norms above 100 percent of the "normal performance." The concrete norms were established in the framework of contract negotiations with the union. In Company B's Mittelort plant, for example, the negotiated degree of performance was 109 percent. Such incentive rates were also agreed to at Company C. These were continually increased as time passed and had reached 134 percent of the normal performance at the end of the 1970s when the company introduced a new wage system. The previous system obviously contradicted the new orientation of union policy which had shifted from a policy of compensation for stress and strain toward a policy of prevention. Levels of performance as high as 130 percent would, if they really were achieved, contradict this goal. The incentive system with 109 percent was retained at the German branch of Company B into the 1990s.

To sum up, we can determine that the idea of regulating performance through individual- or group-related wage incentives was considered to be outdated in all countries and companies in our study. The idea of a system of wage premiums, even though it was discussed repeatedly, could not catch on in the companies, either. The only exception in our sample is Company B's affiliate in the U.K., where a productivity-related bonus was paid on a plant-level performance basis. There was no differentiation according to the production areas and thus no special incentive could be expected from this bonus. Questions of bonus determination and the temporary fluctuations in the amount of the bonus payment led to so many problems in labor and industrial relations that criticism of this system prevailed at the factory level when we made our investigation.

Even where they still formally exist, the traditional incentive wage systems have lost their function of regulating performance. This was true in any case for piece rate systems which would differentiate according to individual or group performance, as the Fordist process lay-out did not have the flexibility to allow for individual variation in performance. But this was also true for incentive wage systems which were tied on to the measured days work system. The (legitimating) connection of wage increases to performance standards led to their being softened up and was dysfunctional from the standpoint of IE tasks for process control. There was no direct relationship between the IE activity and the function of wage differentiation in any of the factories at the time of our study. The objective of IE was, rather, to establish the necessary manning levels on the machines and assembly lines with regard to the agreed to standard performance and to adjust the production schedules accordingly. Work measurement was still seen as an indispensable means for this by the majority of the companies.

7.1.2 Work measurement in the arena of industrial relations

The method of determining standards for the times and methods of performing work in the traditional Western car factory requires that the staff experts, the industrial engineers, be on the shop floor to carry out time studies. These industrial engineers have to observe and analyze the work process at each work station and study all movements and operations necessary to perform the work; they rearrange the process to find better methods to save time and resources; they then measure the time necessary to carry out each single job element, measuring again and again until the deviances between the measurements can be statistically controlled for. The data thus generated are the starting point for defining the time standards for these job elements and – summed up – for the corresponding job. When added up further, the aggregate amount of production time, and thereby also of direct production personnel required for each section, work area, or plant can be derived from these data. The question of whether these standards of time and method are actually adhered to in everyday practice is another question, and controlling this is the responsibility of the production supervisors.

In the time study situation, the direct job-related interests of the workers as objects of the study and the interests of the company in raising efficiency and reducing costs meet in a most direct and obvious manner. It is a "high noon" situation. Conflicts are almost always present, at least in a latent form, and this necessarily shifts the time study into the arena of industrial relations, transforming it often enough into a battlefield.

Thus it frequently comes to a structure of interaction where, besides the industrial engineer and the worker whose work is to be "studied," a shop steward or works council member and the production supervisor of the area also participate.[3] It is a situation which is often seen as threatening by the worker, a testing situation in which the candidate has to present his or her work, a situation of domination where he or she has to obey the instructions regarding the progression and speed of the work. At the same time, it is a disguised situation for negotiating the amount of performance which the individual is prepared to put in or which can be demanded from him. A lot is at stake for the worker affected: it threatens his or her ability to create time buffers which allow for short breaks, for communication, for structuring the course of work according to individual preferences, and even includes the possibility for the worker to lose his or her job at some point in the future and be unemployed altogether. It is thus no wonder that the activity of the industrial engineer has always been a focus of attention for union policy. The conflict potential and sensitivity gave rise to a multitude of rules and customs to control this form of regulating performance. The systems of industrial relations in the three countries we studied each had developed a "typical" pattern.

In the U.S., the master agreements between the companies and the UAW contained the following regulatory pattern:

the standards should be measured according to the principles of fairness, equality, and normal performance;

a revision of the standards can only take place in cases of grievances or of technical and organizational changes;

grievances relating to production standards go through a formalized grievance procedure – if no agreeable solution can be found in this framework, the still open grievance constitutes a legitimate justification for a strike.

The threat of a strike over "production standards," one of the legitimate reasons for a plant-level strike while the national contract is valid (along with grievances related to work safety and out-contracting work), thus represented a means for the unions and work councils to exert pressure on management and can also give them leverage for other demands. It was in the interest of the unions to always have a number of open grievance cases "up its sleeve." In this way, the function of regulating performance became a "hostage" of the union in all types of plant conflicts.[4]

To give an example: in Company B's Greentown plant in 1978 there were 1,044 new grievances filed over "production standards" on the basis of Article 78 of the national contract. This was 30 percent of the total new grievances. In 1982, in contrast, there were only 220 Article 78 grievances and this amounted to 25 percent of the total grievances. This tendency also continued in the years that followed. The drastic decline reflects the change in labor relations described in chapter 4.

We should point out that this regulatory pattern in the U.S. auto industry, although it was still valid in the factories we studied, had been superseded in other plants by regulating systems which, after the model of the Japanese companies, no longer foresaw a right to strike over production standards and where the responsibility for performance regulation had shifted to the lower-level production supervisors and the production teams. These developments were outside the scope of our investigation, though, and we will not be dealing with them more closely in the following account.

There are formal procedures for regulating grievances in British companies, but more important at the time of our research was still the omnipresent threat of an immediate walk-out. In 1976 fifty (out of a total of 310) strikes at Company A's Hartmoor plant had their origin in "performance standards." But there has been a definite decline in strike frequency. At Hartmoor in 1982 only seventeen out of a total of seventy-three strikes were over performance standards and this decline also expressed a tendency here which – although with considerable fluctuations – anchored itself firmly in the following years.

The main instrument of union control over IE in the traditional U.S. and

British plants is thus the strike threat. In West Germany, a totally different pattern of dealing with the whole question of production standards has developed. The basis for this is, on the one hand, the labor law giving the works council the legal right to codetermination over all aspects of incentive wage systems (§87 Works Constitution Act) which we have already mentioned in chapter 4. Master agreements between the IG Metall and the employers' federations in the metalworking industries were reached on this basis and they contained very concise and detailed rules regarding the process and procedures of setting time standards, be it via stop-watch or using other methods. In addition, further details are regulated in plant agreements between the works council and plant management. An integral part of this regulatory structure is the fact that there is no legal possibility for the union and the work force to use the strike as a weapon with regard to speed-up and work intensification. This is why the unions carefully endeavored to put constraints on the industrial engineers by setting detailed rules and standards for all phases and variants of the process to determine time standards.

The attitude of the West German union toward Industrial Engineering has also received a totally different character through REFA ("Reichsausschuß für Arbeitszeitermittlung," National Committee for Work Measurement). The unions were among the major supporters of the "rationalization movement" in the 1920s (Brady 1974; Jürgens 1980). Its key institution was REFA, which was founded in 1924. The unions also backed this institution after the Second World War:

In order to be sure from the start that, in working out the methods of work measurement, the concerns of the company as well as the legitimate interests of all co-workers are taken into account, the unions and the employers associations were both given seats and votes in all committees of the Association for Work Measurement (Verband für Arbeitsstudien) since its founding after the Second World War. Thus began a new era of work measurement in the Federal Republic.[5]

The development of work measurement methods and the training of industrial engineers are among the principal responsibilities of REFA. To work as an industrial engineer it is necessary to attain the required REFA certifications. Because of the joint backing, the unions take part in the decisions over the objectives and contents of this training and, at the same time, legitimate them. The works councils and the unions also take advantage of REFA's course offerings; in each works council of all West German automobile companies one can find experts with IE knowledge and training (which would enable them to work in the IE department). REFA rests on an understanding that the methods and standards of work measurement can be seen as scientific and neutral. This understanding is also prevalent among union representatives and works council members in dealing with IE matters.

The policy of the IG Metall in the 1970s was aimed at increased control over the forms of regulating performance in the factory; a fundamental direction of thrust was to increase the accuracy of work measurement. An example of this is the "small epsilon," introduced as a measure of exactness in some regional master agreements to determine how many repeated measurements would be necessary in the course of a time study to make it statistically safe. The increased demands on the validity of the measurement data were often difficult to resolve in practice. This had the consequence that works council representatives who wanted to make a point of it could often make the measurement process extremely demanding. (According to our findings, the average number of cycles measured in U.S. and British plants for each job element was actually ten to twenty; in the German plants the average was thirty to forty.) To summarize: the policy of a continual strike threat in the U.S. and British plants corresponds with the policy of raising the professional standards of Industrial Engineering in the West German plants.

What were the IE practices for work measurement in the companies of our study and which tendencies for change were becoming apparent? We want to consider this question by focussing on the most crucial areas of the traditional work measurement practice: (1) methods of determining standards, (2) rating the level of performance, (3) time limits for revising standards, (4) the participation of worker-interest representatives, (5) the question of standards for indirect labor, and (6) the emphasis on job design and ergonomics.

(1) Methods of determining standards

A first finding is that the stop watch, as a measuring instrument of time and motions, is losing its followers – also in management. More and more companies are going over to the methods of predetermined times (MTM, WF, etc.) and their derivatives or to "homemade" standards generated within the company. By using predetermined times IE's job will become more and more a desk job and a planner's job.

At the U.S. plants of Company B, both homemade predetermined standard times and stop watches were used to determine standards. It was expected by the divisional headquarters, however, that IE would be gradually be parting from the stop watch: "We are discouraging the use of the stop watch. We tell our people only to time jobs if corporate standards cannot be applied" (Engineer from the Company B U.S. divisional headquarters). Moreover, it was pointed out that the practice of setting performance standards with reference to individual jobs would lose its relevance anyway to the extent that team concepts will spread and that balancing the workload will be organized within the team. This was the objective. The stop watch was, however, still the only way to check over the standard times in the factory when a grievance was filed over performance requirements.

We have found the same attempt to do away with the stop watch at the corporate headquarters level at Company A U.S. Its use was here also criticized as obsolete with regard to NW&M: "In view of NW&M we will have to get away from stop watch measurement. It is regarded as demeaning to have one person stop watch the activity of another. Therefore Industrial Engineering has to adjust and get its data from other sources" (Industrial engineer from the Company A U.S. divisional headquarters). For this reason, the introduction of a method of predetermined times was also being considered here. The stop watch was, however, still the only method of setting standards in the factories.

Methods with predetermined times were not being used in British plants. They were occasionally seen to be desirable by management, but there was a clear position of the unions (TGWU and AUEW) on the subject: "The company has already made the attempt to introduce work measurement by computer. We did not accept this. We want a full time study which takes into account the specific situation at the work place" (Union representative of the TGWU). The unions wanted Industrial Engineering to set and justify its standards on the spot, exposed to the eyes and arguments of the worker affected and his or her union representative. Our interviewees from Industrial Engineering itself did not see any restrictions on this demand which would prevent them from achieving better times. An industrial engineer in one of Company B's British plants explained this:

The entire process of tightening up time standards took place under the old methods. The power relations and the bargaining structures on the shop floor have changed. We are not working with standard times. They would not tolerate that, and it would be a possible reason to strike. We have tried to avoid this because we have had adequate success with the new time allowances. We do not need to fight a battle only over principles in order to tighten up the time standards.

All of the master agreements in the Federal Republic allowed for the possibility to change the methods of standard setting from time studies and the use of the stop watch to predetermined time standard systems. Although these systems are mistrusted by the unions and were criticized as a system of exploitation (MTM: "Make Thousand More"), the readiness of the union and the works councils to introduce predetermined time systems had also been growing. One reason for this was the criticism of "rating" as an integral element of the old stop watch system. Another reason which spoke in favor of the new system was the hope that it would increase the awareness for improved work methods and work design. Thus a pilot project for the introduction of MTM was carried out in B's Mittelort plant at the time of our study and MTM here was introduced at the beginning of the 1990s. Company C had made the use of MTM or the stop watch a matter of discretion to be decided by IE in agreement with the works council in each individual case. We will come back to this aspect later.

(2) Rating the level of performance

Here is the Achilles heel of the traditional time study. The key to a traditional understanding of the function of IE lies in the capability of the industrial engineer to rate the degree of effort the individual worker spends on the job, evaluating each of his or her motions. Through training his eyes and judgment, the industrial engineer should (this is the legitimation for the rating) be able to internalize this objective measure and to mentally make a note of to what extent the corresponding work effort was below or above the norm – for motions which last only a few seconds. The criterion for the rating is a "normal" performance. REFA itself even admitted that "there is no convincing and quantitative proof of the fact that this phenomenon of normal performance actually exists." But "it has been shown that time study people who have sufficient aptitude for rating can obtain a concrete idea of the normal performance through training and through exercises in critical observation and comparison of human performances" (REFA 1978, Part II, p. 135). The industrial engineer usually has to readjust time and again his (or her – but there were no female industrial engineers in any of the plants we studied) "inner scale" for rating through training films and refresher courses. Nevertheless, the claim of the profession to be able to judge and, in fact, quantify exactly the degree of effort of any operation at any time has always been disputed. The rating factors are generally the most controversial part of a time study and worker interest representatives start there when they cast doubts on the results of work measurement. "An aggressive works council member would always question the results of rating" (Industrial engineer at Mittelort).[6]

Rating the level of performance is an opportunity for the industrial engineer to avoid conflicts on the shop floor: If the person being observed does not turn in the normal effort in the opinion of the industrial engineer, the IE can either have the person asked to work faster – his or her foreman would generally give the instruction – or can, without further commentary, record the fact that the given (partial) operation was carried out at, let us say, 85 percent of normal performance. To correct this would then only be an arithmetic exercise. The standards would then be determined on the basis of a 100 percent normal performance.

In the U.S. plants of both companies studied, rating was still being practiced to the extent that the stop watch was still being used. We heard criticism in many cases from both IE and union representatives, especially pertaining to the claim of the objectivity of rating. But the practice of rating was not seen as a noteworthy problem at the time of our study.

In the case of the British plants, Company A U.K. practiced rating and Company B U.K. did not. We do not know what the historical reasons for this difference were, but with the existing conditions in Great Britain it did not seem to be so significant, anyway. In the words of a Company A industrial engineer: "We cannot exclusively correct slow performance by means of rating the level of performance. The problem is that we have to sell our rating to the shop stewards. And you cannot sell ratings at 80. Therefore you have to move the operator up to 100 as much as possible." Under these circumstances the industrial engineer on the shop floor is expected to be able to put up with a lot of pressure. To obtain standards means a battle on the shop floor, in the arena of industrial relations:

When we come to study the job, we have to push the operator up hill. We have to push and push. In Weinkirchen, when the industrial engineer comes, the operator is already on the hill. Here a personality factor comes into play. Some industrial engineers just push and push and push further. They get the abuse, they get called names, but they are tough people and move on. Others give up earlier and try to compensate for this through rating. But you cannot fully compensate through rating if you have not pushed the operator far enough. We would find it very hard to try to sell the ratings to the shop stewards. (Industrial engineer at Company A's Hartmoor plant)

Obviously, an "industrial relations factor" comes into the measurement here, and the industrial engineers in the British plants we interviewed were very much aware of it. The size of this "industrial relations factor" would, of course, be difficult to quantify, although some industrial engineers even had their rule of thumb and a figure for this.

At the plants of B U.K. rating was rejected altogether with the argument that time study was the moment to demonstrate performance and that the expected level should be achieved there:

We don't want rating. We take the job as it is performed if it is performed well. The advantage is that the operator knows exactly what we expect of him. When we come to a result he knows what he is expected to be working all the time. Now with the system in the German plant there are particular problems. If they take some time measurements and consider a certain operation as being badly performed they would then give the operator a rating of say 70 percent. Now in fact the man has to work faster in practice than what he was doing during the time studies. This could and does easily lead to grievances. We will instead make sure that we get a fair demonstration of performance during a period of time studies. (Industrial engineer at Company B's Carborough plant)

Rating the level of performance was also practiced in two of the three German companies studied. The reference point in B's Mittelort plant was, as previously mentioned, not the "normal" performance but the agreed to performance level of 109 percent.

At Company C, rating had been eliminated already in 1979. The last level of performance which had been agreed on in the course of the wage negotiations was 134 percent. This meant that the industrial engineers had to make sure that in every work station, 34 percent more than the normal effort (according to REFA) should be expended in the course of work. This obviously caused extra problems for rating. The "inner scale" trained by the profession had to be adjusted in every single measurement and, as we heard from old practitioners, rating becomes more problematic the further you get from the 100 percent mark.

Production standards at 134 percent of normal performance would mean that the company would need one-third less direct production workers than their competitors working on the principle of "normal" performance for the same operations or, in other words, the work intensity would have to be one third higher than in these other companies. In actuality, however, the contractually agreed to increase in the level of performance was compensated for to a considerable extent by a softening of the standards. An IE representative at Company C had the following comments over the practice at that time:

The works council member stood there during the measuring and exerted quite a bit of influence with remarks like "Give him 130 this time!". Thus the level of performance gets away from you. (...) That was a pure negotiating system, an oriental bazaar. The level of performance was used as an instrument of wage policy.

As a result, the amount of extra performance was actually closer to 20 percent than to 30 percent according to rough estimates of industrial engineers. The reform of 1979 abolished the system of extra performance. All valid time standards were adopted, but in the case of new measurements – be it on the basis of the stop watch, MTM, or other methods – the "normal" performance should be the criterion from then on. Rating was totally eliminated. This reduced the influence of the stop watch method, naturally at the insistence of the works council. In exchange for this management obtained the right to use MTM.

(3) Temporal limitations for the revision of standards

Here we are dealing with the problem of the "piece rate squeeze" ("Akkordschere"). With an increasing amount of practice and experience at the job it becomes increasingly easier for the workers to "beat" the standards and to obtain time buffers within the allotted time frame. In this way the workers can create their small freedoms: for a cigarette break, a short conversation, a glance at a newspaper, or even a detective story – just the things which make the work bearable for many. Informal cigarette breaks, welt working (i.e., one worker temporarily working on two jobs and thus setting a fellow worker free for a while), etc. are a sign for management, however, that the standards have become too loose. Here, the temptation arises for management to try to transform the advantages of the learning curve into a rationalization effect for the benefit of the company by tightening up standards. In order to control this practice, collective agreements, customs, and practices have arisen which limit the possibility to revise a given time standard by specifying preconditions and defining the time period which must elapse before new time studies are carried out.

In the U.S. companies, on the basis of their traditional model policy with yearly model changes, an arrangement emerged in which changes in the time standards were only allowed within a period of 120 days after the start of a new model year. This period of time begins after a short "settling down period" lasting some weeks. After the 120 days, the times could only be changed by means of grievances or technical and organizational change overs. A union representative explained to us that the time saved in this period of "frozen time frame" was like a worker's bank account of time savings which the company could not touch in the current model year, but which was transferred to the company in the next model year; i.e. the standards would be made stricter.

We found no clear and general limitations to revising standards at Company A U.K. Thus we were told in the body shop of one of its plants that there was a "continuous review" and therefore no limitation exists for carrying out time studies. In the assembly area of the same plant it was stated, in contrast, that a revision of time standards was only allowed in the course of the first six months after the introduction of the model. The respondent referred to a local agreement on this point. The manager of labor relations at this plant did not know of this local agreement and disputed its validity. What ever the case was, this ambiguity was characteristic of the British situation. Management's leeway for revisions appeared even greater at Company B U.K.'s plants, in practice, though, it was dependent on the differing attitudes of the shop stewards.

In the German context, management was more interested in a late beginning of time studies after a model change in order to use the effect of the learning curve. Thus in Company A's Altstadt plant, the measurements to revise time standards were begun approximately half a year after the start of a new model. The time validation took place within the following year if possible, although there was no formal limit. At Company B's Mittelort plant, the regional master agreement determined exactly the beginning, duration, and end of new measurements to revise time standards. These studies were only allowed within a one-year period, the period began three months after the start of a model. In order to carry out as many studies as possible within this time, the plant borrowed industrial engineers from other plants in the company. Checking over the time standards in the case of Company C began six months after the start of a model at the earliest, but the main focus of the measurements was later, after about a year, to allow the learning curve to have taken effect. After this, a new measurement could only be done in cases of grievances, errors in the time study, or in the case of technical and organizational changes. Operations not affected by changes or grievances kept their established time standards, and these standards could indeed reach quite an high age in the German context when we regard the frequency of the model change. Thus, ten year old time standards were not unusual here.

(4) Participation of shop stewards or works council representative

In all three countries and companies, the collective agreements stipulated the right of the workers to ask for a shop steward or works council member to be present during his work study. Effectually, in any case, the unions/work councils claimed their right to take part in any time study they wished to.

In the U.S. factories, at the time of our study, time studies were regarded as business as usual. Shop stewards seldom participated in regularly scheduled time studies and frequently limited themselves to attending only the grievance cases. This was true for all U.S. factories studied. The degree of professional IE-knowledge among the shop stewards of the U.S. plants was small. Only a few stewards have had training in IE methods, a joint training along the lines of the German REFA model did not exist. There was a specialized "time study rep" (= representative) on the shop committee only in the two factories of A U.S. On the part of management, especially in the Maple City plant, it was emphasized that this steward category benefitted Industrial Engineering. For conflicts over standards there were clear jurisdictions here. The "time study rep" in question explained to us that production standards were not much of a topic in his local union. They had someone now who was responsible for standards, and dealing with problems was left up to him.

In the British plants, the IE function was much more strongly at the center of union efforts to obtain control. Very few formalized regulations existed and involvement of shop stewards differed considerably between the companies and even between the production areas of the same plant. In the factories of Company A U.K., the shop steward responsible had to be formally notified about the time study five days in advance. In Company

A's Hartmoor plant, the hourly workers union representative insisted that the shop stewards of both the day and night shift had to be present at the time study. In many production areas, stewards regularly took part in every time study. There were also formal advance notice times in Company B's plants, although these were not held to very often. There was also great variance in the participation of the shop stewards in the time studies here.

In the German companies, the works councils were also formally notified about time studies in advance. As a rule, however, works council members or union stewards would not be present during the time studies themselves. They did not deem it necessary to personally attend and control the time study process. This attitude was also confirmed by management: "The works council never had anything against the way of determining time standards. We have also sent the works council to courses and they know that the determination of time standards will take place on the basis that they have learned. And that is accepted" (Personnel manager at Company A's Weinkirchen plant).

Naturally there were also problems connected with time studies. These were sorted out at the shop floor level. At the company level the works council and IE hardly heard about them. "How they reach agreement out there does not come this high up" (IE Manager, Mittelort). Although there were contractually agreed to grievance procedures, the factories we studied responded unanimously that not one time study reclamation had gone before an authority outside of the factory.[7]

At Company C, time studies had a status which was different than in the other two companies: with their signature, the works councils here approved the results of the study. It then had the status of a "mini factory agreement." This came about on the basis of the wage master agreement of 1979. With this, regulating performance formally had become a matter in which the works council had full codetermination rights.

(5) Production standards for indirect labor

Indirect labor would suggest itself as a growing task area for IE. After all, the percentage of indirect labor in the spectrum of jobs in the factory had been increasing with the increasing mechanization of processes, as can be seen in the figures we will present in chapter 8. With the help of work sampling and predetermined motion time this growing area of indirect labor could also be placed under the regime of time standards which had long been used for direct labor. However, a significant shift in the emphasis of IE work and the allocation of personnel into the indirect area had not come about. In part, the converse was true.

Thus the number of industrial engineers for the indirect area in the assembly plants of Company A in all of the countries studied had already been reduced since the early 1970s. At that time around a quarter of the IE personnel was assigned to indirect labor like quality inspection, maintenance, material transport, and janitorial personnel, but this percentage has been reduced ever since. "Everybody wants the control of direct labor" was the critical remark of an IE interviewee at Hartmoor. It was true for all companies that efforts at setting standards for indirect labor had met with little success in the past. This was especially true for the area of maintenance, and thus skilled labor. According to our findings, the attempts of IE to carry out time studies for these jobs had mostly failed. They usually did not fail because of open resistance, but rather because the skilled workers carried out disguised boycotts and misled the industrial engineer (see also Malsch et al. 1982, p. 198ff.). Anyway, studies were often not considered necessary by management of the maintenance departments: "We have already made time studies for skilled workers with the help of multimoment studies. But that did not actually bring us much. There weren't any conflicts, but the workers involved worked slower in any case. I know how long it takes to do a job anyway and when it takes longer, then we look for the reason" (Maintenance manager from a Company A U.S. stamping plant). The reduced importance that IE had been given for indirect labor at A U.S. in the 1980s could not be explained by the resistance of those affected, however. It was rather a result of the strategy of opposing the growth of the indirect areas and of integrating as many indirect tasks as possible into direct production again.

The attempt at extending IE control to the indirect areas was also a sensitive topic in the industrial relations arena. There were no formal limitations in the U.S. and British contexts for management to undertake this attempt, but in practice it could not be achieved against union resistance, especially in the British plants. Legal and contractual regulations (Works Constitution Act and collective agreements) did provide formal limitations on carrying out time studies on indirect work in the German plants. This held true in any case for those companies which had developed a clear division between those jobs under incentive wages (where the works councils have clear codetermination rights on all aspects of performance regulation) and those jobs under straight time pay. Because they could not control the methods of performance regulation for these straight time workers, unions and works councils had insisted on clear rules ensuring that time studies and standards would not be allowed in these areas without their approval. This restriction was another of the ways in which incentive wage systems backfired. It was motivating management in the German companies to get away from these systems, but, at the same time, caused the union to at least formally insist on incentive wages as they only retain their codetermination on performance regulation here.

On the basis of this, time studies for indirect workers were ruled out in the plants of Company B. The situation was different at Company C. In the framework of the wage reform in 1979, an agreement over IE studies of indirect labor and even white-collar work in some areas was reached. Here, we thus had the most far-reaching authorization for time studies for indirect labor at any company we studied. The authorization of IE studies for indirect and white collar labor contradicts in fact the argument that codetermination rigidifies the established practices and restricts management to the given lines of action.

Carrying out those studies in the indirect area was not without problems in practice, though. IE had to ask the works council to be able to carry out these studies, and such requests were always a "hot potato." The approval took three to four months at the time of our research, and because the studies had to cover entire functional areas, not just individual jobs, they were costly. In addition to this, they were a one-time affair. They only took stock of the actual situation, and it was not possible to monitor over a period of time. Thus studies of indirect labor which had been carried out at Windeck between 1979 and 1985 only concerned the areas of shipping and receiving, for instance, not the large and cost relevant indirect labor areas like quality control and maintenance.

(6) The emphasis on job design and ergonomics

The most conspicuous differences in IE practices in our sample were in the area of methods improvements and ergonomics. The professional understanding of the task of an industrial engineer in a time study is first and foremost to make a thorough analysis of work methods, material supply, the quality of tools, and the work environment to optimize the methods and requirements before the time study begins. Due to the pressure to carry out as many time studies as possible within the period of time allotted to revise standards, in many factories IE did not have enough time left over to also analyze work methods and the work environment from an ergonomic point of view.

At least in the period after the start of a new model, during which the checking and revision of standard times were agreed, questions of job design are secondary. An industrial engineer in the Mittelort plant made the following observation about this phase: "Questions of improving methods do not have priority, questions of the time studies have priority, so that as much as possible can be achieved here."

Although there were also significant differences in the importance allotted to methods improvements and ergonomics among the German companies studied, they had become an important topic in all plants here, not least from the background of the "humanization of work" discussion.

According to the wage master agreement at Company C, for instance, the work methods established by IE have to be "physiologically and socially compatible." The work has to be such that it can be handled without undue stress and strain, taking scientifically established ergonomic findings into account. The criterion of "social compatibility" goes further than the dimension of stress and strain. It implies that the methods have to be accepted by those affected. If this were not the case, then the works council would withhold its approval of the study. With this, the measures of work methods and job design actually fall under codetermination too.

In addition, Company C's wage master agreement prescribed that "special environmental influences" at the work station were to be included in the study. With the help of a checklist of environmental influences to be examined, which was agreed to by both sides, and after the provision of the appropriate "tool box" (Lux- and phono-meters, etc.), such studies had been made in around 15 percent of the work measurements at C's Windeck plant at the time of our research.

The introduction of predetermined times, like MTM, was made easier through the union's interest in job design. This aspect of job design was also emphasized by management. Thus it was determined in a comparison at Company C that the time factors obtained using REFA's stop watch method were approximately 5 percent lower than those using MTM. According to an industrial engineer of the central staff, a 5 percent potential for rationalization was thus relinquished with the introduction of MTM. But he added: "The industrial engineer who would then say, though, I have to measure by the watch instead of using MTM so as to tap the rationalization reserves for the company, did not understand MTM. The element of designing with MTM is important" (IE manager at Company C's headquarters).

This aspect was stressed by all interviewees in plants which considered the introduction of MTM. The term "Methods Time Measurement" already implies that the time needed for a certain work routine is dependent on the methods used, which means that each change in work methods has direct effects on the time factor. Assessing a work method only on the basis of time requirements is regarded as insufficient. Further criteria are needed in order to assess the quality of the work design, thereby inducing and instructing the production planner to improve the work methods. And it was in this improvement of the work methods through work and technology planning that management saw the actual potential for rationalization.

Accordingly, the main aim of the production planners would be to simplify and intensify the motions of work. Simplifying means that each single motion is checked for its necessity and to make it easier to find ways to minimize effort and time. Intensifying means to save time by better coordinating the motions, of the right and left hands for instance, in doing different operations simultaneously and overlapping "without additional effort."

For this purpose, checklists had been developed, e.g., on the basis of MTM, in order to systematically exploit the possibilities of methods improvement. Thus the ANABES system used by Company B planners at Mittelort contained the following criteria to evaluate jobs: "recurring elementary operations consuming a large share of the total time": a high percentage of for instance joining on the total time would be an indication that product design and production planning should put a high priority on avoiding and simplifying joining tasks; "indirect movements": these do not directly further the course of work, but lead rather to a disharmonious flow of motions; "degree of overlap": performing movements, e.g., with the hand–arm system simultaneously and coordinated.

Other indicators measured dimensions of stress and strain: "rate of utilization," "effort required to control movement," "degree of complexity," etc. The control efforts and the degree of complexity are important, for instance, with regard to training measures for the respective jobs.

With regard to the different indicators, conclusions about the "potential for improvement" of a work method can be drawn. It is higher,

the shorter the cycle time,

the greater the proportion of indirect movement,

the less the degree of overlapping in the work movement,

the less the degree to which both hands are fully being used in carrying out the work,

the greater the share of highly controlled movements, and

the more unbalanced the relation is between motoric and senso-motoric basic movements contained in the work method.

At Mittelort, a local agreement was reached between the works council and management requiring IE to study the stress and strain related to each individual job. Thus a proportional recovery allowance was given, e.g., for the duration of one-sided dynamic stress per work cycle, for static holding work, for the required degree of attentiveness, unnatural bodily posture, climatic strain, and so on. Making these measurements on the basis of the analytic system for determining recovery times was described by an industrial engineer in the plant as being very costly. But he continued: "The procedure for determining recovery time here requires a great amount of ergonomic knowledge and sensibility." On the basis of relief time determinations, a collective break of sixteen minutes was agreed to in addition to the traditional thirty minutes break.

According to our observations, the traditional system of the yearly model change in the U.S. leaves very little time for problems of job design at the factory level. Usually, the model year begins on September 1. Many factories already begin with time studies at the end of the adjustment period in October; the 120 day limit extends until February; and the planning for the new model year already begins in March. Corresponding to this, ergonomic aspects of job design have a low priority in the factory. At the factory level, we found no ergonomic checklists or goal perspectives, to reduce overhead work for instance. No special attention was given to questions of ergonomics by the union representatives interviewed either. There were frequent union demands, for example in connection with the bargaining rounds, related to "health and safety" as well as to "amenities" at the work station, but none refer to the state of the art in ergonomics.

Observations in U.S. factories confirmed the low priority given to ergonomic design aspects.

The factories are ergonomically not well designed. At present, no one in the division is really responsible for ergonomics. The production planners only work out the specifications for tools and facilities whose design and construction takes place externally, without the interests of the future users flowing into the production there. Work design is terrible in the plants. In Europe and Japan ergonomics get much more attention. (Company A U.S.)

At the time of our study, A U.S. had just requested its assembly plants to list their "ergonomically poor jobs" in order to find the special demand profiles for such jobs. A special "clinic" for those employed in job design was created in one plant. Medical records were referred to for the first time here to evaluate job related stress and demands. The signs for greater consideration of ergonomic aspects were still negligible at the time of our investigation. A broader discussion of ergonomic questions did not come until the end of the decade in the U.S. automobile companies.

Ergonomics was still an underdeveloped area in the British plants also. As an answer to a question about ergonomic objectives, we received the laconic response from an industrial engineer at Blackmoor: "We do nothing about ergonomics in this plant." At Hartmoor we were told "Some of our ergonomic issues are imperative to modify." At the same time, there were many indications that the British unions and work forces had developed a high sensibility for questions concerning the work environment, ergonomics, and work safety.

Our findings on the practice of work measurement can be summed up in six points:

1 In the majority of the factories studied, little had changed in the conventional IE practice of setting standards at the middle of the 1980s; in view of changed work and industrial relations, the traditional IE

function of determining standards in the area of direct production could now be accomplished more smoothly. This gain in terrain for management was especially noticeable in British plants; the divergence from conventional practices was most minor here.

2 The industrial engineers still were the decisive agents for performance regulation in the plants. Transferring IE functions to lower level supervisors and production groups following the Toyotist model was being considered sporadically, but factory practice was still untouched by such considerations. Likewise, there were few attempts in our factory sample at replacing the traditional standards for the individual work stations with group- or area-wide standards in order to give the supervisors or production groups scope to try their hand at work organization.

3 A change in IE methods was observed, however. There was a clear trend toward using methods of predetermined times and less use of the stop watch. This involved a standardization of work methods, time, and personnel planning on the basis of "company data." The trend was most advanced at Company C and Company B (U.S.); in the British plants it was blocked above all by union resistance.

4 The principle held for all factories compared: that properly determined standards would remain "established" as long as nothing changed in the technological and organizational prerequisites of the jobs involved. The standards were thus also a limitation on management's being able to unilaterally use the benefits of the learning curve to their advantage. There was no process of permanent revision of time standards, as we described in our section on Toyotism. Necessitated by the policy of yearly model changes, standards were checked over and revised more often in the U.S. factories than in the European factories, regardless of which company we looked at.

5 The IE arrangements and practices investigated at Company C were a special case. The "IE density," which was comparatively much lower here, was an indicator of this. One could also deduce from the differences in the IE practice that industrial engineering was not directed toward the objective of improving direct work efficiency to the same extent as in the other companies studied. Instead there was more emphasis given to ergonomics and job design.

6 We did not determine a trend toward an increased IE concern with work measurements in the indirect labor areas. The reasons for this can be seen less in the availability of appropriate methods than in problems with those workers affected – above all with the maintenance workers – and with the worker-interest representations.

The most important trend which we have detected in this section was the change in IE work from a shop floor task in the arena of industrial relations to a planning task closely tied to process planning. The aspects of methods improvement which come more strongly to the fore with this correspond to new demands in production itself. We will be coming back to this shortly.

7.2 New challenges and approaches to performance regulation

In this section we will no longer be concentrating on the work of IE itself, but be proceeding from certain factory problems which asserted themselves emphatically at the beginning of the 1980s. These were problems which were crucial with regard to the questions of controlling efficiency and performance and which could not be handled with the existing instruments of IE. New answers were necessary, the limits of an "engineering" approach became visible. This concerned for one the necessity of improved job design and work methods with regard to changes in the structure of the work force, it concerned the necessity for flexibilization of production and it concerned the changed situation in the automation areas of the modernized plants.

7.2.1 Process planning and work improvement

The trend toward moving away from time study on the shop floor with a stop watch and toward determining standards at a desk with the aid of predetermined standard times cannot be explained by the fact that predetermined times would in general be "tighter" than those determined with a stop watch. As we mentioned previously, the majority of the plant practicians did not see a special potential for rationalization here and actually preferred the stop watch measurements when it came down to tightening up the standards. In the literature the advantage of predetermined times is also not seen in their being tighter than stop watch times, but rather in achieving a greater accuracy regarding "normal performance."[8]

The essential point with the introduction of standard time is not to end the "oriental bazaar" of negotiating performance levels and time allowances which often took place with time measurements on the shop floor. A time study man in the Company C plant Windeck explained what had changed in this respect through MTM:

Much has been objectified. On the other hand, the horse-trading has only shifted. What was previously performance rating is seen today in the fact that some operations were written into certain jobs, although they were actually not contained there, in order to reach agreement with the works council about classification ... In favor of the MTM system, one can say that the planners now have exact times and that the negotiations with the works council have become more qualified. (Industrial Engineer, Windeck)

The traditional course of work planning follows the cascade principle: after the basic decisions over product and production technology are made, the production planning department (plant engineering/process engineering) at the company or divisional level draws up the production plans. They include the work to be carried out for each part, broken down to its individual task elements. In this manner, voluminous books of process sheets are produced for all parts and operations. These production plans are processed in the next step by the central IE department where the task elements are assigned time estimates. For this, standard data are generally relied on. The factory level is only reached with the third cascade. The division of tasks between the production (process) planners and the industrial engineers also exists here on the plant level, i.e., the division between those who plan the production process and those who calculate the time and personnel requirement on this basis. The work of the industrial engineers on the shop floor usually begins as soon as "the technology is settled," and assembly lines, machines, and equipment have been installed. With the start of production, the phase of optimizing work operations and correcting planning errors begins. The revision of preliminary times when reclamations have come up also takes place at this stage. The phase of work measurement only begins in the fourth stage in which the preliminary standard times can be revised and in which the "final times" are determined after another optimization of the work process.

This cascade system had long proved to be lengthy and cost intensive. The priority with regard to time and importance placed on technology planning over work planning had often caused problems in the factories, especially at the model start, and had contributed to the waves of *ex post* changes in the planned process design which were so feared in practice: "At the model start it frequently comes to the situation that the time study people accuse the planners: You have really fouled up there again. Work measurement and control knowledge has to thus be built in at the planning phase, the departments for technology planning and time study must cooperate on projects from the beginning" (Industrial Engineer at the company headquarters of Company C), The companies considered new concepts as to how work planning and technology planning could be integrated and how aspects of work planning could be brought into the phase of product development so that problems of manufacturability could already be considered in the product design phase.

The integration of technology and work planning is embedded in the overall trend toward increasing mechanization and results in an increase in the relative share of production engineers. At B's Greentown plant the twenty-six industrial engineers still formed a clear majority compared to

Table 7.1 *The percentage of disabled workers in U.S., British, and West German assembly plants*

	1978	1979	1980	1981	1982	1983	1984	1985
Northtown	n.a.	n.a.	1.24	1.64	0.88	1.29	0.81	1.61
Hartmoor	3.00	3.00	3.00	3.00	3.00	3.00	3.00	3.00
Weinkirchen	5.09	6.12	6.42	8.06	9.74	10.70	11.59	11.87
Mittelort	8.88	10.72	11.57	13.07	14.36	15.06	14.91	14.35
Windeck	8.62	10.37	12.11	11.53	13.42	13.59	14.88	16.75

Source: Company data.

fourteen process engineers; in Company B's Hartmoor plant the relation in the modernized body plant was already six industrial engineers to nine process engineers; in Company C's Windeck plant, the thirty process engineers were a clear majority now compared to the twenty time study men.[9] The trend is toward merging IE tasks with production planning aimed at an optimization of job design with regard both to efficiency and ergonomics.

Against the background of changes in the production work force, it became clear that an improvement in the work place and the aspect of reducing stress and strain, as well as increasing the attractivity of work also corresponded with the interests of management – this above all in the German plants. Behind this was, on the one hand, the increasing number of workers with health limitations and, on the other hand, the increasing number of skilled workers in production.

The share of workers who were officially certified as disabled as a percentage of the work force was in fact much larger in the German plants than in the British and U.S. plants which we looked at, and has almost doubled when one compared the middle of the 1980s with the end of the 1970s (table 7.1).

The deployment of disabled workers has numerous restrictions. Thus the restrictions "no heavy lifting" and "no frequent bending" held for 60 percent of the disabled workers in Company C's Windeck plant; for around 15 percent the restriction of "no assembly line work" existed. Due to the greater protection for disabled workers against loss of job and wages, creating jobs whose profile of demands make efficient employment of disabled workers possible, became especially important. The introduction of predetermined time methods is seen as a starting point for dealing with the problem. Thus an industrial engineer of the central staff at Company C:

These are now being created increasingly in the automated areas because of the decoupling of worker and machine here. This is also true for the (new assembly building) as well as for parts of the body shop and stamping plant. The work stations there are totally designed with MTM and are thus quasi automatically work stations suitable for disabled workers.

The interest in improved job design in the West German plants was not only motivated by the increase in disabled workers, but also, and perhaps even more, by the increase in skilled workers deployed as direct production workers. Thus the personnel manager at the Weinkirchen plant emphasized: "Ergonomic problems have achieved a great deal of attention. This is also because of the problems which the skilled workers now being deployed in production have with the working conditions there. A further training in ergonomics is now being offered and such skilled workers also participated in it." A high and growing share of skilled workers (*Facharbeiter*) deployed as direct production workers is, as we have seen in chapter 4, a phenomena which can be observed in all German plants since the end of the 1970s.

The attempt at creating ergonomically better defined jobs strengthened the expert character and the degree of professionalization of Industrial Engineering in the German plants. This expert orientation was especially characteristic at Company C. Although the shift of responsibility in favor of planning was also unmistakable in the U.S. context, there was clearly a different nexus between performance goals and the goal of better job design. The endeavors in the U.S.A. moved toward involving the workers in planning and designing their own work themselves. Examples of involvement of employee groups in the decisions on work lay-out of their area could be found in most of the U.S. plants of both companies at the time of our research.

Section A of trim assembly in Company A's Motor City plant was the site of such a participation program at the time of our study. It covered one of seven production lines within the trim assembly area. In weekly meetings, the employees discussed improvements of their work area. On their initiative, changes in the sequence of work operations were made, an equal sharing of the workload was ensured, and improvements in tools were brought about. Industrial Engineering determined the basic targets, the list of operations to be carried out, and the time allocated for the whole area. The rest was left up to the group.

The main reason for the experiment was that section A had previously had very poor quality results. One of the group's actions was to introduce a system for the workers to inspect their own work. The experiment resulted in a decline in defects and absenteeism. According to the management, the group now had considerable pride in its work. We also observed that the employees even saw to work discipline among their co-workers. The experiment was also positively evaluated by the union representative interviewed: "The labor relations in section A are now better than everywhere else: The labor relations here have fundamentally improved. The attitude toward work was previously totally different. Some of the other workers had made jokes about things being so messed up here" (Union representative, Company A's Motor City plant).

Examples of this kind could also be reported for other Company A plants in the U.S.A. The local union's assessment was not always positive. A union spokesman from a plant where the union local rejected such projects thus explained: "If management would do line balancing together with the workers involved, then the industrial engineering people would be really happy. Who knows the work better than the people on the line? And the industrial engineers would take advantage of it. They would cash in the increase in efficiency and we would have had 'employee involvement'" (Union representative, Maple City).

Summed up, one could observe clearly different orientations as to the main agents of job design here: on the one hand, toward the specialized planners, on the other hand, toward the workers as concerned persons and "experts" for their work areas. According to our findings, the former was a typical German orientation; the U.S. companies emphasized worker participation instead. In the British factories, the conventional IE role still predominated.

7.2.2 Problems with the increased production flexibility

Despite their great efforts at generating and adjusting standards on the micro-level in the work process, the IE practicians we talked to in the factories saw the main problem at that time to be elsewhere: the problem was not so much in setting the standards for single job elements, but in adding them together to form task descriptions which fit into the cycle time of production, while achieving full utilization of the work force at the same time. Instead of the classical problem with regulating performance, namely the workers "withholding performance," the increasing complexity of production leads to problems of process control. The new problems which come with this very much explain the changes in Industrial Engineering.

The basic problem is not new. After the standards (and thus the time required) have been established for all of the job elements in a work section, these job elements must then be allocated to the individual work stations in such a manner that each worker's labor power is continually utilized to the fullest extent. This goal is often difficult to achieve, especially for the jobs on the assembly line. The summation of all task elements for each job has to exactly fit into the time frame of the production cycle if "over-cycle work," on the one hand, and "cycle loss," on the other, are to be avoided. The former would result in problems in labor relations, the latter in problems in efficiency.

The construction of individual jobs from a multitude of task elements is obviously subject to limitations which arise from essential sequences of operations in the course of the production flow. The carpeting on the floor cannot be laid until the electrical fittings under it have been installed, to give a simple example. This example also shows that process planning and regulating performance are clearly two sides of the same coin. On the traditional assembly line many task elements could be allocated rather freely among the various jobs in the section. Which welds would be made where or which parts would be screwed on at which work place, where certain trim pieces would be installed or where specific gaskets would be fitted, these were decisions to be made pragmatically, and could thus be addressed under the viewpoint of balancing the work load of the various work stations along the line.

To redistribute task elements belongs to the daily routine of the lower level production supervisors anyway, i.e., mostly to the foremen ("*Meister*" or "*Vizemeister*" in Germany), who have to react to miscellaneous changes in the personnel attendance or in the flow of production (see Jürgens and Strömel 1987). The employees themselves also make use of this freedom in order to work ahead against the direction of the line flow ("floating") and thus to create the opportunity for small breaks or to do the work of two in a kind of informal work sharing among co-workers to create even more leeway for free time ("welt working"). The task allocation soon differed in practice in one way or the other from plans which had been carefully worked out by IE. Industrial engineering's setting of performance standards has never automatically meant the control over worker deployment and work organization. The lower level production supervisors are responsible here. But the manning levels required for production are derived from the IE data. If production actually needs more personnel than planned it is "off-standards." On the other hand, the time during which personnel is present but cannot be assigned a full work load is counted as a "necessary loss time" which has to be authorized by IE. This situation arises when the construction of individual jobs from various multisecond operations at each work place does not go smoothly into the cycle time. This means loss time which is planned for, "required idle time" or "unavoidable delay" as it is also called in IE practice. Aside from the waiting and walking times and the "unproductive" movements which are considered to be unavoidable by process or product design, these times are a missed efficiency potential and lead to an underutilization of labor power, which comes, so to speak, at the expense of IE. An indicator for this would be the cycle loss time which remains after all efforts were made to balance a line.

Industrial engineering's successes in efficiency since the beginning of the 1980s can be chiefly traced back to the reduction of cycle losses. We will present our data in this respect in chapter 8. The greatest leaps were made in the British plants, where cycle losses were 40 percent at the end of the 1970s and were reduced to 10 percent and less (Hartmoor) in the mid 1980s. In its German sister plant Weinkirchen the average work load on the assembly lines was already around 85 percent in 1978, in 1983 it had been brought up to 93 percent, though. In Company B's Northtown plant, work load in direct production was estimated at between 70 and 80 percent at the time of our research.

A much higher rate of utilization than 80 percent was seen to be hardly realizable by most industrial engineers we interviewed in the U.S.A. With regard to higher results reported from other plants, we were warned by an experienced industrial engineer at Greentown: "If they tell you they work fifty-five out of sixty minutes, they are lying to you. The most you can get is forty-eight to forty-nine minutes out of the hour." "Of course we are shooting at the 100 percent," reported an industrial engineer at Steeltown, "but with 90 percent efficiency, I would be tickled to death."

We actually reach difficult ground with such figures. The size of the cycle loss time is a critical issue in the performance report and is also an indicator for evaluating the performance of IE itself. There are many different possibilities for reducing the cycle losses times which local IE regards as embarrassing by changing the method of calculation without actually changing anything substantial. Additional tasks such as visual checks can be added to the jobs that are not fully loaded-up in order to raise them some additional hundredths of a minute, even if these tasks are not really necessary. In some plants we saw activities like quality inspection, repair work, and other "free effort" activities on the line being calculated with a flat 100 percent efficiency although a time study had never been made on them. This naturally helped to reduce the cycle losses and to improve the reported efficiency. The use of such tricks to present oneself well in the efficiency reports explains the skepticism which old hands often express about the exact figures in these reports.

Cycle loss times are a continued problem, despite the ground IE has gained here. One cause for this stems from the demands for increased flexibility in production. The Fordist paradigm for regulating performance in mass production called for optimizing the work flow, work methods, and time standards as soon as possible after model change-overs and to keep this optimized "structure" unchanged if possible until the next change-over. The collective bargaining agreements were also aligned to this paradigm. The model mix, the succession of vehicles with differing work requirements on the line, has always been a trouble-maker – especially in the areas of trim and final assembly. Thus already in 1949, Company A U.S. agreed in its contract with the UAW:

To meet its daily production schedules, the Company maintains each line at a constant speed. The Company will space units to provide a uniform flow of work for individual employees. It is recognized that this uniform flow of work contemplates the expected normal ratio of body type from which the work standards are computed and the regular work assignments are made.[10]

Similar arrangements could also be found at Company B. They had not been able to effectively stem the problems, though, which arise from the production schedule and process control. At the time of our study, model mix problems were considered to be one of the main burdens for the factories – with regard to industrial relations and in view of efficiency. According to our interviews the preplanned succession of car types, variants, and options (the model mix) could not be held to in almost all of the factories studied. "You can't control mix" was the resignative conclusion of an industrial engineer at the Motor City plant.

Differences in product diversity were an important influence on plant efficiency. The corresponding extra allowance of time and personnel at Company A U.S. was consequently called "mix penalty." From an option complexity study prepared in one of its plants it could be determined here that the average workload of the operations "without mix" was 55.9 minutes per hour; as opposed to this, the jobs with mix had an average utilization rate of 48.7 minutes, a difference of 12 percent.

Although the Assembly Division of Company A U.S. authorized a "mix penalty" as an unavoidable efficiency loss, the factories frequently did not believe that it completely compensated the off-standards necessitated by the mix. In the words of an industrial engineer at the divisional level: "They all complain." An example could be found in a discussion which was in process at the time of our study. It took place between a factory and its divisional headquarters over the raising of the mix penalty due to the introduction of a second car model at this factory. The change had the result that henceforth a sub-compact car and a full-size model would be run on the same line. The existence of the factory thus appeared secure, but the management feared the adverse effects of the mix on efficiency and quality, and thus on the image and long range perspective of the factory. "We had to argue like a stuck pig to get the mix penalty we needed from the division" (Plant manager, Maple City).

The solution to the model-mix problems cannot be found in the area of competence and problem-solving capacity of Industrial Engineering. The model-mix problems result from developments in customer preferences and from the marketing strategies of the companies. As we have discussed above, the automobile market shifted from a seller's market to a buyer's market in the course of the 1970s. The manufacturers were forced to differentiate between the products they offered to cater to individual customer wishes, and they had to be able to vary their production schedule to follow the changes in sales conditions. The volatility of the exchange rates which we dealt with in chapter 2 also played a role here. Favorable export conditions caused by the exchange rates could only be exploited through the ability to react quickly by changing the model mix, the range of options, or by offering niche products.

The increased flexibility to produce different types, models, and variants on the same production line which was desirable from the marketing standpoint produced enormous problems from a production standpoint. To give an example: at Blackmoor, the upscale variant, had almost one third more labor content than the base model. The range of variance in personnel required in the assembly area of this plant (direct production – without additional personnel necessary to cover absenteeism) was around 250 between the simplest and most expensively equipped models. This was almost 30 percent of the personnel authorized for this area. The mean deviation in personnel requirements of the fifteen variants was sixty-seven direct workers.

Linked to these calculations of variance are very real problems of personnel deployment and flexibility. Thus the margin between the vehicle with the least and the most expensive equipment at the Weinkirchen plant was between nine and fourteen hours of labor. The monthly fluctuation in personnel requirements was 300 in this production area, the weekly fluctuation was around 100, that meant 15 percent or 5 percent of the planned amount of personnel. Added to these fluctuations in personnel requirements due to model-mix variations came the fluctuations in the absenteeism level of the hourly workers. When these fluctuations came together, it was obvious that serious short-term problems with personnel (either a significant lack of personnel or overstaffing) would arise.

The basis for personnel allocation is the production plan or schedule. As soon as the volume of orders is large enough to allow a certain lead time, it may be possible to put together batches of cars with similar specifications to allow for some standardization in production. But in view of the many intervening factors, the shorter the lead time before actual production begins the better the chances that production can "stick to the schedule," i.e., the higher the probability that the planned sequence of auto types, models, and equipment will hold true in practice. Holding to the schedule as much as possible is obviously a prerequisite for orienting plant logistics to just-in-time deliveries, and has important consequences for the investment of fixed capital and thus for costs.

This brings us to the problem of fluctuations in the production schedule. If it is difficult to optimize the line balancing with respect to a production schedule with a broad product mix, it is even more difficult to cope with the continual changes in the production schedule. These changes require continual adjustments in the line balancing if the company does not want to have any efficiency losses. To give a simple example: if the production schedule for the following week were to include 20 percent more vehicles which require a sunroof than in the current week then the personnel allocation must be recalculated for the corresponding work stations. The prerequisite for this is that the production plan is precise enough to exactly predict which customer orders should be worked off in the week in question. According to experience, the shorter the lead time between planning and actual production the greater the degree of correspondence between the planned and the actual schedule. After all, disruptive factors, like machine breakdowns, defective parts or delayed parts deliveries, always come along and spoil things. For this reason it is important that the production plan, which is the basis for personnel deployment, is established as close to the time of production as possible.

In the assembly plants of Companies A and B management used computers to continually actualize the line balancing with respect to the production schedule. Company C used another system which we will be coming back to later in chapter 10.

The computerized line balancing system at Company B was designed with a lead time of one month, the system at Company A had a lead time of one week. The procedure is as follows: the starting point is the data from the current period which contain the optimized line balancing for the given production schedule. The production schedule for the following period is then calculated with this personnel allocation. Because the model-option composition of the new schedule will differ from the current one, the computer will show work overload at some work stations and underload at others. On this basis industrial engineers and also occasionally the lower-level supervisors will rearrange the task/personnel allocation to balance out the over- and underutilization and to minimize the cycle loss time. The result of this effort is the efficiency plan containing the personnel required for each operation. This will be the basis for the efficiency report later on, when planned and actual time/personnel requirements are balanced.

Before this system was practiced, the production foremen/"*Vizemeis-ter*"[11] were responsible for work assignment in all of the companies studied. IE only had a supporting role in this. The systems of computer based line balancing had occasionally reversed this relationship in practice – especially where it was done on a weekly basis. In these cases, the allocation was worked out principally by IE, the foremen had only a secondary role. IE interviewees maintained that the foremen were over-taxed and overburdened with the work of allocation. As the process control department frequently did not give the production plans to IE until the middle of the week, and considering that it took around two days to run the program, the task of line balancing faced by IE and the foremen could become a week-end activity when there were large variations between one week's and next week's production plans. The expenditure for the computer systems was thus viewed critically by individual interviewees from produc-tion management, but also from IE. In the British plant Hartmoor we heard that the introduction of the system there in the middle of the 1970s met with criticism from the foremen, who felt themselves incapacitated and their scope of action restricted through the system.

Lastly, another problem emerges. Despite all the efforts which are made to plan production schedules realistically, in practice they get mixed up time and again. Thus the realization rate at the Windeck plant was around 70 percent for the weekly schedule and 25 percent for the daily schedule at the time of our investigation. We do not have comparable data for the other plants, but we know from the interviewees that problems with the realiza-tion rate also existed there. Planning efforts are frustrated in this time and again and in the end it is left up to the lower level supervisors to bring about an optimal line balancing. Many of the old hands were thus skeptical about the attempts at improving planning through the use of the computer: "I think that we will never bring order there. That's also because there are a number of contradictory demands here. If we meet the requirements for trim assembly then it can well be that we make the requirements for final assembly more complicated." (Industrial engineer, Altstadt)

The fluctuations in the production schedule also limited all attempts to raise the average workload significantly over 90 percent. Attempts at the Windeck plant to exceed this were generally broken off quickly by problems coming from unforeseen changes in the model mix. An interviewee from IE recalls: "In the short term we were also at 96 percent once, and in the course of this around eighty workers exceeded the critical limit from 100 to 102 percent workload. With a stable program, as the Japanese had in their three month program, we could bring our workload up to 3 to 4 percent away from the 100 percent mark." And in regard to the problem of over-cycle work the interviewee added: "One could already almost say that the greater transparency which we have through the ... system has already become a disadvantage. If someone is clever he can spot right away when over-cycle work occurs" (ibid).

The willingness of the workers to also sporadically accept overcycle work was very different in the factories studied. In any case this situation meant strain on the labor relations and led to quality problems. According to the personnel manager at Weinkirchen in Germany:

We had the greatest difficulties – from the point of view of our personnel department – with the program fluctuations. Our output is relatively stable. Under fluctuations in the program which cause us problems, I'm referring above all to the model mix. We try to control the mix, but in the case of difficulties in the supply of certain parts or unexpected repairs, etc. there were adjustments which muddle up this mix planning time and time again. There the people had the impression that they are overburdened, and rightly so. This is a short term situation though, because when many expensive cars in a row come, for example many (upsale versions), then it comes to overburdening which could later be compensated for by many base models in a row. Nevertheless it comes to complaints, the people go to the works council and complain.

And it comes to quality problems, as the personnel manager at C's Windeck plant explains:

Quality problems do not arise through high workloads, but through the extreme variations in job content, through jumping between differing work requirements. The most highly equipped vehicles, for example, do not have more mistakes than others. The most mistakes arise when different models are produced with extreme sequence changes.

There were not only problems with overcycle work at individual work stations. With the short cycle times at some plants, the time was often not sufficient to complete the work within the worker's own station. "The workers float away" was the observation of the production manager of the final assembly area at Weinkirchen which had a cycle time of only thirty-two seconds. This, in turn, leads to an increased worker density in other work stations and the possibility that the workers hinder each other there.

There were arrangements in the Master Agreement as well as in the local agreement to restrict overcycle work in the U.S. plants. Thus it was agreed in the contract between the UAW and Company A:

When additional work is required because the mix of body types differs from the expected normal ratio from which the work standards are computed and regular work assignments are made, the Company will make adjustments which are necessary by one or more of the following means: (a) addition of manpower, (b) greater spacing of units, (c) reducing speed of line, (d) stopping line momentarily, (e) adjusting employee work assignments. (Vol. 1, February 13, 1982, p. 2)

Temporary overcycle work was obviously expected in everyday practice. The intensification of work connected with this was one of the main reasons for countless conflicts over "speed ups" in U.S. factories. Even though such conflicts and grievances did not boil up any longer considering the general economic situation at the time of our study, they still were a significant strain on labor relations. Thus the production management of B's Greentown plant saw their difficulty in achieving line balancing to meet model mix fluctuations to be the greatest problem at that time. The union continually complained about "overcycle operations."

The willingness to do temporary overcycle work existed informally – according to statements of production management – in the plants of the Company A U.S. at the time of our study. Thus a comment of an industrial engineer: "Over-cycle work is accepted if model-mix problems occur. You know we have a very dedicated work force here in the ... shop. But it is expected that this time of overcycle work will be compensated by undercycle work afterwards."

A muddled up model mix was also a severe strain for the labor relations in the British companies. In fact, "loose" standard times, high cycle loss times, and, accordingly, low workloads had functioned as a buffer to cope with overload situations due to an uncontrolled model mix in the past. But with the tightening of the standards and improved line balancing at the assembly plants of A-U.K., overload became a hot issue there. As long as the time standards were "loose," a confused model mix could still be tolerated; this was becoming less and less possible with the elimination of standard allowances. There was an informal arrangement at A's Hartmoor plant for the situation of temporary overcycle operation. This ensured compensation on an hourly basis through corresponding undercycle operation. (The situation was different in the German sister plant where the compensation of under- and overcycle operations was made on a shift basis, which was naturally easier to realize.) A production manager at Hartmoor: "We cannot run overload. That would not do the job. We would run into continuous arguments. We also cannot argue that you had to overload for a certain period and underload for another so that the average workload was right. The people go by the hour."

Unexpected disorders in the model mix and the pressure connected with it, either to accept periodical overcycle situations or – from the side of the union – to refuse them, were among the most important reasons for the hostility of labor relations in the area of trim and final assembly in this plant. This explained the great importance given by an interviewee from this production area to a local contract with the union in which the plant agreed to run gaps in the line (to reduce the number of cars per hour) when necessary if the model mix became confused and the work-intensive models piled up. He regarded this agreement as the first step in the turnaround of the poor labor relations of the past:

One of the key factors that helped to calm down labour disputes was a stability in the model mix. Model mix instability was a very important factor of labour discontent. So everyone, including management, was interested in stabilizing the model mix. So we said to the union: We have to allocate sixty minutes, but we will give you the predicted mix. And to prove the point we had even come to the point where we did run gaps in the line. (Production manager, Hartmoor)

We were told that the improved industrial relations at Hartmoor had not made it necessary to enforce this agreement for quite some time before our investigation, especially since it would be done at the expense of the efficiency targets. This plant was subject to special pressure in this regard from the company headquarters – as we will be describing in more detail later in this chapter. Thus at the time of our study management was looking for a way to better cope with the problems of the model-mix and overcycle work. Remarkable is the fact that group concepts played a prominent role in the discussions which took place between production management, industrial engineers, and shop stewards in the production areas. Thus a suggestion was worked out for forming production groups which would take over the responsibility for dividing their assigned task and time volumes among their members. The size of these groups would vary according to the situation, but would not contain more than eight to ten people. The work groups would organize work and equalize the work load within the group on its own, and thus be more flexible with respect to the uncertainties of production. Within a group of eight to ten workers, a bottleneck situation arising at an individual work place could be more easily coped with because the neighboring workers would step in to help their colleagues in overload situations. It did not come to a realization of these suggestions for group work, though. Interviewees at the plant blamed this on the company headquarters which was not ready to support such concepts with its preference for a standard procedure at all its sites and in view of the problems of pushing this through the system of industrial relations.

In Company B's Seaborough plant, a temporary request for overcycle work by management was not seen to be problematic by our interviewees from production management. If necessary the assembly line could be run a little faster to make up for lost production there. In this respect we were told at Seaborough that management had significantly more leeway there than at the German sister plant. This was confirmed by management at Mittelort. And also the works council resolutely rejected the possibility for increased performance (over the 109 percent norm which had been negotiated here): "More than 109 percent workload is not allowed under any circumstances. If say, five people are in a group and one is at 109.1 percent workload, then a sixth man must be brought in. Even a short term overload is not in the cards, is not allowed" (Works council member, Mittelort). Until 1978 there was a compensation arrangement at Mittelort which made a certain flexibility in the case of model-mix irregularities possible.

According to this, overcycle work up to 5 percent above the contractually agreed to average performance for the duration of one hour per shift, or an overcycle work up to 10 percent for the duration of thirty minutes per shift would be allowed. Excesses would be compensated for in the same shift if possible, within the next three shifts at the latest. Measuring devices were to be installed on certain lines to check over the keeping to this agreement, and these were to be accessible for the works council representative at all times. (Factory agreement 1971)

But such an arrangement proved to be too complicated for practical application and would not be able to handle the growing model mix problem.

Irregularities in the model mix were also seen as a strain on labor relations in the German plants of Company A. There was, in fact, leeway for demanding increased performance and there was "a common understanding that overcycle work would have to be compensated through undercycle work within a certain period of time" (Industrial engineer, Weinkirchen). It was also a strain on the labor relations. Above and beyond this, it was a burden on the position of the supervisor ("*Meister*"), which can be seen in the following answer given by an IE representative to the question of what happens when many expensive models in a row come: "When we have a concentration of expensive cars then the man goes to the works council. It then turns to Industrial Engineering. The *Meister* does not notice this in time. He only notices it when the problem has emerged, when the child has fallen into the well" (Industrial engineer, Altstadt). The quote shows that not only the industrial engineers, but also the lower-level production supervisors are frustrated time and again by the model-mix related problems. We do not want to deal with this point in more detail here.

The many examples of problems and comments from factory practice in this section have made the great problems the factories have with increased production flexibility sufficiently clear. So, what could be done? Contractual agreements, like those which foresee the need for additional operators, running gaps in the line, or slowing down the line do help to reduce work stress and strain which arise though overload situations, but they come at the cost of production efficiency. The companies could, of course, reduce the complexity of the production schedule and thus make the sequence of vehicles more suitable for planning and predicting. Such a move would contradict the goal of an increased flexibility with reference to the market, even though marketing and production managers argue over this. The other possibilities concern the information and production flow. If a deviation from the planned mix is unavoidable, then it should be possible either through early warning systems or through the formation of buffers to ensure that at least the more downstream departments can adjust themselves in time. We will briefly discuss these two possibilities.

Creating early warning systems for overload situations is an old idea, but it cannot be achieved merely by passing on general information. The problem lies in being able to precisely specify an overload warning and give the subsequent work stations the necessary information for their area-specific personnel adjustments which arise through the specific deviations from the mix plan. Software systems for this purpose have been developed at different companies. But even with these "systems," the problem itself would still not be solved because those who have been warned would also have to be capable of carrying the necessary personnel adjustment measures. This presupposes the relevant transfer flexibility and disposal over personnel available with the required qualifications.

Thus the possibility to rearrange the sequence of cars in the event of model-mix disorders does indeed reduce model-mix problems. For this reason all of the factories in our study had set up large buffer areas, especially after the paint shop, which was one of the main factors responsible for the confusion of the preplanned order; buffer areas frequently also existed between trim assembly and final assembly. The following brief description of the process in the trim and final assembly of the Weinkirchen plant should suffice as an example.

The vehicles here came into a buffer after the paint shop which could take in about 100 vehicles, or entailed one and a half hours of production. A worker from the "production control" department directed the car bodies coming from the paint shop into one of ten buffer lines from which they were selectively led into the two trim assembly lines according to certain criteria for sequencing. Thus it was a manual mix regulation. The "mix regulator" did not even attempt to realize the model mix of the weekly production schedule; he could only attempt to avoid extreme situations, e.g., preventing several five door models in a row from coming onto one line. The cycle length on the two trim assembly lines was about seventy-three seconds. After trim assembly, the vehicles came into a buffer which could hold fifty-six units, and could only be partially used for another mix regulation. From here they were directed on to the unitary final assembly line where the cycle time was 36.5 seconds. At Weinkirchen our interviewees regarded the selection possibilities in the buffers to be insufficient. This was, in fact, also true in the majority of the plants studied.

A more comprehensive solution to deal with the problem of model variance was attempted in a change-over which was beginning at the time of this study in Company C's plant Windeck. In this concept, the car bodies were separated after the paint shop according to the work required in the following trim assembly operations. The vehicles with limited options were brought into a newly constructed storehouse. The vehicles which had a labor content of at least twenty minutes more than the base model would go to stationary work stations. Operations like the installation of central locking systems, the sun roof, the trailer hitch, and installing wire harnesses for electronic extras were carried out here. Then these vehicles were also brought into the storehouse. After all vehicles had come into the store-house, where computer-based access to each individual car body was ensured, they were arranged in sequence for the following final assembly. Mix surprises due to the previous departments could not happen any more, the lines could be optimally adjusted.

Thus the creation of buffers helps, but they are expensive. Buffers tie up capital and space. Large buffer zones also produce a management attitude which tends toward covering up problems, for instance in the production technology, the process layout, or the training of workers, and not getting to the roots of them. As the IMVP Automobile Study urgently showed, these disadvantages of "buffered production" are a major cause of the great productivity disadvantage which Western factories have compared to the Japanese (Womack *et al.* 1990, p. 80).

The inefficiencies caused by the buffer systems as a means of dealing with the model-mix problems were seen as more or less inevitable under the given system by our interviewees. The future-oriented considerations were aimed in the following three directions, with characteristic company-specific differences in weighting:

1 to increase in the accuracy of the schedule by removing the causes which bring about confusion in the mix. Logistics and quality control have a central importance here. Missing or qualitatively inferior components from suppliers are an important source of disruptions. Reducing errors and poor quality in production by increasing the line operator's responsi-bility for quality in direct production is planned to reduce the necessity of taking vehicles out of the line flow to perform repair work – an important source of deviation from the planned model mix.

2 to use the increased flexibility potential made possible through group work. The responsibility for work allocation would be delegated to work groups, who could deal with the problem of fluctuating workloads and job contents at individual work stations much more flexibly. An overload situation within a group could be coped with by means of help from co-workers.

3 to create new forms of work organization which diverge from the principle of line work. Work cycles with changing work content could be carried out on individual work stations or separate parallel lines in the area, without the diverse problems of line balancing or over- and undercycle work, etc. appearing.

The first of these strategies aimed at the system of quality assurance in the company. We have dealt with this in chapter 5. It aimed also at the quality control systems at supplier companies and at a fundamental restructuring of the supplier relationships. All three companies made efforts in this direction – at Company A clearly most emphatically. But this is beyond the scope of our research. The introduction of group principles and the delegation of responsibility for time economy and work allocation to the groups was still a largely vague idea for the future; active steps to carry out this principle were taken above all by B U.S. in comprehensive experimental projects. These measures will also be dealt with at a later point in the context of NW&M programs. The approach dealing with process organization, the change in the "structures" of the production flow and work-place design were concepts most likely to be found in West Germany, and more likely at Company C and Company B than at Company A. We will also be dealing with the measures in this area later.

7.2.3 Problems of regulating performance arising with the increased mechanization of production

A further group of problems in regulating performance, which were new at least for auto assembly plants, has arisen from the increased mechanization being carried out in these plants. We will be going into three problems:
1 the increase in the number of jobs which are uncoupled from the direct flow of production;
2 the difficulty in assigning a full workload to the workers deployed in mechanized areas, and
3 the growth of production losses caused by "idle time" in worker utilization due to technology.

(1) In looking at the increase in "uncoupled" jobs we may recall that IE activity in work measurement has traditionally focussed on the activities which could be influenced through individual performance. Where the output is determined by the rhythm of machines, for instance, and cannot be influenced through smarter work methods and higher work motivation, etc., there was less scope for rationalization. In the words of an industrial engineer at Weinkirchen: "Work measurement is most fruitful with purely manual jobs."

With increasing mechanization, the problems of performance regulation and personnel allocation are posed in a fundamentally new manner. The employees who work with high-tech equipment are in fact slipping away from the control provided by the production cycle and IE's standards. Their main task now is keeping the equipment running as trouble-free as possible for the whole shift. The jobs connected with this do not directly contribute to the completion of the product any more and they are not direct production jobs in the traditional sense. An "objective" measure of performance, used to determine the personnel allocation, can therefore not be prescribed any more. This further undermines the principle of regulating performance according to "normal effort" and was consequently regarded as a serious problem in the majority of the plants studied. At the time of our research a solution had only been found at Company C, which undertook an amendment of its wage Master Agreement in 1985 and established the "time constant incentive wage" as a new wage principle (*"Arbeitskenn-ziffer-Lohn"*). Management had at first considered transferring these jobs, which are actually indirect work supporting the functioning of machines, to the straight hourly wage category. But the works councils would never have accepted such a solution as this would have removed precisely the new and desirable jobs of automated systems control from the sphere of codetermination. They would no longer fall under the incentive-wage principle, and the works council has very little influence in the "non-incentive" wage area (Rausch 1987, p. 234).

The agreement now provides more or less for a straight hourly wage in the guise of an incentive wage. It established the measurement of data referring to the equipment (like machine operation times and process times) instead of the workers for determining the basis for the personnel allocation. The personnel level required was established using this equipment-related data in an agreement between management and the works council. This procedure makes a fundamental break with traditional IE principles. Work measurement is no longer related to motions and effort of the human "labor power" required at the individual work place, but was rather based on machining and processing times in a work area. The decision on manning levels has to be reached in the joint wage commission in the factory. In practice, each case was hotly debated in these commissions. Issues of machine uptime and training were dominant in these discussions, no longer the classical issues of workloads and performance levels.

(2) The second problem of regulating performance under conditions of increasing mechanization arises from the loss in personnel allocation flexibility with respect to fluctuating production volume. The jobs in the mechanized areas pose great problems for the work planners. The tasks on the technical equipment, such as filling magazines, taking off parts, etc. are frequently performed at isolated work stations and often cannot be loaded up to make a full workload and thus prevent a 100 percent utilization of the workers deployed here. The number of for example preassembly tasks in the surrounding areas which could be added to such jobs were limited and

receding even further. Beyond this, mechanization has taken away many small tasks which had previously been used to fill out the work cycles. "Thus a typical task to reduce the cycle loss was previously laying nut washers onto screws to prepare for the next operation. Today the washers are threaded onto screws. With this, a productive activity for reducing the cycle loss has been eliminated. We had invested without rationalizing" (Industrial engineer, company headquarters level at Company C).

The biggest efficiency problem arose from the inefficiencies due to minimum staffing requirements. Regardless of how many units per hour were produced, a minimum staffing for certain tasks was required in the automation areas in any case. With a decrease in production the personnel allocation remains unchanged at first and then drops to a lower level. Increased cycle losses with unfavorable capacity utilization arise under these circumstances. As the British plants in our sample produced significantly below their capacities, they were especially affected by this problem. We want to give an example from the body area of Company A's Blackmoor plant which had a capacity of sixty-three units per hour at the time of our research, but produced only thirty units per hour. Nevertheless, the personnel allocation in many areas was determined on the assumption of running at full capacity. Thus thirteen workers were deployed at the welding press for the wheel compartment; if the personnel there were fully used, they would only need nine.

Such minimum staffing limits arise from the fact that there are always jobs which cannot be enriched and enhanced by combining job elements from neighboring jobs. An example of this is rehanging doors from one line to another. Two workers have to stand there, regardless of how many units pass per hour. Thus a proportional elimination would not take place with a reduction in the production volume. If the personnel could be used extensively for a broader range of tasks and had the necessary qualifications, then the problem would not be so acute – for example the "underloaded" production worker could do additional preventive maintenance. Management's considerations also aim in this direction:

What we are doing here is rationalization at any price. And we are under powerful constraints. The Japanese had forced us to an increased speed of rationalization. We had set the goal for ourselves to reduce the direct personnel by 10 percent yearly. That could only be achieved when each minute which could be productively used, is also actually used. Our basic principle is thus to fill the many unproductive times, e.g. which arise through undercycle work or waiting times in the course of a day, with productive tasks. Therefore when someone on an unpaced job has reached his schedule half an hour earlier for example, then I have to be able to give him a task to fill out the rest of his time productively. Important for such a strategy is, naturally, that the people are also qualified to do other tasks. It would be ideal if all of the people were skilled workers. (Production manager in the body shop at Weinkirchen)

This remark shows how the problems in achieving a full work load in the mechanized work sections contribute considerably to management's interest in increasing the level of qualification in production. Thus, problems of regulating performance were also central stimulating interest in "de-Taylorizing" the division of labor in the factory.

(3) The third problem which technology creates for regulating performance was the increase in production losses due to reliability problems. In order to keep to the planned work schedule in spite of disruptions, it was customary practice in all assembly plants that a "reliability factor" was calculated in. The lines and equipment were speeded up by this factor (delay allowance, "overspeed") in order to compensate for the losses caused by machine breakdown, missing or defective parts, etc. In manually dominated job areas this overspeed was generally about 5 percent. In the "old plants" with a low degree of mechanization, such an overspeed was often not needed at all.

The delay allowance of 5 percent means that twenty-two minutes were planned in for machine breakdowns and line stoppages per eight hour shift. If these stoppages do not happen, then the daily production goal is reached a good twenty minutes before the end of the shift. The principle of a measured day's work, which was factually the present wage principle in all of the plants studied, has led to a tradition in many plants that the work was stopped when the schedule had been attained, even if the shift was not over. This was reported from all German plants. In most U.S. plants, management had been able to institute "bell to bell working" again at the beginning of the 1980s. Compared to the restrictions in the German plants, a British manager also referred to the greater flexibility in this regard in his company's British plants: "In Germany, changes in the production plan are agreed to once a month with the works council and can not be changed again afterwards. A loss in production can thus not simply be compensated for with increased line speed. Here on the other hand – if I lose an hour of production my people wind the track up" (Production manager, Company B U.K.).

Compensating for production losses within a shift by increasing the line speed was not practiced in the German plants. The established delay allowance tended rather to become fixed and was made part of the system of performance regulation protected by the works councils: management's attempts to revise delay allowances through work measurement were considered a hot issue and it was debatable as to whether the amount of the delay allowance was a matter for codetermination. In some factories an informal code developed with regard to the usage of the free time gained in the case of fewer stoppages. In Weinkirchen, for example, when the delay allowance was not fully used up by breakdowns, etc., the remainder was used informally to allow the workers to go home a half or quarter of an hour early according to information given by the works council. Only the late shift could make use of this because it was only then clear how well production was adhering to the daily schedule. In some cases the workers of the late shift turned up earlier in order to share the "gains" with the workers from the first shift. We could not determine how widespread this practice was. Plant management was not aware of it and assumed that work was done continually from the beginning to the end of the shift.

Management at Company C also complained that they "could not reclaim lost units from the shift."

When the scheduled volume has been reached then the people go. This is one reason why the lines are stopped earlier here. The company then loses productive time. In some areas this is because the people really pour it on to build up a buffer for themselves in order to go earlier. Good! But in others this earlier end is only because the time lost due to breakdowns is smaller than the delay allowance. This is a big disadvantage in the measured days work wage system in which the fulfilling of a certain scheduled volume is required for the wages paid." (Industrial engineer, Company C central staff)

For these reasons, management also hesitated in carrying out studies of delay allowances, which could only inflame the emotions aroused by this question. Instead of rocking the boat, management preferred to write time credits here. In practice, these credits could amount to much more than the actual delay allowance. This was a step away from "scientific management" with its claim of being able to objectively plan the production targets, but management followed this path in order to avoid arguments over rules and principles. Because of such problems management was considering removing the delay allowance from the time factor altogether.

The problem of how to account for production loss due to things like machine breakdowns was regarded as serious at Company B in Germany. To prevent wages from being reduced, production received special credits for the losses due to disruptions which exceeded the delay allowances. It was also customary in this plant that the work stopped when the scheduled volume was reached.

But also when there were disruptions they stopped work earlier because they had received special credits. Thus the end of work has, all in all, moved away from the formal end of the working time. For example in the stamping plant, where there are facilities with 30 percent delay allowances, the people simply stop when the number of pieces has been run. There they stop around 1:30 PM. although the end of the shift was 2:15. (Personnel manager, Mittelort)

To the extent that it was possible to receive special credits during the shift, the delay allowances could be used as "earned idle time" even when the lost time was due to disruptions.

Just like the cycle losses, the breakdown losses had further increased in the course of mechanization and automation. Time losses of 20 to 30 percent of the daily production time were not uncommon in highly mechanized areas. The basic principles for regulating performance and wages in all plants studied, the measured day's work principle and the principle of job-related standard performance measured by the individual work cycle, were therefore considered more and more dysfunctional from the point of view of management. Management occasionally complained about inequity in this respect. This was because the work force and the unions refused temporary overcycle work, on the one hand, but when, on the other hand, no performance could be demanded – as in the case of lost time due to disruption – the company's interests in having the lost units of this shift be made up were not met. This would presuppose the willingness of the work force to do additional work at short notice, as is often customary in Japanese plants.

To summarize this section we saw the tendencies toward a mechanization and flexibilization of production as the main factors leading to IE's field of operation becoming smaller. New problems arose for which the classical IE instruments were less and less suited. The actual share of direct labor is declining because of changes in the work organization; the share of times which cannot be influenced increases due to the mechanization measures; the "ungovernability" of the model mix requires the willingness of the work force and management's ability to make short-term adjustments and redistributions of workloads. The problems connected with these developments are the background for production management's increased interest in new solutions requiring a greater degree of self-regulation in the work carried out.

This delegation of more competence for self-regulation must also be seen against the background of changes in the industry structures which, on the other hand, give management possibilities for additional, new forms of control. We will be dealing with these possibilities in the last section of this chapter.

7.3 Performance regulation by benchmarking: competing for best practices

Benchmarking and measuring performance competition between factories attained increasing importance in the 1980s. For the company headquarters, benchmarking is a control instrument to evaluate the success of measures for change in the factories; for the management in the factories, it is the possibility to find out for themselves the specific strengths and weaknesses of their own sites and to measure their own production standards against those of the competitors within and outside their own company (see Bailey and Hubert 1980). The essential question for management is: how does it come about that factory b, which produces the same or a similar product with very similar production technology as factory a, can do this with less personnel than factory a?

These questions were often viewed in a more relaxed way under the market conditions of the 1960s and 1970s. "What is one man against 1,000 cars lost?" was the rhetorical question of one of our interviewees in a British plant to explain management's willingness to make concessions in the past. If the production management or the union demanded additional personnel in an area, if strike threats were in the air because of workers being overburdened, it was, without a doubt, less expensive to make concessions. The control over personnel allocation was frequently passed on to the shop stewards of these areas. Starting at the end of the 1970s, however, the tables were turned. The union representatives in all companies worldwide were under pressure to make concessions in order to reduce "off standards." The allocation of investment and the assignment of a new car model to specific factories by company headquarters were increasingly made dependent on the corresponding willingness to make measures for change here. A poor result in the comparison between the factories within the company would now, in view of growing overcapacities, increasingly entail the risk of losing employment or even of being closed down completely.

Benchmarking thus also plays an increasing role in industrial relations. A union official at Company A U.K. referred to the negotiating strategy of the plant management as "a general softening-up process, which contains malicious productivity comparisons."[12] In the "International Metalworkers' Handbook for Ford Workers," under the heading "internal threats of the moving of jobs by the company," the editors had the following comments: "All plant managements use it as a threat. In Belgium, West Germany, Spain, Great Britain, Canada, the U.S.A., and Brazil they openly threaten with the shifting of jobs to other countries. The level of pay and productivity are named as the reason by the plant management in each case."

The use of benchmarking and competition between factories as instruments for regulating performance depends naturally on the product range and the location of the different factories in the company's international division of labor. "World car" conceptions and the increasing interdependencies of worldwide corporate structures give these instruments of performance regulation their increasing weight. There are also technological prerequisites: a flexibility of the production apparatus for adopting models from other plants, the possibility of producing several different models on one production line, etc. Under these conditions there are obvious advantages for central management control, better transparency for evaluating plant performance and exerting pressure on the laggards to match the level of performance of the best factories.

Thus, parallel production also became an important control instrument for management at Company A and Company B in their U.S. and increasingly also their European organizations. Whether in Great Britain or the U.S. the tenor of leading industrial engineers was the same: "We endeavor to achieve a production lay-out and installation which is as comparable as possible. When we now plan new equipment, then the plants will be made exactly the same, even the colors, so that the people in England don't have any more excuses" (Industrial engineer, Company A's European central staff). Or at another company: "The division specified the tooling for all new models and provided the factories with the same equipment in principle" (Industrial engineer, Company B U.S. central staff).

As a rule, factory comparisons are limited to factories of the same level of production: for example, engine plants, stamping plants, or assembly plants. A worldwide spectrum of plants is often covered. This also includes factories of interrelated companies. Comparisons are done using all types of criteria, but "labor efficiency" is certainly at the fore. In the following, we want to give some examples in order to illustrate the strategic role which systematic inter-factory comparison played in the policies some companies pursued to raise plant performance. We will describe these using two examples, the "labor efficiency league" at Company B in the U.S.A. and the "efficiency campaign" at the European branch of Company A which was aimed at the "standards" of the British plants. We will be especially dealing with the labor policy aspects which go along with this competition between plants, and which will bring us back into the area of industrial relations.

7.3.1 The "labor efficiency league" at Company B U.S.

The Assembly Division of Company B U.S. has a whole range of assembly plants in the U.S. Like the other divisions of the company it had developed a standard system to measure and report plant performance. Under this system the divisional headquarters generally did not have to set rationalization targets from the top. It was based on the idea that targets emerge from improvements at the plant level and from competition between plants. The divisional headquarters could take the position of setting the rules and observing the game.

This was also the view at the division's central Industrial Engineering department. Scattered among the factories in the division are small groups of "resident industrial engineers" sent there by the central department and hosted by the plants. Each of these groups concentrated on a certain area, such as engine dressing, body finishing, or final assembly, and determined standard times for these operations after having optimized work methods in the usual manner. Time standards generated in these "parent areas" were then made obligatory for all other plants in the division. If there was no special authorization from the divisional headquarters for additional time and personnel, these parent area standards provided the yardstick against which the plants had to measure their performance. This system not only provided standards for systematic comparison, but it also helped with regard to acceptance and credibility. The standards were not set by lofty central planners, but within the "family" of assembly plants. They had proven their feasibility under real production conditions and anyone could pay a visit to the plant to see how they were achieved.

The measuring and reporting of labor efficiency by the plants in the division took place using the standards thus generated. A division-wide "performance report" was put together each week. From this report, each factory could obtain its current position in the "divisional league" and could ascertain its relative strengths and weaknesses, broken down according to production areas and functional groups. The up- and downward movements in this "divisional league" were carefully followed by many observers – the results went to the factories, appeared on bulletin boards, and were distributed as handouts. Depending on which decisions were on the agenda, the changes in position were followed with satisfaction or concern by the respective factories; by others within the company occasionally with respect, or also they may be gloating. The weekly performance reports were very carefully studied in the entire assembly division of B U.S. We had hardly one conversation in the course of our study in which these reports were not mentioned. Many interview partners referred to the current conversion formula "1 percent increase of efficiency for his department = 3.8 heads that would have to be reduced."

Naturally the factories are not equal in every respect. It was up to the divisional management to decide which differences in the production program and plant technology would be acknowledged by specific allowances, and which would not. Here were the subtle control possibilities for the divisional headquarters:

The factories which manufacture the new car model receive the same standards taking the option differences and a few process differences into account. In regard to the former, we pay attention to see that there is an incentive for measures of automation. The factories should automate their production as much as they can. In a standardized comparison, the automation pioneers naturally do better than the factories which still have manual production. We want this positional advantage. The standards will be adjusted only when the majority of the factories here have followed suit with automation. (Industrial engineer at Company B's divisional level)

If a plant could not get by with the authorized standards there was still the buffer of the "allowances." The authorized time standards defined, so to speak, the net values for time and personnel required to run the operation. By adding "allowances," gross values were arrived at which took various adversities of real life into account. Thus there were allowances for "inevitable" cycle losses due to line balancing problems, for repair work, for personal relief time, for machine breakdowns, etc. All Western companies use a more or less complex system of such allowances – the Japanese companies generally try to do without them and run their operation on a "net basis."

The idea of standards generated in a decentralized manner at Company B was also based on the system for determining the allowances. In this case, the allowances needed by the better half of the plants in the "divisional league" in their best period of the past model year were averaged and then prescribed to all plants in the division for the subsequent model year. The efficiency status of a plant then reflected the differences between the personnel actually required to run the operation in a plant and the personnel requirements derived from the parent area standards plus the allowances authorized by the division, both general allowances and allowances due to plant-specific conditions.

The existence and amount of certain allowances was seen by some respondents as directly connected to strike threats which could be made with regard to paragraph 78 of the national contract with the UAW. This was especially true for the "line balance allowance," which authorized additional personnel in order to avoid overload situations resulting from variations in the model mix. This allowance was repeatedly increased in the 1970s, and in the early 1980s it totalled ca. 15 percent as a factory average – in the area of trim and final assembly ca. 25 percent. An allowance for "attainability" also emerged at this time – for additional personnel required due to special conditions in plant layout, technical equipment, work methods, etc.

Allowances had an outlet function for the dissatisfaction arising from the conditions of assembly line production. With the number of grievances against speed-up and work intensification, the allowances had become increasingly larger. As the "pressure from below" receded at the beginning of the 1980s, the divisional management undertook a "straightening of the front" in all its plants. The allowances for line balancing and attainability were done away with and the average total of allowances was thus reduced by around one third. This measure taken at the beginning of 1983 was a clear expression of the turnaround in industrial relations. All factories were affected equally and it thus had no effect on their rank order in the "divisional league." Only the scale to measure plant efficiency had been shifted. With less allowances, 100 percent efficiency could be less easily achieved. A senior industrial engineer explained to us:

The previous system produced complacency. The best operating plants enjoyed a stable position below 100 percent, now they are over 100 percent efficiency, i.e., optically inefficient. But now they try to make improvements to get below 100 percent again; thus we did create a challenge; the old philosophy was that standards should be obtainable. This has changed now. Now we expect quantum leaps. We set some non-obtainable goals consciously. Nevertheless some of the plants are already approaching the 100 percent mark again.[13] (Industrial Engineer, Greentown)

Thus the management in one of our factories studied, whose efficiency quotient had "sunk" over 120 percent through this change in the measurement scale got together with the local union in order to improve the efficiency performance. To start out, the target was set at the 109 percent mark. The personnel was correspondingly reduced. An industrial engineer at the plant level commented: "This cut has produced pressure to improve methods. Earlier, people could rely much more on allowances: there had been a little gravy for the shop floor" (Greentown). This "gravy" was increasingly taken away at the beginning of the 1980s. In this, the competition between factories, on the basis of the system of efficiency reports described, played a significant role.

The following episode describes the constellation of the turnaround at the beginning of the 1980s much more clearly than any analysis could: the factories discussed in the following account produced cars of the new front-wheel drive generation. This product program was central to the immense investment program the company had launched at the beginning of the 1980s. The expectations of success with regard to this model were high, the production system was generously laid out. Four parallel plants were foreseen for the production of the new model; they were the winners in a bidding competition in which a number of other factories had also made offers. The demand developed disappointingly soon after the model start. One production plant of the product family was thus shut down, the remaining were only working one shift. From the background of the general economic depression in the United States and in view of the locations of the production sites – two in rural regions – the labor market situation of those workers laid off was hopeless. In 1982 more than two thirds of the total work force of Company B's Greentown plant were laid off, at Northtown it was almost 50 percent. Against this background, the actions of the protagonists become understandable when in the 1983 model year signs of a change for the better finally became visible.

At this time the divisional management had decided to bring back the second shift, initially in only one of the three parallel plants. Here was the chance for one plant to bring its laid off employees back to work. Although Northtown considered it had a good chance of doing this – it had always had a good record in the divisional ranking with regard to efficiency, quality, and labor relations – the second shift was not allocated there. The second shift was given to Greentown instead. This was considered in the entire division to be a big coup for Greentown. Three reasons were given to us for Greentown being favored:

1 There had been a turnaround in the labor relations and the division wanted to show the plants that if they can change positively, this will also be rewarded.
2 The president of the company had just publicly declared that the quality performance of the factories would be especially rewarded. In the period in which the decision for the second shift was made, Greentown led the quality league in front of Northtown.
3 In the months before the decision, Greentown had also been able to noticeably improve its position in the divisional league and to considerably increase its "direct labor efficiency." This was considered by our interviewees as being the most important achievement of the plant and crucial in the final decision.

Management and the union at Northtown felt that they had been tricked, especially with regard to the increase in efficiency. The division's "direct labor reports" evaluated plant performance by comparing actual and planned personnel. The basis for this was the line speed in each plant. This was normally set for the length of the model year or even longer and was common knowledge, as it reflected the production volume assigned to each plant by the division. But, "behind the decimal point," there was obviously some leeway for the plant to change the line speed, and even small changes in the line speed had considerable effects on the efficiency data. Information about the exact line speed was contained in the plants' reports to the divisional headquarters, it was not shown in the direct labor reports published by the division, however. The improvements in efficiency at Greentown, seen with amazement by the competing plants, were, however, achieved through a tacit stepping up of the line speed which was decided jointly by local union and management. This could not be kept secret very long; the "hackers" at the other plants were soon able to look into the plant's "computer cards" and find the explanation for the increase in efficiency.

Besides the increase in efficiency and quality, the interviewees at Green-

Table 7.2 *Newly filed grievances in two parallel plants in the U.S.*

	1978	1979	1980	1981	1982
Greentown	13,012	13,584	8,662	10,063	2,071
Northtown	3,279	2,775	1,249	2,302	1,514

town attributed their success above all to the improved labor relations. In fact, Greentown could show spectacular rates of improvement in this respect (see table 7.2), but looking at table 7.2 also makes clear the difficulty for a central authority when it based its decision on performance indicators. Northtown did traditionally have fewer work conflicts, lower absentee rates, fewer grievances, etc., whereas Greentown had the better record in their most recent rate of improvement.[14] With its decision in favor of Greentown, the divisional headquarters thus supported a process of change and did not reward the better past performance. At any rate, 78 percent of the hourly wage workers at Greentown had voted against the "concessions contract" which the company had reached with the UAW in 1982. At Northtown, only 17 percent had done so.

A further reason for the decision of the divisional headquarters to allocate the second shift to Greentown was the plant's entry into a NW&M program. The union had not yet formally decided to participate in this program. Nevertheless, they cooperated in a scheme to introduce the so-called "Quality Audit Representatives." These were hourly wage employees selected by the union and appointed by management who were to have liaison functions on the shop floor with regard to questions of quality. Their task was to talk with their fellow workers about their problems with quality and also get in touch with suppliers and staff personnel about possible solutions. It was consciously decided not to create a hierarchically superior position for this task so that a "dialogue without domination" between fellow workers would be possible. This "Quality Audit Representative" program got off to an excellent start. As the divisional management visited the factory, one of these quality audit representatives gave a presentation which was generally seen as very convincing.

The awarding of the second shift to Greentown was especially a shock to the union at Northtown. A representative explained in an interview:

When there was talk about the possibility of bringing back a second shift, we assumed that the corporation would automatically decide on us. We did not take a closer look into the criteria which the decision was being based on. Greentown is really a fine plant, but they are also opportunists. They took their chance and they made it. After that we decided that we could not sit back any more. Plant management called the union in after Greentown had the second shift and said that we might not get back the second shift, and that we might possibly lose some of our business. Before Greentown got the second shift there were no real demands that management could put forward to us. Management had also assumed that we were in a good position to get our second shift. We both woke up afterwards when it was too late.

Northtown did not want to miss the chance a second time. As the demand situation improved further, the assignment of a second shift was due. In the end, the competing factories Northtown and Steeltown were called upon to make an offer to the division. At Northtown this offer was jointly worked out between management and the shop committee. In the course of this, the union representatives were made familiar with the cost and efficiency calculations. "We were then shown all the cost calculations and efficiency figures. And these figures are reliable. We had them checked out by the International Union (i.e., the UAW – the authors), and everybody in the Assembly Division is calibrated to the same yardstick, so I guess it is a fair comparison" (Union representative, Northtown). Northtown won the bidding in the end, and was awarded the additional shift because of two union concessions:

1 Introduction of the collective break and doing away with the reliefmen. This meant a savings of about 200 reliefmen. The unions originally did not want to give in to the collective break, but became more agreeable as they got the impression that the headquarters could make their decision dependent on this point.

2 In contrast to this, the union was more willing to agree to an increase in the line speed. An acceleration of the line speed by 3.1 units up to 64 units per hour was agreed to. The management committed itself to correct the work allocation on the line in cases of individual overloads. On the part of the union, the question of line speed was publicly discussed in a meeting called solely for this purpose. The laid-off union members were also invited. An estimated 4,000 members took part and it came to heated discussions, especially over the question of competition between the factories in the Assembly Division. In a secret ballot, the concession was then approved with a majority of over 80 percent.[15]

In the middle of the 1980s the goals and criteria for measuring plant performance were being re-evaluated by divisional management. Above all the fixation of the factories on the indicator "direct labor efficiency," thus on the personnel required in direct production, was now being criticized. The divisional headquarters had just developed a new "basic philosophy" which it wanted to see enacted in the factories, and to change the rules of the game of the "divisional league" correspondingly. On the basis of a catalogue of eleven objectives, with differing weighting, a new and more complex indicator for plant performance was developed. Total labor efficiency (not just direct labor efficiency) accounted for only 5 percent in the construction of this indicator; the plant performance in "grievances," "equal opportunity," "work accidents," and "NW&M activities" also accounted for 5 percent each. More weight was attributed to "absenteeism" and "inventory reduction" (10 percent each). "Production costs" counted 15 percent, but quality scored highest in this index making up 40 percent of the total. At the time of our study, this new system had not yet affected management's priorities at the plant level. Our interviewees in the factories hardly mentioned it. But it shows the endeavor to overcome the fixation on direct labor efficiency and to achieve a broader concept of "total factory performance."

Also the "Parent Area System" was seen at the divisional level as quite an expensive way to set standards, and possibilities of performing this function at the headquarters were being considered. According to industrial engineers at the divisional headquarters, standards in their traditional sense were losing their importance anyway. With the spreading of team concepts, decisions over designing work methods and assigning work tasks should mainly be made by the teams. At the time of our study and in the plants involved, however, this was still only a vision for the future.

7.3.2 Measuring stick Japan: the role of competition between factories at Company A U.S.

While the assembly division of B U.S. generated its standards for measuring efficiency primarily through internal comparison, the measuring stick for the assembly plants of A U.S. was set outside the company, at the level of the Japanese "world's leading factories." The model cases were thus considered to be, for instance, Toyota's plants Tsutsumi and Tahara, Mazda's Hofu plant, and Nissan's Zama plant. The interest of U.S. managers in comparison with European plants was small. Labor efficiency of European plants, also those in West Germany, was generally considered to be below that of their own comparable plants: "Our plants are more efficient. We have better methods, better job allocation, better tool allocation" (Manager "Controlling," River City).

The factory comparison with Japan was made easier for the company through its links with a Japanese company. On this basis, the industrial engineering department of the North American assembly division has engaged in an intensive "Japan watching" since the end of the 1970s.[16] Since 1978, extensive reports based on their own factory comparisons have been periodically released. The first of these reports over the differences in manpower requirements met with much skepticism. Later reports, though, corroborated these differences by analyzing each job microscopically, job element by job element, controlling for differences in the degree of mechanization, in the depth of vertical integration, in the process lay-out, etc. These reports finally overcame the skepticism of the divisional management and resulted in a shock which then sent its waves into the plants.

What it meant to use the Japanese factories as a measuring stick is shown in the following figures which are based on one of these factory comparisons, which we could see in the course of our investigation. The study was carried out in 1980. It shows that 2,000 vehicles were produced daily with a personnel volume of 3,300 workers in the Japanese plant; in the U.S. plant it was 3,900 workers who produced 1,120 vehicles. If this is converted into hours of work per car, thirteen and a half man-hours per vehicle were used in the Japanese plant and more than twenty-eight in the U.S. plant. The U.S. plant thus needed more than double the amount of work hours per car; at the same time this meant that the U.S. factory had to rely on twice the amount of personnel per shift to achieve a corresponding hourly output.

As table 7.3 shows, the two plants were hardly different in the personnel required for direct production in the strictest sense; here the difference was only 10 percent. Compared to this, the need for repair workers was about eight times as large as in the Japanese factory, the need for reliefmen about four times as large, and the personnel required to cover absenteeism around fourteen times as large. In addition, a major difference was found in the indirect area. The U.S. factory needed three times as many workers here. The main difference was in the area of quality control.

As we discussed in chapter 2, the productivity advantage of the Japanese production system has many societal, historical, and cultural prerequisites. Nevertheless, close comparison showed the mark which had to be achieved if the Western companies really wanted to "beat the Japanese." Of course this could not be achieved in one step, but in the eyes of divisional management, their own targets should be oriented to the personnel ratios of Japanese plants. By setting targets which could not be achieved by extrapolating the old practices, the plants were put under pressure to explore possibilities of either transferring Japanese management practices or developing functional equivalents to reach the same goal. This was the approach at the North American assembly division of Company A.

Here, the practice of setting rationalization targets was readjusted at the beginning of the 1980s. As opposed to the previous practice of extrapolating the targets yearly – on the basis of the past year, they were now attempting a "great leap forward" in view of the lessons from Japan. The prescribed increases in efficiency for the years 1983 to 1985 were more than 70 percent higher than the targets in the years before. Beyond this, also as a

Table 7.3 Comparison of the personnel requirements in "man-hours" in a U.S. and a Japanese assembly plant (body plant, paint shop, trim assembly, and final assembly), 1980

		U.S. plant (A)	Japanese plant (B)	Relation (A:B)
Direct workers	(a) Personnel required for production			
	direct labor	10.8	9.6	1.1
	relief	1.7	0.4	4.3
	repair	1.6	0.2	8.0
	(b) Absences because of			
	illness	2.7	0.2	13.5
	vacation (and the like)	1.7	0.3	5.7
	other absences	0.5	—	—
	Total direct	19.0	10.7	1.8
Indirect workers	(a) Personnel required for production			
	quality control	2.1	0.9	2.3
	maintenance	1.6	1.0	1.6
	material handling	1.9	0.8	2.4
	other workers	1.5	—	—
	(b) Total absences	1.9	0.1	19.1
	Total indirect	9.0	2.8	3.2
Total		28.0	13.5	2.1

conclusion from the Japan lesson, repair and inspection work was declared to be a special focus for reorganization and rationalization as we described in chapter 5.

Benchmarking with Japanese companies also spread more strongly at Company B in the second half of the 1980s and has joined the above described "efficiency league" system. It finally became a procedure which was discussed worldwide with the publication of the final report of the International Motor Vehicle Program (cf. Womack *et al.* 1990).

7.3.3 The British plants in the pillory of off-standards

In the British context, the problem of plant efficiency had an additional dimension. From the middle of the 1970s on up to the time of our study, the British plants were almost consistently "off-standards" with regard to the staffing levels authorized by the company headquarters. In addition, they almost systematically failed to achieve the daily production schedule. Thus, IE's ability to "objectively" determine personnel levels with regard to planned production schedules had apparently broken down.

Although British plants had shown high off-standards at least since the middle of the 1970s this situation only became readily apparent with the start of new vehicle programs in the middle of the 1980s. This involved the creation of structures of parallel production and, with them, a standard for comparison. The daily production schedule was not always achieved in the plants we studied in other countries either. There were also interruptions in production there which went beyond that which was reckoned with and resulted in the daily production schedule not being attained, either because of material shortages, technical troubles, or high absenteeism. These cases were exceptions, however. In a number of factories outside the U.K., in fact, the situation was rather that the daily production schedule could be easily exceeded, but that no more should be produced in order to avoid a sales glut.

Figure 7.1 shows the discrepancy which existed between the target and the production volume actually achieved in the British plant Hartmoor over the entire period which we studied. In this, as the figure shows, the production targets have been increasingly reduced compared to capacity since 1979. The diagram shows further that strikes (defined as walkouts by three or more employees lasting longer than fifteen minutes) come nowhere close to explaining this discrepancy, except in the strike year 1978.

Regardless of the reasons for not attaining the production target, the fact that they did not attain it placed British plants – local management as well as unions – in a difficult position when they brought their demands for an increased production volume, and thus increased employment for the

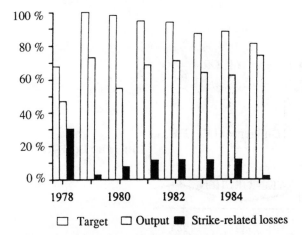

Figure 7.1 Production target, actual production and losses caused by strikes at a British plant, 1978–85 (as percent of capacity)

British sites. As long as they could not show that they could regularly keep to the daily production quota, they could hardly criticize the circumstance that the production volume allocated by the European headquarters to the British plants was still considerably below the sales volume for the corresponding vehicle in the British market. The European central management could always refer to the fact that the production schedule in U.K. could not be reliably set.

Figure 7.2 shows the direct and indirect production personnel necessary to manufacture one production unit (without salaried employees and controlling for the differing level of absenteeism) in three parallel plants of the same company producing largely the same product. One plant is in Great Britain, another in Germany, and the third in the U.S. The European plants are comparable to a great extent with regard to vertical integration and production facilities; the U.S. plant's vertical integration is lower – the integrated press shop found at the two European plants is lacking there.

The diagram shows the striking difference in personnel needed per unit of production. It also shows that the difference has become stabilized with regard to the new model starting at the beginning of the 1980s. The diagram shows, finally, how difficult it is for the British plant to reduce the productivity gap. After all, the number of production workers in the British plant was reduced by twelve per vehicle in the four year period between 1982 and 1985; compared to this, the continental plant was only able to achieve a relative personnel reduction of five. However, both plants have the same percentual increase in productivity – about 10 percent.

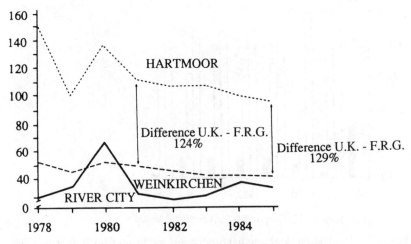

Figure 7.2 Hours of labor per production unit (workers as a whole)

Figure 7.2 illustrates the background for the unprecedented productivity campaign of the British plants. It was waged publicly by the company. In the Hartmoor plant, as described in chapter 4, the campaign had already begun in 1976. The comparison with the German plant acquired a greater significance with the launch of the new model and the establishment of parallel production in plants with largely the same process lay-out. The superior productivity of the German sister plant which, moreover, exported its products to the British market, was a challenge to the British work force. It appealed to their pride in their own workmanship and their national esteem. Management refuted the argument that the comparisons were not fair by inviting members of the work force and union representatives to travel to the German and other continental sister plants to get an idea of the differences for themselves. They could see their parallel work station and work there on a trial basis. At the same time, the industrial engineers carried out an exact matching of jobs between the plants with regard to time standards and work methods in order to transfer the better solutions wherever possible. Thus the "off-standards" for the area of direct production, which were still 90 percent in 1982, were reduced to 60 percent at the beginning of 1985. "Essentially what we did is to measure our efficiency levels on a detailed basis against Weinkirchen" (Production manager, Hartmoor).

The comparison with sister plants on the continent was also an everyday matter for Company B in Europe. It also increased in importance after the introduction of parallel production: "Now with roughly the same equipment and the same car it is more worthwhile to compare with Mittelort than before. We are continuously comparing and trying to find out what causes the variance" (Industrial engineer, Carborough). An industrial engineer in the Seaborough plant told us that they had previously had a model mix there, and when one area did poorly in a comparison they could argue with problems of the model mix. Now the comparability was greater. Not everybody was happy about this because former excuses for poor performance were not working any more. The "like for like comparison," as the IE experts called it, did not only limit itself to continental plants. "In our car-spectrum we are comparing data with every plant in the world, not just with Mittelort, also with Australian plants, and with plants in the United States" (Industrial engineer, Carborough).

The comparison with plants on the continent provoked two reactions from the work force, which we heard in both companies. On the one hand, they referred to the higher wage levels in the plants held up as examples: "With our present British pay don't expect me to perform at the American level. If you want the American level, pay us at the American wage rates" (Industrial engineer, Carborough). For IE managers, the close comparability with the continental European plants was thus occasionally seen as a two-edged sword, because it provided the unions with an argument for equal wages, too. Some managers also looked at continental or U.S. salaries not without envy. The second problem was that the credibility and fairness of the comparison was questioned by the unions and by the work force. It proved to be extraordinarily important for its credibility not to leave the practice and experience of comparison only to the IE experts. We were told in both companies that taking some of the lower-level supervisors into the German sister plant was especially successful:

This had a tremendous effect on their attitude. When they came back they were preaching our gospel about efficiency and time standards, whereas before you could get into continuous arguments with foremen. They very often took sides with the production man, arguing that they could not possibly perform at a certain pace or complete a certain task in a given time. This does not happen any more, or at least not to the extent it happened before. In this case we can often point to their experience at Mittelort: Remember what you saw at Mittelort? (Industrial engineer, Carborough)

At Hartmoor, workers were also involved to a large extent, so that they could get an impression for themselves of the working conditions and design of production in the continental plants. We will be returning to this later in chapter 9.

The pressure to improve their own plant performance which resulted from the factory comparison and the transfer of experience from sister plants were named as important factors by managers as they successfully reduced the efficiency gap in British plants at the beginning of the 1980s. The increased labor efficiency worked out to be a considerable cost advantage for the British plants. In turn, this was now being used by German managers as an argument to urgently consider increases in efficiency in their plants.

There was a further problem of benchmarking and competition between factories, which became especially apparent when one of the competing factories was dependent on the other. In the case of Mittelort and Seaborough, the German plant was a supplier of parts and components for the British plant to a considerable extent. Quality defects were quite a concern with components brought over from Germany: "These things cause quality problems, besides this they result in the fact that the people are occasionally totally frustrated. Thus it has happened that the seats were simply not capable of being installed any more. The workers started after a while to simply throw the seats into the cars. Naturally the workers were made responsible for the problems at first" (Personnel manager, Seaborough).

At the time of our investigation a group of workers in the plant in question was completely preoccupied with repair work on components which had been sent over from Germany and did not fit. One cause was seen in the incomplete or late information which came from Germany. They had the impression of being treated as a second class plant by the sister plant.

One reason for this (for problems with parts) is that changes are made in Germany without our engineers being informed of it. It thus happens that suddenly parts do not fit together any more. We sent a delegation to Germany a while ago in order to find out the reasons for such a case. It was then established that parts had been sent to us which had already been rejected by the German plant. Take the seats, for instance. When we put in seats we found out that the seats would not slide. Now everybody told us: Well, these seats slide at Mittelort: Why can't you make them work. It was suggested that this and that might be wrong. But even then the seats would not slide. Now when we went to Mittelort we found out that they were already using another slide. So we incurred another cost penalty. We found out that we were getting the information too late from Germany. (Manager, Seaborough)

This is one example of the fact that the growing integration of the production structures in companies which operate with parallel plants across Europe often leads to considerable tension between the sites – at the management level and in the work forces. The standardization, organizational and technological differences, and transnationality of the operative processes frequently offended nationally specific sensibilities. Overtones of national stereotypes and prejudices occasionally came up in our conversations.

7.3.4 "Thinking in terms of competition between factories is not as pronounced at our company": the case of Company C

At Company C we did not find any comparable methods and mechanisms for arousing competition between factories. "Thinking in terms of comparison and competition between factories is not as pronounced in our company. There is the competition in the plants between main departments and even between cost areas. But such a competition between plants does not take place" (Finance manager at the company headquarters). There were also performance reports at C and the cross-comparison according to plants for individual reference points. But these comparisons hardly had the function of competitive incentives and of generating the performance or rationalization targets which they had at companies A and B. "I do not think that the results of such studies have a large influence on decisions about investments and the awarding of contracts to the plants. These are political decisions. I do not know where performance criteria should play a role there" (Finance manager at company headquarters).

Although Company C too had the chance to more closely compare production methods and efficiency with Japanese plants in the framework of its joint projects with Japanese manufacturers, there were apparently no attempts to set up the measuring stick "Japan" through comparative studies and reports at the time of our research. In the course of our interviews at the factory level we observed neither particular fears nor expectations connected with factory comparisons, and a large question mark was placed behind the credibility of such comparisons:

But they can not do anything with comparisons because everyone cheats. One has to live with that. It is only important to see that there are no runaways. So it was in our earlier comparisons with (sister plant in Europe). (The sister plant) was once 400 DM less expensive, then we sat down and did some calculations and then we were 400 DM less expensive. There is no transparency. Exact controls are not possible on this point in large companies. They are also not necessarily desirable because they take away the creativity. (Manager of production planning at Company C Windeck)

In contrast to the situation at the other two companies, the parallel production between the plants, which also emerged as a pattern here, had only been minimally used for the purpose of an external performance regulator so far.

7.3.5 Comparison between factories and the fear of losing jobs

Comparing factories and arousing competition between them has, as we have seen, become an increasingly important instrument for regulating performance "from outside" in the course of the 1980s. The most highly perfected system for inner-organizational competition between factories was found at Company B in the U.S. and it already had a long tradition there. The benchmark was set here at the best-practice plants within the organization, i.e., within the U.S. assembly division. As opposed to this, Company A with its U.S. and European organizations had set the standards for comparison at the level of the world's best-practice plants in Japan. At Company C, factory comparison with the goal of arousing inter-organizational competition between factories played a much smaller role. This has changed in the years since our study, especially due to the research done by the IMVP.

The method of benchmarking as a means of performance regulation from the outside will, in our opinion, gain increased importance in the future. For the industrial engineers, the "guardians of Taylorism" who we frequently referred to in this chapter, this also opens up a new task area. Systematic information about the performance of the competitors inside and outside their own company will be required to achieve constant improvements. This information must be detailed, current, credible, and verifiable. It must be explained coherently. These are all new task areas for industrial engineers under post-Taylorist conditions.

The effectiveness of the information is, however, not ensured through credibility alone. The fear of losing sales and jobs are the most powerful levers for pushing through efficiency programs. At the time of our research this fear was heightened against the background of a generally high level of unemployment in all the countries studied. At the sites of the automobile factories, the unemployment rate was frequently even higher than the national average. These figures have generally grown further in the course of the 1980s; in structurally weak regions they were – on the basis of *official* statistics, as table 7.4 shows – up to almost 20 percent. In the U.S. the high point was reached in 1982, and the official unemployment figures had gone down by 1985.

It would be naive to believe that factory comparisons can remain untouched by the influence of interest and power positions. These have an influence on the indicators and methods of comparison itself. Interests and power positions also play a considerable role when conclusions have to be drawn from factory comparisons. It is by no means settled that the factories which do the best in the comparison have to worry the least about the future of their site. Such decisions for the future, as we were told frequently by representatives of local management, are subject in the end to "political" assessments of the expected reactions of the consumers, the unions, and the government in the country affected. The degree of uncertainty over the future of their own site thus does not clearly correlate with its position in the

Table 7.4 *Unemployment rates at selected automobile sites in the U.S.A., Great Britain, and the Federal Republic of Germany, 1980 and 1985*

Site (city/district) of:	1980	1985
Greentown	11.9	11.3
Northtown	13.0	7.2
Hartmoor	14.9	21.0
Seaborough	9.9	13.4
Windeck	7.3	19.9
Mittelort	6.0	15.1
Weinkirchen	6.6	15.4

Sources: U.S. Department of Labor; Department of Employment Gazette; different issues of the Science Center Berlin's "Regionaldatenbank Arbeitsmarkt" (Regional data bank: Employment Market).

comparison between factories. Fears about the future of their own site and fear of losing their jobs were, if we look at the statements of local management and union representatives in the factories studied, just about the same everywhere.

7.4 Conclusions

Let us return to our opening question. This was: what could prompt the powerful institutions and agents of the Fordist–Taylorist production philosophy in the factories to give new forms of work a chance, this in light of the implied contradiction between industrial engineering and employee involvement. In the course of the account in this chapter we have seen at different points how impetus for various changes in the forms of regulation have emerged from the problems of securing efficiency and regulating performance themselves. It was often the industrial engineering staffs themselves who undertook initiatives in the NW&M direction. Even if tensions in the relationship between EI and IE can surely be foreseen for the future, for the period of our investigation we can rather speak of the development of a reciprocal functionalization: industrial engineering saw in the new forms of work opportunities to extract performance potentials from the work force which would otherwise have remained untapped; an example here are the problems with production flexibility – employee involvement required that management experts would provide information and advise problem-solving attempts on the shop floor.

Paradoxically, this development was initiated by a strengthening of the IE position. The weakening of militant union positions in the British and U.S. plants through the depressed situation in the industry in these countries at the beginning of the 1980s and the fear of plant closings has increased the scope of action for IE in the traditional sense. Industrial engineers could again enter areas of the plants where they previously dared not be seen. Nevertheless, industrial engineering's virtual retreat from the shop floor and out of the arena of industrial relations was initiated in this period. The goal was less and less to wring time standards from the workers in a direct confrontation, but with the help of handbooks to determine them in the period of production planning, and to "embed them" into the structures and into the design of the production flow and its technology. This retreat on the part of industrial engineering from the shop floor was by no means complete at the time of our study, and this was also true up until the beginning of the 1990s. There are also nationally specific differences here as we described in section one.

The change in the problems dealt with by industrial engineering, which we have described in the second section (the increased importance of job design due to the changed composition of the production work forces, the increased demands for flexibility in production and personnel deployment, the changed conditions for performance regulation in the mechanized areas), frequently trigger ideas in practice which lead to new forms of work. At the time of our research it was too early to study the practice of performance regulation in group work plants and we still find little literature on this. It is surely no coincidence that we have met with concepts of group work at many points in the factories, but have found little with regard to practical realization of such concepts. This realization would have meant that the representatives of the traditional philosophy of control would have to show their ability to adapt and many plants still tremble at the thought of this leap today.

8 Comparative achievements in labor productivity and changes in personnel structures: trends and development patterns

In this chapter we present an analysis of our quantitative data in a factory comparison. The data include the development in labor productivity in the plants of our core sample and the changes in the personnel structure in these plants for the period between 1978 and 1985. These data reflect to a certain extent the effectiveness of the measures and developments described in the preceding chapters.

We will first show the differences and trends in labor productivity in our factory sample. The comparison shows typical nationally and company-specific influences which we will examine more closely using specific examples. In the second part we will be dealing with quantitative developments in the structure of the production work force. Here we will be looking for trends and differences in the ratio between direct and indirect tasks and then look more closely at the development of individual worker categories.

8.1 Differences and trends in labor productivity

There were great differences in the levels and trends in productivity at the factories we investigated. This will become clear in the following diagrams. They are based on time series data for the employment level (per employee category) on a fixed day each year and the aggregate yearly output of cars per plant.[1] The disparities in the levels and trends of productivity between the factories which are shown in these data cannot be attributed to differences in labor productivity alone. Some plants differ significantly with regard to their degree of vertical integration in production, i.e., to the extent which they rely on parts and sub-assemblies from outside the plant; there are also differences in the labor content of the products. But, as we have chosen plants with the same or a similar product, such features cannot account for the more fundamental differences based on national and company-specific factors. In view of the developmental trend in the industry, changes in the vertical integration and the enrichment of the

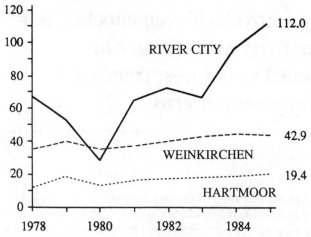

Figure 8.1 Number of vehicles per worker in three parallel Company A plants

model mix with upgraded models and equipment variants could come into play, though, and overshadow increases in productivity (see Hayes and Clark 1985; Flynn 1985; Norsworthy and Zabala 1985; Mayer 1983).

A more comprehensive and systematic comparison of assembly plants was made in the framework of MIT's "International Motor Vehicle Program" in the second half of the 1980s. (Womack *et al.* 1990, p. 84ff.). The information collected in this study of assembly plants allowed a much more accurate standardized comparison than our investigation. But this comparison only applied to one point in time.[2] On the basis of our longer time series we can show, however, that because of the strong fluctuations and shifts in the level of productivity in the same plant over a period of several years, a mere comparison of productivity levels at a certain point in time could be misleading. We are more interested in the pattern of development and the relative changes in the levels of labor productivity.

Figure 8.1 shows the development in the yearly number of vehicles per worker for three parallel plants of Company A located in the U.S., Great Britain, and the Federal Republic of Germany. The U.S. plant had a lower degree of vertical integration than the others (there was no stamping plant on the site), which explains a part of the difference. The British and German plants, on the other hand, were quite similar with regard to vertical integration and production technology.

In spite of the close "relationship" between the three factories, figure 8.1 emphasizes rather the differences:

There was a 100 percent difference in the productivity levels of the German plant and British factories. A large gap had also opened up

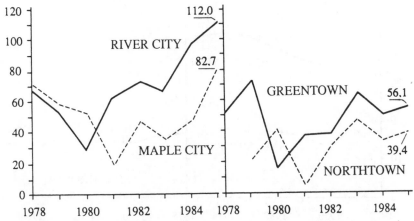

Figure 8.2 Number of vehicles per worker in each of two parallel plants of Company A and B in North America

between the German plant and the U.S. plant since 1983, although the differences were only small up until then (taking the lower vertical integration of the U.S. plant into account).

Whereas development appears to have proceeded steadily over the years in the British and the German plants, the American plant was characterized by furious ups and downs; the enormous upswing starting in 1983 can be traced back to overtime work which had attained a spectacular level here as well as in the company's other American assembly plants. The large productivity gains in the American plant overshadow the increases in both European plants though, which were also quite significant: the number of vehicles per worker increased in the British plant by 46 percent from 1980 to 1985, in the German plant by 28 percent.

The reorganizations in connection with the model change in 1980 brought about a decline in productivity in all three plants. The corresponding break in the American plant was much deeper than in the European plants, however.

Figure 8.2 shows the same development with a comparison between two pairs of plants – Company A's River City and Maple City plants and Company B's Greentown and Northtown plants in the U.S.

All factories in the spectrum of this comparison had a similar degree of vertical integration. Beyond this, they all produced a similar product – it was the same product in the comparison between the twin plants of the same company. The model mix differed between the plants of A though; Maple City was more heavily burdened by the mix of types and models. In

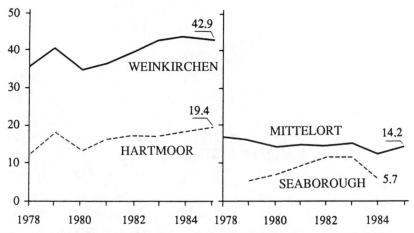

Figure 8.3 Vehicles per worker in parallel Company A and B plants in Great Britain and Germany

the case of the two B plants there was also a difference: greater investments in new technology were made at Northtown in the course of the change-over in 1981 – but, as the diagram shows, without a corresponding personnel saving effect.

The following conclusions can be drawn:

Despite the differences between the parallel plants, the pattern of development indicates a close "family" relationship;

the four plants were similar with regard to their erratic profiles and with regard to the number of vehicles per worker before and after the change-over; a strong divergence first came when Company A's plants started to pull away in 1984.

Figure 8.3 shows the development in parallel plants at Company A and B, located in Great Britain and West Germany respectively. These are the same Company A factories as in figure 8.1. Comparing the employment level of the Company A and Company B plants in this diagram would not indicate much as the differing degrees of vertical integration must be taken into account. In comparing the development in the British and German Company B plants, the fact that the British plant reduced its vertical integration considerably in the period we looked at must also be taken into account.

From this we can conclude:

While the pattern of development in the sister plants at Company A was for the most part parallel, the increase in the level achieved at the British plant Seaborough to bring the number of vehicles produced per

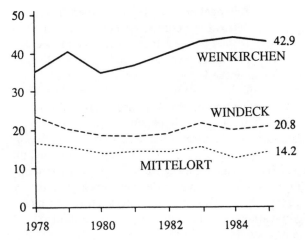

Figure 8.4 Vehicles per worker in three German plants of three different companies

worker up to that of the German plant became quite visible (an increase of 118 percent from 1979 to 1983).

The model change-overs in 1984 led to a significantly greater decline at the British plant Seaborough than in the sister plant Mittelort.

In figure 8.4 we have shown the development of our indicator for the three German plants. Differences in the product must also be taken into account. In the case of Windeck, the product design required more labor hours. The plants also exhibited considerable differences in their vertical integration, this time the other way around: while Windeck was a pure assembly plant without a stamping plant, a stamping plant was also on site at Weinkirchen. Mittelort had a stamping plant as well as comprehensive parts production.

The diagram shows:

Whereas the productivity at Windeck and Mittelort remained largely stable, there was an increase in the level at Weinkirchen starting in 1980 which extended over a four-year period. This was evidently a result of well-directed rationalization measures at the beginning of the 1980s.

The model changes in Weinkirchen (1980) and Mittelort (1984) did not cause such large declines as in the U.S. or British plants.

Table 8.1 contains the productivity data in a slightly different form. It shows the number of workers (referring to a fixed day of the respective year) per 1,000 cars (referring to the yearly production of the respective factory) and the personnel development in the plants (1978 = 100). In the last column we have calculated the changes between 1978 and 1985. These two years appear to us to be best suited for a comparison of the productivity achievements in the plants. This is because these years encompassed a period characterized by very different downward trends in the individual site countries at the beginning of the 1980s as shown in chapter 2.

A close look at the rate of change shows that the three plants from Company A exhibited the largest improvements in productivity during the period we studied. This went along with personnel reduction in the American and British factories, whereas the employment level only changed slightly in the German factories. In both Company B plants the workers needed per car increased, while the number of workers hardly changed. In Company C's Windeck plant the personnel needed also increased with respect to output; this is also the only factory in which a considerable increase in workers took place in the period we studied.

On the whole it can be concluded that:

1 We found enormous differences in the productivity level between factories. We have to take into account the fact that the comparison was not strictly standardized. But the differences we found cannot be explained by differences in the product or by vertical integration. With regard to the differences in the productivity level, the diagrams at least lend plausibility to the hypothesis that nationally specific influences are especially important in this respect.

2 The majority of the developmental patterns in the factories shown in figures 8.1 to 8.4 indicate considerable improvements in productivity in the period studied. The patterns of development at twin factories from the same company show a high degree of similarity. It is apparent that company-specific influences assert themselves especially strongly here, presumably as does the influence of the benchmarking and competition between plants which was discussed in chapter 7.

Differences in the temporal availability of personnel, i.e., the numbers of hours per year in which the employee is actually present at the work place and available for the work process, explain a significant part of the productivity differentials. Here, we have clearly nationally specific patterns of influence. A high rate of absenteeism due to illness, vacation, and reduction of the work week goes along with the German pattern of labor policy and can also be seen in our data. According to our calculations and estimations, the personnel availability, calculated per employee with regard to absences and vacations, was around 20 percent higher in River City than in Windeck; if we include days of extra work and overtime, then the availability in the U.S. plant, e.g., in 1985, was (depending on the basis of our estimation) between around 30 percent and over 40 percent higher than in the German plant. With this we can explain about a third of the

Table 8.1 *Productivity and personnel development in selected assembly plants (total blue-collar workers per 1,000 cars), 1978–85*

	1978	1979	1980	1981	1982	1983	1984	1985	Increase/decrease 1985 versus 1978
River City									
(a)	15.0	19.0	36.4	15.7	13.8	15.3	10.3	8.9	−41%
(b)	100	92	105	93	81	79	75	73	−27%
Greentown									
(a)	16.4	19.4	13.7	66.5	27.0	26.5	15.4	20.3	+23.5%
(b)	100	118	103	117	115	92	99	96	−4%
Hartmoor									
(a)	83.7	53.9	74.2	60.8	57.7	58.2	54.1	51.6	−38.4%
(b)	100	101	100	98	96	86	79	73	−27%
Weinkirchen									
(a)	28.4	24.7	28.8	27.1	25.0	23.3	22.8	23.3	−17.8%
(b)	100	102	110	111	107	107	103	103	+3%
Mittelort									
(a)	59.3	62.6	70.8	67.6	68.5	63.8	80.3	70.4	+18.6%
(b)	100	97	105	99	99	96	96	97	−3%
Windeck									
(a)	42.4	49.0	53.1	54.3	52.8	45.7	50.8	48.1	+13.4%
(b)	100	109	106	121	123	119	121	121	+21%

Notes:
(a) Number of workers per 1,000 cars.
(b) Level of employment (1978 = 100).

Table 8.2 *Lost days (per worker) as a yearly average according to selected criteria in a U.S., a British, and a German assembly plant, 1980–4*

	River City	Hartmoor	Windeck
Lost days because of:			
illness, vacation, working less than			
40 hr/week	25	15	40
strikes	—	7	2
closings because of change-overs			
and demand	33	—	3
Extra days worked	12	n.a.	4
Lost days minus extra days	46	22	41

Source: Company data, own calculations and estimates.

difference in the amount of vehicles per worker in 1985. The remaining difference was probably due to differences in the product, the model mix, and labor efficiency.

Over a period of several years, however, we see a much different picture on the question of availability of the contracted labor. Here, typical restrictions become evident in each of the three countries. The principle of "hire and fire" in the U.S. plants led to the workers being laid off for many days in the year due to the demand situation or because of technological and organizational change-overs. In Britain the absences were less but a considerable part of the yearly work time was lost through work conflicts – strikes, lock-outs, etc. Table 8.2 was based on our calculations and estimates regarding the number of days lost due to absences, labor conflicts, and plant closings due to model changes or slow sales, on a factory average between 1980 and 1984.

The balance of lost work days over the aggregate of days worked overtime was, as a yearly average, about the same in River City as in Windeck, with over forty lost days in each case; the balance in the British plant Hartmoor was lower, even including the strike days. "Hire and fire" (U.S.), illness/vacation/reduction of the work week (West Germany), and strikes (Great Britain) were thus functional equivalents to a certain extent in explaining the restrictions on the workers' availability for work in the three countries studied. But these "functional equivalents" make a great difference when it comes to work satisfaction and the quality of worklife, as days lost through strikes or lay-offs have a different effect on the workers' motivation than days spent recuperating from illnesses or taking vacations. This equivalence relation could change, however, because the weight of the factors behind the lost days is changing. Thus, as we have shown, the companies at the North American location have begun to soften the "hire and fire" policy in favor of a policy of personnel continuity. A clear decline in labor conflicts in the British plants could also be noticed since the beginning of the 1980s. At the same time, Germany faced a further shortening of the working week at the beginning of the 1990s and in 1995 the regular working time per week will become thirty-five hours in the West German metalworking industries. This could bring about a situation – considering the much lower wage level of the British plants – whereby the German companies would face stronger pressure to adjust in terms of costs and productivity in the future.

8.2 Shifting proportions between the direct and indirect areas

8.2.1 Changes in the structure of personnel in direct production

Direct production personnel were, as we have seen, the traditional focus for rationalization attempts in the factory. Measures of mechanization were also aimed primarily at direct production while allowing the relative, and frequently also absolute, share of indirect production personnel to increase. The pressure for efficiency and rationalization of the direct labor areas had, as we have seen, intensified since the beginning of the 1980s in all of the factories studied. The rationalization targets had to be achieved in spite of inefficiencies due to model-mix development and the increased labor content per vehicle, on the one hand, and the trend toward transferring indirect tasks back to direct production, on the other hand.

Table 8.3 shows the development of direct production personnel in selected assembly plants for the period from 1978 to 1985 by means of two indicators: the number of direct production personnel per 1,000 cars produced yearly, and the increase (or decrease) of this personnel compared to the base year 1978. The enormous differences in staffing levels between the plants also become clear here. The most severe personnel reduction in the direct area, seen absolutely, was at the British plant in Hartmoor – by around one third of the direct production personnel. The two North American factories had also reduced direct production personnel. As opposed to this, one can see a significant increase in direct production personnel at the German Weinkirchen and Windeck plants.[3] The increase in personnel needed in the direct area (per 1,000 cars produced yearly) at River City is characterized to a great extent by the lengthening of working time. If we take the year 1983, when overtime was not quite so prevalent, we find a level almost equal to 1978; the personnel level also remains pretty much the same at Weinkirchen. The sharp productivity increase at

Hartmoor came largely from the working time lost due to strikes in 1978; if 1979 is considered a "normal year" there was a growth of about 12 percent over a seven year period. The personnel needed at Greentown and Windeck was at the same level in 1979 and 1985.

The technical and organizational changes did not, however, mean a general reduction in the need for direct production personnel. In relative terms, the need for direct production personnel in the plants we investigated generally remained at the same level during the period examined. There have been considerable changes in the personnel structure in the direct area, however, as we will see in the following.

The overview chart (table 8.4), differentiates six groups of direct production personnel. The chart also contains some examples of the main tasks for each group and gives some of the most important influences on the amounts and types of work requirements in each case. We have attempted to give ranges and estimated dimensions of the relative share of these groups out of the total amount of direct personnel and their tendency toward changing. Finally, we have given the most important innovative concepts and measures for labor deployment which affect this tendency.

The volume of production personnel determined directly by standard time setting (category 1 in table 8.4) only makes up about 60 percent of the total direct production personnel. We have differentiated the category of "standard personnel" further, distinguishing the additional personnel necessitated by the model mix from the regular standard personnel. According to this, the base standard employment level is determined principally by the determination of standards by industrial engineering (and, of course, by the foregoing decisions with regard to product design, production planning, degree of mechanization, and production layout). The employment volume made up by this category of direct productive personnel was generally declining. This was above all due to measures of product and production technology, but also came through as an increase in industrial engineering's ability to assert itself, which contributed significantly to personnel reduction in some plants. This had its limits, however, in a given product and production technology. The innovative concepts for the employee category 1 were above all in the area of product and process planning, and in the increased participation of direct production in production lay-out and work design.

As opposed to the basic standard personnel, the additional personnel necessitated by the model mix (category 2) was growing. When compared to the personnel volume in the direct area of the factory as a whole, a large degree of compensation for the personnel savings in category 1 can be seen in the build-up in group 2. When looking at individual production areas, the picture is different. Although the wave of mechanization at the

Table 8.3 *Development of direct production personnel in selected assembly plants, 1978–85*

	1978	1979	1980	1981	1982	1983	1984	1985	Increase/decrease 1985 versus 1978
River City									
(a)	10.3	13.4	26.5	11.4	9.8	10.9	7.9	6.8	−34%
(b)	100	96	112	99	91	88	84	81	−19%
Greentown									
(a)	13.4	16.1	10.8	54.9	22.3	21.1	12.5	16.2	+21%
(b)	100	120	99	119	117	89	98	94	−6%
Hartmoor									
(a)	54.1	43.6	46.6	37.6	35.5	35.5	32.0	30.5	−44%
(b)	100	100	98	95	91	80	72	67	−33%
Weinkirchen									
(a)	17.0	14.4	17.7	17.1	17.1	16.2	16.0	16.3	−4%
(b)	100	99	113	117	122	124	121	120	+20%
Windeck									
(a)	30.1	35.8	39.3	41.7	39.3	34.3	38.2	35.6	+19%
(b)	100	112	110	130	129	126	128	127	−27%

Notes:
(a) Number of workers per 1,000 cars.
(b) Level of employment (1978 = 100).

Table 8.4 *Structure, determination, and developmental tendencies of the personnel in direct production*

Sub-groups	Basic standard personnel (1)	Additional personnel for model mix (2)	Additional personnel for breaks (3)	Additional personnel for repair work and quality control (4)	Additional personnel for training tasks (5)	Additional personnel created by NW&M measures (6)
% of pers.	60%	15%	1–10%	5–10%	0–3%	0–2%
Term for function	Assembler, welder	(like 1)	Reliefman	Repair worker, quality upgrade worker	Trainer, utility man, kolonnenführer	Quality upgrade operator group leader/team leader Anlagenführer
Determining factors for the number and content of jobs	Product and process design (technology, layout); work organization work studies (IE)	Market situation and sales strategy	Factory break routine, rules concerning allocation of relief men	Quality control system, supplier relations	Personnel fluctuation; mobility/job rotation within the factory; measures for qualification	New forms of work; new production concepts
Main determining dept. or function	Production planning, industrial engineering	Production control, IE, production supervisors	Collective agreements, works councils/shop committees; production depts.	Quality control; material and production control; production	Production; personnel	Organisational development; corporate strategy

Innovative concepts	Integration of product and process planning/mixed planning teams/ integration of technology and job design	Computer based information and production control systems; module production; team formation	Change from individual to collective break	Total quality management; self-inspection; integration of inspection and repair	Integration of direct and indirect labor in the course of new job descriptions; formation of production teams

Increased input of the production department in production planning and job design (e.g., quality circle) beginning of the 1980s with its focus on welding technology in the body plants had reduced the production time per unit and the labor input in the paint shop, the areas of trim and final assembly had gained in labor input. The reason for this is, as we have seen in chapter 7, primarily the growth of the model mix. The difference between the two groups, base standard personnel and additional personnel necessitated by the model mix, is not one of function and job content. These remain the same. The additional personnel need arises through increased walking and waiting times, as well as through cycle losses and other inefficiencies which come from unforeseen fluctuations in labor requirements.

The base standard personnel and additional personnel necessitated by the model mix are, so to speak, the immediate "clientèle" of the industrial engineering departments and the starting point for all efficiency analyses and reporting systems. The work studies were traditionally concentrated on these groups. These were the activities which were directly subject to the production rhythm of the assembly line, the machines, and the work organization. Industrial engineering's control in the factory was weaker, though, with respect to the additional requirements necessitated by the model mix than with respect to the "base standard personnel". This was also expressed in the fact that the provisional times for group (1) were generally set at the central level. For group (2), on the other hand, the factories only received allowances from control staff.

All remaining categories of direct production personnel were based on such allowances as were authorized by the central or factory management. Thus the relief-time allowance authorizes extra personnel (3), who come in to allow workers to take their breaks without interrupting production. This personnel supplement to the "hard core" was the most important reserve of flexibility in the traditional production organization. This had several reasons:

> The position of reliefman represents one of the few possibilities for promotion for the "ordinary" workers in direct production;
> the reliefmen have to be qualified to carry out all tasks in their work area and thus represent a flexible labor reserve;
> as breaks are not required at all times in a shift the reliefmen can be at the "particular disposal" of the lower-level line supervisors for special tasks, especially at the beginning of a shift;
> the reliefmen can fill vacancies or break in workers to allow for job rotation and on-the-job training;
> finally, the personnel volume represented by the group of reliefman itself forms a flexibility reserve for situations with an unexpectedly high rate of absenteeism or an unexpectedly heavy workload. This reserve can be tapped by changing the break routine and temporarily going over from individual breaks ("tag relief") to a collective break ("mass

Table 8.5 *Forms of break-taking in selected factories*

Factory	River City	Greentown	Hartmoor	Seaborough	Weinkirchen	Mittelort	Windeck
Paid breaks per shift (in minutes)	48 IB	46 CB	40 CB/ 15 IB	20 CB/ 24 IB	34 CB	26 CB/ 13 IB	64 CB

Notes:
CB = collective break.
IB = individual break (with reliefman).

relief" or "shut-down relief"). When production is interrupted for a collective break the group of reliefmen becomes redundant and can be used for other tasks.

This flexibility was not found in all of the factories. Company strategies and industrial relations come together in this area so that a very diverse picture appears with regard to the use of reliefmen (see table 8.5).

Company B's factories in the U.S.A. generally had collective breaks since the beginning of the 1980s, while individual breaks were the rule at Company A. We found mixed systems of collective and individual breaks in the British plants. The collective break predominates in the German plants. The possibility of a short term change to individual breaks had been negotiated at Windeck and, incidentally, the longest paid break time was found here. On the question of collective versus individual break arrangements, aspects of employment security, capacity, and quality control come together. The transition to a collective break routine means capacity losses for the moment. This can be desirable or undesirable, depending on the company's volume of orders. The decision in favor of individual breaks, and thus the system of reliefmen, at A U.S. can be explained by the tighter capacity situation of this company. Employment protection was also involved due to the fact that the abolition of the reliefmen would do away with a desirable position for advancement in production; in the U.S. context this would also mean laying off personnel. (These were not the reliefmen themselves, but rather those on the bottom end of the seniority chain whose jobs were taken over by the reliefmen.) A further problem follows from the effects of the changed break routine on product quality. Management in the factories in which the change to collective breaks was carried out had observed a noticeable improvement in quality. The increased stability at the work place led to a reduction in the number of mistakes. A Company B representative connected a 20 to 25 percent increase in quality with the transition to collective breaks (Ward's Automotive Review, No. 62, December 22, 1986, p. 404).

As a whole, there was a clear trend in our factory sample toward reducing or largely doing away with the group of reliefmen. With this, we would see the disappearance of a significant flexibility reserve of the traditional factory organization.

The second large traditional group of additional personnel in the direct production area are the repair workers (4). The required personnel volume here is determined by the organization of quality control, the systems of material supply, the quality of parts, and by work practices and care in production as well. The tasks performed by the repair workers are not direct production tasks in the strictest sense. To reduce the number of repair workers and quality inspectors (only the latter are generally considered to be indirect productive personnel) was at the center of the strategies for job integration as we have seen in chapter 5. The proportion of repair workers in direct "standard personnel" shows a declining tendency: on the one hand, due to the extent to which company programs and goals oriented toward Japan are pushed further, and, on the other hand, due to increased mechanization and changes in product technology. As a whole, reduction could be expected in this group of direct production personnel, which still made up an average of 10 to 20 percent of the standard personnel in the factories we studied and we do not see a drastic decrease in more recent years here. The decline was toned down at the time of research, if not temporarily compensated for, by measures for integrating repair work with quality control tasks. Thus the quantitative importance of the second traditional possibility for advancement by the direct "standard personnel" was also being reduced. This was an activity which was less line-paced and repetitive, and offered a greater "time-sovereignty" to the worker.

The third category of additional personnel in the traditional factory context are represented by the trainers utilitymen, "Kolonnenführer," etc. (5). These jobs are frequently now being redefined and used as starting points for the job descriptions given under (6). As a whole, the three categories of additional personnel, the reliefmen, the repair workers and the traditional group leaders, form a recruitment base for these new jobs in production in all countries due to their high transfer mobility and production experience.

The personnel for new tasks in direct production (6) has played a quantitatively small role up to now. These are generally new combinations of previous direct jobs with indirect production tasks:

the integration of quality inspection and repair work to the "detect and correct" (e.g. "Kontroll-fertigmacher") jobs,

the integration of the jobs of machine supervision and servicing with some maintenance tasks to the position of "automated systems controller" ("Anlagenführer"),

jobs with partial management and disposition tasks in small groups in the case of the "Kolonnenführer," group leaders, etc.

Table 8.6 *"Anlagenführer" and similar jobs[a] in production in the body shop of selected German assembly plants*

Factory		Number	Share of "Anlagenführer" on the total direct production personnel
Windeck	(1986)	24	2.5%
	(1988 planned)	74	19.0%
Weinkirchen	(1985 planned)	n.a.	10.0%
Südstetten[b]	(1987)	104	34.0%

Notes:
[a] "Straßenführer," "Anlagenbediener," "Kolonnenführer."
[b] Südstetten is an assembly plant from a company not included in our core sample.

The new job descriptions, e.g., that of "Anlagenführer," which show an integration of skilled work and production tasks and are generally filled by skilled workers, are at the center of a debate over reprofessionalization of production work which is being intensely fought out in West Germany. A critical argument referred to the very small number of corresponding new positions. As table 8.6 shows, this quantitative argument no longer holds true for individual German companies and their change-overs starting at the middle of the 1980s.[4] According to more recent investigations of the "Soziologischen Forschungsinstitut Göttingen" (SOFI) the number of *Anlagenführer* (called "*Systemregulierer*" here) at the German automobile manufacturers at the beginning of the 1990s was 8 percent – with considerable variance in the different production areas: in the press shops, the share of automated systems controllers was 26 percent; in parts machining shops 28 percent; in body and paint shops 6 percent, and in final assembly areas only 1 percent of the productive work force. (Schumann *et al.* 1992; p. 179)

8.2.2 Change in the personnel structure within the area of indirect production

Table 8.7 shows the development of the indirect production personnel in selected assembly plants of our core sample.

On the basis of this data we want to make two observations:
1 The development in the factories of Company A deviates sharply at all three locations from that in the other factories. A reduction in indirect production personnel can be established, relative to output as well as absolute with reference to the base year 1978, and this reduction exceeds

Table 8.7 Development of indirect production personnel in selected assembly plants, 1978–85

	1978	1979	1980	1981	1982	1983	1984	1985	Increase/decrease 1985 versus 1978
River City									
(a)	4.8	5.6	9.9	4.3	3.3	3.7	2.4	2.2	−55%
(b)	100	85	90	80	61	60	56	55	−45%
Greentown									
(a)	3.0	3.3	2.9	11.7	4.8	5.4	2.9	4.1	+35%
(b)	100	109	118	111	110	101	100	105	+5%
Hartmoor									
(a)	29.6	19.3	27.6	23.2	22.5	22.8	22.0	21.0	−29%
(b)	100	102	105	104	104	97	91	84	−16%
Weinkirchen									
(a)	11.4	10.2	11.1	10.0	8.0	7.2	6.8	7.0	−39%
(b)	100	105	105	101	85	82	77	77	−23%
Windeck									
(a)	12.3	13.2	13.8	12.6	13.5	11.4	12.6	12.7	+3%
(b)	100	101	95	96	108	103	103	103	+3%

Notes:
(a) Number of workers per 1,000 cars.
(b) Level of employment (1978 = 100).

– with the exception of the British plant Hartmoor – the reduction in direct production personnel (see table 8.3).

2 In contrast to this, the indirect production personnel grew, relative and absolute, in the plants of B and C; the increase compared to the direct production personnel is overproportional at B, and underproportional at C, where the indirect production personnel remained almost constant in the period examined.

Table 8.8 shows the development of personnel for quality inspections which we examined in detail in chapter 5. The observation we made there of a special development in the factories of Company A is confirmed here. Quality inspection, as an indirect productive activity, was drastically reduced in all factories of this company in the period examined, most strongly in the German plant, but almost as drastically in the British and U.S. plants. This holds true absolutely, as well as relative to the number of quality inspectors per vehicle.

The number of quality inspectors as an indirect job group was also reduced in the Greentown and Windeck plants, although not as drastically; in contrast to this, one can see a slight increase here when measured per vehicle. One should note, however, that the line inspection at Company B was already partially counted as direct production, and thus the starting level was lower here. When we compare the other plants for the year 1983 (in order to exclude the effect of overtime at River City), it can be seen that the number of quality inspectors per vehicle was lowest in the German plant, at one inspector per 1,000 vehicles. In relative terms, the U.S. sister plant needed about 50 percent more quality inspectors per vehicle of yearly production, the British sister plant four times as many.

Differences also appear in a comparison of the skilled workers assigned to the indirect area, i.e., mainly to the maintenance departments. Table 8.9 shows the number of skilled workers in the maintenance departments of some assembly plants. The number of skilled workers per vehicle differs significantly without a specific company profile becoming apparent. River City had, with a relation of 1.2 skilled workers per 1,000 cars, the lowest share of skilled workers; Greentown was more than 50 percent above this; the German plant Windeck used exactly double the number of skilled workers per car. (We are not counting the skilled worker deployed at non-skilled jobs here.) River City's German and British sister plants used (with a greater vertical integration) 1.5 times as many or – in the case of the British plant – more than five times as many skilled workers per vehicle.

As table 8.9 shows, there can be no talk of a general tendency toward increasing the share of skilled workers in the course of the modernization of factories. The table shows that the technological modernization of individual sections of production did not mean an increase in the skilled worker

Table 8.8 Development of quality inspection personnel in selected assembly plants, 1978–85

	1978	1979	1980	1981	1982	1983	1984	1985	Increase/decrease 1985 versus 1978
River City									
(a)	1.54	1.76	3.51	1.52	1.30	1.38	0.85	0.74	−52%
(b)	100	83	99	88	75	70	61	59	−41%
Greentown									
(a)	1.08	1.19	0.91	4.07	1.22	1.50	0.91	1.16	+8%
(b)	100	110	104	109	79	79	89	83	−17%
Hartmoor									
(a)	6.22	4.06	5.56	4.57	4.12	4.23	3.68	3.46	−44%
(b)	100	102	101	99	92	84	72	66	−34%
Weinkirchen									
(a)	2.16	1.87	1.95	1.76	1.31	1.04	0.94	0.96	−56%
(b)	100	101	98	95	73	63	56	56	−44%
Windeck									
(a)	2.99	3.10	3.21	3.09	3.42	2.82	2.92	3.04	+2%
(b)	100	98	91	97	113	104	98	97	−3%

Notes:
(a) Number of workers per 1,000 cars.
(b) Level of employment (1978 = 100).

Table 8.9 Development in the number of skilled workers in the indirect area in selected assembly plants, 1978–85

	1978	1979	1980	1981	1982	1983	1984	1985	Increase/decrease 1985 versus 1978
River City									
(a)	0.84	1.20	2.07	1.01	0.97	1.19	0.84	0.76	−10%
(b)	100	104	107	106	101	110	109	110	+10%
Greentown									
(a)	1.04	1.29	1.31	4.42	1.91	1.90	1.21*	1.91*	+83%
(b)	100	123	154	122	128	103	123*	143*	+42%
Hartmoor									
(a)	7.70	5.17	7.59	6.54	6.29	6.78	6.77	6.68	−13%
(b)	100	105	112	115	113	109	107	103	+3%
Weinkirchen									
(a)	3.04	2.78	3.01	2.86	2.62	2.39	2.39	2.46	−19%
(b)	100	107	107	109	104	103	101	101	+1%
Windeck									
(a)	3.35	2.64	3.45	3.29	3.61	3.08	3.38	3.14	−7%
(b)	100	74	87	92	106	101	101	100	0%

Notes:
(a) Number of workers per 1,000 cars.
(b) Level of employment (1978 = 100).
* Values estimated through interpolation with data for 1986/7.

share in the factory as a whole. In the British plants and in the two German plants, the number of skilled workers in the skilled labor departments stagnated; it went down with reference to vehicle output. In the River City the number of skilled workers grew by 10 percent over the seven year period; the use of skilled workers went down relative to the vehicle output. A clear strategy can only be recognized at Greentown: compared to 1978, the number of skilled workers increased by over 40 percent, with reference to the vehicle output by over 80 percent. This peculiarity of Company B U.S. was also confirmed, as we will see in chapter 9, in the area of initial vocational training for skilled workers.

In looking for the driving forces and determining factors for the development in the area of indirect labor the same influences emerge as in the direct area. A characteristic feature of the situation in the 1980s was that the dividing line between the direct and indirect job areas was in a state of flux. A share of the indirect jobs was "descending" into the area of direct productive tasks, and that required new solutions for work organization. At the same time, the relation of indirect to direct tasks was being restructured. In this, the individual indirect task areas were open to different degrees for an exchange with the direct productive or salaried jobs. This will be demonstrated in more detail for the case of quality control and maintenance. Here we will briefly recount our own findings from the previous chapters.

(1) The development in quality inspection

The most personnel-intensive indirect area was traditionally line inspection, where the work in each production unit was checked over for its quality in order to initiate necessary repairs (which are generally controlled again afterwards). In addition to this came the entry inspection for component parts and random checks, tasks in the measurement rooms, carrying out quality analyses, etc. While line and entry inspection were semi-skilled tasks, skilled workers and salaried employees predominated in the measurement rooms and in the task area of quality analyses.

As we have shown, a decline in the quality control requirements took place in the 1980s, even considering the increased importance of the quality goal itself. This reduction in functions was due to the following reasons:

Entry inspection of incoming parts and material could be drastically reduced at many manufacturers by reorganizing relationships with the suppliers. The corresponding inspection tasks were delegated to the suppliers along with detailed instructions.

These and more comprehensive standards and controls which affected the production of the suppliers themselves, along with more stringent procedures for selecting suppliers brought about noticeable improvements in the quality of component parts. Quality defects in the component parts were traditionally one of the most important sources of mistakes in the assembly plants.

Changes in product and process technology further reduced the inspection requirements. Thus the amount of mistakes with robots was smaller; and if a mistake was made it was made more consistently and thus easier to diagnose than human mistakes.

This also made the automation of inspection operations easier.

Finally, the responsibility for quality in production was increased by measures such as having the production workers report their own mistakes and eliminate the sources of mistakes in production themselves.

As a consequence, the personnel levels of the quality control departments were scaled down in most plants. The erosion of job demarcations in the area of skilled labor and the shift of minor maintenance tasks to production also played a role: the largest part of the traditional quality inspection work was being taken over by direct production, where it was either carried out more or less unchanged or merged together with direct production tasks; a small part of line inspection remained in the area of the quality control organization and was integrated there with qualified tasks of measuring room work, quality analyses, etc. A further, likewise quantitatively small, share of what was previously line inspection was being merged with other jobs by some manufacturers, above all with repair work. New job descriptions, like that of "Kontrollfertigmacher" (control finisher), were thus being created. The taking over of quality control functions in direct production forms the starting point here, be it for the creation of new job descriptions, be it for the enrichment of the previous job spectrum. At the same time, it offers a starting point for the formation of production groups or teams with the possibility of job rotation between inspection and production tasks.

(2) The development in maintenance

In the area of maintenance, the indirectly productive area with predominantly skilled-labor jobs, a picture can be seen which is clearly different than in quality control. Here, a loss in function of traditional maintenance tasks is accompanied by a considerable growth in new tasks due to increased degrees of automation and the change to electronic technology. The loss in function is brought about through:

a decline in the amount of mechanical maintenance tasks and tool maintenance due to measures in product and process technology and the shifting of tasks to outside firms and

a transfer of maintenance tasks to production (small repairs and servicing tasks).

According to our findings, an overproportional growth in the personnel levels of the skilled-worker departments did not take place. This follows from the fact that the thrust of mechanization in many plants at the beginning of the 1980s had been limited to individual sections of production and often only involved the replacement of production equipment which was already highly mechanized. Furthermore, the shift of minor maintenance tasks to production had evidently played a compensatory role. In the German plants, the growth of the traditional skilled-worker departments in indirect production was limited by the fact that skilled workers were in some cases transferred into production to take over the new jobs of "Anlagenführer" and group leader.

With regard to skilled work we see a general tendency: on the one hand, simple maintenance tasks were becoming more differentiated and transferred to production where they have influenced the design of new job descriptions and new forms of work organization; on the other hand, a group of specialists is developing through the new demands of electronics, control technologies, etc., "nutcrackers" – who are forcing their way into the status of salaried employees. From the point of view of traditional maintenance this means a polarization of qualification demands with regard to their previous spectrum of functions. From the perspective of direct production, the transference of maintenance tasks and the creation of new job descriptions mean the possibility of creating jobs which demand higher qualifications.

At the end of this section dealing with changes in the personnel structures we would like to particularly emphasize three findings which concern differences in our factory sample:

1 Whereas the share of indirect production workers in comparison to direct workers clearly increased at Companies B and C in the period we studied, the indirect tasks were reduced even more than the direct ones at Company A. The decisive factor here was primarily the strategy of the integration of quality control; this tendency also appears more weakly in the development of skilled workers.

2 With regard to skilled workers, the distinctive development at Company B's U.S. plant Greentown stands out. While the manning levels in the maintenance departments in the other plants hardly changed in the period we studied, we observed a considerable increase in the maintenance capacity here. The share of skilled workers and developmental tendency here in comparison to Company A's River City plant points to a clear difference in the role of technology as a problem-solving strategy. The stagnation in the number of skilled workers in the indirect areas in the German factories can be primarily explained by the fact that skilled workers there are increasingly being transferred from the maintenance areas into production in order, e.g., to take jobs such as *Anlagenführer* (automated systems controllers) there.

3 In the traditional plants there were a large number of jobs with better working conditions and better pay, above all with regard to the task complex inspection/repair/relief, which embodied the potential of factory experience and decentral problem solving competence. At the same time they were advancement opportunities for production workers. These jobs are becoming more scarce due to the new concepts we described. At the same time, new job categories like group leader and *Anlagenführer* emerge – from which the production workers are excluded in many cases, as we described for in the German plants. Here is a very serious motivational problem for the production workers. The extent to which this can be counteracted through the creation of structures of team work is an open question for development in the 1990s.

9 Tapping new resources: skill levels and worker participation

"Human resources development" was often a stated goal of the companies at the beginning of the 1980s. This expression was used to describe two types of corporate strategies: "employee participation" which aimed at the "attitudes" and "behavior" of the work force, on the one hand; and training measures geared toward increasing skill levels, on the other. In the following we will be dealing with both of these with respect to human resources.

The first two sections in this chapter deal with the training strategies of our companies. First we will look at initial training for skilled workers, thus primarily apprenticeship training. In the second section we are dealing with continuous training, both for skilled workers and for non-skilled workers. As we will show, the companies had very different focal points in their training strategies and these focal points reflect – although not very clearly – the production concepts we found in the factories. Especially interesting for us was to see to what extent the training concepts already reflected future conceptions for new forms of work. We will be investigating the different training strategies as always comparatively within our factory sample.

The third section of this chapter deals with the human resources strategies which aim at employee participation and team work. These strategies naturally also include training measures. We have often pointed out the fact that such NW&M concepts were discussed here and there at the time of our study, but had not yet been implemented anywhere. Our empirical findings could thus only apply to the processes leading up to implementation. Correspondingly, we will be referring in this section primarily to the different conditions and controversies concerning the NW&M in the different locations where we did our research. The final section of the chapter will put the new concepts of work and motivation into a broader context of company reorganization, especially the trend toward decentralizing the management areas of responsibility.

9.1 Differences in the systems and emphasis of vocational (apprenticeship) training

The process of skill formation must also be seen as a process of socializing the workers to working life. There are very considerable differences in this respect between the U.S. and the European systems of vocational training for skilled workers, as we will show in the first part of this section. The traditional U.S. system consisted of three paths for attaining the skilled-worker qualification. These were, first, proof of having worked eight years as a skilled-worker at another company, second, a four-year apprenticeship in the worker's own factory, or, third, participation in an eight-year training program in the factory (Employee in Training, EIT) to the extent that such programs existed in the factory or company.

The young man or woman who wants to become a skilled worker in a car factory would hardly look for his or her first job there. One reason for this is the low numbers of workers trained up to now. Another reason is that filling the apprenticeship positions mainly takes place through factory-internal applications, and then chiefly according to seniority. Under these conditions, someone who definitely wants to become a skilled worker is better off starting his or her career in a non-union company in order to attain the prerequisites for being a skilled worker and then applying for a skilled-worker position in a car plant. Even the stepping up of the apprenticeship programs in some factories during the 1980s did not open up chances for young high school graduates. There were thus 3,000 applicants for thirty apprenticeships in the "Greentown" plant in 1982, two thirds of those chosen were workers in the plant. Out of seventy-five apprentices in the "Northtown" plant in 1987, all were previously employed as workers in the plant.

The applicants for an apprenticeship at Company B in the U.S. have to be between eighteen and forty-four years old (at A U.S. the age limit is thirty), had to have a high school degree or its equivalent, and to pass an entry test. In contrast to the British and German plants, there are rarely full-time trainers in the plants. Thus the quality of the training is heavily dependent on the existing skilled workers and supervisors who have to look after the apprentices at the individual training stations. The companies have pretty much a free hand in designing the training program – the government hardly has any influence on the contents of the vocational training[1] – and there was no direct union influence on the training. The length of the factory training at the car companies in the U.S. amounted to four years. Decisive is that the contractually allotted number of hours for the different training elements and areas are completed. The number of training hours for the majority of the trade programs is about 8,000. Of these about 93 percent were "on-the-job training" and only 7 percent took place "off-the-job," away from the work place at the time of our investigation.

In addition to the standardized apprenticeship training programs there was a program for further training for attaining the skilled-worker status at one of the U.S. companies we studied, which was set up for eight years and involved an even greater amount of "on-the-job" training. The total number of hours of classroom training prescribed for the normally eight-year training period was only 275. The EIT program opened up a possibility for advancement within the factory. The formal selection criterion for applicants was the worker's qualification and – with the same qualification – seniority; seniority actually played the deciding role in the majority of cases. The EIT system was – aside from outside recruiting – the predominant form of skilled-worker recruitment at Company B in the U.S.A. up until the beginning of the 1980s. It offered the advantage that the factory would virtually have skilled workers in production at its disposal in the person of the more senior participants of this program (after four years they attain the status of Employee in Training Seniority, EITS).

In contrast to the U.S. practice, the apprenticeship positions in Great Britain, as in West Germany, are filled exclusively by recent school graduates. There was an upper age limit of eighteen for the acceptance in the apprenticeship program at Company A and B in the U.K. The period of training was four years and, at the time of our research, was carried out according to the general standards of the Engineering Industry Training Board (EITB).[2] In the years following our research the EITB was dissolved in favor of more decentralized control institutions. As far as we can determine without carrying out our own empirical research, this has not affected the factory-related training systems to a great extent – at least in the companies we studied. The share of training at the work place made up approximately 40 percent at the time of our research, the share in the factory training workshop was also around 40 percent, and the share of classroom training at a state technical college was about 20 percent. In both companies, the factories studied have their own training departments and full-time instructors who supervise the apprentices in the first two apprenticeship years. In the third and fourth years, they are attended to by the skilled workers and supervisors at their work stations. After completion of the training, a transfer is only possible to a skilled job. The unions would not have agreed to a transfer to production. It was just as clear that the new skilled workers would remain employed.

The recruiting for apprenticeship programs in German companies also takes place out of the group of new school graduates.[3] The majority of the occupations in the automobile industry have a three to a three and a half year training period; with the reform of the training system in the metalworking and electrical trades, all apprentices are completing a three and a half year training period. We will come back to this.

All of the factories studied have a training workshop at their disposal. Between 40 and 50 percent of the training activities takes place here – depending on the company and profession. Almost 30 percent of the training is spent in the state vocational training school, the remaining time is made up of training at the work place. The focus of the training program is, with regard to time spent and to content, instruction in the training workshop where basic and specialized training in the trade was carried out. The apprentices spend the last part of their training mainly in the factory. But they are seldom drawn directly into production work; for the most part they worked in maintenance workshops (at "Altstadt," for example, 95 percent worked in maintenance, 5 percent in production). With this, there is the danger that the training could tend to be somewhat removed from production practice. The instructors often do not have direct personal experience with the most modern production technologies and have to first acquire the relevant knowledge themselves. This problem was seen in practice by the interviewees from the training departments – although the arguments against a stronger on-the-job orientation were that maintenance in production generally takes place under intense time pressure which does not allow skilled workers enough time to give the necessary instructions and explanations, or that it takes place during the night shift. At the close of the apprenticeship training there is a test which is carried out by the industry and trade chamber with the participation of union representatives and professional vocational instructors.

With regard to the apprentices being accepted for regular skilled-worker positions in the factory, the situation in the German factories was fundamentally different than that in the U.S. and Great Britain. In principle, the training relationship does not establish a right to continued employment for the workers in the factory. After the expansion of the training programs in the factories since the beginning of the 1980s as we described in chapter 4 the factories increasingly found themselves incapable of retaining the apprenticeship graduates as skilled workers. All of the German factories studied thus have adopted the practice of transferring their finished apprentices into the areas of direct production first. If skilled-worker positions open up, then the transferees have the possibility of applying within the factory. In certain trades it has come to a waiting period of more than four years. The mechanical trades like tool and die maker and millwright are especially hard hit by this problem.

The differing systems of vocational training – especially in the comparison of the U.S. and German systems – obviously have important consequences for the integration of the skilled workers into the factory and in the establishment of a specific "socialization type" of skilled worker. In the U.S.A., training at the work place dominates, carried out by skilled workers who must also perform their regular job at the same time. Production experience and requirements are emphasized in the training. The workers to be trained are themselves "established" workers who are now going to become skilled workers.

The apprentices in the German factory find themselves in a transitional phase from pupils to workers, without personal work experience. They are trained by special instructors in training workshops, far away from the shop floor. They have no opportunity to develop criteria with respect to the practical relevance of the knowledge they received, whereas their U.S. colleagues are more familiar with the requirements of production. The rationale for the traditional U.S. system – and we met this argument frequently in factories – is that 90 percent of the jobs of skilled workers consist in performing tasks which could be mastered with a much lesser qualification than that provided by a complete apprenticeship. As opposed to this, a narrowly understood utilitarian interest has not been able to establish itself in the dual governmental-private system of vocational training in the Federal Republic. The connection between the system for vocational training with the general educational system has remained there, and with this also the reference to the general educational goals of this system.

There was a broad consensus at the time of our research on the importance of vocational training for securing a company's future and guaranteeing its ability to adapt to changing technological and organizational developments. Therefore, the specific corporate strategies for deploying labor and technology should determine the distribution of apprentices among employment categories. By adjusting the structure of its apprentice training, a company could enhance its ability to cope with changing technical and organizational requirements. In the following we will be determining the extent to which the companies have used these opportunities to expand their future-oriented potential for action.

As shown in table 9.1, the relation between apprentices in vocational training and the number of skilled workers varied widely, indicating very different emphases in the various companies and countries. In fact, the table shows enormous differences in training efforts. We found above all a very low training intensity at Company A U.S. Thus only eight apprentices were trained at River City in 1986 (it was twelve in 1980) – this also corresponds to the number at other plants of A U.S. At River City in 1986 there was one apprentice per thirty skilled workers or one per 380 production workers; at Company C's German plant Windeck the relation was one apprentice to 2.4

Table 9.1 *Initial vocational training (skilled trade) in selected assembly plants*

Factory	Number of skilled workers per apprentice	Number of workers per apprentice
River City 1986	30:1	380:1
Maple City 1986	100:1	1,730:1
Greentown	10:1[a]	92:1[a]
Northtown 1986	4:1[b]	63:1[b]
Hartmoor 1985	8.3:1	64:1
Seaborough 1984	5.7:1	30:1
Weinkirchen 1985[c]	4.8:1[d]	46:1
Mittelort 1985[c]	n.a.	36:1
Windeck 1986[c]	2.4:1[d]	41:1

Notes:
[a] All in formal apprenticeship programs.
[b] Ca. 60% in apprenticeship programs, 40% in Employee in Training (EIT) programs.
[c] Own estimations of the share of production-related apprenticeship training out of the total apprenticeship training which also included business-related apprentices.
[d] Refers to the number of skilled workers in all skilled-labor departments (i.e., "indirect" labor).

skilled workers deployed in the indirect area or one per forty-one production workers.

Although there was no change in the extent of initial vocational training at A U.S. in the course of the 1980s, B U.S. exhibited a fundamental change in the type and scale of its training in this period. For example, whereas fifty-five apprentices were employed at Greentown in 1986, the plant had yet to set up its formal apprenticeship program in 1979. At that time, twenty-three workers were undergoing continuous training to attain the skilled-worker status (Employee in Training, EIT). The EIT program was discontinued here in 1983. These changes correspond to developments at a sister plant, Northtown. In 1980, ninety-four workers were trained as skilled workers in the EIT program. In 1986, seventy-five employees were in the EIT program and fifty-four in formal apprenticeships. EIT programs were only carried out for skill classifications with no formal apprenticeship programs.

In contrast to A U.S., "modern" apprenticeship programs were established in the plants of B U.S. in the first half of the 1980s and by 1986 the relation of apprentices to skilled workers or total workers in B's U.S. plants was almost the same as in European plants. The British companies have also stepped up their training activities in the 1980s, thus the British factory Hartmoor had 115 apprentices in 1985, a 13 percent increase over 1978. The training efforts were also intensified at Seaborough. Still, the number of apprentices in the German plants was higher than in most British and U.S. plants. At Weinkirchen there were 150 trade apprentices in 1985, at Windeck they numbered approximately 220. There was nearly one apprentice for every forty production workers. This ratio signified an increase since the 1970s – 33 percent more at Mittelort, 28 percent at Weinkirchen, and 11 percent at Windeck.

There are four areas of emphasis in training the skilled trades specific to assembly plants: (1) skilled workers such as the millwrights responsible for general plant maintenance tasks, (2) mechanically oriented trades for machine repair, (3) electrically oriented trades such as electricians and electronics mechanics who are responsible for production equipment, and, finally, (4) skilled workers like the industrial mechanic for production technology ("Mechaniker in der Fertigung"), who were prepared to work in production jobs and were only found in German plants. Table 9.2 shows the distribution of trade apprentices according to mechanical, electrical/ electronic, and other trades in U.S. and German plants. The "WEMR" group is the hybrid category referring to mechanical and electrical tasks associated with welding equipment which we dealt with in chapter 6. Table 9.2 shows in particular the large percentage made up of the new mechanic in production at Windeck and the separate training for electronics mechanics ("Elektroniker") with a large share of training slots in the German plants.

From these patterns in the training structure and shifts in the focus of vocational training we come to the following conclusions:

(1) Because of technological developments, the demand for electrical/ electronics related skills is increasing. This has led to a clear restructuring in apprentice training, away from mechanical in favor of electrical trades in all European plants. Thus, for instance, out of the thirty-one new apprentices in the Hartmoor plant in 1981, fourteen were assigned to electrical and seventeen to mechanical trades; in 1985, twenty-eight of the newly hired apprentices went to electrical and only seven to mechanical trades. The shift can also be seen in the German plants. Here, there used to be a differentiation between power electronics mechanics ("Energie – Anlagenelektroniker"), who are especially trained for electronic control, and various types of industrial electronics mechanics ("Elektro – Anlageninstallateur"), who do more traditional electrical tasks.

We did not find similar changes in the emphasis of vocational training in

Table 9.2 *Distribution of the skilled trade apprentices in selected assembly plants according to vocational groups*

Trade	Factory	River City	Greentown	Weinkirchen	Windeck
Mechanical trades	Millwright		13		53
	Pipefitter, plumber	2	11		
	Machine repair	1		39	25
	Other metalworkers	1		8	
	"Mechanic in production"				80
	Welding equipment maintenance and repair (WEMR)		12		
Electrical trades	Electricians	3	13		24
	Industrial electronics mechanics			50	17
	Power electronics mechanics			34	
Tool and die maker			6		
Other		1		6	
Total		8	55	137	199

the U.S. plants. In the assembly plants of A U.S. only minimal training activities existed anyway and they reflected almost no changes in the skill structure. In the plants of B U.S., the number of apprentices clearly increased in the course of the 1980s, coupled with a change in the system of apprentice training as we have shown. However, there were no noticeable changes in the distribution of training between the different skill classifications. Table 9.3 gives the numbers of skilled workers, apprentices, and trainees according to skilled trades classifications at Greentown for 1979, 1984, and 1986. The employee in-training program was abolished altogether between 1979 and 1984. Training of apprentices was doubled between 1984 and 1986. Compared to the 1979 EIT program the apprenticeship program of 1986 concentrated on fewer skilled classifications, but if we control for the general increase in apprentices we do not see differences in emphasis such as the training of certain skills in connection with the introduction of new computerized production systems between 1979 and 1986.

(2) A further tendency set off by increased automation in production has been the trend toward stationing skilled workers closer to the equipment. This is shown in the gradual disappearance of the boundary lines between maintenance and production in the automation area which was of particular concern in coping with the demands of automated equipment. This was also one reason for the attempt at reforming vocational training in the Federal Republic since the beginning of the 1980s. In 1987 the industrial metalworking and electrical trades were newly classified. A goal of this reform was to broaden the range of tasks of the individual workers and to reduce their number. The number of apprenticeship options for skilled workers in the metalworking industries was reduced from forty-two to six. A further goal was the creation of new job profiles for skilled workers deployed in direct production.[4] For example, the new job description of industrial mechanic/subject area – production technology ("Industriemechaniker/Fachrichtung Produktionstednik") covered the previous work areas of machine repairmen, millwrights, precision engineers, and mechanics. The curriculum of the apprenticeship training in this area includes the following skills and types of knowledge:
(a) maintaining machines and equipment or systems;
(b) thermal separation;
(c) setting up and testing hydraulic circuits for control technology: checking the functioning of numerically controlled components, machines, or systems, and of electro-technical components as well;
(d) checking and adjusting the functioning of components, machines, systems, and production equipment;

Table 9.3 *The number of skilled workers, EITs, and apprentices at the Greentown plant, 1979, 1984, and 1986*

	1979			1984			1986	
	Skilled workers	EITS	Apprentices	Skilled workers	EITs	Apprentices	EITs	Apprentices
Air conditioning and refrigerator controler	3	—	—	3	—	—	—	—
Carpenter	11	—	1	12	—	4	—	13
Electrician	84	3	—	85	—	7	—	13
Millwright	100	5	—	97	—	—	—	—
Painter/glazier	19	—	—	18	—	—	—	—
Pipefitter	71	2	—	78	—	—	—	11
Tool repair – portable power driver	13	—	—	15	—	—	—	—
Tool repair gas + electric	26	—	—	28	—	—	—	—
Welder maintenance – gas + arc	18	1	—	15	—	—	—	12
Welding equipment maintenance/repair	73	9	—	100	—	7	—	—
Machine repair – machinist	19	—	—	14	—	—	—	—
Power house repairman	8	—	—	8	—	—	—	—
Tool maker – jig and fixture	62	2	—	72	—	3	—	6
Welder gas and arc – tool and fixture	7	—	—	6	—	—	—	—
Total	514	23	1	551	—	27	—	55

(e) preventative maintenance: assessing, containing, and rectifying defects and disturbances;
(f) breaking in machines and production equipment;
(g) equipping and retooling machines, systems, and production equipment, securing and supervising supply and waste management;
(h) operating and programming machines and production equipment, supervising the course of production and securing the quality of the products (Ordinance for vocational training in the industrial metalworking occupations 4, chapter 2).

A further new occupation which was being trained for deployment in production was the industrial electronics mechanic with the subject area production technology ("Industrieelektroniker, Tachrichtung Produktionstechnik"). The areas of deployment foreseen in the training plan were automated production and quality control. Their jobs include setting up, recommissioning, supervising, and maintaining automated equipment for production and quality control. When disturbances occur, it is expected that they can locate the cause of the defect and overcome the disturbance by replacing components.[5] The new types of skilled trades were geared primarily to the new jobs in the high-tech areas of production, i.e., "automated systems controller" ("Anlagenführer").

The reform of the apprenticeship system for the metalworking trades can be regarded as an example of the adaptability and flexibility of the labor policy institutions in Germany. In the "dual system" of vocational training, new training policies require that a consensus be found between the employer's associations and the unions (Streeck 1989). But the great number of institutions and regulations governing the policies in the field of vocational training did not cause the system to become rigid, but rather acted as guidelines at the company level. At the same time, the new skilled job profiles were an expression of the importance given to the initial vocational training as a problem-solving strategy in West Germany.

As table 9.1 shows, the level of apprentice intakes in the British plants was similar to that of the German plants. The EITB's training system which existed at the time of our research also exhibited a greater flexibility in adapting the training programs to changes in job demands. There were no job descriptions for skilled workers deployed in production, however, as in Germany.

Governmental training regulations hardly played a role in the initial vocational training in the U.S. companies. The unions also had little influence on the design of training courses with regard to the skilled trades classifications listed in the national contracts. The changed technical requirements could of course be taken into account by expanding training times "on the job" in areas with new technologies – but only to the extent that the factory already had the appropriate equipment. The possibilities for raising the necessary qualification potential in anticipation of problems with future mechanization were thus limited. Finally, the creation of new job descriptions for workers to be deployed in direct production would have needed the approval of the union, which could hardly be expected in view of the attitude held by the UAW's skilled-worker representation.

Another aspect of the skilled-worker oriented strategy and the thrust behind the initial training which we observed in West Germany would probably be even less acceptable in the eyes of U.S. unionists. This is the fact that it is in many cases the graduates of the apprenticeship training who were seen as the most suited candidates for the new enhanced jobs in production. Such a "built-in right of way" with regard to the better jobs in the modernized production areas would contradict the traditionally high value given to the seniority principle and meet with the resistance of the work forces and the union in U.S. plants. In the German factories, on the other hand, a competition frequently arose between experienced production workers and young skilled workers over the chances for advancement in production.

9.1.1 Measures for further training in the factory

Starting at the beginning of the 1980s, all of the companies we studied enacted measures of continuous training for target groups in the non-skilled area who had up to then been almost untouched by such measures. Programs for continuous training, within and beyond the factories, increased rapidly in number and intensity. This is true for all of the countries and companies studied, even if they had their typical differences. Three points of emphasis have to be distinguished in these programs: (1) the continuous training of skilled workers in view of the requirements of the new technologies, (2) training for non-skilled workers in order to qualify them for the demands of the new technologies, and (3) training measures with regard to the NW&M programs of the companies.

At the U.S. companies we studied, funds and institutions for the NW&M programs were established particularly in the 1982 and 1984 bargaining rounds. They were supported both by the union and by management. Joint committees were established at the national and factory level which decided on the target groups, and the type and extent of these training measures. At the time of our investigation, these institutions and programs for continuous training were in their early stages. Yet measures for continuous training associated with the introduction of new technologies were almost exclusively aimed at the skilled workers, whereby measures for continuous training for the non-skilled area mostly concerned the topic NW&M. The

technology-related qualification measures in the unskilled area were limited
to the breaking-in of employees who were directly affected by the use of new
technologies.

The NW&M-related qualification measures were often huge organizational projects. Thus in the years 1981 to 1983, the entire hourly wage work
force at Northtown was sent on a three day course to familiarize them with
the NW&M program and its objectives. In 1984 and 1985, only one-week
courses for upper management and local union leadership were given.
There was a total of twenty hours in courses for the hourly wage work force
and their supervisors in 1987. The following subject areas, for example,
were being offered in the factory courses: NW&M principles; goals,
functions, and structures of the union and management; communication
and group-related problem-solving techniques; procedures at group meetings; presentation techniques.

On the whole there has been a considerable increase in further training
activities in the U.S. factories[6] reflecting the new production concepts on
the basis of NW&M principles. It should also be mentioned that the
companies were discovering that the "lay-off" situation characteristic of
the U.S. employment system also provided flexibility for training purposes.
As we have seen, large portions of the work force of many plants were laid
off in the 1980s – unemployment compensation being paid mainly by the
companies. The training plans were beginning to recognize the possibility
of freeing workers for training measures by calling back laid off personnel
to fill their jobs during this time.

In the factories which we studied in Great Britain, continuous training
was also increasingly receiving more importance. Of the three focal points
for further training named above (skilled workers for new technologies,
non-skilled workers for the demands of the new technologies, and NW&M
training), the emphasis was almost exclusively on the continuous training
of skilled workers. NW&M related programs were strictly refused by the
blue collar unions. Agreements for jointly supported training programs,
like in the U.S.A., did not exist. The emphasis on activities for continuous
training was related to measures of restructuring, especially before the
introduction of a new car model.

In the West German companies, the emphasis on continuous training
was also placed with the skilled workers. Training activities related to
NW&M concepts played a marginal role here. The fact that many workers
with skilled trades certificates were working on non-skilled production
jobs, and thus in danger of "delearning" their skills seemed to be the most
important factor leading to an increased awareness of the importance of
additional training. To cope with the employment effects of restructuring,
continuous training became the central element of a wave of "rationaliza-

tion agreements" at the plant and company level in German companies at the beginning of the 1980s. These agreements stipulated the individual right to retraining for workers who were made redundant from their jobs due to technological and organizational measures and were transferred to jobs with lower pay and qualification requirements. The details for arranging this were agreed to by the works council and management. The unskilled workers were included as a specific target group, especially in the agreements dealing with technological and organizational restructuring. This corresponds to the "training offensive" which in principle was seen to be necessary by all societal organizations and parties. To achieve training measures for production workers was one of the central objectives pursued by the "IG Metall" in their 1984 "Aktionsprogramm Arbeit and Technik" ("Program for action regarding work and technology").

Thus in view of the upcoming restructuring at Windeck, the training for the position of automated systems controller ("Anlagenführer") has also been opened up for semi-skilled workers. According to the job description, there were two ways to qualify as an "Anlagenführer": skilled workers received a one stage training, non-skilled workers received two stages, whereby the first stage should give them enough knowledge to allow them to take the course for skilled workers. At the time of our research, 106 of the around 1,200 production workers in the body shop, the section where the "Anlagenführer" were to be primarily deployed, had completed this two stage course.

In contrast to the other two countries, continuous training for skilled workers in West Germany went beyond the conventional boundary lines between the skilled trades. Thus in the area of maintenance in the stamping and body plants at Weinkirchen, it was possible to train 80 to 85 percent of the mechanical tradesmen in control systems, hydraulics, and pneumatics; and about 70 percent of the electricians attained certificates in electronics and digital technology through continuous training. Mechanical tradesmen were trained to work with robots by means of a teach-in procedure, and electricians frequently completed a hydraulic and pneumatic training. The willingness of skilled workers to enlist in the training programs was depicted as extraordinarily great. Thus many of the skilled workers who were deployed in production below their qualifications also obtained this additional qualification in evening courses on their own initiative and in their own time. That is why a considerable percentage of the skilled workers employed in non-skilled areas at Weinkirchen have their "electronics pass."

In many cases, only the consideration of safety set a limit on the attainment of hybrid skills. Differing opinions and solutions could be found on the question of whether skilled mechanical workers should be allowed to open the electrical switchboards. For safety reasons, only workers who had the so-called "E1-key" were allowed to do this. These were the electricians and the "instructed persons" who had taken part in a brief continuous training course. The training time necessary to become an "instructed person" was estimated differently. At Windeck they assume almost 600 hours; other companies considered shorter training time to be sufficient. At the time of our study, Windeck was considering the separation of high and low voltage switchboards and also allowing the mechanical trades access to the latter. After all, the robot controls had a low voltage level (24 volts) and thus did not present a safety risk. Debates like this and the introduction of positions like the "instructed persons" are typical for the West German context with its extremely high flexibility in the tailoring of trades. Carrying the example of the E1 switch key further, we were told off the cuff that it was typical in many factories for a great number of direct production workers to have such a switch key in order to be able to intervene more rapidly in critical situations. The factories frequently took advantage of opportunities provided by near-by publicly financed vocational training centers for their further training measures. The trend in Germany and to a lesser extent also in the U.K. was that the plants were establishing their own training centers. This was made easier through the fact that, in contrast to the U.S. factories, these are as a rule still considerably larger production sites (with 10,000 employees and more).

Although the programs for apprentice training had been flexible in meeting technological changes, they have been far less flexible in reflecting changes in organizational concepts – neither in the U.S. nor West Germany. The head of the newly appointed staff function for employee participation at Weinkirchen remarked critically on this point: "A true 'training boom' took place in this plant, especially in 1984. It was very impressive when measured by the expenditures of time and money. I have my doubts concerning the contents. I miss an orientation of these qualification activities in the direction of the NW&M objective" (NW&M coordinator, Weinkirchen).

The situation was changing, though, at the end of the 1980s. At least in Germany, where we could observe further development, apprentice training has become more team-oriented and more related to realistic production situations with the large-scale technological and organizational adjustments for model changes. As more factories have gone through this process in the meantime, we see a more widespread recognition of exactly how important training is for a smooth start of production with the new system. The planning and preparation for such change-overs is becoming increasingly long term, thorough, and systematic – and central management is increasingly willing to supply the necessary resources. We would like to give an example in which the attempt was made to make the change-over and start-problems themselves the main topic of a NW&M project.

At Altstadt, the employee participation process, which had just been initiated by the company, was geared totally to the demands and problems of the production start-up for the new model coming up in 1985. At this time the management program had been accepted by the workers' representation in the factory but had not been actively supported. "It was also through the impulse of NW&M that we could begin much earlier with preparations for the model start, namely already at the middle of 1983. The NW&M project had contributed significantly to the fact that such a short and successful starting phase could be realized" (NW&M coordinator, Altstadt). The goal was to organize an exchange of experiences between the workers of the future work areas, the production engineers and possibly the suppliers of components in order to achieve improvements in the planning of the process layout. This team formed project groups for specific task areas. A start-up team formed at the plant level was included in the process of pinpointing problems and considering solutions as early as the design and development phase. The model start was planned for the beginning of 1985. Presentations and test runs for individual employee groups had already begun in the spring of 1983. In addition, there were various training measures in connection with the introduction of problem-solving groups and supervisor training in participative leadership.

Training measures affecting the production workers began about six months before the model start. The average length of further training per production employee was more than three days, for the indirect area it was 3.9 days. Measures for further training for "skilled workers in production" ("Kolonnenführer" and electronics mechanic) received a good third of the "man-days" of further training in these areas.

New in this was above all the further training of direct production personnel, especially in the areas of trim- and final assembly. There were six projects for comprehensive technological and organizational changes for trim and final assembly. It was expected that for the new model every second worker in the area of trim assembly was to be taken from other areas – the body plant or other trim assembly areas. A pilot line for trim and final assembly was set up on the factory grounds, on which 60 to 70 percent of the later assembly workers were trained. Process engineers and industrial engineers from the management start-up teams were present at this test area. As a result of the initial experiences on the test line, the assembly workers were able to voice their concerns and make suggestions for improvement. About 350 out of 600 proposals were implemented. Ergonomic questions played a substantial role in this. According to a management account there was often a real workshop situation on the pilot line, where workers, supervisors, and production engineers discussed process details, repeatedly assembled and disassembled components, and intensively discussed possibilities for improvement.

This example makes clear the growing awareness of the companies of the necessity to involve their work force in dealing with the large technical and organizational transitions and to use the experience and knowledge of the work force in setting-up new processes. Production change-overs are no longer only seen as matters for the technicians and production planners. The majority of our management interviewees in the above case saw the increased emphasis on "social engineering" to be a significant contribution to the success of the model start. In the case of the change-over described above, however, a "snag" arose as the lines were speeded up to achieve the planned output.

If you now go through the factory, you see that many foremen slipped back into the old authoritarian leadership style in order to reach the output. The NW&M people do not see that. They don't see that the pressure for output increases and that performance is needed in the acceleration phase. And one cannot always get the upper hand on this through NW&M. But many foremen are now destroying that which was supposed to be developed over months. (Personnel manager, Altstadt)

9.2 Approaches for new work and management concepts

9.2.1 In the U.S.

I'm tired of hearing about Japan. Let's do it!

This was the exclamation of a worker in an "awareness workshop" at River City, as quoted in the plant's NW&M brochure (Vol. 1, No. 5). It is characteristic of the determination, not only of management but also of the union and many members of the work force, to do whatever was necessary to meet the Japanese competition. And NW&M was seen as a necessary antidote. The goal was to beat the Japanese with their own weapons, "to out-Japanese Japan."

But it was not only the fear of losing their jobs that was behind the willingness of the work force in the U.S. plants to break with old habits and to accept the offer of participation. Many of the participation offers tied up with the genuine interests of the work force. "Some call us the quality circle jerk-offs" explained a quality circle member in a stamping plant of Company A we visited, "they think that we are only wasting our time. But we as a group think that if we are going to spend a good part of our life and possibly thirty years in this plant, then it is worth it to be concerned with the improvement of working conditions" (Worker, Company A's Goodhaven stamping plant). The workers in this plant had formerly made a game out of seeing how long it took for management ("those white collar dummies") to find out about mistakes which had been clear to the workers for some time: "Management simply didn't listen, and that has cost the company a lot. Now it listens." One worker gave a vivid example from his own experience: "I knew that I would ruin the press if I did what the foreman had told me to do. The foreman said then, no, let it go, do it like I told you. What happened, was that the press actually was ruined and a lot of money went down the drain" (Worker, Goodhaven stamping plant). It is obvious that the irrational aspects of everyday production, e.g., production of faulty parts, inadequate tools, misdirected materials, the withholding of information, are frequently seen by the workers as nuisances and that the work force also has an interest in providing remedies, not only in the U.S. plants. Some of the euphoric comments of the participants could otherwise not be accounted for, even assuming that disillusionment may take place in the course of time. Being taken seriously as experts in their own work, and being included in problem-solving often did produce increased commitment by the workers, as was confirmed time and again by production management in our interviews.

There were a multitude of initiatives in this vein in the factories we visited and we have already presented many examples in chapters 4 to 7, such as:

the involvement of quality circles or problem-solving groups in job design in connection with technological and organizational change-overs;

the involvement of workers in solving quality or production flow problems, the establishment of "quality interest representatives" (Greentown);

the inclusion of workers from affected production areas in negotiations with the manufacturers of machines and equipment on which these workers will later be working;

and their participation in discussions with suppliers over the quality of component parts with which they had experience. Thus problem-solving groups at Northtown visited dealers or repair shops to have a closer look at customer complaints, etc.

These initiatives had led to a process of change in consciousness and behavior in the U.S. plants which was assessed by many of our interview partners as being irreversible. At the beginning of the 1980s, however, the NW&M process had affected little change in work organization and labor deployment patterns in the factories we investigated. The focus was rather set on questions of labor relations – the attitudes and behavior of management, the union, and the work force.[7] There was no team plant in our U.S. sample through which we could look at the practice of team organization. Since the middle of the 1980s, the local contract parties at an increasing number of sites in the U.S.A. have agreed to revise their local contracts in the spirit of the team concept and make a new beginning. The decisions were frequently made under considerable pressure on the part of central management and the central union organization. In fact Greentown and Northtown have also become "team plants" since the time of our study. The change was frequently connected with conflicts within the union and severe factional battles at the local level (cf. Parker and Slaughter 1988). These conflicts, and the attempts by management and the union leadership themselves to show the successes in "direct labor efficiency" frequently ran counter to the proclaimed objectives of the NW&M process. The extent to which battles within the union and the strategy of forcing NW&M through central channels endangered the NW&M process at Company B cannot be determined at this point.

In the U.S.A., the NW&M process and team concept aim above all at the non-skilled employees. Whereas fundamental "human resources" in the German context were seen in the stock of skilled workers, a different perspective dominated in the U.S. factories. The approach to human resources aimed at the non-skilled workers, and we did not get the impression that they were basically seen as a dying species. An explanation for this difference can be found in the status differences and vocational training system for skilled workers. An integration of skilled workers into non-skilled teams in which rotation was practiced would not currently be conceivable in the U.S. plants at this time. A strategy of qualification "from below," which starts with the non-skilled workers and strives at raising their qualifications, appeared to be a more promising – although longer term – path. The introduction of the compensation principle "pay for knowledge" aimed in this direction. It offered a wage incentive for further qualification "on-the-job," and thus increased the breadth and flexibility in labor deployment. The "pay-for-knowledge" or flexibility wage is an hourly wage with a flexibility bonus. Newly hired workers are taken on at the lowest wage level. To the extent that a worker masters the demands at other work stations within his or her area (or team) as well as those in other areas (teams) and receives the appropriate flexibility points, she or he will then reach the higher wage levels.[8] In contrast to the previous wage rates, which were contractually fixed at the central level, this new system creates leeway at the factory level to take its objectives into account in differentiating wages (e.g., by defining the criteria for giving out points). The traditional wage systems often stood in the way of decentralized solutions. With the flexibility wage system, the planning of personnel deployment in the factory received a basis different from the traditional seniority criterion. At the same time it created an incentive for increased worker flexibility.

This mobility allows workers to be transferred or temporarily assigned to other areas.

As a whole, we found the NW&M process in the U.S. plants proceeded more dynamically than in the Company's British and West German plants. In the U.S. this had already changed the traditional work and social organization in the assembly plants to a considerable extent at the time of our research. This process was duplicated and reinforced in the second half of the 1980s by the establishment of an increasing number of Japanese "transplants." Up to now there are very few reports on the situation in these new plants (for an update of our description see, in particular, Turner 1991).

The problem of bridging the gap between skilled and non-skilled workers in the U.S. still remained. The qualification strategy "from below" will probably not be sufficient to cope with the future process of mechanization. Here integrated teams of skilled and non-skilled workers and new quasi-skilled job descriptions in production are needed. The NW&M process thus threatens to remain limited to the manual labor areas.

9.2.2 In Great Britain: Union blockade of the NW&M process

The enactment of management programs for participation was especially difficult in Great Britain. Although the 1980s may turn out in hindsight to be the years of decisive turnaround in industrial and labor relations (see Cahill and Ingram 1987), adversarial labor relations predominated on the shop floor at the time of our research, a system of direct interest representation by shop stewards or occupational groups which often followed narrow self-interest without considering the effects of their actions on other groups, to say nothing of the effects on the company. The outcome was a situation in which coping with the difficulties of everyday work conflicts absorbed a good deal of energy of both union representatives and management. In fact, the management of B U.K. refrained from even attempting to introduce the NW&M concepts which were widespread in this multinational company's plants outside the U.K. during the period we studied. The following account is thus limited to the initiatives at Company A in the U.K.

The central management of A's European organization ordered the establishment of quality circles in the plants in 1979. As a conclusion drawn from the Japan reception, they saw improvements in the activities of the small groups in the Japanese companies as one of the main explanations for the Japanese productivity success. Thus the British plants were also required to take part in the quality circle movement. Corresponding to management's leadership style, the extent to which quality circles had spread became a main item in the factory reports to the headquarters. The company's objectives aimed at as rapid a diffusion as possible in the number and activity levels of quality circles. The union rapidly clamped down on this, however. With reference to the job descriptions in the national contract, which did not involve participation in quality circles, they demanded stoppage of such activities until a central agreement had been reached.

The overloading of expectations ("Quality circles were regarded as universal panacea for all our problems" – a remark of a management representative at Hartmoor) and introduction from above ("We essentially established the quality circles according to orders from above" – Hartmoor) were criticized in retrospect by many British management interviewees in the course of our investigation. Obviously, management had learned that the cooperation of the British workers in solving factory problems was not to be achieved by means of a decree. The large scale participation of workers in some continental plants was often also criticized by managers in British plants – as "cooperation on command" and therefore a "contradiction in itself" if one took the goal of increased worker participation seriously. Behind this was the suspicion that only a superficial behavioral adjustment had been achieved there, and, at the same time, the assessment that worker participation could only be attained through a long-term comprehensive process of change. "At Weinkirchen (the German sister plant) they could naturally implement quality circles quite quickly. This has a lot to do with the German disciplined work force. If you order quality circles you will get them" (Personnel manager, Hartmoor).

The introduction of a program of worker participation without the union could not succeed in view of the strength of the unions in the companies investigated. Because of the type of union representation in Great Britain it was also hardly possible for the union to silently accept the introduction of such a program, as the unions in the West German companies had at this stage. The shop stewards still controlled communication on the shop floor in some areas. "We can't even speak to our operators," was the complaint of a quality control manager at one plant. The union position was that when management wanted to discuss problems of say, product quality, with the work force it should talk to the shop stewards. Participation programs for workers were thus seen as an attempt to deprive shop stewards of their power base.

According to an industrial relations manager, this attitude led to the situation when even production management's right to stop the assembly line for a while to talk over problems with regard to ensuring quality was disputed "We are working in an atmosphere of total and complete suspicion. The attitude generally is: if the company wants to do it, it must be against the interest of organized labor. And I say organized labor because the ordinary working men are tremendously interested in these approaches" (Personnel manager, Company A's European headquarters). At the time of our study, signs of a change in both local management and union representatives' willingness to cooperate in decentralized factory problem-solving in the spirit of NW&M objectives were increasing. To illustrate this we will describe two episodes.

At Hartmoor, the first step toward obtaining the cooperation of the unions and reducing mistrust was a change in management's behavior regarding information. The union representatives in this plant saw the former (dis-)information policy as one of the main reasons that the quality circle was mistrusted. When restructuring for a new vehicle model in this plant was imminent at the end of the 1970s, the union had received little information as to what they could expect: "They did not give us much more information than the new lay-out chart. In this country, Company A doesn't tell about their thinking and their choices. They will only inform you when the equipment is already ordered" (Union representative, Hartmoor).

The awareness that they must be prepared for everything, and could not believe what management said was only strengthened by management's miscalculations concerning the extent of the personnel reductions: "When they gave us the presentation over the introduction of the new technology and what it would mean for the work force, they said that they would have 80 surplus people. (...) But it turned out that we had 800 people surplus. I do not think that they had actually given us the true facts" (ibid.). The effects of the selection of personnel for reduction (trouble-makers were the first to go), the replacement of personnel within management, and the fears which had been growing since 1982 regarding the future of the factory as a whole initiated a process of reconsideration at this point, by management as well as by the unions. Management lost its fears that its already weak position would become weaker:

Yes, we were very skeptical. In the old days we used the baseball bat. Then we had to recognize that we had come to a point where force did not pay anymore. If you have a reduction of the head count by a hundred and lose a week of production that is okay. But we moved to a point where we were losing one week for one man. That is where you have to start to think about another way to achieve these goals. And there is another important fact: we don't have to worry about being seen as weak. If we had introduced employee involvement in the bad old days the union would have regarded this as a sign of management weakness. But now they know our strength as we know theirs. Now they see that we are not introducing new work and motivation concepts out of weakness, and this is important. (Personnel manager, Hartmoor)

The rethinking process by management and the union would have hardly taken place without the Damocles sword of off-standards and the closing of the site. For the union, a significant stage was reached when management agreed to allow its highly publicized comparisons with the continental plants to be checked over by those workers affected. The following account is from a union representative of the TGWU:

It began with the Joint Works Council going to (Weinkirchen) and that they noticed a couple of things there where relevant differences between the plants existed, even though management still said that both plants were the same. After they returned from Weinkirchen they demanded that the workers themselves should be allowed to go to (Weinkirchen) and, as experts for their own work station, get a picture for themselves of the differences that exist.

Management agreed to this demand. Groups of twenty were put together – on the average twelve hourly wage workers, one shop steward and, representatives of management. A total of twenty-five to thirty such trips were made, which meant that ca. 600 employees were sent to a sister plant on the continent in which they could study the working conditions and the course of work at "their work stations" for two days. The union representative said that, to a certain extent, the workers were presented with a facade. "But the trips were by and large successful. The participants pointed time and again to individual things and asked management 'Why don't we have something like that?' Management had always argued with the fact that they had identical means of production. They could not get away with this so easily after these trips" (Union representative of the TGWU). The action of letting the workers themselves make the comparison, of taking them seriously as experts for their work stations, was called "controlled employee participation" by this union representative, participation which did not only serve management interests.

The impetus for the entry into the next phase of NW&M development was given by a factory comparison with a sister plant on the continent. Although all those involved at the Hartmoor plant had thought that they had achieved an enormous leap in productivity and in quality performance in the plant since 1983, this comparison still showed a large gap between the plants. (We have dealt with these efforts in chapter 7.3.3 and with the results in terms of productivity development in chapter 8.) A management presentation which informed the plant's unions of these results gave the impetus. The unions announced their support for necessary measures to close the gap in productivity. Joint committees with representatives of management and the unions were formed at the level of the production area to discuss production related problems and to give work assignments to project groups which the committee introduced. A labelling of these activities as "employee participation" was rejected by the management. But they were an "indicator of the willingness of the unions to sit down with management to discuss future necessities" (Personnel manager, Hartmoor). It was actually only a union- and not worker-participation program at this point.

The union's attempt to retain control over the process of employee participation in management problem-solving programs was clear. Its own goals or interests in structuring were still undeveloped. The involvement was largely defensive. Measures which affected the workers, such as the carrying out of NW&M training, were blocked by the unions. A process was set off, however, in which management and unions in the factory could jointly work out concepts for future work practices and forms of work organization. Concepts of semi-autonomous work groups were being discussed. Drafts for necessary adjustments of the wage system, which was seen as a central obstacle, were worked out jointly by management and the unions in the factory and then sent to the company headquarters. From the factory perspective, it was frequently the company headquarters which hindered the success of these endeavors. For instance, in its attempt at keeping wage costs down it did not allow exceptions to the general principles of the wage system.

The development had a somewhat different course in the British sister plant Blackmoor. The unions were involved at an earlier stage in the process, in part because they let their willingness to cooperate be known earlier. This is an almost ideal example of the phases which characterize the transformation of traditional work and industrial relations in the British context. The timing here also stemmed from an impending plant change-over for the generation of a new model (1984).

A disciplinary phase began in 1980/1. The main goal was for management to win back control over the availability of workers during the working time. "We started out with a one week suspension for being ten minutes out before lunch break. This is a severe penalty for a man. Since the men are dependent on their income it really amounts to a heavy fine. The conflicts following this certainly created agony in the plant" (Personnel manager, Blackmoor). A main management goal was to do away with the practice of "job and finish" which meant – especially on the night shift – that a major portion of the employees had already left the plant before the end of the shift, and that a few workers would punch out for all. This practice was also criticized by the unions, and a joint "Statement of Basic Disciplinary Controls" was agreed to which set penalties for absence from the work station during working hours, leaving the factory during the working hours, doubling up, punching out for others, etc. On this basis, ca. 250 firings for disciplinary reasons were carried out between 1981 and 1982. The conflicts took place according to the "four times four policy" we described in chapter 4. In 1982 management began to proceed more moderately.

The second phase was the disclosure of company goals and the involvement of the unions in discussions on securing the future of the site. In the words of the above quoted personnel manager at the Blackmoor plant: "This was our first attempt to be participative: Giving them information they had never had in their whole life, we involved them to the greatest degree possible." It becomes clear that the word "involvement" had become very stretched in this process, and it was no wonder that this gave rise to the criticism that NW&M was only accompanying music to large-scale rationalization measures. At any rate, the information also included the British company's plan for personnel reduction amounting to 33 percent of the work force in the period from 1981 to 1985. On the basis of the management presentation, a joint statement from the factory and the unions emerged regarding necessary adjustment measures to rescue the factory. "There was unanimous commitment to insuring the survival of Blackmoor as a viable competitive manufacturing unit, capable of reliably meeting a production goal set at its capacity. In this context, the need for a properly trained and motivated work force working constantly for the whole shift was agreed to" (June 1982, Project documents).

The document contained the demands which were raised by management and the unions regarding these objectives. Points listed by management were: changes in job delimitation between direct and indirect areas; solving certain demarcation problems; achieving higher quality in production and following agreed-to procedures in conflicts, e.g., over performance standards. From the unions came above all demands for a revision of the wage structure and for bonuses. Repeated meetings between management and the unions were held on the basis of this document. A discussion partner in the IE department made the following comments: "Disagreements over efficiency measures have become minimal. The major problem here is not the union but the attitude of the work force" (Industrial engineer, Blackmoor).

The third stage of employee participation had just begun at the end of our investigation. These episodes indicate how far the situation had improved at the factory level in the British industrial relations since the "Riot Act" in 1976 until the middle of the 1980s, which period we described in chapter 4. The extent of the changes in labor relations and in industrial relations was greater at Blackmoor than in most of the others in our sample. The main driving force was the fear that the site could be closed; the skepticism of the unions was still not entirely overcome and the agreements between the contract partners over goals and procedures, which the unions had demanded, had yet to take place. But the consciousness of the necessity for changes was there, as a result of the dramatic economic situation. This can hardly be demonstrated more vividly than in an open letter to the work force, written by a union representative who was considered to be militant. Commenting on a management presentation which dealt with the future of the site and the company, he wrote:

All of us therefore need to recognize a very serious threat to our livelihoods and work towards the elimination of those problems that are within our control. The facts as we have them are not very palatable, but we would be failing in our responsibility to you – our members – if we turn away, ignore or try to wish them away. This is the first occasion in which the unions and management at the site (...) have indulged in such a frank exchange of views. (Letter of July 6, 1982, Project documents)

Development in Great Britain has also proceeded further in the time since our investigation – also simultaneously with and reinforced by the developments in the Japanese "transplants" since the second half of the 1980s (for an account of the developments toward NW&M at the traditional British manufacturers up to the beginning of the 1990s, see Müller 1991).

9.2.3 In the Federal Republic of Germany: competition and convergence of NW&M ideas of management and the union

Management in the German plants investigated in our study had frequently shown skepticism about the concept of production groups. They referred to their experiences with resistance against rotation, but also expressed their fears that establishing production groups could result in management's loss of control.

Teams are very dangerous in the course of production because one can never know what sorts of group dynamic processes will take place. If you are lucky, it will turn out good, but it can just as well happen that a dynamism forms which leads to group egoism, withholding performance, and esprit de corps which you no longer have under control. (Production manager, Windeck)

Skepticism and restraint in this respect predominated among the management representatives we interviewed. This was also true with respect to the point and usefulness of quality circles which, by the way, were only widely diffused at one of the German companies we studied. Resistance from the works council had led to the fact that quality circles had not yet appeared in the Mittelort and Windeck plants at the time of our study. There had only been wide-scale quality circle activity in the plants of Company A in Germany since 1980. These plants were in the midst of a transition period at the time of our study; thus the opinions expressed by the interviewees were very critical of the previous activities of the quality circles. But there was no talk of discontinuing them; they were to be taken up in the framework of a more comprehensively conceived program for employee participation and be continued in another form.

The high time of the quality circle at Weinkirchen was 1981/2. Upper management saw quality circles as a central productivity concept and expected that the factories also "perform" in this respect. In retrospect, management representatives saw the setting of quantitative goals for the development of quality circles in this phase as a big mistake. "In this, the process of reporting had been carried to an extreme; everything was counted: the number of quality circles, the goals and topics, the solved and unsolved problems, etc. There was a statistic over anything and everything. We suffered under the delusion of sometime being able to achieve a 100 percent quality circle participation" (NW&M coordinator, Weinkirchen).

By 1982, Weinkirchen with its 8,000 employees could show 531 quality circles. This also brought up the question of their voluntary nature, the initiative for the formation of a quality circle rested with the first level supervisors ("*Meister*"), who also took over the leadership of the quality circle. The works council did not intervene; the union stewards ("*Vertrauensleute*") were asked not to take part in the quality circles to avoid a conflict of interests. The insufficient qualification of the "*Meister*" as leaders of the quality circles, the question of their voluntary nature, and the skeptical restraint of the workers' interest representatives proved to be significant hindering factors. The circle activities received an upswing when agreement was reached with the works council, who then sent representatives to the factory steering committee on quality circles.

The main task of the small group activity was, according to an agreement with the works council, to address the question of product quality. The organization of the circles and the initiative of the supervisors, who could nominate each of the employees of their area for participation if they wanted to, also reproduced the dividing line between indirect and direct job areas in the circle activities. This meant that the quality circles could only really solve problems within the competence area of the "*Meister*" leading the discussions. As soon as the questions brought up touched on the competence of the indirect departments, production planning, or product development they could not be meaningfully dealt with any more. The participation of quality control personnel in the quality circles in direct production was also avoided, as a works council member at Weinkirchen explained: "because of the conflict of purposes between quality and quantitative performance and to avoid that these conflicts be carried out in the quality discussions, where dirty linen would be washed."

A further dilemma of the quality circle in this period was the lack of cooperation between middle and upper management in the factories. A representative of upper-level factory management at Weinkirchen explained: "Here, problems such as questions of communication and informational advantages and the fear of a loss of power are involved. It is difficult to change traditional communication structures in the spirit of the participation program."

Thus with regard to the program, the main problem was seen by one of the NW&M coordinators in the cooperation of management not in that of the works council: "This willingness is more pronounced in the works council than in management. I would estimate that ca. seventy percent of the management is still not ready to take part in the change. My conversations with management are much more elaborate and time-consuming than those with the works council" (NW&M coordinator, Weinkirchen). We also gained the impression that there were still few allies to be found in management. This was especially true for the management of the quality control area, who apparently saw the quality circle as only a marginal contribution toward realizing the quality objective. A representative of management said openly: "I am almost tempted to say that there is no connection between quality and quality circles. A connection would be almost coincidental. Quality circles should produce more long-term changes. That is simply too long for our purposes" (Quality control manager, Altstadt).

The industrial engineers we interviewed at Altstadt and Weinkirchen assessed the positive contribution of quality circles in the past to be similarly small. The opinions of production managers, however, were more positive. The managers we interviewed generally recognized the quality circles as a good means for communicating with and informing the work force and as an aid in reducing tensions. In the longer run, the production managers did not see them to be very efficient without guidance and instruction from outside the circle. For them it was necessary that the quality circles not be left to their own initiatives, and that they should be given suggestions with regard to the problems to be solved (Production manager, Altstadt). Their experience was that the quality circles often ran out of meaningful topics after a while. The works council's observations that the quality discussions had the tendency to "increasingly infringe on social questions within the competence of the works council" (Works council member, Weinkirchen) had at the time of our investigation led to the consensus that the formation of "problem-solving groups," established for dealing with specific problems and dissolved again after completing their task, was a more sensible concept than the establishment of quality circles as permanent institutions with a stable membership.

At the beginning of 1985, the infrastructure for entering into the new employee participation program was being created at Weinkirchen. A coordinator was appointed and placed directly under the plant management;

steering committees were being established at factory and production area levels. The works council had announced its willingness to support the program and send delegates to the committees. At the production area level, they were aiming at creating positions for coordinators to oversee the participation process. Participation in problem-solving groups or quality circles was being made strictly voluntary. With this, an important precondition for the further development of the participation program was seen in changes in the job and hierarchy structures of production itself. Below the first line supervisor (*"Meister"*) level, a new "half" supervisory level was emerging with the establishment of group leaders. These would be supervisors who worked alongside the other group members, with a maximum of 25 percent supervisory and leadership functions – for a group of eight to ten employees. These group leaders were considered to be the natural leaders for quality circle activities. It was expected of the first line supervisors that they also be capable of giving directions to skilled workers and, with this, to take on tasks dealing more directly with technology. This demanded comprehensive measures for further training. Management also tried to hire young engineers for *Meister* positions, in the hope that they would bring the appropriate comprehensive technical knowledge from the university. This strategy was abandoned after initial experiences showed that these young engineers as *Meister* could not command the necessary authority from the shop floor personnel. The process of realizing the new concepts slowed down in the following years anyway, both in Weinkirchen and Altstadt. We do not know to what extent this slowing down could be explained by the fact that management in the European division of Company A did not want to diverge too much from the British plants, where NW&M developments were being blocked (for the development up to 1990 see Müller 1991).

In contrast to Company A the other West German automobile companies had no preliminary phase with quality circle activities when they started to introduce or discuss group concepts at the end of the 1980s. The union was more skeptical of quality circle activities here. Quality circles were considered clever social technologies employed by management with the aim of furthering the workers' identification with management's goals. They feared that the workers would lose their solidarity and become estranged from their union organization.[9] But in 1986, group work was demanded as the core element for future work organization in several resolutions at the IG Metall union congress in 1986 (Resolutions 5, 10, and 12). Up until then the criticism had predominated in the union that the group principle would above all amount to an increase in work intensity and that humanization effects would, in contrast, play a secondary role in practice – a view which had been confirmed by earlier sociological studies (Altmann *et al.* 1981).

Despite the remaining skepticism, both the union and management were becoming increasingly positive in their assessment of the group principle in the second half of the 1980s. The broad terrain for reaching compromises offered by the group principle was recognized. The three (alternative or complementary) objectives of management are to increase machine up-time, work efficiency and the responsibility for quality in production. The interests of the union and the workers are in raising the skill demands of the work, in increasing wage and employment security through the increased skills and expanded deployment area of the group members and, finally, in using the skilled worker potential already existing in the factory, but deployed at non-skilled jobs. These interests do overlap, especially in the area of using skilled-worker qualification.

In the concrete application of the group principle in the German companies, however, the objectives of the interested parties conflict. The controversies often center on a differentiation between "groups" and "teams" as two different concepts for work organization:

The members of a "group" form a cooperative relation, in which it is attempted to achieve a situation where all group members can be deployed as universally as possible in all of the group's job areas, and in which a greater importance is thus attached to rotation and qualification alignment;

the "team" forms, on the other hand, a cooperative relation in which the members retain their differing specialization and in which an alignment of skills is at best sought after as a long-term goal. The team concept would thus allow differences in formal qualifications and pay between the team members (an example would be a team which encompasses an automated systems controller, maintenance staff, and simple machine feeder jobs).

The union has a clear preference for the "group," as it corresponds to the goal of aligning qualification and wages at a higher level. In management, at least in the high technology areas, there is a preference for the teams in which the members are assigned differing jobs and have differing qualifications. At the same time, a certain overlap of tasks and a certain degree of job rotation was also sought here to increase the flexibility of labor deployment within the teams.

Obviously the question "group" or "team" was closely related to different process requirements. The main goals for production groups were an increased deployment flexibility on similar work stations and the reduction of cycle loss time on the lines. Thus, in the eyes of management interviewees, the group principles were seen as appropriate for the manually dominated areas, like trim and final assembly and the finishing area of the body shop, whereas teams were seen as appropriate for the highly mechanized areas, like in the body shop. The point of reference for team formation was first and foremost the machine up-time. The job spectrum extended from skilled work to "automated systems controlling"; from monitoring machines and equipment to tool and die setting. To the extent that the team area included skilled-worker jobs, a critical point in forming them was the question of being able to fully deploy the skilled workers, thus also for less demanding tasks like machine feeding or material handling. Here considerable resistance from skilled workers, especially those who were transferred from maintenance departments into production teams, also existed under German conditions. This was one of the reasons why companies proceeded quite slowly in implementing team concepts, although innovative solutions already existed at the time of our research, as we have shown in chapter 6. A more group-oriented approach toward new forms of work organization was implemented more recently in the Mittelort plant.

The distinction we made above between groups and teams was, in fact, not pursued further in the course of discussion in Germany and it does not play a role any more in factory agreements between the works council and company management at the beginning of the 1990s. (The Japanese companies, by the way, also distinguish between "groups" and "teams," although in a different manner; see Jürgens and Strömel 1987.)

9.3 Programs for worker participation in the context of company reorganization

The developments in the area of work organization, the stress that has now been put on integrated job descriptions, on increased responsibility and self-regulation at the level of work performed, on group formation, and on employee participation cannot be understood if they are not seen in a larger context as they only form an element of the sweeping movement for reorganization which includes all levels and functioning areas of the companies. In this process we are dealing with questions of centralization and decentralization, of autonomy and control, of power and influence (cf. also Dohse, Jürgens and Malsch 1985; Jürgens 1986).

A central theme which runs through these developments is the trend toward decentralization, in the spirit of forming smaller, self-regulating units; a further theme is the creation of integrated areas of responsibility, which transcend the given departmental boundaries and levels of hierarchy in their "project orientation." Both of these levels are closely tied together and are connected with the change from a rigid to a more flexible form of mass-production. Increased demands for coordinating all of the "parties" involved in the development, production, and sales of the individual product lines and an increased time pressure for model changes and product innovations are characteristics of this regulatory model:

The increase in cooperation agreements between the manufacturers, the reduction in the degree of vertical integration, and the increased market-orientation under the imperatives of the just-in-time principle and quality in production make it more and more important that development, planning, and production expertise be closely coordinated.

The traditional lines of segmentation between departments and processing stages also appear dysfunctional due to the increasing time pressure under which the product-related innovations are placed. The traditional processing sequence for new model lines, with product development, process planning, and manufacturing, as processing stages which are departmentally separated from each other, and deal with the new product one after the other, has proven itself to be too time consuming and inefficient. Fundamental points for decision, which could easily have been integrated into the process if they had been considered earlier, are brought up too late; belated modifications have to be made in many cases, which, if they do not totally upset the time planning, lead to commotion during the phase of the model start at the latest and result in poor compromises in process design. A reduction of the lead times for new vehicle types, which are presently at ca. six years in Western companies, to the standards of the Japanese companies, that is to three to four years (cf. Womack *et al.* 1990, p. 118), requires increased communication between all functions and organizational units which take part in the process "from product to market."

As a reaction to these developments the decentralization of decision-making structures and the formation of project teams with representatives of management from different departments and areas can be found in all companies. Team formation and self-regulation are not only topics with regard to restructuring in the factories, but also for the companies themselves. But at the factory level, we are not only dealing with changes at the level of direct production. Also the functions which were previously centralized in the plants, like industrial engineering, maintenance, and supply, are now being decentralized and given to the heads of the individual production areas.

This development toward "area management" or "cost centers," and thus the creation of "self managing units," can be called "job enrichment" of middle management. But the movement toward task integration has a tendency to trickle down to lower management and supervisory positions. This tendency would eventually bring integrated task profiles down to the first line supervisor (*Meister*) level. These supervisors would then not only be responsible for direct production, but also for quality control, maintenance, and other formerly indirect functions and personnel categories. Such

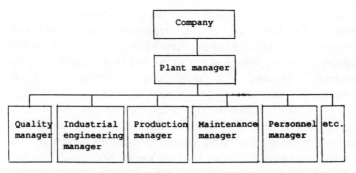

Figure 9.1 Organizational diagram of the factory management organization at Company B

a tendency towards a de-Taylorization of management structures must be seen as an important correlate and prerequisite of the tendency toward job integration and self-regulation in the form of group work at the shop floor level.

At the factory level, there were differing management structures in the three companies we studied. These could be differentiated according to their degree of centralization or decentralization. At the time of our investigation, the first model, a centralized plant management, predominated at Company B; the second model, decentralization, characterized the plant management at Company A; and the third model of vertically functional specified centralization held true for Company C. Figures 9.1, 9.2, and 9.3 show the corresponding organizational diagrams.

At Company B, the plant manager – who had integral responsibility for all activities of the production site – was the central point of coordination between corporate management and the factory. The managers of production, quality control, material and production control, maintenance, industrial engineering, and the other staff functions were directly responsible to this plant manager.

The powerful role of the plant manager went hand-in-hand with the company management's interest in the divisional headquarters only having one clear counterpart at the plant level. In the course of a restructuring at the divisional level in the 1980s the position of plant manager was strengthened even more through the enrichment with responsibilities from the sales area. This shifting of competence could also be seen as an additional burden, however, because the plant management was then even responsible for the vehicles after they had left the plant. Customer complaints and guarantee costs were, according to the principle of direct responsibility, charged to individual factories.

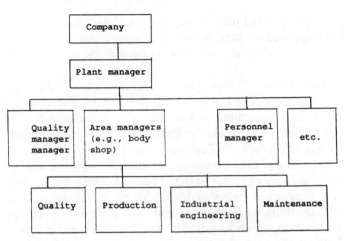

Figure 9.2 Organizational diagram of the factory management organization at Company A

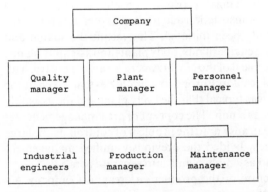

Figure 9.3 Organizational diagram of the factory management organization at Company C

In our sample Company A had gone farthest in decentralizing its management structures. In fact, Company A's "area management" served as a model for other companies when they started to decentralize their management later in the 1980s. Until the end of the 1970s Company A and B had a similar management organization with production managers reporting on equal footing with the managers of the staff functions to the plant manager. Under the new system of area management the production managers attained a key position. The managers of the support functions were hierarchically subordinate to the managers of the production areas now. Each area manager had his own support functions, thus had direct access to his maintenance workers, industrial engineers, quality engineers, etc. without having to coordinate their deployment with the other production areas.

Different considerations obviously came together to explain the move toward area management. The history of this new organizational model makes this clear. It is interesting to note that this decentralization of production responsibility and its concentration at the area level had already been introduced in the company's European operation in 1977. This was three years before participative management was introduced into company philosophy worldwide. We can surely speak of a certain complementarity of the idea of participation initiated in 1980 with the decentralized area management. Decentralized area management arose from more mundane considerations, however, which did not have anything to do with the idea of participation at first. The goal of top management was to create clearer and more manageable production units. This problem was more evident in Europe at the end of the 1970s than in the U.S.A. There, the move away from the old industry structures with gigantic production sites encompassing all the functions of automobile construction and toward a spreading out of the production sites had already been initiated. This meant the spatial and organizational separation of engine plants, body plants and assembly plants. This structure, which was typical of the North American auto industry, had, until then only established itself in Europe to a limited extent. Even at the newest production sites it was typical that the body plant and the assembly plants be brought together as a unit. The concept of area management was thus Company A's European answer to the problem of controlling the large production complexes: they divided the previously unified management hierarchy of their body and assembly plants into separate tiers.

In comparing the structure of the production areas in Company A's European plants in 1985, the reorganization of a German plant shows the clearest decentralization. There were initially five independent areas. In 1980 the number was reduced again to three: the body and press shops were merged again, the paint shop and the assembly areas remained separated. At the same time, the functions "controlling," "production planning," and "material supply" (except for "linefeeding") were centralized again at the plant level. Quality control, maintenance, and industrial engineering remained under the area managers.

Two of Company A's British sites received four management areas each: press shop, body shop, paint shop, and trim and final assembly. The organizational separation of the production areas "press shop" and "body shop" was the result of a difficult decision. This had its basis in the industrial relations in the British automobile industry. With the separation of the press shop and the body shop, management was pursuing the goal of establishing smaller, and thus more "governable," production units. At the Hartmoor plant, for instance, there were over 6,500 direct production workers in the organizational unit press/body shop alone before the introduction of area management. Against the background of conflict-prone industrial relations, this organizational area had gotten out of hand for management.

In the German plant, on the contrary, there was a fundamentally different situation. Industrial relations did not play a role here. Based on the experiences of 1977, there were two arguments which spoke in favor of a renewed *integration* of the body plant and press shop areas. First, their separation in the first phase of area management from 1977 to 1980 had led to an expansion of personnel at the level of management and salaried employees. And, second, coordination problems between the press and body shop had appeared. These had inhibited the smooth flow of materials and information. The overstaffing and such coordination problems were to be eliminated by joining the two areas.

When compared to Companies A and B, Company C had a factory management organization which could be described as vertically centralized functional management. The management organization at Company C exhibited a high degree of centralization when compared to the other two companies. This centralized company structure had a long tradition. The company was ruled from its central headquarters. The other locations, as satellites, had a low degree of autonomy and were kept on a tight rein in all matters. This centralism was seen most clearly in the fact that the company departments "personnel" and "quality control" were hierarchically structured from the executive board on down to the department or plant level. This meant that the board member responsible for personnel was the direct supervisor of the personnel manager at the plant level, the board member for quality control that of the quality control manager at the factory level. The quality manager and the head of personnel of the satellite plant were thus not directly responsible to their plant manager, this meant that the plant manager did not have full authority over them. The figure of the strong plant manager, like at Company B, who had integrated responsibility in all factory matters, did not exist here. The plant manager was not only a production manager, however. In the triumvirate: plant manager, quality manager, and personnel manager the plant manager functioned as "primus inter pares" (first among equals). He had a strong position because all remaining plant functions – production, logistics, maintenance, production planning, and work measurement – were directly responsible to him.

The strong position of the plant personnel department in the organizational system of Company C was directly related to the importance of

personnel policy in company policy. This personnel policy was characterized by a close interdependency between management and the works
council, by continual coordination and cooperation with the union and the
works councils, and by a corresponding consideration of the interests of the
work force. This policy was to be seen against the background that the
works council was a very powerful institution which could not be ignored
by management. In this respect, the exalted role of personnel in the
company hierarchy was the direct expression of the fundamental importance of personnel policy in the company's strategy.[10]

The relationship between the company's quality policy and its quality
organization was similar to the situation in personnel. Historical development was more varied in quality organization than in the personnel
department because quality control only became a central department
again in 1979 as a strategic answer to the increasing competition in the area
of product quality. This management model, which consisted of a thoroughly centralized linear organization, corresponded to a quality policy of
strict hierarchical control. This was in contrast to other companies, where
quality responsibility was increasingly being delegated to the direct production workers. At Company C, quality control was primarily still a control
function – institutionally safeguarded and given executive power. This
traditional understanding of control conflicted with a new understanding
of quality responsibility which would correspond to the area management
and participation philosophy at Company A. At Company A, area
management was primarily designed to strengthen the quality responsibility of the production areas. The fact that this was not without problems in
factory practice does not discredit the strategy of decentralization. It could
be observed, however, that the traditional control philosophy at Company
C had started to crumble. Signs could be seen of quality responsibility
becoming primarily a production task.

The fact that the centralism at Company C is not undisputed despite its
dominance could be illustrated using the example of maintenance. Like
personnel and quality control, maintenance had been centralized to a large
degree in the 1970s. The local maintenance managers of the satellite plants
were directly responsible to the maintenance management at the company
headquarters. This centralization proved to be impractical. A reorganization process lasting several years began at the beginning of the 1980s. A new
balance of power which took all of the differing interests into account was
to be reached through arduous negotiations between the different departments. In the course of the reorganization of maintenance, the decentralization was achieved at C's large plants and part of maintenance was given to
the production areas.

At the end of this chapter we will briefly deal with the question of organizational transfer within the company. This transfer consisted of organizational concepts being taken over from other divisions and factories within the company. It was the question of the "management of change" at the company level, and was linked with the management systems of the companies. Here, we had the impression that diffusion and implementation of new concepts within a company could take place more rapidly and more successfully when the management of a company and its production plants were compact and centralized. It could be seen here, however, that the structural and functional dimensions of the management organization did not coincide: structural centralism could go together with rigidity, and decentralized structures did not exclude rapid, centrally influenced organizational change – indeed, they may depend on this.

Company C offers an example of slow organizational change and a high persistence of the established structures. This had been especially visible with regard to the lengthy process of decentralizing the management organization. Compared to the organizational change at Company B, this could almost be considered paralysis. At B, the divisional level was restructured twice in a relatively short period of time. The structures at the plant level were left relatively untouched, however.

When compared with the other two companies, Company A can be characterized by relatively rapid organizational change at both levels. This was clear in the implementation of the new decentral area management: the new organizational model was first tried out in two of its continental plants in 1977 and then in a modified form in the remaining assembly plants of Company A Europe from 1980 to 1981. After a successful evaluation of this reorganization in Europe, Company A U.S.A. also began the implementation of area management in 1983. Such patterns for implementation within and between the two company divisions could also be shown in other matters. They were an expression of a compact management system which facilitated a methodical evaluation of new strategies and structures and then their large-scale implementation. Decentralized area management and centralized company management were thus two contrasting sides of a process of reorganization which was very effective in the entire corporate organization.

With regard to its willingness for innovation, Company B was aiming at slower organizational change. This change could have more far-reaching results than that at Company A in the long run, though. Company B was characterized by a conspicuous discrepancy between far-reaching organizational experiments in individual factories, on the one hand, and the persistence of traditional organization in the majority of its assembly plants, on the other. The company management was piling up a considerable fund of experiences with new organizational models in its experimental factories. These models were preferably tested at new production sites which were built from the ground up. At the end of the 1980s the company was about to enact these programs on a large scale and also introduce them into the old production plants with their traditional structures. The success of this endeavor remains an open question.

10　Is the assembly line obsolete?

The classical core of Taylorist–Fordist system has always been the assembly line. Critical writers have described the assembly line as being primarily responsible for the alienated character of work in mass production. Many observers were hoping that the assembly line would become obsolete with restructuring in the 1980s. Overcoming Taylorism and Fordism appeared to be synonymous with the abolition of the assembly line. In this chapter we will discuss the extent to which this expectation was fulfilled in the modern factories of the 1980s and look at which alternatives to the assembly line were chosen. In this we will be referring to the trim and final assembly areas in our sample of assembly plants.

A surprising observation for us was that even in the modern plants of the 1980s the assembly line hardly lost its centrality for the production organization. On the contrary, a further perfecting of the assembly line organization could be observed, above all in the American plants. This will be described in the first section of this chapter. We will be contrasting the reasons we were given for the advantages of this production layout in the American plants with a plant in Germany which also had conventional assembly line work which was, however, designed totally differently from the standpoint of the quality of work, and thus represents an alternative within the framework of conventional assembly line work.

In the second section we will be dealing with the possibility of automating assembly tasks as a consequent alternative to assembly line work. On the basis of the problems which emerged in the case we describe we will be pointing out the limits of this strategy given the technology available in the 1980s.

In the third section we will describe another alternative which could be considered as a compromise. This is the attempt at partially moving away from the assembly line organization by setting up stationary work places for individual tasks. These work stations supply their partial product (modules) to the still existing main line. We will be focussing especially on the extent to which the workers can influence their work process and the changed forms of control in the module production areas.

10.1 Alternatives within the framework of conventional assembly line work

A number of plants in North America were either fundamentally restructured or newly constructed, in connection with the change-over to the new generation of front-wheel drive passenger cars. In contrast to this, the plants for rear-wheel drive cars were primarily excluded from the modernization. When comparing the new generation of plants for front-wheel drive cars with the plants for rear-wheel drive cars, we see a clear shortening of the cycle times in production. The average output in Company B's North American assembly plants for front-wheel drive vehicles was sixty-six units per hour in 1985, the rear-wheel drive factories, on the other hand, produced at a rate of forty-nine units per hour. This situation existed in the assembly plants of A in North America as well, where front-wheel drive cars were produced at sixty units per hour in 1986, compared to forty-seven for the rear-wheel drive cars.[1] In view of the dominant type of assembly plant in the U.S., in which parallel production on several lines in the trim and final assembly areas generally did not exist, we can assume that an increased hourly production output also defines the cycle time; sixty units per hour thus means a work cycle of sixty seconds for the workers on the line. It becomes clear from the above figures that short cycle times were still considered by the planners in the U.S.A. to be the optimum in efficient work layout for new plants at the time of our research.

The situation in Company B's Greentown plant, which we will be describing in the following account, can thus be considered typical for the production philosophy which was still dominant in North America in the 1980s. A short cycle was traditional at Greentown. At the time of our study, it had an hourly output of seventy units from the assembly line. This corresponds to a cycle time of 0.86 minutes or 51.4 seconds. The actual line speed was, taking into account the overspeed, even higher: 82.5 units hourly, that meant a cycle time of 43.6 seconds in the body plant and 80.6 units hourly (a cycle time of 44.7 seconds) in trim assembly. The high "overspeed" allowances of about 18 percent in the body area, 20 percent in the paint shop, and 15 percent in final assembly indicate that the high speed had its price and went along with a high rate of breakdowns (see table 10.1).

We did not meet with any criticism of the short cycle times from management at that plant. A high line speed was seen to be advantageous in itself, because, the lower the line speed, the more task elements have to be carried out in a work cycle and, with this, the chances of a mistake increase. In addition, temporary reassignments cause fewer problems with a higher

Table 10.1 *Cycle times on the lines of trim and final assembly in minutes, 1985*

Factory	Length of the individual work cycle[a]
Company B Greentown	0.86
Company A Maple City	0.91
Company B Seaborough	2.0
Company A Hartmoor[b]	1.9
Company A Weinkirchen[c]	1.3/0.64
Company C[d]	2.6/1.9

Notes:
[a] Without the overspeed.
[b] Parallel lines with the same staffing.
[c] Trim assembly: parallel lines; final assembly: one line.
[d] Parallel lines with differing and variable staffing.

line speed due to the fact that short cycle tasks are easier to learn. Management also referred in this respect to the bumping system on the basis of seniority rules which we described in chapter 4 which results time and again in extensive turnovers. Moreover, with a greater line speed the work is carried out so habitually that a slight additional increase in speed is hardly noticed: "If you increase the line speed from, let us say, twenty-five to thirty jobs per hour, the workers would immediately find out and would raise hell. If you increase the line speed from seventy to seventy-five jobs per hour, however, they would not know, they would not notice that" (Industrial engineer, Greentown).

According to our interviews, management neither saw problems with quality with regard to the short cycles, nor in the endeavors toward a high degree of capacity utilization. An industrial engineer explains:

According to my experience, you have to give the people a good workload. When people have a good workload they do a better job. Underloading people is bad for quality. People would hang around, would be less concentrated on their job, losing their work rhythm, and quality would suffer. To achieve good quality you should rather aim for 100 percent workload. (Industrial engineer, Greentown)

The advantages of shorter cycle times for management were also emphasized in other plants with a high-speed tradition, especially with respect to the need for training. The IE interviewees in one of A's U.S. plants, in which an hourly output of sixty-eight units per hour was run until 1980, used a production volume of seventy-five units per hour as a rule of thumb for the optimum utilization of assembly plants under the perspective of efficiency. More units of output per hour automatically mean less, shorter and, generally, also more simplified tasks for the worker on the line. "If you have low volume and longer cycle times, it is hard on the operator to remember all the elements and the sequences of work. This is much more fatiguing for the operator than shorter cycle times" (Industrial engineer, Motor City). For this reason, the industrial engineers we interviewed in the American plants were very skeptical of minimum cycle times of over one minute in duration. But the Taylorist–Fordist world was also not fully in order for American production management. Thus, as we saw in chapter 7, increasing difficulties in achieving an efficient line balance were also seen here in connection with the increasing model mix. The reorganization considerations aimed, however, more at the introduction of team work on the line than at the abolition of the assembly line organization.

At Company C in Germany we found a totally different "philosophy" regarding the question of cycle times. Based on the discussion of assembly line work and cycle times in West Germany in the 1970s, management and the union agreed in the wage master agreement that "within the bounds of economic feasibility and befitting the state of technology" the company would redesign conveyor systems so as to "plan the work contents at 1.5 minutes per cycle." This cycle time regulation referred to the work cycle, not to the cycle time of production. At Heidedorf, this was at almost eighty-six seconds at the time of our research, only a little under the 1.5 minutes sought after with an hourly output of forty-two units. But most of the workers actually worked a "double cycle," which meant that he or she worked on the same car over two (or three or more) stations and thus only worked on every second or third vehicle. At the same time, his or her fellow worker(s) did the same operation on the car(s) in between. In this way multi-cycle work had become a widespread alternative to single car work in the designing of assembly line jobs.

Production at Windeck took place on two assembly lines. Both had a capacity of about 300 cars per shift and the same technical equipment. The parallel assembly line layout, which was also customary in the company's other plants, was used systematically for mix control. The "expensive" models were assembled on line 1 and the standard models – like the vehicles for public services (post office, police) – on line 2. The assembly lines were staffed differently corresponding to the different labor requirements. The staffing on the assembly lines was flexible, however, and could be changed daily according to the volume of orders and the personnel situation (level of absenteeism). It had been agreed that when the cycle times went below 1.5

Table 10.2 *Work volumes in an assembly section of Company C Heidedorf, 1983*

Length of the cycles	Number of jobs
2.774 min.	20
4.161 min.	10
5.548 min.	10
6.935 min.	1

minutes due to a change in line staffing, work operation would be switched to double cycles.

As opposed to the short cycle operations of the high-speed plants, the assembly work in this company has changed significantly. The tendency was, rather, toward even longer work cycles. In the Heidedorf plant, for example, in view of a production cycle of about 1.4 minutes we found the work cycles in an assembly section as shown in table 10.2.

Although management was originally very skeptical with regard to the efficiency of the work organization with long cycle times, this arrangement has apparently initiated a process of rethinking. The inefficiency which other observers see in this was disputed here:

If we bear in mind the goal of involving the people in the work process and the fact that people are motivated by more information, then I don't see this inefficiency. More meaningful work tasks mean more motivation. Especially since we have more skilled workers in production. They must be offered more challenging work. 60 second cycle times are not desirable in the spirit of the humanization goal. They lead to an increase in repair work and higher absenteeism. (Industrial engineer, Windeck)

Incidentally, the industrial engineer referred to the fact that problems with balancing the line increased with reduced labor requirements. From the standpoint of IE, a time of about two minutes was seen here as a reasonable lower limit for the work cycle. Regarding the upper limit, we were told that at the time of our research stationary work places in assembly were being set up with labor requirements of fifteen to twenty minutes. The argument of higher walking times was also rejected: "In the beginning, the argument of walking times was used against the double cycle. But the worker has to go between one cycle and the next anyway, and with a double cycle he only has to pick up material or tools once. The walking times can only be tackled by setting group standards. We haven't come that far yet" (Industrial engineer, Windeck). IE at the company level also referred to the advantages of decoupling the work cycle from the production cycle:

The flexibility of labor deployment is greater. The people are more capable and know more because they have to do more than just "a few turns."

With an expanded work cycle there are fewer interfaces to other operations and thus fewer problems with quality control.

Longer work cycles also allow the more efficient usage of tools, and make better line balancing possible, and thus a reduction in cycle losses.

The industrial engineers rejected the arguments that longer work tasks would bring about increased training times and problems with flexibility by pointing out that most of the employees at that time exhibited a high length of service, both in the plant and at their individual work sections. A further advantage was seen in the fact that with longer work cycles the personnel allocation can more easily be adjusted to fluctuations in the production schedule. It is then not necessary to completely rebalance the line. Instead, people can be taken out or brought in, depending on whether production is to be reduced or increased. With the double cycle work, two workers were alternating in performing the same job at each work station anyway. The system of parallel lines and double cycles at Company C was a major reason why model-mix problems did not become as much a problem for industrial relations here as in the other plants we investigated. At the same time, it helped Company C deal with its own problems: in view of the high absenteeism level and its fluctuations, the system was also designed to ease problems connected with the fluctuations in attendance of personnel. C's Windeck plant showed the highest average absenteeism level in our core sample.

With regard to the weekly planning of labor deployment, the model mix appeared rather to be secondary to the expected situation with regard to attendance. Computer assisted programs for rebalancing the lines with respect to the changing model mix, as we have seen in the other two companies, did not exist here. Personnel allocation was determined on the basis of a plan which showed the personnel requirements of the two assembly lines for different output levels. It was an easily understandable sheet which was part of the handbooks of both the production supervisors and the works councils in the factory. The plan which was valid at the time of our study had been in force for several years already. It was based on an optimized line balance, developed by the industrial engineering department, to determine the conditions under which assembly lines 1 and 2 would operate most efficiently with regard to a certain output level and to determine the required personnel for both lines. Additional calculations showed the personnel requirement for different output levels and the most favorable split between the numbers of units run on each assembly line for a given average production volume. Thus with a production program of 380 vehicles per shift the combination of 160 units on line 1 and 220 on line 2 was generally selected. This corresponded to cycle times of 2.3 on the "little line" and 1.5 on the "big line." The plan was not specified for differing model mixes. Part of the additional work content was done at stationary work stations separated from the assembly lines anyway, such as the installation of central locking systems, the sun roof, and power windows. On the basis of this plan, the principle of "running according to the number of workers in attendance" was introduced. Under an agreement with the works council, management could determine the production level according to the absenteeism level in the first half hour after the beginning of the shift.

The system described gives the assembly line organization considerable flexibility with respect to unexpected personnel and model-mix situations. Added to this is the possibility of making short-term personnel reassignments between the parallel lines and from the off-line work stations to the lines. A prerequisite for this flexibility in deployment at Windeck was the high level of qualifications: 28.5 percent of the direct workers had learned a metalworking or electrical trade; 29.5 percent had another skilled trade; only 42 percent were unskilled. A further prerequisite was created with the reform of the wage system. The new system combined a certain number of work stations which had similar job contents and (at least in the area of direct production) were situated in the same area, into "work systems." Within these "work systems" full flexibility of job assignment could be expected. For the transfer to a job with the same pay level but in a different "work system" a mobility allowance of 1.8 percent of the hourly wage was paid; in case of a transfer to a job at the same pay level in another department, this allowance increased to 3 percent. The agreement also regulated cases of transfers to higher- or lower-graded jobs, but we will not expand on this.

The mobility allowance gave the company built-in flexibility in labor deployment. This flexibility had indeed increased. At the same time it made the administration of transfers easier. Previously, the notification of a wage change had to take place in each case of a reassignment. This was a considerable administrative expense in a wage system with over thirty wage groups. By unifying jobs into work systems, management achieved a full reassignment flexibility within these systems, not only in theory but also in practice.

The systems of production organization in the German plants of Company A and Company B differ considerably from the system we just described at C's Windeck plant. The cycle time for the line workers was shorter. Thus in final assembly at A's Weinkirchen plant it was less than one minute (see table 10.1) – totally corresponding to the American high-speed ideal. In the area of trim assembly, however, there were also parallel lines designed to relieve production and improve quality.

The high-speed layout of American assembly plants did not necessarily mean an increased speed and pressure in carrying out individual work tasks; but it was definitely an expression of a stronger orientation toward the Taylorist–Fordist principles of simplification, routinization, and standardization of work. In the German plant Windeck these principles were clearly modified and toned down in favor of higher skill requirements and longer work cycles, even though the assembly line still formed the backbone of the production organization here.

The effect of Taylorist–Fordist principles on the qualification requirements and the possibilities for skill development were still eclipsed by the effects of the seniority system in the American plants. We will only mention this aspect here. As we have seen in chapter 4, the variety of job classifications which developed in the traditional American automobile plants was one of the main points of attack for management's attempts at work reform since the beginning of the 1980s. Under this traditional system the mobility for transfer within the job classifications would be guaranteed while assignment to other job classifications would lead to demarcation conflicts if it was not covered by the seniority system.

As we described above, Company C's German plants "work systems" were set up in order to define areas within which unlimited mobility in personnel development was expected. In principle, mobility between the work systems was also possible, however a mobility allowance must be paid in this case. Structuring the job spectrum according to work systems thus invites a comparison with the job classification system in American plants. In fact, a comparison shows that the German plant Windeck is not so different from the traditional American plant in this respect. In table 10.3 we look at the number of "work systems" or job classifications for the area of trim and final assembly of a Company C plant in W. Germany and a Company B plant in the U.S.

It can be seen that the average number of employees per work system/job classification were fairly comparable with thirteen in the German plant and eighteen in the U.S. plant. There is a considerable difference in the variance of job types with respect to the qualifications required and with respect to compensation. Although the degree of differentiation in the area of assembly jobs was still comparable, there were a multitude of additional direct production jobs in the German plant however, which either did not exist in the U.S. plant because of different technical equipment or were covered by skilled-worker departments. This brought about a much greater degree of wage differentiation over the spectrum of direct production jobs in the German plant than in the U.S. plant. The hourly wage rate of the highest group represented (L) was, with 21.75 DM (according to the monthly pay contract of January 15, 1985) about 34 percent above the lowest wage group of the area (C = 16.19 DM); in the U.S. plant the highest wage rate of $10.40 (utility dingman) was only 8 percent higher than the wage rate for the lowest paid job of the area, that of simple assembly work.

Similar variations in the degree of differentiation between job and wage groups existed between the other German and American plants. In the U.S.A., management's standardization efforts and its goal of securing control on the shop floor, on the one hand, and a union policy of levelling the wage differentiation, on the other hand, have led to a job spectrum in direct production which is rather "egalitarian" with regard to wage differentiation and the required qualification levels. This is true despite the multitude of job classifications in these plants. Thus there is little "substance" which could be used to design more qualified and rewarding jobs in this context. Egalitarian job structures at a low qualification level and management's attempt at optimally using the efficiency advantages of routinization and habitualization in mastering the work operations limit the possibilities for job enrichment in these plants. The potential for dealing with technology leaps or with requirements coming from a change in the design of the production flow could hardly be developed internally in these circumstances.

10.2 The risks of venturing into high technology

Manual labor on the assembly line dominated in the trim and final assembly areas in the majority of the plants in our investigation. Only a few tasks were automated, generally less than 3 percent; the number of robots was minimal. There was only one factory in the framework of our investigation where the leap into high technology had been attempted for assembly operations; and the character of work had changed fundamentally here. This was Company C's German plant Heidedorf. The company paid a high price for this. In the following account we will take a closer look at the problems relating to assembly automation and the way in which they were dealt with at Heidedorf.

The company had built a new facility for final assembly operations for its new car model which went into production in 1983. The increasing model and option variance had inflated the number of assembly operations, and the old assembly plant was more and more overcrowded. The worker density per work station amounted to five, in some cases even eight persons, and this caused many labor and quality problems. The new facility was planned with a worker density of less than three workers per work station and all overhead work was selected to be the target of mechanization

Table 10.3 Comparison of the job classifications in direct assembly in a German and an American assembly plant (trim and final assembly)

	Windeck (1986)			Steeltown (1982)			
Job	Number of work systems[c]	Wage groups[a]	Average number of employees[a]	Job (job code)	Number of job classifications[c]	Hourly pay (in dollars)	Average number of employees[b]
Assembly workers	43	D–G	23	Assembler (0101 ff)	12	9.63–9.00	41
Install wiring harnesses	2	E–F	9	Assembler (0201 ff)	4	9.69–9.00	8
Cutting-out fabric	1	E	4	Assembler (0301 ff)	2	9.79	7
Sewing	3	D/F	35	Driver unlicenced cars (1600)	1	9.63	31
Cushion making	5	E–G	15	Hang, fit, adjust, repair doors (2000)	2	9.79	6
Equipment assembly	1	F	1				
Parts assembly	37	C–F	15	Hood fit and adjust	1	9.79	1
Group leaders for production workers	6	E–H	1	Prepare body apply transfer (4200)	1	9.73	11
Repair workers	34	E–L	7	Stockmen (5400)	1	9.79	4
Testers	1	E	12	Washer and/or cleaner (5900)	1	9.63	8
Parts handling	1	D	16				
Equippers	10	E–F	8	Water test (6000)	1	9.90	1
Controlling parts	9	E–F	8	Auto repair mechanic (7600)	1	9.93	5
Tracking down programs and orders	2	F–G	1	Repair assembly line (8300)	2	9.90	19
Controllers	4	F–G	1	Repair auto general (8400)	2	9.90	15

Equipment operators	2	E–F	3	Repair auto general	2	9.90	15
Machine operators	2	D–E	18	Repair body final trim (8658)	1	9.93	5
Machine controllers	1	E	2	Utility (8700–8800)	8	9.79–10.40	5
Systems controllers	7	F–I	1	Replacement operators	4	9.79–9.90	15
Set-up workers	2	G–H	3	(8800 ff)			
Equipment monitors	1	F	3	Repair trim and hardware (9800)	2	9.90	18
sum/average	174	—	13		46	—	18

Notes:

[a] Calculated for single shift operation.

[b] Single shift operation.

[c] The same jobs in different departments (hard trim; soft trim; chassis; final process) are counted as separate job classifications.

measures. The new technology went into an area called the mechanized section. Because of the large volume and the high speed of through-put which the planners wanted to achieve, the flexibility of the equipment was restricted to one body and the majority of its variants. We will first of all describe the production layout as we found it in a follow-up investigation in 1988.

The mechanized section was spread over two areas: the first was on the ground floor where the preassemblies of the engine, gear box, and suspension system took place. The complete drive train was mounted on a special assembly frame, then brought up to the main lines on the upper floor where it was joined to the car body, including parts and components like battery and wheels, brake line and gas lines, exhaust tail pipe, etc. There were about fourteen preassemblies and about twenty automated work stations for car body assembly in the mechanized section. Most of the assembly operations took place in the final assembly stage. Most of these operations required overhead work and heavy lifting in the previous process layout.

The heart of the mechanized section consisted of two parallel lines, each of which consisting of two separate automation complexes separated by a buffer area. Each of these automated transfer lines carried out about ten operations, each within the cycle time of twenty-five seconds and strictly in sequence. Whenever something went wrong at one station, the whole transfer line stopped operating. There was some flexibility though, as there was one empty station after each work station. Therefore, whenever the process stopped at one station, the subsequent stations could continue until the next cycle was over. This provided about thirty seconds, which could be of great value. Of course, the process came to a halt if the preassembled components, either from the ground floor or from other plants (or storage areas) were not there in time. This whole process was controlled by computer systems, designed to make sure that the cars arrived in the right sequence and were coordinated with components arriving from elsewhere in the proper sequence. They made sure that parts were correctly joined, and, if not, recorded errors or stopped the operation.

The mechanized section was not a manless production though. Including the maintenance personnel stationed in the surrounding work environment, there were approximately thirty workers at each transfer line. But the human element was dwarfed in comparison to the enormous proportions of these complexes. It would, however, be a mistake to only focus attention on the impressive technology of the mechanization area. As has been said, this area was a sort of automation "island" within the larger production flow. Before and after the mechanized section we found the classical manual assembly operations. There were around 3,500 hands-on workers in the trim operations before the mechanization and about the same number of workers in the final assembly operations that followed it. For most of them, the "mechanization" was a critical bottleneck of the process. In order to ease the effects of a breakdown in the mechanized section huge buffer areas were created.

As is customary in assembly plants, there was a big buffer area behind the paint shop, from which the car bodies were sent to the assembly area. At this point, the car bodies passed a control station where an electronic scanner read the name plate of each car body and passed the data on to an "assembly-order information system." This system carried all necessary data for the construction of this specific car, including all options and specifications. Thus, at that moment it gave an order to other areas of the parts production system to send the corresponding engine, transmission, etc. for the car. The car body travelled about seven hours from there to the "marriage point" in the "mechanization," where the drive unit and the car body were mated. This was a very critical point from the logistical perspective of synchronizing the various processes of parts and body production.

After arriving in the assembly area the car body was channelled into five parallel assembly lines, each planned for a daily output of 600, although they have been run at 700 since 1988. One of these lines, it should be noted, was planned for manual production only and bypassed the mechanization area. After passing through buffer areas where the sequence was checked against the criteria of line balancing, the cars moved into the trim area. After another buffer area, the four assembly lines converged into two lines, each of which led to yet another buffer area. Then, each of the two remaining lines passed through the first automated transfer line for a good hour of production and entered the second transfer line. After this, each of the mechanized lines split again and four lines left the new facility for another building where other final assembly operations, final quality checks, and preparations for sales operations took place. The buffer areas were closely watched by computers at several control stations to provide early warnings to the manual work areas whenever the buffers were overfilled (before the mechanized section) or had dried up (after this section) due to a breakdown in technology.

Compared to other assembly plants, the characteristic traits of this layout process could briefly be summarized as follows:

a fair degree of systems integration, especially with regard to the assembly-order information system and the various systems controlling the equipment, manufacturing machinery, and transportation devices;

the process was highly buffered, both before and after the mechanized section;

within the mechanized section a large number of the complex operations were rigidly connected and, thus, a breakdown in one station could quickly bring the entire transfer line to a halt.

We would now like to deal with the problems which emerged from this high-tech production organization. With all the new technology, the interdependencies of the various logistical flows and the new demands on the work force, breakdowns and delays were inevitable. Of course, there were the buffers. In fact, most of the breakdowns of machinery lasted only a few seconds. Moreover, as there were empty stations within the transfer lines production could go on to the next station, i.e., continue for around thirty seconds. And then, of course, the mechanized area worked faster than the manual lines – in addition to the fact that it worked double speed because each mechanized line took up two manual lines – and thus ground could be won back from the trim line after a short disturbance. But even if it was only for a second, such a breakdown in the mechanization of the sub-assembly or main assembly equipment caused a minor crisis. The people responsible scurried with questions: Can we fix it in a few seconds? Will it occur again? What was the cause?

But, thanks to the buffers, even a twenty-minute breakdown could be coped with. But if the breakdown occurred frequently, the shift "crashes." (The English term is actually used in the German factory.) Typically, a "crash" is a breakdown that lasts more than one to two hours. At this point, the buffers before the mechanized section are full and those behind it are empty, while in the manual areas thousands of workers stand idle. The people responsible for the equipment not only have to fix the breakdown but at the same time reallocate personnel. They also have to report to all the white collar workers who turn up on the shop floor to watch the money going down the drain. "This is a black day," as one engineer put it.

In view of the volume of production, the mechanized section could become a serious bottleneck for the corporation. The loss of one hour's production runs easily into millions of DM. For the superintendents, *Meister*, and automated systems controllers responsible for the mechanized section, this translates into enormous stress. They have to be on the alert at all times. They must know what emergency strategy should be used in what kinds of situations. They have to know how best to fix all sorts of breakdowns. This requires a good technical understanding of the functions and pitfalls of the technology. Unfortunately, "crash" situations were not infrequent. They happened again and again, especially when changes were introduced, new options included, logistical flows rearranged, etc.

The most fundamental decision to be made by the supervisors in a crash situation was whether to gamble on a short repair time and risk the loss of some production or to rely on an emergency strategy and "assemble by hand" that which the mechanized section failed to produce. Of course, this decision depended on a prognosis as to how long the repair would take and on which operation had been affected. Some operations could be carried out in one of the empty stations within the transfer lines, some could be arranged in a repair area behind the mechanized lines, while still others could be done in the final assembly area in the other building. The manual line was loaded up to capacity and could not serve as a stand-by in such cases.

Emergency point strategies had been developed for all stations in the mechanized section except for the "marriage." Each case had to be dealt with differently. Some operations could be done within the "mechanization," like installing the bumper. Others, such as installing the exhaust pipe, the brake, and gas lines, etc., had to be done in the final assembly area. Finally, still others had to be carried out on repair platforms which had recently been installed behind each of the two mechanization lines. On each platform, around twenty workers complete what the machinery had failed to do. The finishers, for example, took the place of the traditional repairmen whose task was to correct the errors of their fellow workers. Because of the automatic stopping devices, the machine did not make errors, it just ceased to operate.

"Crashes," as already indicated, were normal to the production process, even though the new facility had now been in operation for more than six years. As could be expected, the problems accumulated in the first years. But, rather surprisingly, relatively few of these problems were related to technical hardware. Most of these were brought under control after teething problems had been worked out. The two main problem areas were the software systems and workers' qualifications. We will now be considering these two factors.

Computerized control systems have to ensure that the various material flows and the advancement of the car body take place sequentially so that exactly the right part comes to the right point at the right moment. If not, there are big problems. The situation could be seen analogous to a zipper connected with the wrong teeth. The zipper improperly closes all the way up. To disengage the teeth can be a painful process.

There are all kinds of reasons why the "systems" can and do make errors. In the early years, there were some very large crashes, causing the whole assembly-order information system to break down. When this happened, chaos broke out because no one knew which part had to be joined to which car body and "the whole factory assembly line had to be cleared up." At the same time, thousands of workers sat idle, waiting and smirking about management's incompetence.

But breakdowns need not have spectacular reasons. Thus, it happened that a transmitter counted further when a worker walked past it with his safety shoes. As a consequence, the wrong part arrived at the wrong vehicle, creating the zipper problem. Another case occurred when a vibration of the conveyor caused the transmitter to count improperly. Errors in bar code reading were additional reasons, and this became increasingly problematical because of the explosion in part specifications. Other reasons for crashes were insufficient knowledge or other small matters, such as employees putting parts back which had fallen down from a conveyor in the wrong places. Finally, another cause was insufficient preventive maintenance, especially due to increased overtime and extra-shift production in recent years. Too little time was devoted to maintaining the equipment.

The exploding variety of parts and specifications ensured that there was no shortage of reasons for crashes. As compared to the initial planning stages in 1982, by 1987 the number of engine block variants had risen from twenty-eight to fifty-one, the number of different suspensions from thirty to 380, and the number of different drive train combinations from 450 to 18,000. The introduction of these new options often required changes in the hard- and software of the mechanized section, thus the next series of crashes.

A deeper reason for problems was the lack of coordination among those units involved in product development, production planning, and production. Product development occasionally "designed" parts without taking care to ensure that the mounting hole separation, the threaded hole or the handling points of the new part variants remained the same. Taking into account the errors in the system of electronic parts identification, for instance, would reduce the burden of adjustment in the production facilities considerably. If representatives from "production" could participate in the earlier phases of the "design" and planning processes, they could increase the awareness for such requirements. The explosion of variants, and thus the flexibility of change demanded from the facilities, was not foreseen by the planners and strategists in the late 1970s.

The second problem concerned insufficient training. The figure of 100 million DM was cited as the total loss in units of production in the first years of mechanized production due to breakdowns. A good part of this was attributed to training deficits. It was, of course, anticipated that the mechanized lines required different skills and job classifications to run and to maintain the operation. The company, for example, had long-term experience with automated transfer lines from its body shop. Here, as we described in chapter 6, the classification of an automated systems controller ("*Anlagenführer*") had been created.

The task of this automated systems controller ("*Anlagenführer*") is to take charge of operating equipment, observe its functioning, carry out

small repairs and preventive maintenance and to make necessary disposi-
tions in case of impending or actual trouble. The additional need for
qualified workers resulting from the "mechanization" amounted to
between forty and seventy new employees according to information
provided by management. In particular, this involved *Anlagenführer* and
maintenance personnel. In the original plan, the need was grossly under-
stated. By 1990, the number of *Anlagenführer* exceeded the plan by more
than 150 percent. Some of this increase can be explained by reductions in
the working time and to the increase in scheduled output.

Thus, with an investment in the hundreds of millions of DM for
technology, personnel requirements were calculated rather tightly and the
training courses had to be developed at the last minute. As to the question
of who would get the upgraded and well-paid jobs, management and the
local works council followed the strategy of selecting workers internally
from the assembly areas. However, the differences between equipment in
the body shop and in the assembly areas proved to be so great that neither
the training programs nor the people from the body shop would fit the new
job requirements.

The training course took six weeks. In addition to this the first generation
of *Anlagenführer* had the advantage that they had participated in the build-
up of the new facility and thereby knew the equipment "from the inside"
when they later worked there. But the pressure of the hectic first years was
so great that many of them gave up and turnover among automated systems
controllers was high. Especially the fear of making mistakes with such
expensive machinery caused them to quit. Moreover, as there had been no
ongoing training for *Anlagenführer* for many years, the number of experts
in production grew thin. In any case, training would not have been the
panacea for all situations. Because the various real and potential crash
situations and the corresponding emergency strategies could not be foreseen, there was no way to train workers for all eventualities.

The availability of skilled personnel with experience in assembly operations and the training measures taken were not the least important factors
explaining why, despite all of the problems, the mechanized section
operated relatively successfully in the years after the launch. Some interviewees saw the failure to consider how to select and train the rest of the
work force for "low-qualification" jobs to be a mistake. The less-qualified
workers handled parts, fed the machines, and filled magazines. Their
selection was largely determined by foremen in other sections of the
assembly area who wanted to get rid of particular workers. But with such
complicated machinery, and only a few workers scattered around, mostly in
isolated places, every eye, ear, and mind was needed to observe the process,
anticipate problems, and to help diagnose their causes (among the 400

direct workers at the upper floor "mechanized" area 180 were automated systems controllers, most of the remaining workers performed the lower qualified jobs – figures for the end of 1989). In more recent times, it has been recognized that the role of these workers had been underestimated and management attempted to draw more skilled workers into these jobs. But as long as the work organization restricts them to poorly qualified operations and no rotation with the system controlling functions takes place, there is not very many opportunities in these jobs.

Automation islands of such giant proportions as described here have generated a new generation of control concerns for management. In classical car production, assembly operations had always been the most difficult area for work regulation. This changed for a variety of reasons after technology had been brought in and labor became more cooperative. Heidedorf had a great potential for coping with the situation in its new assembly facility. As we have seen, the skill level even among the direct hourly workers was high, the in-house technical know-how was enormous, earlier experiences with automated facilities existed and central staff was at hand on the site.

Nevertheless the experience has shown: the full automation of assembly operations in car production is not in sight, for technological as well as economic reasons. The kind of automation we described precludes a "smooth" operation. The threat of a crash is always present. It requires enormous buffers. The most efficient assembly plants in Japan and elsewhere do without a systematic buffering of the process and they do without "automation islands." The philosophy here is that smoothness of the production flow and the balancing of the various phases of production takes priority. Buffers put a heavy burden on plant efficiency (see Krafcik 1988). And buffers are regarded as covering up problems which should be traced back and solved at their roots. Technology, as management learned from the Japanese in the 1980s, often stands in the way of a harmonious, fully efficient production.

10.3 The compromise solution with off-line module production using AGVs

In view of the difficulties of a leap into high technology in the assembly areas, off-line module production using AGVs was an alternative for the technical and organizational restructuring of assembly processes. This alternative was pursued above all in Company B's European assembly plants, but Company A also chose this solution for the change-over to its new model at its German Altstadt plant in the middle of the 1980s and for its second model line at Heidedorf. Additional German assembly plants were restructured accordingly by the end of the 1980s. The organization of assembly work with partially stationary work stations in pre- (module) assembly areas has thus also established itself in Germany as an alternative to the high-tech strategy.

In module production, certain parts of the operation are removed from the central line flow. Many operations which have now gone into module production areas were also previously independent of the line, in the so-called preassemblies. Among these is especially the assembly of the instrument panel and the doors. The advantages of module production are

an increased flexibility of types, variants, and production volumes;

increased possibilities for introducing new forms of work organization and improving ergonomic aspects,

creating possibilities for mechanization or automation in specific sub-areas,

the reduction of inventories and of the production lead-time for the entire system. (Hesse and Oelker 1986)

The solution of module production was chosen in the plants Mittelort and Seaborough. Two module areas were created in the last big change-over before our study. One was for the separate door assembly, the other for cockpit assembly. We want to briefly describe the new process with the example of the new door assembly area at the Mittelort plant.

After the cars came out of the paint shop the doors were taken off the bodies again and loaded in pairs on automated guided vehicles (AGVs, also called "robocarriers"). The AGVs brought the doors past four different work areas where they were provided with windows, mirrors, padding, handles, etc. Each work area consisted of up to fifteen work stations and the AGVs automatically sought a station. After inspection the completed doors were returned to the main assembly line and reconnected to "their" bodies which, in the meantime, had been further assembled (see the process outline in figure 10.1).

There were 140 AGVs in the door assembly system of the Mittelort plant, and they went through four work islands, each with a set of parallel work stations. One person worked on both sides of the AGV. Each side had a door attached. There were 3,000 different door variants if the different paint options are counted. The average labor content on work island A was 5.17 minutes per unit at the time of our study. Control lamps installed at each work station lit up after a certain period, indicating that the programmed time had elapsed at this work station and that the carrier should move on.

These control lamps were a visible sign of the close relationship between the functions of process control and performance regulation. There was a column at each work station of the AGV system with a button to press and a "time overrun lamp" at the top. After completing the prescribed operation it was the task of the production worker to push the button to send the AGV

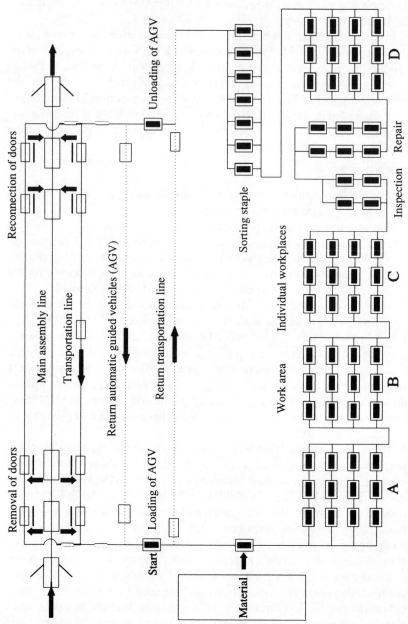

Figure 10.1 Schematic representation of modular door assembly

further. It then drove to the next production island automatically. The intent of the control lamps was to visualize a delay. They could thus be programmed to light up as soon as the precalculated work time for the workpiece in question had elapsed and "lost time" occurred. These signals were also registered in the module area's terminal room, in which the control center of the system was located.

With the system of control lights, it was possible to regulate the appearance of the light to match predetermined times for the respective variant. In this manner, delays caused for technical reasons, by restrictive practices or by an attempt of the worker to establish his or her own rhythm were made openly visible to all. A works council member remembered: "At first it was a big ambition of the supervisors not to have any lights on. They flipped out when the lights were on regularly anywhere" (Mittelort). The "introduction and use of technical equipment which was intended to monitor the behavior or the performance of the worker" were however, according to §87, paragraph 1.6 of the German Plant Constitution Act, subject to codetermination. As a result of discussions, management and works council agreed to keep the lights in operation, but to set them at the average standard time for the work to be performed at the respective island. Thus they would not be differentiating according to the length of the operations actually required for each workpiece. After some debate they agreed to generally program the control lamps at the average time of 5.17 minutes. This created new problems, however.

The Achilles heel of the concept of module production was being able to keep the sequence of the workpieces parallel to the production progress of the respective car body on the main line. When the door or the cockpit which belonged to the car body in question did not reach the station on the line where the doors had to be installed at the right time, then the entire flow of production was disrupted. The control lamps could play a critical role here. As the lights were programmed for five minutes with a range in labor requirements of about three to eight minutes per variant it was possible to wait with the "cheap variants" (under five minutes) and take an informal break until the light went on and the supervisor would notice. A cumulation of delays resulting from such a practice at different work stations could result in the module not coming out of the area in time to be installed into the proper car. Even if such an abuse did not take place often – due to control by foremen and co-workers – the problem that the time was too short for necessary repair work still remained. This was an especially serious problem in the cockpit module area, thus for the electronics, which had become a focus of quality problems anyway because of their increased complexity. The situation was depicted as follows by a works council member:

Delays are a main problem at present. It even happens frequently that cockpits are put on the lift and brought past checkout, only in order to supply cockpits to the line in time. If the hangers are empty, then all hell breaks loose. Then reliefmen come in, new work stations are opened, an enormous pressure is exerted. And because the vehicles bypass the checkouts, an enormous number of repairs arise later. (Works council member, Mittelort)

Time-sovereignty at work obviously appeared as a terrain of conflict as another works council member pointed out:

An important problem is that working ahead is not possible here. If one has a carrier with fewer labor requirements than the cycle for which the control lamps are programmed and waits until the light goes on, it can happen that someone else, for example the foreman, comes by and pushes it off himself. There is always trouble in such a case. There are now certain tricks though, for example someone does not send the carrier that he has just finished further but rather goes to the second carrier that is waiting before his station and works ahead. Then he sends the first carrier further and has practically the entire time for the second carrier as a time buffer for himself. But the problem is that everything is now totally obvious because everyone sees when you work outside your station. Previously on the line, no one was concerned if you worked ahead. The foreman knew it when he saw you smoking a cigarette somewhere, but at the same time he knew that you had worked ahead and that everything was running. Now it can happen that they immediately send the first carrier further when they see you working on the second one. Otherwise there are small delays in the system. (Works council member, Mittelort)

Company B had already had experience with module production and the AGV system in its other German assembly plant in the course of an experimental project in the engine dressing area. Such a concept had, however, not yet been tested on a larger scale and in the framework of mass production in the trim assembly area. The Mittelort and Seaborough plants thus also had a pilot role for the company. Correspondingly, the cost/benefit calculations with respect to the system were doubtless influenced by long-term strategic considerations for the company. This system layout was much more costly than, e.g., separate door assembly with conventional line organization. Management also saw the step away from the conveyor belt as the backbone of the production organization as a preliminary stage for future automation projects.

Cost/benefit calculations for new production concepts can be deceptive, though. Many of the savings realized on the basis of the new system were not recognized at first in these calculations for the cases described. Actually, more was saved than had been expected, e.g., through the fact that production took place on the main line without doors parts could be fitted more accessibly, there was less damage, and thus a reduced need for repair work. Area management at the Mittelort plant emphasized some of the reasons for introducing the new production concepts:

1 advantages with regard to model variance (reduction of cycle losses, etc.);
2 preparation for automation,
3 improved job design and increased transparency of the work flow in the area.

An important economy factor was the elimination of the walking and waiting times. At Mittelort, the savings in personnel compared to the previous allocation for the same operations on the line was 15.7 percent in the door assembly module (thirty-four people out of a previous 216 per day), and 19.1 percent in the cockpit module (41 out of previously 215 per day). The labor content had been significantly expanded and enriched. In the door area they were between 3.5 and 10.5 minutes at the time of our research, in the cockpit area between 4.5 and 8.5 minutes. The restructuring of work also brought about significantly simplified movements and reduced stress and strain. The workpieces were transported on AGVs which were programmable at three different heights and adjusted themselves accordingly as soon as they come into certain work stations.

Better working conditions in the spirit of humanization of work was an explicit goal of this layout. Cockpit work was particularly characterized by miserable work requiring especially unfavorable bodily postures: workers assembling while lying on their backs, bent over, crawling in the car body. Such operations could only be replaced by introducing new assembly principles. Module production thus provided better working conditions. It was estimated that between eighty and one hundred ergonomically unfavorably laid out work stations were improved through setting up the module areas.

Being tied to a stationary work station was, as we were told, seen as a disadvantage by the employees who had previously worked on the line: they had the feeling of working "on a serving tray," individual work and performance became more easily visible and transparent. For management, though, tying workers to a stationary work station involved a potential limitation to work flexibility. In order to prevent the emergence of barriers caused by qualification or a policy of restrictive practices, they thus took precautions with the work organization at plant Mittelort. This was in contrast to the British sister plant Seaborough even though management there had experienced far more problems with restrictive practices in the past. Certain work stations at Mittelort were combined to form "groups" within which the workers would rotate. Organizing the work rotation was the responsibility of the area *Meister*.

In the door assembly area, the group included the production islands A, B, and C – about sixty work stations between which the workers could rotate; in the cockpit module the group encompassed about eighty work stations at the islands A, B, and D. The breaking-in time at new work stations on different islands was estimated by the *Meister* we interviewed from this area at around one week. A definite procedure for rotation had not yet been established. The goal of the works council was to work out a plan so that all participants could determine when they would be deployed at which work stations. At the time of our study, the department only had a list of who had already been at which work stations. Was there resistance against rotation?

"Because the different work stations now have the same wage classification, a refusal to change work station does not have any wage consequences. Surveys on the shop floor show, however, that, in contrast to previous attempts with job rotation, there exists a great deal of consent today" (Works council member, Mittelort). The works council also wanted to introduce group work on the assembly line. Its goal in this was to get a higher classification for the other group members through the inclusion of more qualified jobs. Nevertheless, the possibilities given in module organization for the formation of semi-autonomous group work remained largely unused in Mittelort at the time of our study. This changed, however, with the large-scale introduction of group work at Mittelort and in the British factory Seaborough at the end of the 1980s.

To conclude, while the principle of the assembly line was still completely in force in the U.S. plants (at the middle of the 1980s, the GM plant in the Detroit suburb of Hamtramck was the first and only assembly plant in which the line was done away with on a larger scale), the European plants went differing ways: in the British plants of Company A we studied, the principle of assembly line work was still fully valid. At Company A's German plants in Altstadt, whose technological and organizational restructuring took place one year after the Mittelort plant, the path of module production was taken as well. Management also decided to assemble the doors and instrument panel separately from the main line. The process layout was different, though. No automated guided vehicles were used. Assembly took place on conventionally organized sub-assembly lines, whereas the instrument panel was assembled on an intermittent carousel line.

In the British and German plants of Company B, special work areas were, as we have seen, created for specific traditional trim assembly operations. Automated guided vehicles served as work platforms and transport for the workpieces. At Company C, after its experience with large-scale automation of assembly work, this concept was regarded as the most promising option for the organization of assembly work in the future also.

Classical assembly line work was not eliminated in these measures; the new work structures were only established where problems had occurred because of increased variance in production: this was especially true for the instrument panel and the electrical components. In addition to the module areas in trim assembly, the main line, where the majority of the blue-collar workers were employed, still existed. Thus at Mittelort, for example, out of the about 1,600 employees in trim assembly, 73 percent worked on the main line and about 21 percent in the module areas. A little more than 5 percent worked at off-line trim assembly work stations outside the module areas. In this manner, a maximum of one third of the traditional tasks in assembly were performed without an assembly line at the time of our research. Thus the module areas served to reduce the complexity of the remaining assembly line tasks so that they could be continued in their traditional form. But, due to the module areas, work on the line could thus be more heavily standardized again and the problems of line balancing described above could thus be reduced.

The new process layout actually did create new working conditions in the module area:

There was no longer a unified work pace which determined the rhythm of all jobs.

The work was ergonomically much better designed.

The labor contents of individual jobs were higher.

The difference is significant, but not so great that it would be legitimate to speak of an elimination of Fordism. The pace of the main line still determines the rhythm in the module area because the individual modules must be ready at the end to be installed in the proper car body. The work pace is no longer forced, but it is still controlled by predetermined times stored in the process control programs.[2]

11 Modern times in the automobile factory: trends toward new forms of work (summary and conclusions)

It is not easy to summarize our investigations with regard to the questions we posed in the introduction. We were witnesses in the 1980s to a far-reaching radical change in the world automobile industry, not only with regard to the forms of work. The signs of dissolution of the Taylorist–Fordist production regime were obvious: flexible production designs took the place of the rigid standardized production organization; the reintegration of work tasks emerged as a dominant strategy and took the place of highly fragmented task structures; control and responsibility were decentralized and given back to the operational areas. We have seen many examples of such processes in the preceding chapters.

But what will come after the Taylorist–Fordist regime? In view of the many facets of the changes in the automobile industry which we have described in this book, we are faced with considerable difficulties in interpreting the direction and pace of the change and getting to its essence. It is difficult to track down the actual changes, despite, or perhaps because of, the loudly proclaimed objectives of the companies. One of the problems in this is to properly assess the inertia of the established structures, institutions, and attitudes. A further problem lies in the fact that at the time of our research there was no established model for the new forms of work in the future, only many controversies about the direction to be taken. The factor "industrial relations" proved to be an extraordinarily important influence. But also within management there were many different ideas – about the necessity as well as the path of the reforms to be pursued.

In the concluding discussion of our findings we would like to address the following questions:

1 What are the general trends which can be established from the most important aspects of our investigation with regard to the forms of labor deployment in the factory?

2 What influence do company affiliation and national affiliation have in regard to the differences observed in the spectrum of our study? Are there

converging or diverging developments in the company- and nationally specific forms of regulation?

3 What are the models for future forms of labor regulation and what are the prospects for their stabilization and spread?

11.1 Directions of change

In summarizing our findings about trends in the forms of work in the factory we see the following directions of change:

(1) Change in the forms of control over production work

In the traditional Taylorist–Fordist organized automobile factory, everything was geared to prescribing the course of work to the last detail from above and beyond the "shop floor" level. Machine-pacing of work through the assembly line, standardization of work performance by the industrial engineering experts and direct monitoring by the line supervisors – this control structure of Taylorism–Fordism did not tolerate self-regulation by the workers themselves.[1] This constellation, which stifled the initiative and any sense of responsibility in the workers, is now beginning to loosen up in the course of developments which soften the deterministic character of the traditional control structure:

An increasing number of work stations are being freed from strict machine-pacing through alternative work design and mechanization.

The production standards are increasingly being set in the phase of production planning, and thus direct confrontation of the experts on the "shop floor," as was the case in the traditional work study, is avoided.

Increased demands for technical expertise require a different type of supervisor, who has to be able to deal with problems of process control, material flow, and the technical equipment of his area; routine matters of labor allocation, work organization, and personnel mobility are, in part, being given to the shop floor for self-regulation.

With this, scope is opened up for self-regulation of the operative tasks in the production process. The question of how much autonomy should be "delegated" to the shop floor is being debated in all the companies of our sample. Control functions, like in the area of quality inspection, have already been given over to the workers on the shop floor to a large extent. But the development goes beyond this. The goal is that the employees themselves accept the operational goals of improving quality and work efficiency – external control will be "internalized," so to speak.

At the same time, the power of the corporate headquarters to exert external control over the results of this self-regulation are increasing:

through computer-aided information and control systems and through comparison and competition between factories, which can be used as instruments for performance regulation. These elements make it possible for the corporate headquarters to observe the performance profile of their independently operating organizational units and to measure them against the most highly efficient and most successful examples in their own global company ("best practice"). The competition between factories contributes toward externalizing the pressure to adapt, and toward strengthening the consciousness of common (survival) interests in the factory. Parallel production of the same product at differing sites, growing overcapacities in the industry, modularization of production, and increased pressure to make a decision on the question of "make or buy" intensify this external pressure on the factories and work forces to adjust. An increase in self-regulation of the tasks to be carried out thus does not mean a reduction in control, but rather a change in the form of control.

(2) Change toward job integration

"Integration" is a key concept used to describe the restructuring of car production in the 1980s. Common to all integration measures is the understanding that the forms of specialization enforced by Taylorism–Fordism has turned out to be dysfunctional, obsolete, or driven too far. The costs of control and coordination required by separating functions and competences have become too high. Flexible production and high technology require a more integrative approach.

Integration refers both to the horizontal and vertical separation of tasks and functions. And it refers to management and supervisory jobs as well as rank and file production or administrative jobs. In fact, many of the new concepts for management organization (like project teams, computer-integrated manufacturing, and group work) aim at a functional integration, too. But at this point we are only referring to the job design aspect, i.e., the work structure of the individual employee.

According to our findings, the main focus of the measures undertaken by the companies was on the horizontal aspect of work structuring and, in particular, the integration of direct and indirect tasks. This classical differentiation has increasingly become a hindrance to a more effective and efficient work organization. Tasks which had become the basis for separate departments and lines of hierarchy, such as quality control, equipment maintenance, and material handling, are being partially merged again with direct production tasks. Shop floor policies of "job control," which were based on the formalized structures of the division of labor, are increasingly losing ground to measures for "job enrichment."

The aspect of vertical integration was often touched upon when it came to measures for dismantling hierarchies and decentralizing authority. But, in practice, we only observed timid and mostly symbolic steps toward "enriching" the jobs of operators with planning, budgeting, and control functions.

(3) Change toward car production becoming the domain of skilled workers

It has often been stated that work in the modernized factories of the car industry will increasingly become the domain of skilled labor. With increasing levels of automation, more direct work would be done by machines anyway, and tasks of controlling and maintaining these machines would become dominant, thus requiring qualified skilled workers. In these statements, skilled workers would normally be synonymous with *Facharbeiter*, workers who had gone through apprenticeships as mechanics, electricians, etc. According to our findings, it is too early to speak of car production as the domain of skilled labor. One reason for this is that we found a polarization of qualification requirements in the areas of high-tech production. On the one hand, new jobs of automated systems controlling and systems management with more demanding qualification requirements are emerging; but, on the other hand, there was also the emergence of less qualified jobs, like feeding parts ("residual work"). Compared with the type of qualified semi-skilled labor which predominated before the mechanization (e.g., welding) we see a polarization of qualification requirements. Thus there is a tendency toward a relative increase in qualification in high technology areas. Against this background, there were differing options for combining or separating maintenance, monitoring and "residual work." From the perspective of minimizing wage costs, everything would speak for a segmentation of the few highly qualified jobs from the many lower qualified jobs (thus following the Babbage principle). But the increased importance of avoiding machine down times would demand, on the other hand, that all of the workers assigned to the installation could detect process irregularities as early as possible, intervene preventively, and support the experts in the event of a disruption. That is why production managers often preferred to keep qualified skilled workers at these "residual work places," even if they would be overpaid for what they were doing most of the time. This would require a new type of skilled worker who could be assigned simple "residual jobs" in addition to their more demanding tasks of controlling the automated systems. This development has been most characteristic in the West German automobile industry. It is made easier through a considerable expansion of apprentice training in German automobile companies which has led to an oversupply of qualified skilled workers. This oversupply forms an important potential for coping with the technological modernization. At the same time, the oversupply of skilled workers produces a weakening of the skilled worker status which is laden with conflicts.

In the U.S. and British plants there was the clear tendency for skilled workers to take over the qualified jobs in the high-tech production areas. Yet the gap still existed between the unskilled production workers and the skilled maintenance workers who were only moved closer to production. The step from the decentralization of maintenance and thus the stationing of qualified skilled workers close to the automated systems to actually letting them run the system and thus perform production jobs has not yet been made.

(4) Change toward decoupling work from the line pace

Tying work rhythm and performance to the pace of the assembly line has been a central characteristic of the Taylorist–Fordist production organization. In the 1980s, some companies began to abolish the assembly line as the backbone of their work organization, even in mass production assembly plants. Whole modules of assembly operations were taken off the main line in order to be performed at stationary work places. Such organization can deal more efficiently with the increased variety of car models and options produced in the same plant.

Thus, the number of work places which were uncoupled from the flow of the assembly line was increasing in many plants. The gradual abolition of the assembly line in favor of stationary work places and the establishment of work areas outside the main line flow allows job design to be more oriented toward meaningful holistic tasks and less dominated by the priorities of the moving conveyor belt. This reduced the proportion of extremely short-cycle, repetitive operations. Nevertheless, the classic assembly line still governs the majority of jobs in assembly operations; as we have shown in chapter 10, the new modules (preassembly areas) only comprise up to one-third of the assembly jobs, even in these factories.

But not all companies share the view that the reign of the assembly line is coming to an end. This is definitely not the message that could be received from the Japanese car plants at the time of our research. Since Japanese ideas of production organization were increasingly becoming a model of "best practice" in the 1980s, advocates of the assembly line still had a strong position. None of our American sample plants had reduced the share of line-paced jobs or had made an attempt at creating longer work cycles on the assembly line, as we found in some German plants.

Moreover, uncoupling work from the flow of production and establishing stationary work places do not per se mean greater "time-sovereignty" of the workers with respect to the rhythm and intensity of work over the course of the shift. Of course, the job cycle at stationary work places varies according to the differing work contents of the respective workpieces. But nothing has changed with respect to the predetermination of time. The time requirements for each workpiece are recorded in the computerized system for process control, and this system registers deviations from the standards more mercilessly than the lower-level supervisors in the traditional course of work could ever hope to. Holding to the preplanned labor time for the flow of production is here just as necessary as on the assembly line.

(5) Change toward emphasizing employee participation

Measures for increasing employee participation were widely discussed at all of our research sites. The existence of all kinds of small group activities such as quality circles, problem-solving groups, and voluntary study circles, were regarded by many interviewees as an essential difference between Japanese and Western companies and as a major factor explaining the success of the Japanese. The actual activities in the factories exhibited considerable differences in this area, however. In this, two aims can be seen in management strategy:

The first aim is at individual work behavior and work motivation and at the quality of labor relations. In the process, management strives to reduce individual and collective resistance (e.g., absenteeism, strikes), and to inspire or improve the identification of the work force with the company's goals.

The second aim is to exploit more fully the capabilities and experiences of individual workers and their informal personal networks. These resources are to be mobilized for work-related solutions to problems and for improvements in the operative work process.

We found the first aim to be prevalent in those cases where the problem scenario was seen very much in an industrial relations context; the second was found to be prevalent in those cases where the problem scenario was defined more in terms of new tasks and new qualification requirements due to the introduction of new technology and higher automation levels.

(6) The change toward group and team work

Group work principles played an important role in the future oriented work concepts at many sites. In theory, group work could be a means to achieve many objectives at the same time: greater job flexibility among individuals (by practicing job rotation), enhanced responsibility of shop floor workers for cost and quality (by delegating quality control, equipment maintenance, and process control responsibilities to the group), and improved social relations in production (through less control and more mutual help and support between workers and supervisors).

Group work meant task integration at both the horizontal and vertical dimension and it meant giving shop floor workers a certain degree of self-regulation with regard to their work. The range of tasks to be delegated to the group and the extent of self-regulation varied widely in the discussions of group work in the different companies, but at the time of our research we could only observe a few cases where group work had actually been introduced.

These general findings send out a clear message. The work reforms of the 1980s can neither be interpreted as a purely symbolic policy or even as cheap propaganda by management in order to ensure that the workers and the general public accept personnel reductions, the introduction of new technologies, and the restructuring of the industry. Nor can a sweeping renunciation of the traditional Taylorist–Fordist production model be observed. Referring back to table 1.1 in our introduction, we can observe an unfinished process of development in which differing configurations of the Taylorist–Fordist mode *and* its functional alternatives are visible. Our empirical results also make the limitations of the functional alternatives to the Taylorist–Fordist work organization clearly visible: stationary work stations do not necessarily mean increased time sovereignty; internal self-regulation of partially autonomous groups is not to be equated with the weakening of external controls; job integration does not mean the abolition of the division of labor, status differentiation, and the segmentation of labor markets within the factory.

Formulated positively: we can observe a growing decoupling of the system elements of the Taylorist–Fordist mode as we presented them in table 1.1. This contrasts sharply with the tight connection of these elements which existed well into the 1970s. A standard product, mass production and economies of scale, rigid single-purpose mechanization, strict hierarchically structured chains of communication, fragmented and low-qualified work content, stressful working conditions, and conflicting labor relations formed a seemingly insoluble package. According to our observations, this structural connection began to break up in the 1980s. This situation offered considerable scope for design and a corresponding mood of change could be observed at many sites.

11.2 The influence of company strategies

Clearly, the companies cannot be seen as just adapting and reacting to the trends described above. In strategically choosing a specific direction of work reform and in giving priority to certain measures they actively influenced the trend itself. But none of the companies opted to remain outside the trend and preserve the well-established Taylorist–Fordist ways of work.

Table 11.1 *Emphasis of change measures in the individual companies*

	Company		
Directions of change	A	B	C
(1) Task integration	+		
(2) Employee participation	+	+	
(3) Shop floor self-regulation via group work		+	
(4) Automation as much as possible		+	+
(5) Reduction of line-paced jobs			+
(6) Skilled workers for direct work			+

The clearest and most important difference between the companies could be found in the question of whether they oriented their strategy toward human or technical factors as the supposedly "decisive" productivity resource. This was indeed a strategic decision, although it is true that the companies were in very different positions with regard to their financial strengths and thus their ability to purchase new technology at the beginning of the 1980s. But it would be overly simplified to explain the companies' decision of whether they would give priority to "technology" or to "people" as merely a matter of the power of the purse. More important was the different degree to which the companies were rudely awakened at the beginning of the 1980s. The companies which perceived their very survival to be at stake were presented with the option of making a more fundamental break with past practises or perishing.

Company A clearly emphasized the "people potential" in its reorganization measures. The focus of the measures in its factories was on decentralizing management responsibility and on integrating direct and indirect production tasks. Along with this went the institutionalization of a program for employee participation and involving employees in problem-solving activities on the shop floor. The concepts were based on a human relations approach, group work principles did not play a central role in this. A further characteristic of this strategy was the remarkable emphasis that Company A placed on increasing efficiency and rationalizing labor deployment. The use of new technologies was secondary in this strategic concept. Finally, Company A did not venture into new production concepts which do away with the assembly line.

Table 11.1 shows the differences in the directions of change taken by our three companies. Of course there are differences in the emphasis put on each of these measures by the companies and the extent to which all of the company-specific measures could be found in all of its plants, even in the same country. Table 11.1 shows the company profile which was characteristic in the country where the companies had their headquarters as it appears plausible that company strategies would find their most authentic expression here.

In contrast to Company A, Company C clearly emphasized automation in its measures. As a complementary measure, C expanded its programs for initial and continuous vocational training considerably and adapted them to the new technological requirements. Less importance was attached to questions of task integration, employee involvement, and group work principles at the time of our investigation. It was a clear policy to reduce the number of directly line-paced jobs through the use of various measures. The most important of these, however, was assembly automation. Finally, there was a clear strategy to let skilled workers run production in the highly automated areas.

Company B's strategy could be characterized as maximizing its options. Different paths were being tested in pilot plants within the company. To this end, the company introduced programs of employee participation, but also programs of high-tech automation aiming at the "unmanned" factory, as well as socio-technical programs for restructuring work on the basis of group work principles. But this multi-faceted strategy was only valid at the company level. On the level of individual plants, we found insecurity as to which direction the development should go.

Just as important as the differences in the main emphasis of the strategies were differences in the way they were being implemented. Profiles which were typical for the different companies as a whole could also be observed here. As far as Company A is concerned, the human factor strategy was pursued in the factories – company-wide – with remarkable consistency and speed. This was true for the goal of job integration as well as for employee participation. A campaign, also carried out publicly in the company, attempted to secure the acceptance or toleration of the work forces and the local managements for the program. The speed and the breadth of this process of reorganization can be summed up in a paradoxical formula: the strengthening of management and employee participation on the shop floor was pushed through by means of a tightly centralized company organization. This paradox of a new combination of highly centralized company management and the strengthening of decentralized self-regulation at the lower levels is the key to understanding the organizational change in Company A. The highly centralized form of control was, admittedly, faced with the limits of national industrial relations. The measures could be rapidly introduced and enjoyed initial success in the company's American and German factories, whereas NW&M measures were blocked for a time by union objections in the British factories. Nationally specific factors come into play here.

Company B, with its strategy of maximizing its options, i.e., simultaneously testing several alternatives, increased the variety of forms of factory labor regulation within its global organization. In contrast to the far-reaching innovations in production technology or in work and social organization in some pilot plants, the bulk of the assembly plants remained limited to an onlooker role at the time of our empirical investigations. At the level of local management, a greater insecurity over the goals of future development existed than that which we had observed in the case of Company A's local management. The diffusion process of new organizational concepts into Company B's factories proceeded in a less centralized fashion and was more strongly oriented toward individual local initiatives. In view of this pattern of diffusion it is no wonder that the influence of the national affiliation of the factories showed through to a greater extent than at Company A.

At Company C there seemed to be no ambiguity and hesitation about how the factory of the future was to be envisioned. The future was automation and the personnel considerations were concentrated on the necessary training requirements. At the time of our final investigations, however, the shortcomings of this strategy were already being recognized.

Differences in emphasis and priorities as to the directions of change described above – whether companies focus on human factors or technology factors – do not say anything about the quality of these measures as seen from a worker's perspective. Company A's strategy was designed to take advantage of a potential for rationalization which could obviously be attained in the shorter run. Holding back with automation meant at the same time that the layout of production technology remained largely unchanged, so that possibilities for improving working conditions through technology and process design could not be realized. Company A thus still retained the traditional forms of assembly line organization in the factories we studied. On the other hand, Company B and C's factories had already transferred a considerable share of their assembly tasks to production areas without an assembly line. These new work structures, generally introduced in connection with new production technologies, provided significantly improved working conditions, at least from an ergonomic point of view.

11.3 The influence of national affiliation

The national affiliation of the factory site turned out to be a strong intervening factor which often came through more strongly than the influence of company affiliation. Table 11.2 shows considerable differences in the directions of change found in the various plants of the same company located in different countries. (There were also differences between plants of

Table 11.2 *Emphasis of change measures according to companies and countries*

Country	U.S.	U.K.	F.R.G.
Company			
A	(1) (2)	(1)	(1) (2) (6)
B	(2) (3)	(5)	(5)
C	—	—	(4) (5) (6)

the same company in the same country but the influence of location was clearly weaker than the influence of company or country affiliation.)

As can be seen in table 11.2, Company A's American plants emphasized task integration and employee participation; in its British plants, task integration was the only major direction of change; in the German plants we found task integration, employee participation, and the deployment of skilled workers at direct production jobs as characteristic directions of change.

Employee participation and the introduction of group work were dominant features in the American plants of Company B which we investigated. Other Company B plants ventured into "as much automation as possible" and partially abolished the assembly line. Thus, the intra-country differences between Company A and B were in fact greater than expressed here. In any case, Company B's British plants were characterized by new assembly concepts as were the German plants. The direction of people-oriented measures, i.e., task integration or group work or the deployment of skilled workers in direct production jobs, was quite unclear in these European plants at the time of our study.

Company C focussed clearly on automation and the work organization concepts it devised for these automation areas centered around skilled workers deployed in production. A third package of measures aimed at diminishing the role of the assembly line for determining the speed and rhythm of the individual workers: first, the introduction of automated transfer lines in assembly areas had the effect of decoupling human labor from the direct production process; second, areas with stationary work stations linked by automated guided vehicles were created, though to a smaller extent than at Company B's European plants; third, due to union demands line work was organized in such a way that individual work cycles became three to four times longer than at the assembly plants in most other companies we investigated.

Among the national factors which most conspicuously influenced the direction of change in the various countries were the policies and institutions of industrial relations and of vocational training.

In the U.S., the companies made the transformation of industrial relations to a central element in their strategy for work reform. Since the beginning of the 1980s, the purposeful change of industrial relations has been formulated and supported jointly by the top representatives of the companies and the unions. This policy was also jointly supported at the local level in the majority of cases because the company headquarters made it perfectly clear that the decisions over future investments, and thus over the survival of the production sites, were strongly influenced by the demonstration of their willingness and ability to change. Under these conditions the change strategy focussed mainly on human factors. The employee participation programs played a central role in securing the compliance with job integration or the introduction of group work.

The strategy of transformation from above had already taken root at the factory level in the American automobile industry at the time of our investigation. The traditional structures for regulating labor deployment (seniority and demarcation rules) were still partially in force. They had already lost their unconditional validity, however.

Where advanced automation projects were implemented in the U.S. the importance of vocational training policies and institutions became clear, though in a negative sense: not only were there too few qualified skilled workers (especially electronics-related), production workers were also incapable of coping with the new technologies. Due to the status consciousness of skilled workers and union policy, the deployment of qualified skilled workers as direct production workers (as in the German plants) was out of the question in the American plants at the time of our study.

The decisive importance of union cooperation for such a strategy of institutional change can be seen in the case of the British companies. Here it was not possible to obtain a consensus between the companies and unions at the top level so that they could jointly support programs for change as in the U.S.A. Due to differences in union structures, however, a strategy "from the top down" would hardly have had a chance of success anyway. The influence of the unions on the process of change in work has always been strong in the U.K. But this was limited to establishing and consolidating the unions' veto power. This led to a special selectivity which furthered traditional strategies for rationalization through industrial engineering and mechanization which, because of the shift in the balance of power, could be pushed through almost unimpeded by management. Programs to develop employee participation or group work, on the other hand, were blocked by the unions since they required a formal agreement in the arena of industrial relations. In its inability to develop its own concepts, British management apparently perceived its scope of action to be especially limited by dependency on the European networks of their companies. We observed a growing consciousness of heteronomy at the British sites. Production organization and technological equipment were seen as "German concepts" imposed upon the British factories by the European company headquarters.

But the prerequisites for greater autonomy in developing their own solutions would have been better performance and a process of institutional change jointly supported by the unions and management. These prerequisites did not yet exist at the time of our study, despite remarkable examples of change in behavior within individual plants. Independent innovations in work and in social organization for regulating work could not emerge under these conditions. Concepts like employee participation, group work, or production concepts without the assembly line were regarded as foreign imports from either the U.S.A. or the continent. The British constellation was apparently not particularly fertile soil for developing independent non-Taylorist forms for regulating labor in the 1980s.

Characteristic of developments in the German context was that changes in labor were being carried out in and through existing institutions. The companies' restructuring process in the German automobile industry did not include a specific strategy for transforming the institutions. The system of industrial relations remained, so to speak, outside the scope of the restructuring. The dual system of interest representation by the union and codetermination by works councils elected by all workers as the central institution of industrial relations turned out to be supportive of recent trends toward de-Taylorization. Along with this came a specific preference for mechanization and forms of labor deployment which focussed on skilled workers.

The statutory rights of the works councils to information and participation had entrenched a pattern of cooperative problem-solving at the factory level. At the same time, the works council members and union representatives had been able to develop their own concepts and alternatives for organizing work, not least because of the institutions of codetermination. We did not find a comparable pattern of union involvement in job design in either of the other countries studied. It was possible on this basis to negotiate future oriented arrangements between the two sides. With this, the institutions for labor policy and vocational training have had the function of a societal productivity resource for the restructuring process of the 1980s.

The institutional peculiarities in the German context seemed to foster specific solutions with regard to work organization and patterns of labor deployment. Three indicators supporting the thesis of special German development could be observed:

1 The exceptional vocational training and labor market situation provided the factories with skilled-worker potential which was also deployable for direct production tasks, and could thus be used for new forms of work organization and new job descriptions in direct production. The growing use of skilled workers (*Facharbeiter*) in direct production increased the necessity for and the possibility of creating "intelligent" work structures. Corresponding to this, a close connection has emerged between the surplus of skilled workers and the degree of innovation in work organization in the German assembly plants.

2 Due to legal and contractual regulations, absentee rates arising from illness and the percentage of disabled workers in German plants were much higher than in the British and American plants (about three times higher as we have shown in chapter 4). In order to overcome the restrictions for labor deployment which this situation created, management was more dependent on job design and the use of technology. Management had to improve working conditions and job design in order to make work more attractive. In the American and British plants, restrictions lie more in the area of informal work practices and are tackled by management in the arena of industrial relations.

3 The particular profile of demands by the unions and works councils in the Federal Republic of Germany is clearly aimed at reducing line-paced work or at least loosening the link between the individual's work rhythm and machine or assembly line cycle times. This has led to alternative solutions in process design and work organization being considered. In contrast, a one minute cycle time was still considered by the production planners in the U.S.A. to be the ultimate in work layout for the 1980s. The average work cycles in West German plants, which are much longer than in American plants, are in line with qualification requirements, even for simple line work, which are considerably higher than those in the U.S. plants. With this, the gap between assembly line work and the work requirements at stationary work places with more comprehensive tasks is clearly smaller, and that is why a change-over to forms of labor without an assembly line faces fewer difficulties there than in the American context.

Let us summarize: the national systems of industrial relations and labor policy institutions in each of the three countries were connected with systematic cross-national differences in the objectives and priorities of restructuring. Our study reveals three different nationally specific types of rationalization strategies. Thus, in the U.S.A., rationalization strategies were generally accompanied by New Work and Motivation programs aimed at the non-skilled workers; in Great Britain, Taylorist rationalization was still dominant; and, in the Federal Republic of Germany, a rationalization strategy oriented toward the *Facharbeiter* potential could

Table 11.3 *Paradigms for the production organization of the future*

German	Japanese
Deployment of skilled workers in direct production	On the job trained workers with high general base qualification
Decoupled from the production cycle	Work determined by the production cycle
Large/holistic job content	Short, line-determined job cycle
Mixed teams (skilled/unskilled)	Homogeneous teams (On the job trained workers)
High degree of team autonomy in process-design	Low degree of team autonomy in process-design

be observed. These broad national patterns of selection overlapped with the company-specific patterns.

11.4 Models for future development

With the dissolution of the Taylorist–Fordist control system there are primarily two lines of development which could fulfill the function of a model for future developments: the "German model" of labor regulation revolving around the use of qualified skilled workers and the "Japanese model" of group-oriented labor regulation. (We are not discussing the "Swedish model" here. It is in many ways similar to the German model but it differs considerably in terms of training systems and measures to upgrade skills on the shop floor (see Berggren 1991)). Both developmental models are characterized by a degree of self-regulation of shop floor work. And both employ a type of worker who, through his/her competence and willingness to accept responsibility, is clearly different from the unskilled mass laborer. Despite these common features, there are important differences between the two models.

Table 11.3 shows some of the basic differences between the models.

At the center of the "German model" is the skilled worker and a specific understanding of skilled work as a "profession." This understanding includes several features: interest in the work, a willingness to accept comprehensive responsibility (also crossing over the borders from one's own task area), and a large degree of self-regulation in carrying out the work. This model presupposes a "training offensive," above and beyond the direct company needs for skilled workers, which in turn is dependent on institutions and policies of vocational training. With this we are referring to the societal prerequisites for a specific form of labor regulation as they exist in the educational system in the Federal Republic of Germany. It is clear that the model of skilled-worker centered work regulation is especially important for modern technology management. The ideal typical goal of the German way is qualified labor, uncoupled from the production cycle, and the rhythm of the machines. Uncoupling work from the flow of production is the prerequisite for a type of labor with increased possibilities for self-regulation and with increased responsibility.

The Japanese way also gives a central role to skilled labor, though not in the sense of uncoupled skilled labor. Rather, the ideal typical of the Japanese model is self-regulation under the pressure of the assembly line and the production pace. Characteristic is an allocation of personnel which aims at the best possible performance and its permanent improvement, i.e., the continual intensification of labor. This stands in contrast to the industrial engineering practices in Western companies which aim for "normal" performance ("fair day's work principle") and are restricted in their possibilities for a continuous review of the established time standards. In the Japanese automobile industry, the work group is the starting point for an integrated job understanding, for the flexibilization and expansion of labor deployment, and for the qualification of the workers. Self-regulation is thus not based on skilled worker competence and a professional ethic.

The question of the transferability of group or skilled-worker oriented organizational alternatives is also posed for the British and U.S. companies in view of the increasing technological requirements of the future. The considerable increase in vocational training in British factories hints at the German way. Although such a development is not yet achievable in British labor policy, it could come to an expansion of the skilled-worker potential beyond the needs of the skilled labor departments in British factories, with similar consequences as can be seen in the German automobile industry. Such a development is being furthered by the centralization and creation of European company branches and the corresponding standardization of production and rationalization concepts.

In contrast to this, considerations in the U.S. companies are more and more influenced by Japanese concepts. The formation of production groups in the unskilled area and a flexibilization and expansion of the workers' areas of deployment is being sought. Training measures with the goal of forming groups and the teaching of group problem-solving techniques also play a much more important role in policies for worker qualification than does the training of skilled workers. In the German context a potential for dealing with technology by using skilled workers, can be observed which arose through a "softening up" of the skilled-worker status from above. In the long run the strategy of group-related retraining for unskilled workers could allow the necessary qualification potential to emerge in the American plants too.

Transferring either the German or the Japanese management concepts poses problems. Social and cultural prerequisites play an important role in explaining the Japanese concepts. In fact it is quite disputed among "Japanologists" whether these concepts can be transferred to the West at all and whether it makes sense to isolate certain elements and use them as "recipes." Nevertheless, most Western companies are more inclined toward transferring Japanese concepts than German concepts. The strong anchoring of the German way in the structures of codetermination and the corporatist system of vocational education would set greater institutional and legal limits on the scope for action and decision making by the company headquarters. Such infringements on managements' prerogatives seem to be more threatening to most Western companies than the risks associated with borrowing from Japan.

On the question of the use of skilled workers and skilled-worker supported solutions, it is important not only to consider the circumstances that promote them in the German automobile industry, but also the circumstances hampering them in the U.S.A. and Great Britain. The distinct skilled-worker status in the Federal Republic has changed significantly in the 1980s. While the march of the skilled-worker into production is already quite far advanced in the German factories, the classical separation between production tasks as non-skilled labor, on the one hand, and technical support functions as skilled labor, on the other, still dominated in the British and American assembly plants. This "German path" of labor regulation centered on skilled workers has shown itself to be advantageous for coping with the requirements of new technologies. The German factories have, in fact, been able to meet the new technological requirements resulting from the wave of modernization at the beginning of the 1980s with less friction, thanks to their skilled-worker potential.

11.5 Outlook for the 1990s

The investigations which we are recounting in this book deal with a critical developmental phase in the history of the world automobile industry. The period from 1983 to 1986, in which most of our factory studies took place, was the eve of secular change in the hegemony of the world automobile industry. If it was the U.S. companies who had dominated the industry up until then and essentially determined the forms and speed of development in the industry on the strength of their resources and multinational production structures, this role now passed over to the Japanese companies.

In the 1980s it was still possible to consider Japan as a "background factor" on the question of developmental tendencies and design options with regard to new forms of work, as we did in our investigation. This procedure would no longer be possible in the 1990s. A considerable share of the pressure to change did come from Japan during the period of our research, but the reference to Japan still played a minor role in this phase for the actual concepts and measures for change at the factory level. Most concepts were, as we have seen, "homemade" and developed within the company and within nationally specific traditions. We did not observe any revolutionary upheavals, even if management literature talks a lot about revolutions nowadays. But the wheels are moving rapidly in the development of the world automobile industry and we face changed conditions at the beginning of the 1990s. In this final section we would like briefly to deal with the development after the conclusion of our research up until the beginning of the 1990s.

How did the "Modern Times" continue up until the end of the decade?

First of all, the world automobile industry had the good fortune of experiencing an extended "Indian summer" in the second half of the 1980s. The upswing phase of the business cycle beginning in 1982 was unusually long and lasted almost to the end of the decade. The five-year period between 1985 and 1990 was not a phase in which hard decisions had to be made; it was rather one of consolidation and recovery, above all for the companies which had been previously losing money and for the countries and plants which had been having problems. In 1989, the new car sales in the EEC countries were 30 percent higher than in 1985.[2] The British automobile industry increased its output by 24 percent in this period, and the auto industry in West Germany would increase its production by 10 percent. In the United States there was already a 9.5 percent decline in the registration of new cars and a 16.5 percent decrease in the production level in 1989 compared to 1985; though compared to 1982 the registrations were still 27 percent higher and the production level 33 percent higher. The first years of the 1990s mark a deep recession for almost the entire world automobile industry. In the U.S. the production levels plunged to 6.5 million in 1991, almost the same level as its lowest point in 1982; in the U.K. the decline was even steeper. Only Germany has been an exception in this development so far as it has profited from the affects of reunification and the exploding demand for Western cars in what was formerly East Germany.

The increasing importance of the Japanese manufacturers in world car industry continued undiminished in these years, however. In the U.S. the capacity of the "transplants," which had been projected at the beginning of the decade, started to come into play. The transplants made ca. 1 million cars in North America in 1989 and the sum of their capacities should be around 2.5 million cars a year by the middle of the 1990s – one quarter of these would appear to be excess capacity from today's perspective. Plant closings are on the agenda now. General Motors is primarily affected. GM has lost market shares in the U.S. since 1979, from 46.5 percent to 35.6 percent in 1991. Ford, on the other hand, had a market share of 20 percent in 1991, almost the same as in 1979 (20.3 percent). The Japanese manufacturers received the lion's share, however, their share increased from 15.8 percent to 30.2 percent (Japanese derived: 36 percent) during this time. Production from the transplants already amounted to 45.5 percent of the Japanese car sales in the U.S. in 1991. While the U.S. companies experienced the cold gust of wind from the economic decline with tremendous sales losses, and this holds true for GM as well as for Ford and Chrysler, the sales figures of the Japanese companies continued to increase.

By 1990, the economic upswing had also come to an end in Western Europe. But capacity bottlenecks are still regarded as more pressing than the fear of excess capacities. The formation of a common European market and the saturation of the North American market have channeled the stream of Japanese direct investments toward Europe. Great Britain is getting the lion's share here and thus experiencing a renaissance as a production site. From the investment plans of the Japanese manufacturers it can be expected that the Japanese transplants will account for more than 10 percent of the Western European car production starting at the middle of the 1990s.[3] A significant increase in market shares is also being forecasted for Japanese imports on a free Western European market.

In the course of this development Great Britain is becoming one of the most important countries for new investments. Nissan, Toyota, and Honda have selected the sites for their first European plants here. But Germany has also been the site for a wave of new plants, after BMW's Regensburg plant, which opened in 1986, Daimler-Benz's new Rastatt plant which will begin production in 1992, and the two new plants from Volkswagen and GM-Europe in Eastern Germany, which are currently being built. The latter plants are totally oriented on Japanese models in their production and work organization and thus mark the change in industry hegemony described above.

As far as we can see, the changes have continued to be evolutionary in most of the plants we investigated. Two plants from our core sample have become "team plants," one has completed the step to a sweeping adoption of Japanese management methods. But two plants out of our North American sample have been closed in the meantime. In Europe, two plants from our core sample are on the verge of introducing team work as their new paradigm principle for work organization, preparations are being made for this in others.

The tendency toward new forms of work has been strengthened in more recent years for the following reasons: the leap into "high-tech" production processes and the huge, often unexpected, mostly underestimated problems resulting from it – training and work organization had obviously not received the amount of attention which this experience showed to be necessary; second, the success exhibited by those companies which had placed their priority on work organization measures. The prime example for this is Ford, a company that trimmed its plants in this manner for higher productivity in the 1980s and came closest to the productivity level of Japanese plants; and, finally, it was and is the expectation of increased pressure to adapt in the future. This concerns the Big Three, as the build-up of transplant capacities in the U.S. is continuing, this concerns Europe, as trade restrictions will be successively eliminated with the creation of the common European market and sizeable transplant capacities are being established in Europe itself in the meantime.

Also, MIT's International Motor Vehicle Program has played a very important role in pushing modernization programs and new production concepts at the traditional Western manufacturers. The results of the comparisons which were made of the performance differences between plants (cf. Krafcik 1988; Krafcik and Mac Duffie 1989) led to the realization that the modernization efforts of the 1980s, which were the topic of this book, had thus far not eliminated the fundamental performance differences between the producing regions. In a comparison of fifty-eight assembly plants in the mass automobile segment which was carried out in 1989, the Japanese plants came out as the best by far. The average productivity here was 16.8 hours per vehicle; the U.S. plants of the "Big Three," on the other hand, needed 25.1 hours per vehicle, the average of the plants of the car manufacturers in Europe was 35.5 hours (Womack *et al.* 1990, p. 85). Similar differences in performance appeared when comparing the quality results (assembly defects per 100 vehicles): an average of fifty-two defects in the Japanese plants compared to an average of seventy-eight in the U.S. plants and an average of seventy-six in the European plants.

These and similarly unflattering results for Europe and the U.S. have entered public discourse and the internal discussions in many companies through various channels. Dertouzos *et al.* (1989) used these results in their analysis of the causes of the competitive weakness of the U.S. industry, the EEC High Commissioner for economic affairs, Bangemann, drew on them to support his argument that protectionism only leads to the conservation of weak competitive structures. In some companies, the data have had an instrumental function in justifying rationalization; internal company demarcations and calculation methods have been changed in order to ensure a better comparability in the framework of the IMVP and the authors have been invited by companies to analyze their relative competitive positions and "survival chances."

With an eye on the differences which they documented in their report the MIT authors formulated a clear "change or die" message to the Western automobile companies: either they adopt the methods of the best Japanese plants, which the authors generalized as a "lean production system" or they would not survive the competition of the 1990s. If the superior performance of the lean production system proves to be so strong that the Western companies cannot survive the competition with their home-grown solutions, then these cannot be seen as equally functional and there would no longer be alternatives for future-oriented work organization. There would only be "one best way" toward which company and nationally specific differences would be forced to converge.

The impression that the different paths to the "modern times" could converge does suggest itself if the companies' measures and points of emphasis since the second half of the 1980s are examined. The one-sided orientation toward technology and the fascination with the possibilities of flexible production technologies and computer-aided control systems have made way for a more prosaic assessment. All companies are now emphasizing the prime importance of human resource development and work organization. Another common tendency is a decentralized management organization. The same is true for integrated quality responsibility and the organization of quality control. The function of quality control is now being integrated into the area of responsibility of decentralized "cost-center" managers. Looked at more closely, however, typical profiles of and differences between countries and companies are already developing within the wide current of consensus again and these tend to correspond with the typical differences we described above.

Thus for the authors of the IMVP, teams are the basis of work organization for the fragile/lean plant type. Groups form the key element in the framework of a "human centered" (Auer and Riegler 1988) production organization in Swedish plants, however. A large number of U.S. plants have declared themselves to be "team plants" in the meantime; although most of them are oriented toward the NUMMI model, there are also great differences (cf. Turner 1991). In Germany, the conflict between the union and management over how to organize the group principle is still going on (cf. Roth and Kohl 1988). To the extent that the designs have not been patterned after U.S. or European prototypes within the multinational companies, as was the case with GM, the unions tend to favor the Swedish model and management favors the Japanese model. In the British plants, with the exception of the Nissan plant in Sunderland of course (cf. Wickens 1987), the team concept has still not cleared the hurdle of union acceptance. We do not know, though, to what extent this has really been put to the test and how hard management has really tried to introduce the team concept in the years following our research (cf. Müller 1991).

In the U.S.A., the question of team organization is still contested within the union. The "new directions" movement which has formed here sees team organization primarily as an attempt by the company to reduce and neutralize past union achievements. The criticism (cf. Parker and Slaughter 1988) is primarily concentrated on the "give away" of rules and practices previously pushed through to protect against work intensification or favoritism in personnel decisions. These critics do not find the offer of opportunities for participation to be sufficient compensation.

Up to now, the critical opposition to the team principle and "new industrial relations" within the union has been able to block the introduction of teams in some plants, but as a whole this position has not been able to assert itself. The shock of unemployment at the beginning of the 1980s, the insight that new approaches would be necessary to secure the competitiveness of the respective production sites, and, to a certain extent, also the satisfaction which workers experienced through successful participation programs and improvements in work and communication relations still sustain the process of change. This is still one of the differences in the company profiles of Companies A and B, while B has made great efforts to establish the team principle in all of its plants, A has – with the exception of local pilot projects – refrained from introducing production teams. The priority here has been set on improving work and communications relations and decentralizing management and decision-making structures – important prerequisites for the introduction of the team principle in any case, if this were to be decided in the future.

It is also not entirely certain as to whether a new "productivity pact" dealing with the form of team organization can be reached between the union and management in West Germany. This would be easier in the high-tech areas, where the interests of both sides coincide in their desire to utilize excess skilled-worker potentials and where tasks which are uncoupled from the production cycle and involve more demanding qualifications would promise a clear improvement in work content and working conditions. It is more difficult with manual tasks, especially where they are still structured by an assembly line. There are estimates that calculate up to a 25 percent increase in productivity through the introduction of production teams. This applies especially to the areas with manual tasks, where considerable reductions are expected through the elimination of cycle losses and waiting times with team organization. But how can the interests of workers and management be balanced out in these areas? There are only limited possibilities for using "job design" to create jobs which require more sophisticated qualifications and thus offer better pay. To completely abolish the assembly line, either in favor of high-tech transfer lines or in the form of low-tech production islands, does not appear very attractive at present from the point of view of the companies. Thus the above described mixture of largely conventionally organized assembly lines with "assembly islands" uncoupled from the line for specific tasks where variance of the model mix leads to especially large deviances in work content, appears to be the most probable direction of development for production organization. But we doubt that the young *Facharbeiter*, often regarded as the most valuable productivity resource for the future, will find the work structures to be in keeping with their qualifications and stimulating enough and assume that they will thus leave these areas as soon as they have a chance. Team structures are no compensation for working conditions suitable for skilled workers and the tensions coming in factory practice with an integration of skilled and semi-skilled workers show that viable solutions have yet to be found in this area.

The clearest turn away from the Taylorist–Fordist production organization occurred in the context of the construction of new plants in Sweden in the second half of the 1980s (Berggren 1991). The Volvo plant in Uddevalla represents a hallmark here and, at the same time, can be interpreted as an affirmation of the separate path of a human-centered production organization which Sweden has been following since the 1970s. This encompasses the consequent abolition of the assembly line, a factory structure based on group work and clear task areas, process control that can be influenced by the production groups, sovereignty over time and far-reaching possibilities for the group to control the planning and execution of its own work, far-reaching autonomy of the groups to regulate their own personnel matters, holistic work cycles lasting up to several hours, and a one and one-half year training phase for all semi-skilled workers. Here, the attempt was indeed made at returning to a work organization following the craft model of qualified production work.

It must be emphasized that this Swedish concept aims primarily at semi-skilled tasks in areas with a low degree of mechanization. The planned training measures for unskilled assembly workers far surpass those which we have seen for unskilled workers elsewhere, also in the Federal Republic of Germany, but do not match the demands of skilled-worker training here. The concept foresees a far-reaching autonomy of the group. Management and hierarchical functions have been transferred to the group, which itself is structured in a very egalitarian manner. It is still unclear what is actually meant by "full responsibility" for questions of personnel, amounts and quality, though, and what consequences the group and the individual will have to bear if this responsibility is misused. This Swedish model is viewed with great skepticism by other Western manufacturers – also by some Swedish managers – though, not to mention Japan, as it is connected with a clear relinquishment of control on the part of management. This surrender of control is without guarantees, as no one knows whether the expected improvements in quality, efficiency, absenteeism, and work acceptance will also emerge in a long-term, stable manner.

This is why the chances for transferring this model, which is currently still in its preliminary stages, to other companies and countries do not look good. It will be interesting to see what effect the recent alliances – Volvo with Renault and Saab with GM – will have on the future development of the Swedish path. The closing of Saab's newest assembly plant in Malmö, which was organized totally in accordance with this path, does not bode well for the future. Above and beyond this, the Swedish companies are currently increasing their foreign activities and justifying this step with the high production costs in Sweden.

As we have already indicated above, the companies are also shying away from investment in higher degrees of automation. The enormous problems with the operation of "high-tech" equipment, the delays in production and equipment failures – which almost appear as normality in the factory routine – have made it clear that, at least in the assembly areas, the extent to which the system of "high-tech" mass production has been mastered has turned out to be lower than the planners had expected. Thus, the newest generation of assembly plants in Germany, Mercedes Benz's plant in Rastatt and the two plants of Volkswagen and Opel (GM) in Eastern Germany, have rather low-tech assembly areas.

Under these circumstances, Western management continues to look toward Japan or the Japanese transplants at the beginning of the 1990s. But the likelihood that new solutions and simple recipes will be found there is much less than at the beginning of the 1980s – especially since much has already been transferred.

What are the perspectives for the 1990s? Here we would like to touch upon three aspects, the first aspect again concerns Japan:

(1) In Japan, the limits of the most successful production regime in recent times are becoming more and more apparent, and are a cause of great concern for the companies. This has led to the fact that, in Japan itself, the discussion is more directed toward "post-lean concepts" and that new solutions are being sought in this respect. The background for this development is formed, first, by the chronic labor shortage which plagued the Japanese automobile industry throughout the 1980s, second, by a

change in values in the younger generations through contact with Western values and growing prosperity, and, finally, by clear indications of exhaustion especially of the, in principle, more privileged group of the core work force at the well-known leading companies in the Japanese economy. The consequences of this development are serious recruiting problems, both for the leading companies and, above all, for the supplier companies, who are increasingly competing with the leading companies for workers. A further consequence are growing fluctuation rates, which have, in part, reached Swedish levels in the meantime.

In view of these problems the Japanese companies now see themselves forced – whether they like it or not – to adopt some measures which they would rather have avoided:

these are, first of all, a stepped-up automation of production operations and the use of computers in areas where previously they had especially appreciated the flexibility of human labor. Thus currently we hear about projects in which assembly automation of the magnitude of Volkswagen's *Halle 54* and more are sought after.

Second, it concerns the legal and in part illegal employment of migrant workers, who stream inexorably into the country. Especially the supplier companies cannot survive without this reserve.

Third newest generation of Japanese assembly plants in Germany at the beginning of the 1990s thus exhibits many characteristics of assembly organization which we described above for Western plants: high-tech transfer lines for large assembly sections, stationary assembly islands, work on stationary assembly platforms, and automated guided vehicles.

The problems and the measures aimed at coping with them lead visibly to the erosion of the previous basic principles of Japanese production and work organization. Along with the leap into automation comes the necessity of carrying out more extensive training measures for maintenance personnel and automated systems controllers, at the same time migrant workers tend to take over simple production tasks. Will it come to the emergence of polarized structures of work organization and status differences? We do not believe that the Japanese will repeat Western mistakes, but they are faced with the great challenge of developing "post-lean" concepts which retain the basic principles of lean management but expand it to fulfill new goals of increased attractiveness of work and dealing with the demands of computer-integrated manufacturing.

(2) The development in Europe in the 1990s is a further point which plays a significant role in the consideration of perspectives. Here, at least the European manufacturers seem to have found compensation for their varied

losses in market shares in the U.S. and the developing countries. Although the topic "EEC 92," the creation of a unified market and thus the lifting of national regulations, aimed at protecting the domestic automobile industries in individual countries, had been dominated primarily by the question of how the Japanese companies would use their newly found freedoms and how the domestic automobile industries could hold out against the intensified competition, the sudden and unexpected opening of the Eastern borders has opened up a new market where, in addition, there is no serious established domestic competition for the companies forcing their way in. As Daihatsu's fruitless attempts at establishing a production site in Poland show, the Western European companies have a clear starting advantage to the extent that they can now decide to establish production sites in the Eastern European countries. At present, though, the car manufacturers are quite reluctant to invest in new plants and capacity in Eastern Europe.

The opening of the Eastern borders did not only create new markets. Eastern Europe has a tremendous potential of workers who have had skilled training in metalworking occupations and, in view of the labor market and the differences in the standard of living, would be willing to work for very low wages. This created a situation in Europe which was characteristic for Japan in the past and was an important prerequisite for the Japanese competitive success. Under these changed conditions there will in the foreseeable future not be pressure from the labor market toward high technology, as could be seen clearly in the German automobile industry in the 1980s. It is not possible today to determine how this changed situation will affect the future development of production concepts. In Volkswagen and General Motors' new plants, we see a consequent turn toward Japan-oriented production forms, strongly influenced by NUMMI and the automobile industry's first European assembly "transplant," the Nissan plant in Great Britain.

Fundamental for the question of the future chances for the "German way" is thus the appraisal of the potential savings of future technological development. If the assumption is made that competition on the world market will be decisively fought out in the arena of technology, then the goal of short-term cost savings through traditional measures for increasing efficiency would only have secondary importance. According to our findings, this assumption has more supporters in German companies than in U.S. companies. In this we are not speaking of reducing wage costs in direct production through the use of technology. We are rather referring to computer integrated manufacturing (CIM), that is as a means of achieving integration and flexibilization of the production processes, to cost savings through new logistics systems, and to the speeding up of product and process innovation. At present, none of the automobile companies has achieved a decisive breakthrough in the field of computer integration. The strategy of a determined leap into the age of high technology thus remains risky. A concentration on technological solutions to future problems could lead to similar experiences as we have described for the 1980s. The possibilities for the new technologies were overestimated and the chances of innovations in work and social organization were underestimated.

In the near future, with intensified competition on the world market, those companies and production sites will be able to assert themselves which are able to effectively combine computer integration and the development of human resources, new forms of group work and work efficiency. It is possible that we will even be experiencing a synthesis of the Japanese and the German models: group formation, job integration, and high labor efficiency in manual mass production according to the Japanese example; skilled-worker oriented team formation and professionalization in the high technology areas and in the service functions according to the German example. In the present state of the industry, such a scenario is not without chances for the 1990s. Whether it will be realized in some form or another, or whether another type of model will determine the future of labor in the automobile industry, can hardly be predicted in view of the continued high dynamics of development in the world automobile industry. Today, at the beginning of the 1990s only one thing is certain: we are at the end of an age in the auto industry and the contours of the new production regime are barely visible.

Notes

1 The restructuring of the world automobile industry

1 Project title: "Challenges and Opportunities for the Employees in the Present Restructuring of the World Automobile Industry. An international comparison of changes in the pattern of factory level labor deployment practices." The research was carried out by Knuth Dohse, Ulrich Jürgens, and Thomas Malsch. The project was financed by the Science Center Berlin for Social Research with additional funding from the Deutsche Forschungsgesellschaft.

2 The following gives the distribution of our expert interviews according to countries and companies. The countless interviews which we carried out with workers, union representatives at the central level, in other plants (parts plants) as well as at companies which were not included in the sample for our investigation and with government representatives, representatives of the scientific community, etc. are not included here. The same is true for the interviews in the Japanese automobile industry.

(a) *Expert interviews in each country*

U.S.A.	172
G.B.	104
F.R.G.	183

(b) *Expert interviews at each company*

A U.S.	73	A G.B.	91	A F.R.G.	60
B U.S.	99	B G.B.	43	B F.R.G	40
C F.R.G.	83				

3 See Mintzberg 1987 for the strategy concept

4 The method of comparing "matched" pairs was used specifically by those studies aimed at criticizing the hypothesis of technological determinism. This hypothesis assumes that it is technology which primarily determines the pattern of labor deployment and work organization. It could be demonstrated in various studies,

397

however, that the influence of societal differences, union policies, the systems of education and training, cultural norms, and government policies are also important independent variables for explaining differences in work organization and labor deployment patterns. In order to isolate the influence of these variables, as in the studies of the Aston-School (Pugh and Hickson 1976), it is necessary to analytically control for factors such as the level of technology, the size of the plant, and the type of production process (like special order production/large series production/continuous process production). Therefore, a sample of cases which are as similar as possible should be selected in order to be able to trace back the differences caused by the aforementioned factors.

Ronald Dore (1973), who compared the practices of worker deployment, gratifications, and the methods of dealing with conflicts in the factories of large companies in the electronics industry in Great Britain and Japan, can be considered to be a classic in the comparison of matched pairs. In his selection of factories he attempted to find plants which were as similar as possible in both countries – both with regard to the technology used and with regard to the size of the plant. Dore could show significant variation in country comparisons in all of the dependent variables that he investigated. This country variation was corroborated and elaborated more precisely in the empirical studies of Gallie (1978). Lutz (1976), Maurice *et al.* (1979), Dubois (1980), Malsch (1982), and Sorge *et al.* (1982).

In our opinion, the greatest and, with regard to the automobile industry, the most relevant weakness of these factory comparison studies lies in the fact that they have neglected the variable of company affiliation. All of the factories investigated by Gallie were from one company, but this fact was not made fruitful for the analysis. Thus, the theory of technological determinism, with its implications of convergence beyond national boundaries, was refuted; the question of to what extent the companies, on their part, promote convergence has not been investigated. The influence of company affiliation on the organization of factory processes (also in the company's subsidiaries in other countries) was generally labelled as weak in the few existing studies on this question (see the investigation of Kujawa 1975 and the contributions in Peninou *et al.* 1978). There were strongly diverging positions on this issue; the union generally asserted that an extensive control through the company headquarters did exist (see Woodcock 1977; Woodcock was president of the UAW); representatives of management, on the other hand, emphatically denied such an influence (see Copp 1977; Copp was the Overseas Liason Manager for Ford). In the ILO's comparative factory survey of the practices of subsidiaries of U.S. multinational companies, it can clearly be seen that there are company-specific ways to approach and solve problems, even though the nationally specific context has a considerable influence on the structure of the factory processes in the subsidiaries (see International Labor Organization 1977; see also Eichner and Hennig 1978). In case analyses of individual factories or national subsidiaries, reference to the importance of the variable of company affiliation is frequently found as well (e.g., Beynon 1973).

Because these methodical considerations and our starting assumptions led us to attach great importance to the question of company affiliation and the inclusion of factories in company strategies, we also carried out surveys at the central staff level of the companies and corporations.

2 Changing markets and the rise of Toyotism

1 Standard Industrial Classification (SIC) 3711, the statistical data base for the following presentation is documented and discussed in Atzert 1987.
2 Sypro 3311-Workers; Sypro is a classification system similar to SIC (cf. Atzert 1987).
3 The same is also true for the South Korean export potential, which is still being built up. According to a prognosis of the South Korean Ministry for Trade and Industry in 1986, this potential will reach 1.25 million vehicles annually (predominantly passenger cars) in 1990 and will increase to 2.5 million vehicles in the year 2000 (KIET 1985, p. 10). This would be more than the export volume of West Germany in 1986 (2.3 million passenger cars). We thus see a new competitor with highly modern production facilities entering the world market. This export venture's main direction of thrust will be the market segments of lower and middle sized cars: just the market segments in which the Japanese auto industry has had the most success. The Japanese producers will be forced to shift their product range to the territory of upper middle-class and luxury automobiles, the area where the Western manufacturers had been able to protect themselves in the face of the Japanese attack, and have, boosted by the development in oil prices and buyer preferences, been able to make good profits.

3 Company strategies for answering the challenges

1 At Ford it was considered important to omit the second "e" in employee in order to avoid the connotation of dependence in the employee-employer relationship; cf. Halberstam 1986, p. 253.

4 Industrial relations in the process of change

1 Management and union representatives who had taken part in these conflicts and who we interviewed in the course of our background studies in the U.S.A. preferred a different explanation, referring to an organizational change that General Motors had just carried out in its assembly plants. General Motors had united all of the assembly plants of its five divisions (Chevrolet, Cadillac, Buick, Oldsmobile, Pontiac) into one assembly division. At the same time, their degree of vertical integration was increased as the bulk of the body work (welding of body parts and assembly of the chassis), which had previously been carried out (together with press work) at a separate division, the Fisher Body Division, was transferred to the assembly plants (see also FT, September 16, 1970, Business Week, July 7, 1970, The Wall Street Journal, December 6, 1972). Although this measure took place in 1968, its results were still fresh in the memories of our respondents at the time of our study.
    Neither the new organizational concept nor the method of the reorganization

took into account the structures of industrial relations, rules, and "organizational cultures" which had developed in the previously independent organizations. As a result of the specific power constellations and conflicts over labor policy in each plant, fairly complicated systems for regulating demarcation and seniority had developed over time. This was especially true in the Chevrolet Division plants to which Lordstown belonged.

We were told that before the reorganization in these plants, task assignment according to job categories had been extended so far that practically every task in trim assembly had its own job category and was, correspondingly, compensated for differently. This went so far that exactly the same jobs were paid and classified differently depending on whether they were performed on the right or left side of the car body.

The management of GM attempted to use the embryonic situation to clean house and push through greater flexibility in labor deployment. Added to this came the fact that through the fusion of the organizational cultures a general insecurity and uncertainty with regard to the validity and continued existence of previous customs and practices arose. This could hardly bode well for a system of industrial relations which traditionally placed high emphasis on substantive arrangements (and not on procedural rules, as in the German context), even though the basis for the validity of these arrangements was often unclear (as was the case with many demarcation rules). The reorganization did not proceed without problems in any of the plants where a fusion with Fisher Body occurred. It was often remembered by our respondents as a battlefield of industrial relations, a "bloodbath" of labor relations. Lordstown was one of the factories in which the organizational fusion was carried out.

Looked at from this perspective, the conflicts at Lordstown pointed less toward a syndrome of a new generation of workers rebelling against assembly line work and the conditions of automobile work in general and more toward problems of securing the traditional stock of work rules of the old organization in a new organizational context.

2 Ford had neither built any new plants in North America (excluding Mexico) in the 1970s nor planned any for the 1980s.

3 An indication of this is a local union document issued in the course of factory negotiations in 1982 and in which the members listed their "concerns," that is, their demands on management. This appears to have been the normal practice here. Management was confronted with a list of 277 demands, and had, in turn, listed thirteen of its "concerns," at the center of which were questions of seniority and demarcation. The union list had contained 900 points in 1979, of which – according to the union representatives we interviewed – 300 in 1982 were to be understood as "serious" demands. In looking at the union's catalogue of demands one must consider that there was no representation of skilled workers on the shop committee at the time of the study. The list of 277 concerns thus did not contain any that were specific to skilled workers. Out of the total about 250 concerns remained when contract technicalities, administrative problems and borderline cases are excluded. Approximately half of the demarcation concerns referred to distinguishing between repair work, inspection, assembly line work, and material transport, that is, the division of tasks which management would

like to see broken down in the spirit of "new production concepts." The demand that repair workers do not do inspection work and vice versa, and that line workers do not do inspection and repair work (and vice versa) appears several times in the catalogue. The second largest group were problems of demarcation, in the sense of retaining the established work assignments for individual groups of workers, clearing up gray areas, as well as questions of work assignment and classification for specific types of work tasks were mentioned in fifty-six "concerns." Thus demarcation was a big issue, even though the skilled workers hadn't even brought their demarcation problems into the catalogue.

The third largest group, with twenty-eight concerns, consisted of questions dealing with the regulation of working time. More than the half of these were questions of taking breaks and the job descriptions of reliefmen. The demands in this area were not aimed at fundamental questions such as the legitimacy of overtime, shift work, etc., but rather more directed at "small changes" such as the time which certain job groups are allocated for washing, shifting the coffee break in the event of an interruption of production, etc.

Problems with seniority formed a small percentage of these with twelve concerns. This is not because these questions were considered secondary, but rather that this problem complex appeared to be sufficiently regulated.

Questions of organizing and structuring work, with nine concerns, were next to the last on the list and the problems here dealt with the availability of tools, etc. Such questions beyond problems with work safety – do not fall into the union organization's area of concern.

It is clear that the union's representation of interests was still rooted deep in the trenches of previous conflicts with the companies at the time of our investigation. Neither the concerns of the skilled workers, who would surely oppose all attempts of consolidating the classifications, nor the ideas of management with regard to the enlargement and enrichment of work in the task complex "assembly line – repair – inspection – material transport" are considered here. This is also true for forms of participation like quality circle. Thus the union succinctly demanded: "that daily (quality) audit meetings involving employees be done away with."

4 Bhaskar 1979, p. 390. Bhaskar theorizes that the insufficient degree of modernization in the plants, the carelessness of the work done, and the poor labor relations in British plants are closely connected as causes: "the older plant is frequently incapable of producing work of acceptable quality, which in turn means that rectification work must be carried out. Breakdowns are more frequent, leading to stoppages during and between shifts (which, due to the cramped layout of British plants, can bring the entire plant to a standstill while repairs are being carried out). More maintenance staff are required to keep the equipment operating (up to 78 percent more, according to the CPRS-report). Older machines are usually incapable of working as fast as newer ones and often require more men to operate them, leading to higher manning levels and slower working. And, finally, plant lay-out itself can affect productivity through lack of space or costly misuse of existing space. All of which affects the entire production process and, indeed, the morale of men who are obliged to work in far from perfect conditions."

5 This was regretted by this manager, because "experience has shown time and again that important resources were often tied up with breaking in and training at

the work place when they were most needed elsewhere" (see also Dombois 1982b).

6 In addition, there is a tacit understanding by both sides in West Germany that the wage safeguards are indefinitely valid, regardless of how the agreement reads: "This arrangement foresees wage security for a certain time. Up till now we have arranged things so that no loss of wages takes place . . . We also have no plans to discontinue this policy. The guarantees will be extended. . . There is a time limitation for the younger workers, in principle, which has however not been held to and will not be held to. We will take care of that in another way" (Personnel manager, "Mittelort").

7 The question of the degree of freedom for structuring work or, conversely, the extent to which work organization is determined by technology, was thus central for the theoretical discussion in the Federal Republic but hardly appeared in the U.S. discussion.

8 The employers' response to the perspective of a shortened work week has been the demand for a lengthening of weekly plant utilization hours through shift work. This can be achieved by uncoupling the employees' working hours from the hours in which the plant facilities operate. The first agreement on such an uncoupling was at BMW's new Regensburg plant in 1986. A nine hour shift was introduced with four individual work days and thus a work week of thirty-six hours for the employees. At the same time, the plant utilization time amounted to ninety-nine hours per week, including one Saturday shift. The highest plant utilization time achieved in this manner in Germany can be found at Opel's (GM) Kaiserslautern engine plant, where an agreement was reached in the spring of 1988 that in the planning of future investments, management could assume a utilization time of 140 hours per week for its facilities. This agreement includes round the clock production from Monday to Friday without stopping the line for breaks, two possible six-hour overtime shifts and a sixth night shift on Sunday night.

5 Reorganizing quality control

1 The defect code had eight digits, and was therefore more complex than the five digit code at Company A.

2 The new card was different from the old one as it did not have any defect characteristics which were manually marked, but was rather a clear record, which explicitly identified each defect in plain language and made a control over the repairs carried out considerably easier. Whereas the defect markings and subsequent imprints of the rectifiers were often misleading on the old inspection card due to the large amount of items and the limited space on the card, the danger of improper markings and false interpretation had been largely eliminated with the machine readable card.

6 Coping with new technology

1 This assessment of the WEMRs was also underscored by German experts from Company C on the basis of their own experience in the U.S.A.

7 Regulating work performance and plant efficiency

1 The figures on the IE density were based on our own estimations and calculations. Included was the entire IE personnel with the exception of the IE manager and his office staff. These relational figures are given with limitations. On the one hand, there were differences in the task assignments and differing jurisdictions of IE between the companies and factories, there were different divisions between central and factory IE functions, etc. In calculating the "IE density" we also did not account for IE's responsibility for the indirect production areas, which was differently organized in different companies. In any case, one cannot attribute the entire IE personnel to regulating performance in the direct production area.

2 REFA 1978, Part 2, p. 136. In older contracts there were attempts to provide a substantive definition for the "fair day's work" norm. Thus the following definition can be found in a contract of an U.S. automobile company in the 1950s: "A fair day's work involved using a pace which a man could best attain for an eight hour shift without undue fatigue. It was neither immoderately fast nor immoderately slow. It was a pace at which a man walks over smooth level ground without load at a rate of three miles per hour" (quoted by Hutchinson 1961, p. 37).

3 We use "shop steward" here as the general name for the workers' interest representative. In the German context it could either be the works council member elected by the area or a "Vertrauensmann" to whom the works council has delegated the competence to formally take part in the practice of time study.

4 The contracts of the Canadian plants of both companies did not allow the possibility for a strike in the case of unsolved grievances over "production standards." The volume of the corresponding open grievances in the statistics there was considerably lower than in the U.S. sister plants at the time of our study.

5 REFA, 1978, Part I, p. 24. The organization which backs REFA today is the *Verband für Arbeitsstudien und Betriebsorganization* (Association for Work Measurement and Factory Organization).

6 "With the rating of the level of performance, it's a bit of a problem." A member of the works council in a German plant thus related his experiences with the training in REFA methods. "We also went to REFA courses, and it came up again and again that the works council members rated the level of performance most poorly, I mean most disadvantageously for the worker. We had such a factor in our heads: as a member of the works council you have to attempt to be as objective as possible, if you set the level of performance too high, then it will appear that you were partial here. And there we unconsciously set the level of performance too low. It also happened to others. We were really upset with ourselves."

7 A typical remark of an industrial engineer in a German company: "We could generally agree rapidly with the works council representatives that one cannot leave the decision up to Adam, the village judge, who doesn't have the vaguest idea what MTM and rating were. Then one could just as well draw lots right

away. The concept of 'Adam, the village judge,' was really a familiar quotation if we were trying to press for an agreement in the company" (IE Manager, Heidedorf).

8 In the magazine *Industrial Engineering* this was confirmed in a comparison with other methods of setting standards as the following table shows:

Accuracy of different IE measuring methods

Methods for setting standards	At the close of the work study	Customary trends after the work study
Adoption of past values	+/−30%	20% too tight to 60% too loose
Estimates on the basis of valid assumptions	+/−20%	10% to 45% too loose
Measurements with the stop-watch	+/−10%	5% too tight to 35% too loose
Methods of predetermined times	+/−5%	5% too tight to 20% too loose

Source: Sellie 1984, p. 84.

9 Differing task assignment of the two groups in the different companies were not taken into account; the same was true for differences in the delimitation of functions between company headquarters and the factories; see, e.g., the Parent Area System at Company B U.S. which we describe later in this chapter.

10 Agreements between the UAW and the (A) Company, Vol. 1, February 13, 1982, p.2.

11 The foreman in the U.S. and British plants corresponds in status and function in the strictest sense most closely to the "Vizemeister" (the deputy of the "Meister") in German plants. In any case, it would be misleading to equate foreman and "Meister" due to the very different degrees of responsibility. See Jürgens and Strömel 1987 regarding the differences in responsibility.

12 IMB 1986, p. XVI.

13 Industrial engineer at the divisional level at Company B. The Division's calculation of efficiency is so constructed that the improvements in efficiency lead to a reduction of the percentage, and vice versa.

14 This sudden improvement in regard to grievances was criticized quite sarcastically at Northtown "From one day to another they worked out a whole lot of grievances: This is just not a kosher thing to do. We are more sincere in grievances, when we have grievances going we feel there is a cause behind them and we do not just use them for technical purposes as Greentown seems to do. How can you really settle your whole grievance load almost overnight if you were sincere in the first place?" (Union representative, Northtown)

15 In explaining why the union headquarters does not undertake anything against the competition between factories, and why the local union organizations do not consult with each other, a union spokesman explained: "The question was put to the international: Why did they not put a lid on the competition of the local unions against each other? But it was argued that under the free enterprise system there was a possibility of a liability case being brought forward by the

company against the union. They had a bunch of lawyers around who said that the company could sue the union if they would coordinate to fight against efficiency improvements. There was another argument and this is that Company B's supplier plants have always worked under the system of competing against each other. Now just because a system moves into the assembly plants, it does not necessarily mean that it is wrong or has to be evaluated differently."

16 We have borrowed this term from the "America watching" of traditional Japanese practice.

8 Comparable achievements in labor productivity

1 This data base was not ideal (yearly averages of the personnel level would be more appropriate). Distortions arose above all in using data for fixed days in plants where the employment volume underwent considerable changes within a year. In the framework of our study this was only the case for the U.S. factories in the years 1981 and 1982, as the work force of the second shift was laid off temporarily here.

2 The data published in Womack *et al.* 1990, p. 85 refer to the year 1989; a number of papers from Krafcik refer to the years before, but due to the annonymization they do not allow for the conception of a time series.

3 We have not included the plants Seaborough and Mittelort in this consideration for reasons of data quality or, respectively, the strongly deviating vertical integration.

4 The size of the shares of these jobs of "Anlagenführer," "Straßenführer," "Anlagenbediener," "Kolonnenführer" or whatever they are called in the different companies is naturally dependent on the quantity of reference. The numbers given in table 8.5 refer in each case to the body shop of the corresponding areas, and here also, as far as possible, to the sections where "Anlagenführer" were used at all – thus without the area of body finishing. The share of jobs which were similar to that of "Anlagenführer" shot up to as much as one third of the jobs in the areas where a high degree of mechanization and automation had been reached.

9 Tapping new resources

1 General standards for the apprenticeship programs of the companies are set by the Bureau of Apprenticeship and Training of the Department of Labor and the Federal Committee of Apprenticeship – on which the states, the unions, and the employers are represented. The Bureau of Apprenticeship and Training formulates the minimum criteria for apprenticeships and thus attempts to attain a certain standardization. An apprenticeship must thus fulfill the following criteria in order to be recognized and registered:

at least 144 hours per year spent on related instruction away from the work place,

the numerical relation of skilled workers to apprentices must be such that a reasonable supervision and instruction is possible, the length of the training should not be under one year or 2,000 hours. This regulation (BNA, Vol. 2 1980, p. 171ff.) opens up for the companies a wide scope for structuring.

2 As the companies were represented in the EITB they could influence the contents of the training. The industry training boards were abolished in the second half of the 1980s. According to our information, this did not entail significant changes in the content and conditions of skilled-worker training at the established car companies in the U.K.

3 In practice, as in the British factories, the children of plant members are given preference. There is an entrance test, but, according to a works council member, "Out of those who pass the test only the children of plant members will be taken. If around 800 apply, then perhaps 400 will pass the test and out of these then only the plant children will be selected. But heaven forbid if the workers' children don't pass the test – then the works council will get the heat. According to the accounts of their parents, their children must be true prodigies, but if they don't pass the test here, then all hell breaks loose" (Mittelort).

4 The corresponding training programs were already prepared at the company headquarters level in anticipation of the introduction of these new job descriptions for skilled workers in production. At Windeck, ca. 40 percent of the apprentices in 1986 were being trained for the job "mechanic in production." The category of "parts finisher" was created at Weinkirchen and Mittelort several years ago, above all for deployment in production. Knowledge and skills of the mechanical crafts were supposed to be transmitted in the course of a short, two-year training period. The quantitative importance of this trade (which was also known in practice as a "crippled trade") remained small.

5 The training curriculum for the industrial electronics mechanic in the specialized area of production technology encompasses:
   (a) mounting automated production equipment;
   (b) setting up and supervising automated production equipment;
   (c) checking, measuring, setting, and adjusting function and process flows in automated production equipment;
   (d) recommissioning units and automated production equipment;
   (e) maintaining automated production equipment.

6 A focal point for the activities of further training was formed by the model start phase in all plants. At Greentown the following totals of "man days" were spent on further training in the years 1981 to 1986:

	1981	1982	1983	1984	1985	1986
man days	1,765	4,599	2,255	1,379	1,092	577

The above shows that the maximum further training was in 1982. In this year, each employee participated in an average of one day of training. It was the year of the start of a new car model.

7 The focal points of many "NW&M schedules" at the factory level correspond to this. Thus at Greentown, the focal points of the action plan for the next period (at the time of our investigation) were:

interpersonal skills and group dynamics,
decision analysis and decision-making process,
goal setting and planning,
positive management – the use of behavior modification in business,
principles of attitude change,
understanding human motivation and behavior/stress management and
   coping behaviors,
conflict resolution/positive responsible assertive behavior,
encouragement of self-development through tuition refund, professional
   organization affiliation, etc. (1982 report, Company B U.S., p. 71).

8 An example from the Aspern plant where the flexibility wage system so far has
only been used for workers in direct production (Scheinecker 1988). The entry
wage is the wage level F 0; by obtaining additional qualification the workers can
climb the wage scale from F 1 to F 8*. The maximum wage F 8* is about 40
percent higher than the base wage F 0.

This system assigns the first point when the worker can operate a machine and
carry out measurements or when he or she can perform the work at an assembly
station. In normal cases, three points can be given per work station with one
additional point for inspection.

Work stations in parts production		Work stations in assembly areas
Servicing and measuring	1 point	Assembly/joining
Tool change	1 point	Master sequence of automatic stations, be able to perform servicing and deal with minor problems
Maintenance and small repairs	1 point	Recognize assembly mistakes, be able to carry out repairs and recognize rejects
Qualification for an inspection job	1 point	Qualification for an inspection job

The maximum number of points which a worker can achieve is obtained by
multiplying the number of machines, machine groups or assembly by the points
given for the criteria listed in the table.

After a worker has reached 75 percent of the points possible in one team, a
change into a second team can take place and four further flexibility stages can
be attained. The distinct level F 8* is given to especially qualified workers who
are flexible within two teams. The maximum number of points that can be
earned is made up by the number of machines/groups of machines or assembly
places multiplied by the number of the allocation criteria.

The allocation of points for flexibility takes place in the Aspern plant through
the "Meister", who is required to consult with the central personnel department
to make sure that the target distribution which is striven for is not exceeded (in
fact, the planned staffing of the higher flexibility levels F 5 and F 6 were already
exceeded in August 1987, see Scheinecker 1988). There is, however, no right to

flexibility in the sense of a claim of the employee to the flexibility point if the qualification can be proven.

A plan for personnel usage for each team is submitted to the meister and to the personnel department. This plan documents the flexibility stage and the level of training of each individual team member. This personnel usage plan is thus an instrument of control in order to be able to react immediately to program changes or absences. The usage plan contains the number of machines in each team, the number of the points achievable, the names of the workers, the number and percentage of the points which each team member has, and with this his corresponding flexibility level.

9 See Antrag 139 "Konzept gegen Qualitätszirkel," in IG Metall 1986a, 15. ordentlicher Gewerkschaftstag der IG Metall, Protokoll Band II, Teil III, p. 74f.
10 Cf. Brumlop and Jürgens 1986.

10 Is the assembly line obsolete?

1 Calculated from data in Ward's Automotive Yearbook 1986, pp. 81f.
2 At Volvo's Kalmar plant, this command is given centrally by the system without regard to the situation of the individual work station. See Berggren 1988, p. 141.

11 Modern times in the automobile factory

1 It did coexist to some extent with "self-regulation" through the British shop steward movement, an effect which created a special situation in the British context.
2 Spain and Portugal were also included in 1985 for reasons of comparability.
3 AN, November 29, 1989, p. 128 – projected Western European car production in 1995: 14.067 mill.

Bibliography

Abegglen, J. 1958, *The Japanese Factory*, Glencoe: Free Press.

Abernathy, W.J. 1978, *The Productivity Dilemma. Roadblock to Innovation in the Automobile Industry*, Baltimore/London: John-Hopkins University Press.

Abernathy, W.J., Harbour, J.E., and Henn, J.M. 1981, "Productivity and Comparative Cost Advantages: Some Estimates for Major Automotive Producers," Report to the Department of Transportation; Transportation System Center, Cambridge.

Abernathy, W.J., Clark, K.B., and Kantrow, A.M. 1983a, *Industrial Renaissance. Producing a Competitive Future for America*, New York: Basic Books.

1983b, "The New Industrial Competition," in Kantrow, A.M. (ed.), *Survival Strategies for American Industry*, New York: Harvard Business Review Executive Book Series, pp. 72–131.

Abholz, H., Hildebrandt, E., Ochs, P., Rosenbrock, R., Spitzley, H., Stebani, J., and Wotschak, W. 1981, "Arbeitswissenschaft ohne Sozialwissenschaft," Discussion Paper IIVG/dp 81–222, Berlin: Science Center of Berlin for Social Research.

Aglietta, M. 1979, *A Theory of Capitalist Regulation. The US Experience*, New York: New Left Books.

Altmann, N., Bechtle, G., and Lutz, B. 1978, *Betrieb – Technik – Arbeit. Elemente einer Analytik technisch-organisatorischer Veränderungen*, Frankfurt: Campus.

Altmann, N., Binkelmann, P., Düll, K., Mandolia, R., and Stück, H. 1981, *Bedingungen und Probleme betrieblich initiierter Humanisierungsmaßnahmen*, Forschungsbericht BMFT – HA 81–007(1)–(4), Eggenstein-Leopoldshafen.

Altmann, N., Deiß, M., Döhl, V., and Sauer, D. 1986, "Ein 'Neuer Rationalisierungstyp' – neue Anforderungen an die Industriesoziologie," *Soziale Welt*, Vol. 37, No. 2–3, pp. 191–207.

Altshuler, A., Anderson, M., Jones, D., Roos, D., and Womack, J. 1984, *The Future of the Automobile. The Report of MIT's International Automobile Program*, London: George Allen & Unwin.

Anthony, R.N. and Dearden, J. 1980, *Management Control Systems*, (4th edn), Homewood, Ill.: Irwin.

Armstrong, P.J., Goodman, J.F.B., and Hyman, J.D. 1981, *Ideology and Shopfloor Industrial Relations*, London: Croom Helm.

Aronowitz, S. 1973, *False Promises. The Shaping of American Working Class*

Consciousness, New York: McGraw-Hill.

Atzert, L. 1987, "Die Automobildatenbank. Betriebsdaten und Länderdaten des Projektes 'Risiken und Chancen der gegenwärtigen Umstrukturierungen in der Automobilindustrie für die Arbeitnehmer'," Discussion Paper IIVG/dp87–221, Berlin: Science Center of Berlin for Social Research.

Audi 1970–87, *Geschäftsberichte*, Annual Editions.

Auer, P., Penth, B., and Tergeist, P. (eds.) 1983, *Arbeitspolitische Reformen in Industriestaaten. Ein internationaler Vergleich*, Frankfurt: Campus.

Auer, P. and Riegler, C.H. 1988, *Gruppenarbeit bei Volvo: Aktuelle Tendenzen und Hintergründe*, Berlin/Stockholm: WZB/Arbetsmiljöfonden.

Ayres, R.U. and Miller, S.M. 1983, *Robotics. Applications and Social Implications*, Cambridge, Mass.: Ballinger.

Bailey, D. and Hubert, T. (eds.) 1980, *Productivity Measurement. An International Review of Concepts, Techniques, Programms and Current Issues*, Westmead/Englewood Cliffs, N.J.: Gower.

Bailey, J. 1983, *Job Design and Work Organization. Matching People and Technology for Productivity and Employee Involvement*, Englewood Cliffs, N.J.: Prentice Hall.

Barnes, R.M. 1980, *Motion and Time Study Design and Measurement of Work*, (7th edn), New York: Wiley.

Barth, H.-R., Muster, M., Ulich, E., and Udris, I. 1980, *Arbeits- und sozialpsychologische Untersuchungen von Arbeitsstrukturen im Bereich der Aggregatfertigung der Volkswagenwerk AG*, Vol. 1 and Supplement, Forschungsbericht: BMFT HA 80–016/017, Eggenstein-Leopoldshafen.

Batstone, E. 1984, *Working Order. Workplace Industrial Relations Over Two Decades*, Oxford: Basil Blackwell.

Batstone, E., Boraston, I., and Frenkel, S. 1977, *Shop Stewards in Action. The Organization of Workplace Conflict and Accomodation*, Oxford: Basil Blackwell.

Bayer, K. 1982, "General Motors in Aspern: Grundstein einer neuen österreichischen Industriepolitik," in Abele, K. *et al.* (eds.), *Handbuch der österreichischen Wirtschaftspolitik*, Wien: Manz, pp. 427–40.

Benedict, R. 1946, *The Chrysanthemum and the Sword*, Boston: Houghton-Mifflin.

Benz-Overhange, K. 1982, *Neue Technologien und alternative Arbeitsgestaltung. Auswirkungen des Computereinsatzes in der industriellen Produktion*, Frankfurt: Campus.

Benz-Overhage, K., Brumlop, E., v. Freyberg, T., and Papadimitriou, Z. 1981, "Der Einsatz von Computer-Technologien in der Fertigungstechnik und Möglichkeiten der Arbeitsgestaltung," *Beiträge zur Arbeitsmarkt- und Berufsforschung*, No. 53, pp. 39–68.

Berggren, C. 1988, "'New Production Concepts' in Final Assembly – The Swedish Experience," in Dankbaar, B., Jürgens, U., and Malsch, T. (eds.), pp. 133–66.

1991, *Von Ford zu Volvo: Automobilherstellung in Schweden*, Berlin: Springer-Verlag.

Beynon, H. 1973, *Working for Ford*, London: Allen Lane.

Bhaskar, K. 1979, *The Future of the UK Motor Industry*, London: Kogan Page.

1980, *BL: Tomorrow's Economic Miracle*, Bath: Sewells.

1983, *The Future of the UK and European Motor Industry*, Bath: Sewells.

Bhaskar *et al.* 1986, "Japanese Automotive Strategies: A European and US Perspective," The Motor Industry Research Unit, Norwich: University of East Anglia.

Blauner, R. 1964, *Alienation and Freedom: The Factory Worker and his Industry*, Chicago: University of Chicago Press.

BMW 1970–87, *Geschäftsberichte*, Annual Editions.

BNA (Bureau of National Affairs), *Collective Bargaining. Negotiations and Contracts*, Washington.

Bolt, J.F. 1983, "Job Security: Its Time has Come," *Harvard Business Review*, No. 6 (November/December), pp. 115–23.

Bosch, G. and Lichte, R. 1982, "Die Funktionsweise informeller Senioritätsrechte – am Beispiel einer betrieblichen Fallstudie," in Dohse, K., Jürgens, U., and Russig, H. (eds.), pp. 205–35.

Brady, R.A. 1974, *The Rationalization Movement in German Industry. A Study in the Evolution of Economic Planning*, New York: Fertig.

Braun, S. 1968, *Ablauf und soziale Folgen von technischen Umstellungen in der mechanischen Fertigung und Endmontage eines Automobilwerks*, Göttingen: SOFI.

Braverman, H. 1978, *Die Arbeit im modernen Produktionsprozeß*, Frankfurt: Campus.

Briam, K.-H. 1986, *Arbeiten ohne Angst. Arbeitsmanagement im technischen Wandel*, Düsseldorf/Wien: ECON-Verlag.

Brown, W. 1972, "A Consideration of 'Custom and Practice'," *British Journal of Industrial Relations*, Vol. 10, No. 1, pp. 42–61.

Brown, W. (ed.) 1981, *The Changing Contours of British Industrial Relations*, Oxford: Basil Blackwell.

Bruggemann, A. 1980, *Arbeits- und sozialpsychologische Untersuchungen von Arbeitsstrukturen im Bereich der Aggregatfertigung der Volkswagenwerk AG*, Vol. 2: Zur Entwicklung von Einstellungen und sozialem Verhalten in den untersuchten teilautonomen Gruppen, Forschungsbericht: BMFT HA 80–018, Eggenstein-Leopoldshafen.

Brumlop, E. 1986, *Veränderungen der Arbeitsbewertung bei flexiblem Personaleinsatz. Das Beispiel Volkswagen AG*, Frankfurt: Campus.

Brumlop, E. and Jürgens, U. 1986, "Rationalisation and Industrial Relations: A Case Study of Volkswagen," in Jacobi, O., Jessop, B., Kastendiek, H., and Regini, R. (eds.), *Technological Change, Rationalisation and Industrial Relations*, London: Croom Helm, pp. 73–94.

Bundesminister für Forschung und Technologie (ed.) 1980, *Gruppenarbeit in der Motorenmontage*, Schriftenreihe "Humanisierung des Arbeitslebens," Vol. 3, Frankfurt: Campus.

Busch, K.W. 1966, *Strukturwandlungen der westdeutschen Automobilindustrie. Ein Beitrag zur Erfassung und Deutung einer industriellen Entwicklungsphase im Übergang vom produktionsorientierten zum marktorientierten Wachstum*, Berlin: Duncker & Humblot.

Cahill, J. and Ingram, 1987, *Changes in Working Practices in British Manufacturing Industry in the 1980s*, London: CBI.

Cappelli, P. 1985, "Plant-Level Concession Bargaining," *Industrial and Labor Relations Review*, Vol. 39, No. 1, pp. 90–104.

Cassell, F.H., Juris, H.A., and Roomkin, M.J. 1985, "Strategic Human Ressources Planning: an Orientation to the Bottom Line," *Management Decision*, Vol. 3, No. 4, pp. 16–28.

CDG (Carl Duisberg Gesellschaft) (ed.) 1984, *Berufliche Bildung des Auslands*, Stuttgart: ECHO-Verlag.

CPRS (Central Policy Review Staff) 1975, *The Future of the British Car Industry*, London: HMSO.

Cherry, R.L. 1982, "The Development of General Motors' Team-Based Plants," in Zager R. and Rosow M.P. (eds.), pp. 125–48.

Child, J. 1978, "The Myth at Lordstown," *Management Today*, 150th issue, pp. 80–4.

Child, J. and Partridge, B. 1982, *Lost Managers. Supervisors in Industry and Society*, Cambridge: Cambridge University Press.

Chinoy, E. 1955, *Automobile Workers and the American Dream*, Garden City: California Press.

1964, "Manning the Machines – The Assembly Line Worker," in Berger, P.L. (ed.), *The Human Shape of Work*, New York: Regnery, pp. 51–81.

Clark, R. 1979, *The Japanese Company*, New Haven: Yale University Press.

Cole, R.E. 1971, *Japanese Blue Collar. The Changing Tradition*, Berkeley: University of California Press.

1979, *Work, Mobility and Participation: A Comparative Study of American and Japanese Industry*, Berkeley: University of California Press.

Copp, R. 1977, "Locus of Industrial Relations Decision Making in Multinationals," in Banks, R.F. and Steiber, J. (eds.), *Multinationals, Unions, and Labor Relations in Industrial Countries*, Ithaka: Cornell, pp. 43–8.

Coriat, B. 1980, "The Restructuring of the Assembly Line: A New Economy of Time and Control," *Capital and Class*, No. 11, pp. 34ff.

Craft, J.A., Abboushi, S., and Labovitz, T. 1985, "Concession Bargaining and Unions: Impacts and Implications," *Journal of Labor Research*, Vol. 6, No. 2, pp. 167–80.

Cray, E. 1980, *Chrome Collossus. General Motors and its Times*, New York: McGraw-Hill.

Crosby, P.B. 1986, *Qualität ist machbar*, Hamburg: McGraw-Hill.

Cusumano, M.A. 1985, *The Japanese Automobile Industry. Technology and Management at Nissan and Toyota*, Harvard, Mass.: Harvard University Press.

Cummings, T.G. and Molloy, E.S. 1977, *Improving Productivity and the Quality of Worklife*, New York/London: Praeger.

Daimler-Benz 1970–87, *Geschäftsberichte*, Annual Editions.

Damm, H. 1978, "Ansätze zur Arbeitsgestaltung in der Automobilproduktion," *Zeitschrift für Betriebswirtschaft*, Vol. 48, No. 1, pp. 72–6.

Daniel, W.W. and Millward, N. 1983, *Workplace Industrial Relations in Britain. The DE/PSJ/SSRC Survey*, London: Heinemann.

Dankbaar, B., Jürgens, U., and Malsch, T. (eds.) 1988, *Die Zukunft der Arbeit in der*

Automobilindustrie, Berlin: Sigma.

Demes, H. 1989, "Beförderung und Entlehnung in einem japanischen Automobilunternehmen – Eine Fallstudie," Discussion Paper Fs II, 89–201.

Denise, M.L. 1974, "Industrial Relations and the Multinational Corporation: the Ford Experience," in Flanagan, R.J. and Weber, A.R. (eds.), pp. 135–45.

Deppe, J. 1986, *Qualitätszirkel – Ideenmanagement durch Gruppenarbeit. Darstellung eines neuen Konzepts in der deutschsprachigen Literatur*, Bern: Peter Lang.

Dertouzos, M., Lester, R.K., and Solow, R.M. 1989, *Made in America: Regaining the Productive Edge*, Cambridge, Mass.: MIT Press.

Deutschmann, C. 1986, "Economic Restructuring and Company Unionism – The Japanese Model," Discussion Paper dpIIM/LMP 86–17, Berlin: Science Center of Berlin for Social Research.

1987, *Arbeitszeit in Japan. Organisatorische und organisationskulturelle Aspekte der "Rundumnutzung" der Arbeitskraft*, Frankfurt: Campus.

Deutschmann, C. and Weber, C. 1987, "Das japanische 'Arbeitsbienen'-Syndrom. Auswirkungen der Rundum-Nutzung der Arbeitskraft auf die Arbeitszeitpraxis am Beispiel Japans," Discussion Paper IIM/LMP 87–4, Berlin: Science Center of Berlin for Social Research.

Dieckhoff, K. 1978, *Ausgewählte Indikatoren der ökonomischen Entwicklung und der Arbeitssituation in der westdeutschen Automobilindustrie*, Marburg: Görich & Weiershauser.

Dohse, K. 1982 (in cooperation with Jürgens, U. and Russig, H.), *Hire and Fire? Senioritätsregelungen in amerikanischen Betrieben*, Frankfurt: Campus.

1987, "Innovations in Collective Bargaining through the Multinationalisation of Japanese Automobile Companies: the Cases of NUMMI (USA) and Nissan (UK)," in Trevor, M. (ed.), pp. 124–49.

Dohse, K. and Jürgens, U. 1982, "Statussicherungen bei Personalbewegungen. Regelungsansätze im internationalen Vergleich," in Dohse, K., Jürgens, U., and Russig H. (eds.), pp. 11–52.

1985, "Konzernstrategien und internationale Arbeitsteilung in der Automobilindustrie am Beispiel Ford und General Motors," *Mehrwert*, No. 26, pp. 30–48.

Dohse, K., Jürgens, U., and Malsch, T. 1984a, "Reorganisation der Arbeit in der Automobilindustrie – Konzepte, Regelungen, Veränderungstendenzen in den USA, Großbritannien und der Bundesrepublik Deutschland – Ein Materialbericht," Discussion Paper IIVG/dp 84–220, Berlin: Science Center of Berlin for Social Research.

1984b, "Vom 'Fordismus' zum 'Toyotismus.' Die Organisation der industriellen Arbeit in der japanischen Automobilindustrie," *Leviathan*, Vol. 12, No. 4, pp. 448–77; also *Politics & Society*, Vol. 14, No. 2, pp. 115–46.

1985, "Fertigungsnahe Selbstregulierung oder zentrale Kontrolle – Konzernstrategien im Restrukturierungsprozeß der Automobilindustrie," in Naschold, F. (ed.), *Arbeit und Politik. Gesellschaftliche Regulierung der Arbeit und der sozialen Sicherung*, Frankfurt: Campus, pp. 49–89.

Dohse, K., Jürgens, U., and Russig, H. (eds.) 1982, *Statussicherung im Industriebetrieb. Alternative Regelungsansätze im internationalen Vergleich*, Frankfurt: Campus.

Doleschal, R. 1985, "Zur internationalen Reorganisation der Produktions- und

Absatzkonzepte im Volkswagenwerk," *Mehrwert*, No. 26, pp. 49–66.

Doleschal, R. and Dombois, R. (eds.) 1982, *Wohin läuft VW? Die Automobilproduktion in der Wirtschaftskrise*, Reinbek bei Hamburg: Rowohlt, rororo.

Dombois, R. 1976, "Massenentlassungen bei VW: Individualisierung der Krise," *Leviathan*, Vol. 3, No. 4, pp. 432–64.

1979, "Stammarbeiter und Krisenbetroffenheit," *Prokla*, No. 36, pp. 161–87.

1982a, "Die betriebliche Normenstruktur. Fallanalysen zur arbeitsrechtlichen und sozialwissenschaftlichen Bedeutung informeller Normen im Industriebetrieb," in Dohse, K., Jürgens, U., and Russig, H. (eds.), pp. 173–204.

1982b, "Beschäftigungspolitik in der Krise. VW als Modell großbetrieblichen Krisenmanagements," in Doleschal, R. and Dombois, R. (eds.), pp. 273–90.

Donovan-Report 1968, Royal Commission on Trade Unions and Employers' Associations 1965–1968, Cmnd 3623, London: HMSO.

Dore, R.P. 1973, *British Factory – Japanese Factory: The Origins of National Diversity in Industrial Relations*, Berkeley: University of California Press.

Dubois, P. 1980, "Niveaux de main-d'oeuvre et organization du travail ouvrier. Etude de cas francais et anglais," *Sociologie du Travail*, No. 3, pp. 257–75.

Düe, D. and Hentrich, J. 1981, *Krise der Automobilindustrie – Das Beispiel des Multi General Motors/Opel AG*, Frankfurt: IMSF Informationsbericht No. 35.

Dunlop, J. 1958, *Industrial Relations System*, Carbondale: Southern Illinois Universitiy Press.

Dunnett, P.J.S. 1980, *The Decline of the British Motor Industry. The Effects of Government Policy, 1945–1979*, London: Croom Helm.

Dyer, D. Salter, M.S., and Webber, A.M. 1987, *Changing Alliances*, Boston: Harvard Business School Press.

Edwardes, M. 1983, *Back from the Brink? An Apocalyptic Experience*, London: Collins.

Edwards, P. 1982, "Britain's Changing Strike Problem?," *Industrial Relations Journal*, Vol. 13, No. 2, pp. 5–20.

Eichner, H. and Hennig 1978, *Die sozialen Aspekte der Tätigkeit der multinationalen Unternehmen*, Berlin: Duncker and Humblot.

Euler, H.P. 1977, *Das Konfliktpotential industrieller Arbeitsstrukturen. Analyse der technischen und sozialen Ursachen*, Opladen: Westdeutscher Verlag.

Expenditure Committee 1975, House of Commons Expenditure Committee, Fourteenth Report: *The Motor Vehicle Industry*, London: HMSO.

Fisher, A.B. 1985, "Behind the Hype at GM's Saturn," *Fortune*, November 11, pp. 34–42.

Flanagan, R. 1984, "Wage Concessions and Long-Term Union Wage Flexibility," *Brookings Papers on Economic Activity*, No. 1, pp. 183–216.

Flanagan, R.J. and Weber, A.R. (eds.) 1974, *Bargaining without Boundarie. The Multinational Corporation and International Labor Relations*, Chicago: The University of Chicago Press.

Flynn, M.S. 1985, "U.S. and Japanese Automotive Productivity Comparisons: Strategic Implications," *National Productivity Review*, Vol. 4, No. 1, pp. 60–70.

Ford UK 1976–87, *Annual Reports*.

Ford US 1970–87, *Annual Reports*.

Ford-Werke AG 1970–87, *Geschäftsberichte*, Annual Editions.

Form, W.H. 1976, *Blue-Collar Stratification. Autoworkers in Four Countries*, Princeton: Princeton University Press.

Fricke, E., Notz, G., and Schuchardt, W. 1982, *Beteiligung im Humanisierungsprogramm. Zwischenbilanz 1974–1980*, Bonn: Verlag Neue Gesellschaft.

Fricke, W., Peter, G., and Pöhler, W. (eds.) 1982, *Beteiligen, Mitgestalten, Mitbestimmen. Arbeitnehmer verändern ihre Arbeitsbedingungen*, Köln: Bund Verlag.

Friedman, G. 1964, *Industrial Society. The Emergence of the Human Problems of Automation*, Toronto: Free Press.

Friedrich-Ebert-Stiftung 1981, *Qualifikation und Beteiligung. Das "Peiner Modell,"* Schriftenreihe "Humanisierung des Arbeitslebens," Vol. 12, Frankfurt: Campus.

Gallie, D. 1978, *In Search of the New Working Class. Automation and Social Integration within the Capitalist Enterprise*, Cambridge: Cambridge University Press.

Garbarino, J.W. 1985, "Unionism Without Unions: The New Industrial Relations," *Industrial Relations*, Vol. 23, No. 1, pp. 40–51.

Garson, B. 1975, *All the Livelong Day. The Meaning and Demeaning of Routine Work*, Harmondsworth: Doubleday.

General Motors US 1970–87, *Annual Reports*.

Genth, M. 1981, *Qualität und Automobile. Eine Untersuchung am Beispiel des westdeutschen Automobilmarktes 1974–1977*, Frankfurt: Peter D. Lang.

Ginsburg, D.H. and Abernathy, W.J. 1978, *Government, Technology, and the Future of the Automobile*, New York: McGraw-Hill.

Glaser, E.M. 1976, *Productivity Gains Through Worklife Improvements*, New York/London: Harcourt Brace Jovanovich.

Gold, Ch. 1986, *Labor-Management Committees: Confrontation, Cooptation or Cooperation*, New York: New York State School of Industrial and Labour Relations.

Goldschmidt, N. 1981, *The U.S. Automobile Industry, 1980. Report to the President from the Secretary of Transportation*, Washington D.C.

Goldthorpe, J.H. 1966, "Attitudes and Behaviour of Car Assembly Workers: A Deviant Case and a Theoretical Critique," *British Journal of Sociology*, Vol. 17, No. 3, pp. 315–32.

Goldthorpe, J.H., Lockwood, D., Bechhofer, F., and Platt, J. 1969, *The Affluent Worker in the Class Structure*, 3 volumes, Cambridge: Cambridge University Press.

Gora, W. 1986, "Anwenderfunktionen und -protokolle in MAP," *Automatisierungssystem MAP*, Workshop on MAP, Berlin, November 25/26.

Guest, R.H. 1982, "Tarrytown: Quality of Work Life at a General Motors Plant," in Zager, R. and Rosow, M.P. (eds.), pp. 88–106.

1983, "Organizational Democracy and the Quality of Work Life: the Man on the Assembly Line," in Crouch, C. and Heller, F. (eds.), *Organizational Democracy and Political Processes*, New York: Wiley, pp. 139–53.

Haag, I. 1986, *Arbeitskommunikation – Kommunikationsarbeit. Neukonzeption industriesoziologischer Arbeitsanalyse durch die systematische Einbeziehung arbeitsbezogener Kommunikation*, Berlin: Schelsky und Jeep.

Haas, V. 1983, "Team-konzept – Mitarbeiter planen und betreiben ihr Arbeitssytem," in Bullinger, H.J. and Warnecke, H.J. (eds.), *Wettbewerbsfähige Arbeitssysteme, Problemlösungen für die Praxis*, Stuttgart: Verein zur Förderung produktionstechnischer Forschung e.V., pp. 129–89.

Halberstam, D. 1986, *The Reckoning*, New York: Avon.

Hall, J.L. and Leidecker, J.K. 1981, "Is Japanese-Style Management Anything New? A Comparison of Japanese-Style Management with U.S. Participative Models," *Human Resource Management*, Vol. 20, No. 4, pp. 14–21.

Hammer, M. 1959, *Vergleichende Morphologie der Arbeit in der europäischen Automobilindustrie*, Basel/Tübingen: Mohr.

Hayes, R.H. and Clark, K.B. 1985, "Exploring the Sources of Productivity Differences at the Factory Level," in Clark, K.B., Hayes, R.H., and Lorenz, Ch. (eds.), *The Uneasy Alliance, Managing the Productivity – Technology Dilemma*, Boston: Harvard Business School Press, pp. 151–88.

Heizmann, J. 1984, "Neue Arbeitsstrukturen in automatisierten Fertigungssystemen," in Zink, K. (ed.), *Soziotechnologische Systemgestaltung als Zukunftsaufgabe*, München: Hanser, pp. 109–21.

Hesse, R. and Oelker, K.-C. 1986, "Zukunftsorientiertes Montagesystem mit automatischen Flurförderzeugen," *REFA-Nachrichten*, No. 6, pp. 5–10.

Hildebrandt, E. 1982, "Der VW-Tarifvertrag zur Lohndifferenzierung," in Doleschal, R. and Dombois, R. (eds.), pp. 309–49.

Hirsch, J. and Roth, R. 1986, *Das neue Gesicht des Kapitalismus. Vom Fordismus zum Postfordismus*, Hamburg: VSA.

Hoffmann, R. 1968, "Erweiterung der innerbetrieblichen Mitbestimmung durch Arbeitsgruppen," *Gewerkschaftliche Monatshefte*, No. 19, pp. 719–28.

Holleis, W. 1987, *Unternehmenskultur und moderne Psyche*, Frankfurt: Campus.

Hübner, K. and Mahnkopf, B. 1987, "École de la Regulation. Eine kommentierte Literaturstudie," Discussion Paper FS II 88–201, Berlin: Science Center of Berlin for Social Research.

Hunker, J.A. 1983, *Structural Change in the U.S. Automobile Industry*, Lexington, Mass./Toronto: Lexington Books.

Hutchinson, J.G. 1961, "The Measurement of Production Standards and the Administration of Systems of Production Standards: An Analysis of Selected Firms in the Automobile and Auto Parts Industries," Dissertation: University of Michigan.

Hyman, R. and Elger, T. 1982, "Arbeitsplatzbezogene Schutzstrategien: Englische Gewerkschaften und 'restrictive practices'," in Dohse, K., Jürgens, U., and Russig, H. (eds.), pp. 407–42.

Iacocca, L. 1984, *An Autobiography*, New York: Bantam.

IG Metall, Bezirksleitung Stuttgart 1979, *Werktage müssen menschlicher werden!*, Stuttgart.

IG Metall 1983, *23. Untersuchung über Löhne und Verdienste der Arbeiter in Automobilbetrieben*, Frankfurt.

1984, *Beschäftigungsrisiken in der Autoindustrie. Vorschläge der IG Metall zur*

Beschäftigungssicherung und zur Strukturpolitik in diesem Industriebereich, Frankfurt.

1986a, *Protokoll des 15. ordentlichen Gewerkschaftstages,* Vol. II, Part I: Stellungnahmen und Erledigungsvermerk zu den Anträgen und Entschließungen des 14. ordentlichen Gewerkschaftstages München 1983, Frankfurt.

1986b, *"Betriebliche Daten": Vergleichstabellen aus Werken der Automobil-Industrie,* Frankfurt.

(undated), *Automobilindustrie. Eine Sammlung praktischer Handlungshilfen,* Aktionsmappe.

I.G. Metall (eds.) 1987, *Zukunft der Automobilindustrie,* Symposium der IG Metall Wolfsburg in Zusammenarbeit mit dem Betriebsrat der Volkswagen AG Werk Wolfsburg, Wolfsburg.

Imai, M. 1986, *Kaizen. The Key to Japan's Competitive Success,* New York: Random House.

IMB (Internationaler Metallgewerkschaftsbund) 1986, *IMB-Handbuch für Ford-Arbeitnehmer,* Genf.

International Monetary Fund (IMF): International Financial Statistics (annual).

International Labor Office 1977, *Social and Labor Practices of Some US-based Multinationals in the Metal Trades,* Geneva.

Jacobi, O. and Kastendiek, H. (eds.) 1985, *Staat und industrielle Beziehungen in Großbritannien,* Frankfurt: Campus.

JAMA (Japan Automobile Manufacturers Association, Inc.), *Motor Vehicle Statistics of Japan,* Annual Editions.

JMA Consultants Inc. (Japanese Management Association) 1985, *Key of Productivity: Work Measurement,* International Survey Report, Tokyo.

Japan Management Association (eds.) 1986, *Kanban. Just-In-Time of Toyota. Management Begins at the Workplace,* Stamford/Cambridge, Mass.: Productivity Press.

Johnson, R. 1989, "Volvo's New Assembly Plant has no Assembly Line," *Automotive News,* July 10, pp. 22–4.

Jones, D.T. 1981, *Maturity and Crisis in the European Car Industry: Structural Change and Public Policy,* Sussex: University of Sussex, European Papers No. 8.

Jürgens, U. 1980, *Selbstregulierung des Kapitals. Erfahrungen aus der Kartellbewegung in Deutschland um die Jahrhundertwende,* Frankfurt: Campus.

1986, "Kontrollierte Autonomie – arbeitspolitische Strategien in der internationalen Automobilindustrie," *ASI-News* (Arbeitsgemeinschaft sozialwissenschaftlicher Institute), No. 10, pp. 32–57.

1987, "Entwicklungstendenzen in der Weltautomobilindustrie bis in die 90er Jahre," in IG Metall (eds.), pp. 15–49.

Jürgens, U. and Dohse, K. 1982, "Statussicherung durch Seniorität. Senioritätsregeln als Dreh- und Angelpunkt betriebsnaher Gewerkschaftspolitik in den USA," in Dohse, K., Jürgens, U., and Russig, H. (eds.), pp. 289–319.

Jürgens, U., Dohse, K., and Malsch, T. 1985a, "Japan als Orientierungspunkt für den Wandel der industriellen Beziehungen in der US-amerikanischen und der europäischen Automobilindustrie," in Park, S.J. (ed.), *Japanisches Manage-*

ment in der Praxis. Flexibilität oder Kontrolle im Prozess der Internationalisierung und Mikroelektronisierung, Berlin: Express, pp. 127–48.

1985b, "Der Transfer japanischer Management-Konzepte in der internationalen Automobilindustrie," in Park, S.J., Jürgens, U., and Merz, H.P. (eds.), *Transfer des japanischen Managementsystems*, Berlin: Express, pp. 109–32.

Jürgens, U., Dohse, K., Malsch, T., and Strömel, H.-P. 1987, "The Communication Structure between Management and Shop Floor: A Comparison of a Japanese and a German Plant," in Trevor, M. (ed.), pp. 92–110.

Kalmbach, P. *et al.* 1980, *Bedingungen und soziale Folgen des Einsatzes von Industrierobotern*, Sozialwissenschaftliche Begleitforschung zum Projekt der Volkswagen AG Wolfsburg: Neue Handhabungssysteme als technische Hilfen für den Arbeitsprozeß, Bremen.

Kamata, S. 1983, *Japan in the Passing Lane*, London: George Allen & Unwin.

Kanter, R.M. 1983, *Change Masters. Corporate Entrepreneurs at Work*, London: George Allen & Unwin.

Katz, H. 1984a, "Collective Bargaining in 1982: A Turning Point in Industrial Relations," *Compensation Review*, No. 1, pp. 38–49.

1984b, "The U.S. Automobile Collective Bargaining System in Transition," *British Journal of Industrial Relations*, Vol. 22, No. 2, pp. 205–17.

1985, *Shifting Gears. Changing Labor Relations in the U.S. Automobile Industry*, Cambridge, Mass.: The MIT Press.

1986, "Recent Developments in the U.S. Auto Labor Relations," in Tolliday, S. and Zeitlin, J. (eds.), pp. 282–304.

Katz, H. and Sabel, C.F. 1985, "Industrial Relations and Industrial Adjustment in the Car Industry," *Industrial Relations*, Vol. 24, No. 3, pp. 295–315.

Keller, M. 1989, *Rude Awakening: The Rise, Fall, and Struggle for Recovery of General Motors*, New York: William Morrow.

Kelly, J.E. and Clegg, Ch.W. (eds.) 1982, *Autonomy and Control at the Workplace. Contexts for Job Redesign*, London: Croom Helm.

Kern, H. and Schumann, M. 1970, *Industriearbeit und Arbeiterbewußtsein*, 2 vol., Frankfurt: Europäische Verlagsanstalt.

1984, *Das Ende der Arbeitsteilung. Rationalisierung in der industriellen Produktion*, München: Beck.

1989, "New Concepts of Production in West German Plants," in Katzenstein, P.J. (ed.), *Industry and Politics in West Germany*, Ithaca: Cornell University Press, pp. 87–110.

KIET (Korea Institute for Economy and Technology) 1985, *Long Term Perspectives of the Korean Economy up to the Year 2000* (Part: Industry), Seoul.

Koch, G.A. and Hackenberg, W. (1971), Organisatorische Umstellungen In der industriellen Produktion-Objeute, Umtang, Teuden-zen, Frankfurt: E.V.A.

Koch, H.C. and Gericke, E. 1986, "Produktplanung und Produktionsforschung für die Montage von Automobilen," *Zeitschrift für wirtschaftliche Fertigung*, Vol. 81, No. 4, pp. 180–84.

Kochan, T.A. and Cappelli, P. 1984, "The Transformation of the Industrial Relations and Personnel Function," in Ostermann, P. (ed.), *Internal Labor Markets*, Cambridge, Mass.: MIT Press, pp. 133–61.

Kochan, T.A., Katz, H.C., and Mower, N.R. 1984, *Worker Participation and American Unions. Threat or Opportunity*, Kalamazoo: Upjohn Institute.

Kochan, T.A. and McKersie, R.B. 1983, "Collective Bargaining – Pressures for Change," *Sloan Management Review*, Vol. 24, No. 4, pp. 59–65.

Köhler, C. 1981, *Betrieblicher Arbeitsmarkt und Gewerkschaftspolitik. Innerbetriebliche Mobilität und Arbeitsplatzrechte in der amerikanischen Automobilindustrie*, Frankfurt: Campus.

Köhler, C. and Sengenberger, W. 1983, *Konjunktur und Personalanpassung. Betriebliche Beschäftigungspolitik in der deutschen und amerikanischen Automobilindustrie*, Frankfurt: Campus.

Koopmann, K. 1979, *Gewerkschaftliche Vertrauensleute. Darstellung und kritische Analyse ihrer Entwicklung und Bedeutung von den Anfängen bis zur Gegenwart unter besonderer Berücksichtigung des Deutschen Metallarbeiter-Verbandes (DMV) und der Industriegewerkschaft Metall (IGM)*, München: Minerva.

Krafcik, J.F. 1987, "Trends in International Automotive Assembly Practice," International Motor Vehicle Program, Massachusetts Institute of Technology.

1988, "Triumph of the Lean Production System," *Sloan Management Review*, Vol. 29, No. 5, pp. 41–52.

Krafcik, J.F. and MacDuffie, J.P. 1989, "Explaining High Performance Manufacturing: The International Automotive Assembly Plant Study," IMVP International Policy Forum, May 1989.

Kuhn, R. and Spinas, P. 1980, *Arbeits- und sozialpsychologische Untersuchungen von Arbeitsstrukturen im Bereich der Aggregatefertigung der Volkswagen AG*, Vol. 4: Determinanten der Einstellung zu Neuen Formen der Arbeitsgestaltung, Forschungsbericht: BMFT HA 80–020, Eggenstein-Leopoldshafen.

Kujawa, D. 1975, *International Labor and the Multinational Enterprise*, New York: Praeger.

1980, *The Labor Relations of United States Multinationals Abroad: Comparative and Prospective Views*, ILO Research Series, No. 60.

Kugler, A. 1981, "Gesellschaftliche Hintergründe der Rationalisierung und der Humanisierung der Arbeitswelt in der amerikanischen Automobilindustrie seit Ende der 60er Jahre," unpublished (Diplomarbeit Freie Universität), Berlin.

Landen, D.L. and Carlson, H.C. 1982, "Strategies for Diffusing, Evolving and Institutionalizing Quality of Work Life at General Motors," in Zager, R. and Rosow, M.P. (eds.), pp. 291–335.

Lawler, E.E. III 1978, "The New Plant Revolution," *Organizational Dynamics*, Vol. 6, No. 3, pp. 3–12.

1986, *High-Involvement Management*, San Francisco: Jossey Bass.

Lee, S.M. and Schwendiman, G. (eds.) 1982, *Management by Japanese Systems*, New York: Praeger.

Leibenstein, H. 1987, *Inside the Firm: The Inefficiencies of Hierarchy*, Cambridge, Mass.: Harvard University Press.

Lichtenstein, N. 1986, "Reutherism on the Shop Floor: Union Strategy and Shop Floor Conflict in the USA 1946–70," in Tolliday, S. and Zeitlin, J. (eds.), pp. 121–43.

Linhart, R. 1981, *The Assembly Line*, Amhurst: University of Massachusetts Press.

420   Bibliography

Lünzmann, F. 1989, "Montage im Umbruch," *Automobilproduktion*, April, pp. 64–70.

Lutz, B. 1976, "Bildungssystem und Beschäftigungsstruktur in Deutschland und Frankreich. Zum Einfluß des Bildungssystems auf die Gestaltung betrieblicher Arbeitskräftestrukturen," in Mendius, H., Sengenberger, W., Lutz, B., Altmann, N., Böhle, R., Asendorf-Krings, I., Drexel, I., and Nuber, C. (eds.), *Betrieb – Arbeitsmarkt – Qualifikation. I. Beiträge zur Rezession und Personalpolitik, Bildungsexpansion und Arbeitsteilung, Humanisierung und Qualifizierung, Reproduktion und Qualifikation*, Frankfurt: Aspekte, pp. 83–151.

MacDonald, R. 1963, *Collective Bargaining in the Automobile Industry*, New Haven: Yale University Press.

Mallet, S. 1969, *La Nouvelle Classe Ouvrière*, Paris: Ed. du Seuil.

Malsch, T. 1982, "Technologietransfer und betriebliche Arbeitsorganisation. Ein industriesoziologischer Beitrag zur Entwicklungsländerforschung am Beispiel eines ägyptisch-deutschen Betriebsvergleichs," in Schmidt, G., Braczyk, H.J., and von dem Knesebeckij (eds.), *Materialien zur Industriesoziologie*, Kölner Zeitschrift für Soziologie und Sozialpsychologie, Sonderheft 24, pp. 494–515.

1983, "Erfahrungswissen versus Planungswissen. Facharbeiterkompetenz und informationstechnologische Kontrolle am Beispiel der industriellen Instandhaltung," in Jürgens, U. and Naschold, F. (eds.), *Arbeitspolitik*, Leviathan, Sonderheft 5, pp. 231–51.

1987, "'Neue Produktionskonzepte' zwischen Rationalität und Rationalisierung – mit Kern und Schumann auf Paradigmensuche," in Malsch T. and Seltz R. (eds.), pp. 53–80.

Malsch, T., Dohse, K., and Jürgens, U. 1984, "Industrieroboter im Automobilbau. Auf dem Sprung zum 'automatisierten Fordismus'," Discussion Paper IIVG/dp84–217, Berlin: Science Center of Berlin for Social Research.

Malsch, T. and Seltz, R. (eds.) 1987, *Die neuen Produktionskonzepte auf dem Prüfstand. Beiträge zur Entwicklung der Industriearbeit* (2nd edn), Berlin: Sigma.

1987, "Zur Einführung: Die aktuelle Diskussion über die Entwicklung neuer Produktions- und Rationalisierungsmodelle," in Malsch, T. and Seltz, R. (eds.), pp. 11–34.

Malsch, T., Weißbach, H.-J., and Fischer, J. 1982, *Organisation und Planung der industriellen Instandhaltung*, Frankfurt: Campus.

Marchington, M. and Armstrong, R. 1983, "Typologies of Shop Stewards: A Reconsideration," *Industrial Relations Journal*, Vol. 14, No. 3, pp. 34–48.

Marsden, D., Morris, T., Willman, P., and Wood, S. 1985, *The Car Industry. Labour Relations and Industrial Adjustment*, London: Tavistock.

Marsland, S. and Beer, M. 1983, "The Evolution of Japanese Management: Lessons for U.S. Managers," *Organizational Dynamics*, Winter, pp. 49–67.

Maurice, M., Sorge, A., and Warner, M. 1979, "Societal Differences in Organizing Manufacturing Units. A Comparison of France, West Germany and Great Britain," Paper IM/79–15 Berlin: Science Center of Berlin for Social Research.

Mayer, G.E. 1983, *Past and Projected Labor Productivity. Trends and their Potential Impact on the Structure of the World Automobile Industry of 1990*, München: Florentz.

Meyer III, S. 1981, *The Five Dollar Day. Labor Management and Social Control in the Ford Motor Company 1908–1981*, Albany: State University of New York Press.

Meyer-Dohm, P. and Schütze, H.G. (eds.) 1987, *Technischer Wandel und Qualifizierung: Die neue Synthese*, Schriftenreihe: "Humanisierung des Arbeitslebens," Vol. 90, Frankfurt: Campus.

Meyer-Larsen, W. (ed.) 1980, *Autogroßmacht Japan*, Reinbek bei Hamburg: Rowohlt.

Milkovich, G.T. and Glueck, W.F. 1985, *Personnel/Human Resource Management: A Diagnostic Approach*, (4th edn, 1. 1974) Plano: Business Publ.

Mill, U. 1986, "Organisation als Sozialsystem. Ein Kommentar," in Seltz, R., Mill, U., and Hildebrandt, E. (eds.), pp. 199–218.

Milton, D. 1986, "Late Capitalism and the Decline of Trade Union Power in the United States," *Economic and Industrial Democracy*, Vol. 7, No. 3, pp. 319–49.

Mintzberg, H. 1987, "The Strategy Concept I and II," *California Management Review*, Vol. 30, No. 1, pp. 11–24, 25–32.

Mitchell, D.J.B. 1986, "Alternative Explanations of Union Wage Concessions," *California Management Review*, Vol. 29, No. 1, pp. 95–108.

Monden, Y. 1981, "What Makes the Toyota Production System Really Tick," *Industrial Engineering*, January, pp. 36–46.

1983, *Toyota Production System. Practical Approach to Production Management*, Atlanta: Institute of Industrial Engineers.

Müller, F.U. 1991, "The 'New Employee Relations': A Comparative Study in Automobile Engine Plants in Germany, Britain, Austria and Spain," Thesis submitted to the Faculty of Social Studies, University of Oxford.

Müller, T. 1983, *Automated Guided Vehicles*, Berlin: Springer.

Muster, M. 1983, "Breite Qualifizierung ist auch Angelernten vermittelbar," *Die Mitbestimmung*, Vol. 29, No. 12, pp. 550–2.

1984, "Moderne Qualifizierung der Produktionsarbeiter. Betriebspolitik zum Schutz vor Entwertung der Arbeitskraft," in Buhmann, H., Lucy, H., Weber, R. *et al.* (eds.), *Geisterfahrt ins Leere. Roboter und Rationalisierung in der Automobilindustrie*, Hamburg: VSA, pp. 32–48.

MVMA (Motor Vehicle Manufacturers Association of the U.S., Inc.) 1986, *Economic Indicators. The Motor Vehicle's Role in the U.S. Economy*, Detroit.

Naisbitt, J. 1982, *Megatrends. Ten New Directions Transforming Our Lives*, New York: Warner Books.

Naisbitt, J. and Aburdene, P. 1985, *Reinventing the Corporate Future*, New York: Warner Books.

National Economic Development Office/Manpower Services Commission 1984, *Competence and Competition – Training and Education in the Federal Republic of Germany, the United States and Japan*, London.

Negandhi, A.R. and Balige, W.B. 1981, "International Functioning of American, German, and Japanese Multinational Corporations," in Otterbeck, L. (ed.), pp. 107–17.

Norman, G. 1972, "Blue-Collar Saboteurs," *Playboy* (American Edn), September, pp. 96ff.

Norsworthy, J.R. and Zabala, C.A. 1985, "Responding to the Productivity Crisis:

A Plant-Level Approach to Labor Policy," in Baumol, W.J. and McLennan, K. (eds.), *Productivity Growth and U.S. Competitiveness*, Oxford: Oxford University Press.

OECD 1983, *Long Term Outlook for the World Automobile Industry*, Paris: Organization for Economic Co-operation and Development.

1985, *Costs and Benefits of Protection*, Paris: Organization for Economic Cooperation and Development.

Ogden, S.G. 1982, "Bargaining Structure and the Control of Industrial Relations," *British Journal of Industrial Relations*, Vol. 20, No. 2, pp. 170–85.

Olle, W. 1986, "Neue Dimensionen der Produktionslogistik. Die Zukunft hat schon begonnen," *WSI-Mitteilungen*, No. 4, pp. 312–16.

Opel AG 1970–87, *Geschäftsberichte*, Annual Editions.

Otterbeck, L. (ed.) 1981, *The Management of Headquarters – Subsidiary Relationships in Multinational Corporations*, Aldershot: Gower.

Ouchi, W.G. 1981, *Theory Z. How American Business Can Meet the Japanese Challenge*, Reading, Mass.: Addison-Wesley.

Palmer, G. 1983, *British Industrial Relations*, London: George Allen & Unwin.

Parker, M. 1986, *Inside the Circle. A Union Guide to QWL*, Boston: Labor Notes Book.

Parker, M. and Slaughter, J. 1988, *Choosing Sides: Unions and the Team Concept*, Boston: South End Press.

Pascale, R.T. and Athos, A.G. 1981, *The Art of Japanese Management. Applications for American Executives*, New York: Simon and Schuster.

Peninou, G., Holthus, M., and Kebschull, D. 1978, *Who's afraid of the Multinationals. A Survey of European Opinion on Multinational Corporations*, Westmead: Saxonhouse.

Piore, M.J. 1982, "American Labor and the Industrial Crisis," *Challenge*, March/April, pp. 5–11.

Piore, M.J. and Sabel, C.F. 1984, *The Second Industrial Divide. Possibilities for Prosperity*, New York: Basic Books.

Poole, M. 1981, *Theories of Trade Unionism: A Sociology of Industrial Relations*, London: Routledge & Kegan.

Prais, S.J. 1981, "Vocational Qualifications of the Labor Force in Britain and Germany," *National Institute Economic Review*, No. 4, pp. 47–59.

Przeworski, A. and Tenne, H. 1970, *The Logic of Comparative Social Inquiry*, New York: Wiley.

Pugh, D.S. and Hickson, D.J. 1976, *Organizational Structure and its Context. The Aston Programme I*, Westmead: Heath.

Rausch, J. 1987, "Wechselbeziehungen zwischen neuen Technologien und Tarifverträgen," in Meyer-Dohm, P. and Schütze, H.G. (eds.), pp. 232–6.

REFA 1978, *Methodenlehre des Arbeitsstudiums, Teil I: Grundlagen, Teil II: Datenermittlung*, München: Hanser.

Reitzle, W. 1983, "Der Trend beim Einsatz von Industrierobotern," *Management-Zeitschrift industrielle Organisation*, Vol. 52, No. 6, pp. 267–70.

Reynolds, M.O. 1986, "Unions and Jobs: The U.S. Auto Industry," *Journal of Labor Research*, Vol. 7, No. 2, pp. 103–26.

Robert-Bosch GmbH u.a. 1980, *Entkoppelung von Fließarbeit: Techniken in der teilautomatisierten Montage*, Schriftenreihe "Humanisierung des Arbeitslebens," Vol. 2, Frankfurt: Campus.

Robson, M. 1982, *Quality Circles. A Practical Guide*, Aldershot: Gower.

Ross, I. 1982, "The New UAW Contract. A Fortune Proposal," *Fortune*, February 8, pp. 40–5.

Roth, S. and Kohl, H. (eds.) 1988, *Perspektive: Gruppenarbeit*, Köln: Bund.

Rothschild, E. 1973, *Paradise Lost. The Decline of the Auto-Industrial Age*, London: Random.

Sämann, W. *et al.* 1978, "Erfahrungen mit der Arbeitsstrukturierung in der Automobilindustrie," *Zeitschrift für Betriebswirtschaft*, Vol. 48, No. 1, pp. 76–82.

Sakurai, T. 1979, "Entwicklungsstand von Pressenstraßen in der japanischen Automobilindustrie," *Werkstatt und Betrieb*, No. 7, pp. 477–80.

Saturn-UAW-Agreement 1985, "Special Report LV: Saturn-UAW Memorandum of Agreement," Supplement to *Labor Trends*, July 13.

Savoie, E.J. 1982, "The New Ford-UAW-Agreement: Its Worklife Aspects," *The Work Life Review*, Vol. 1, No. 1, pp. 1–10.

Schäuble, G. 1979, *Die Humanisierung der Industriearbeit*, Frankfurt: Campus.

Schauer, H., Neumann, U., and Sperling, H.J. 1981, *Tarifvertragliche Regelungen zur Verbesserung industrieller Arbeitsbedingungen*, Zusammenfassender Endbericht zum HdA-Projekt V-TAP 6015 und SGA 0003, Göttingen.

Scheinecker, M. 1988, "Neue Organisationskonzepte in der Automobilindustrie: Entwicklungstendenzen am Beispiel General Motors Austria," in Dankbaar, B., Jürgens, U., and Malsch, T. (eds.), pp.167–84.

Schonberger, R.J. 1982, *Japanese Manufacturing Techniques. Nine Hidden Lessons in Simplicity*, New York: The Free Press.

Schumann, M., Baethge-Kinsky, V., Kuhlmann, M., Kurz, C., and Neumann, U. 1992, "Neue Arbeitseinsatzkonzepte im deutschen Automobilbau – hat lean production eine Chance?," *Mitteilungen*, Soziologisches Forschungsinstitut Göttingen, January, pp. 15–27.

Schumann, M., Baethge-Kinsky, V., Neumann, U., and Springer, R. 1989, *Breite Diffusion der Neuen Produktionskonzepte – zögerlicher Wandel der Arbeitsstrukturen*, Zwischenbericht, Göttingen: SOFI.

Schultz-Wild, R. 1978, *Betriebliche Beschäftigungspolitik in der Krise*, Frankfurt: Campus.

Schweizer, W. 1986, "Der lange Weg zum Roboter," in von Fersen, O. (ed.), *Ein Jahrhundert Automobiltechnik-Personenwagen*, Düsseldorf: VDI-Verlag, pp. 504–45.

Seaman, B. and Redman, C. 1980, "Detroit's Uphill Battle. New Cars, New Plants and a Strong Emphasis on Quality for U.S. Autos," *Time*, September 8, pp. 46ff.

Sellie, C. 1984, "Better Use of Better Tools Should Make Work Measurement Increasingly Valuable in Future," *Industrial Engineering*, July, pp. 82–5.

Seltz, R., Mill, U., and Hildebrandt, E. (eds.) 1986, *Organisation als soziales System. Kontrolle und Kommunikationstechnologie in Arbeitsorganisationen*, Berlin: Sigma.

Serrin, W. 1984, "Giving Workers a Voice of Their Own," *New York Times*

424   Bibliography

Magazine, December 2, pp. 126–32, 136–7.

Shimada, H. 1983, "Japanese Industrial Relations – A New General Model. A Survey of the English-Language Literature," in Shirai, T. (ed.), *Contemporary Industrial Relations in Japan*, Madison: University of Wisconsin Press, pp. 3–27.

Shingo, S. 1981, *Study of "Toyota" Production System from Industrial Engineering Viewpoint*, Cambridge, Mass.: Prod. Press.

Simmons, J. and Mares, W. 1983, *Working Together*, New York: Alfred E. Knopf.

Skinner, W. 1981, "Big Hat, No Cattle: Managing Human Resources," *Harvard Business Review*, September/October, pp. 106–14.

1985, *Manufacturing. The Formidable Competitive Weapon*, New York: Wiley.

Sloan, A. and Miles, C. 1980, "GM's Chance of a Lifetime," *Forbes*, September 1, pp. 110–12.

Sorge, A., Hartmann, G., and Nicholas, S. 1982, *Mikroelektronik und Arbeit in der Industrie. Erfahrungen beim Einsatz von CNC-Maschinen in Großbritannien und der Bundesrepublik Deutschland*, Frankfurt: Campus.

Sorge, A. and Streeck, W. 1987, "Industrial Relations and Technical Change: The Case for an Extended Perspective," Discussion Paper dp IIM/LMP 1987–1, Berlin: Science Center of Berlin for Social Research.

Sorge, A. and Warner, M. 1986, *Comparative Factory Organization*, Aldershot: Gower.

Soziologisches Forschungsinstitut Göttingen (SOFI) 1981, *Industrieroboter. Bedingungen und soziale Folgen des Einsatzes neuer Technologien in der Automobilproduktion*, Frankfurt: Campus.

Spanyar, R. 1979, "Der 'Mercedes-Effekt'," *Management-Zeitschrift*, Vol. 48, No. 11, pp. 479ff.

Sperling, H.J. 1983, *Pause als soziale Arbeitszeit. Theoretische und praktische Aspekte einer gewerkschaftlichen Arbeits- und Zeitpolitik*, Berlin: Verlag Die Arbeitswelt.

Strauss, G. 1984, "Industrial Relations: Time of Change," *Industrial Relations*, Vol. 23, No. 1, pp. 1–15.

Strauss-Fehlberg, G. 1978, *Die Forderung nach Humanisierung der Arbeitswelt. Eine Sicht aus der Sicht der Tarifvertragsparteien*, Köln: Bund-Verlag.

Streeck, W. 1984, *Industrial Relations in West Germany. A Case Study of the Car Industry*, London: Heinemann.

1988, "Successful Adjustment to Turbulent Markets: The Automobile Industry," Paper FS I 88–1, Berlin: Science Center of Berlin for Social Research.

1989, "Successful Adjustment to Turbulent Markets: The Automobile Industry," in Katzenstein, P.J. (ed.), *Industry and Politics in West Germany*, Ithaca: Cornell University Press, pp. 113–56.

Streeck, W. (ed.) 1985, "Industrial Relations and Technical Change in the British, Italian and German Automobile Industry," Discussion Paper IIM/LMP 85–5, Berlin: Science Center of Berlin for Social Research.

Sumiya, M. 1981, "Japan: A Survey of Industrial Relations Series," in Doeringer, P.B. (ed.), *Industrial Relations in International Perspective*, London: Macmillan.

Terry, M. 1983, "Shop Stewards Through Expansion and Recession," *Industrial Relations Journal*, Vol. 14, No. 3, pp. 49–58.

Therborn, G. 1980, *The Ideology of Power and the Power of Ideology*, London: Veiso.

Tolliday, S. 1986, "Management and Labour in Britain 1896–1939," in Tolliday, S. and Zeitlin, J. (eds.), pp. 29–56.

Tolliday, S. and Zeitlin, J. 1986, "Shop Floor Bargaining, Contract Unionism and Job Control: An Anglo-American Comparison," in Tolliday, S. and Zeitlin, J. (eds.), pp. 99–120.

Tolliday, S. and Zeitlin, J. (eds.) 1986, *The Automobile Industry and its Workers. Between Fordism and Flexibility*, Cambridge: Polity Press.

Trade Union Research Unit (TURU) 1984, "The Decline of the U.K. Motor Industry. The Strategic Consideration for Motor Industry Unions," A report by the Trade Union Research Unit for the TGWU Automative Conference – July 5–6, Oxford, Ruskin College.

Trevor, M. (ed.) 1987, *The Internationalization of Japanese Business. European and Japanese Perspectives*, Frankfurt: Campus/Westview.

Triebe, J.K. 1980, *Arbeits- und sozialpsychologische Untersuchungen von Arbeitsstrukturen im Bereich der Aggregatefertigung der Volkswagenwerk AG*, Vol. 3: Untersuchungen zum Lernprozeß während des Erwerbs der Grundqualifikation (Montage eines kompletten Motors), Forschungsbericht: BMFT/HA 80–019, Eggenstein-Leopoldshafen.

Tsuda, M. 1974, "Personnel Administration at the Industrial Plant," in Okochi, K. et al. (eds.), *Workers and Employers in Japan. The Japanese Employment Relations System*, Princeton/Tokyo: Princeton University Press/University of Tokyo Press, pp. 399–440.

Turner, H.A., Clack, G., and Roberts, G. 1967, *Labour Relations in the Motor Industry*, London: George Allen & Unwin.

Turner, L. 1991, *Democracy at Work. Changing World Markets and the Future of Labor Unions*, Ithaca/London: Cornell University Press.

U.A.W. 1986, *Research Bulletin*, Special Conventional Issue, Detroit.

USITC (United States International Trade Commission) 1985, *The Internationalization of the Automobile Industry and its Effects on the U.S. Automobile Industry*, Report on Investigation, USITC Publication 1712, Washington D.C.

Vauxhall 1978–87, *Annual Reports*, Annual Editions.

VDA 1970–87, *Tatsachen und Zahlen aus der Kraftverkehrswirtschaft*, Frankfurt, Annual Editions.

VDA 1980–7, *Das Auto International in Zahlen*, Frankfurt, Annual Editions.

Volkswagen AG 1970–87, *Geschäftsberichte*, Annual Editions.

Wagner, K. 1986, *Die Beziehungen zwischen Bildung, Beschäftigung und Produktivität und ihre bildungs- und beschäftigungspolitischen Auswirkungen – ein deutsch-englischer Vergleich*, Berlin: CEDEFOP.

Walker, E.R. and Guest, R.H. 1955, *The Man on the Assembly Line*, Cambridge, Mass.: Cambridge University Press.

Walker, J.W. 1980, *Human Resource Planning*, New York: McGraw-Hill.

Weißbach, H.-J. 1988, "MAP als 'entwicklungsleitender Standard' von CIM-

Projekten in der Automobilindustrie," in Dankbaar, B., Jürgens, U., and Malsch, T. (eds.), pp. 114–29.

Weißbach, H.-J. and Weißbach, R. 1987, "Logistiksysteme in der Automobilindustrie," Discussion Paper IIVG/dp87–215, Berlin: Science Center of Berlin for Social Research.

Weltz, F. and Schmidt, G. 1982, "Rationalisierung und Betriebsratstätigkeit," in Dohse, K., Jürgens, U., and Russig, H. (eds.), pp. 55–90.

Whitehill, A. and Takezawa, S. 1968, *The Other Workers*, Honolulu: East-West Center Press.

Whitman, M. 1981, "Automobiles: Turning Around on a Dime?," *Challenge*, May–June, pp. 36–44.

Wickens, P. 1987, *The Road to Nissan. Flexibility, Quality, Teamwork*, Houndmills, Basingstoke: MacMillan

Widick, B.J. 1976, *Auto Work and its Discontents*, Baltimore: Johns Hopkins.

Wildemann, H. (undated), "Rechnerunterstützte Informationssysteme in der Qualitätssicherung (CAQ). Technisch-organisatorische Konzepte und Fallbeispiele," FMT-Report No. 4, München.

Wilks, S. 1984, *Industrial Policy and the Motor Industry*, Manchester: Manchester University Press.

Williams, K., Williams, J., and Haslam, C. 1987, *The Breakdown of Austin Rover. A Case-Study in the Failure of Business Strategy and Industrial Policy*, Leamington: Berg.

Willman, P. 1986a, *Technological Change, Collective Bargaining and Industrial Efficiency*, Oxford: Clarendon Press.

1986b, "Labor-Relations Strategy at BL Cars," in Tolliday and Zeitlin (eds.), pp. 305–27.

Willmann, P. and Winch, G. 1985, *Innovation and Management Control. Labour Relations at BL Cars*, Cambridge: Cambridge University Press.

Windolf, P. 1981, *Berufliche Sozialisation*, Stuttgart: Ferdinand Enke Verlag.

Womack, J.P., Jones, D.T., and Roos, D. 1990, *The Machine that Changed the World*, New York: Rawson.

Wood, S. 1986a, "Neue Technologien, Arbeitsorganisation und Qualifikation. Die britische Labor-Process-Debate," *Prokla*, No. 62, pp. 74–104.

1986b, "The Cooperative Labour Strategy in the U.S. Auto Industry," *Economic and Industrial Democracy*, Vol. 7, No. 4, pp. 415–47.

Wood, S., Wagner, A., Armstrong, E.G.A., Goodman, J.F.B., and Davis, J.E. 1975, "The 'Industrial Relations System' Concept as a Basis for Theory in Industrial Relations," *British Journal of Industrial Relations*, Vol. 13, No. 3, pp. 291–308.

Woodcock, L. 1977, "Labor and Multinationals," in Banks, F. and Stieber, J. (eds.), *Multinationals, Unions, and Labor Relations in Industrialized Countries*, Ithaka: Cornell, pp. 21–8.

Woodward, J. 1968, *Management and Technology*, London: HMSO.

Wright, J.P. 1979, *On a Clear Day you Can See General Motors. John Z. De Lorean's Look Inside the Automotive Giant*, London: Sidgwick & Jackson.

Yamamoto, K. 1975, *Nihon no Jidosha Sangyo* (The Japanese Auto-Industry, Jap.), Tokyo: Kodansha.

Yankelovich, D. and Immerwahr, J. 1984, "Putting the Work Ethic to Work," *Society*, Vol. 21, No. 2, pp. 58–76.

Yates, B. 1984, *The Decline and Fall of the American Automobile Industry*, New York: Vintage Books.

Zachert, Ü. 1979a, *Betriebliche Mitbestimmung. Eine problemorientierte Einführung*, Köln: Bund-Verlag.

1979b, *Tarifvertrag: Eine problemorientierte Einführung*, Köln: Bund-Verlag.

Zager, R. and Rosow, M.P. (eds.) 1982, *The Innovative Organization. Productivity Programs in Action*, New York: Pergamon Press.

Periodika

Assembly Automation
Automobil-Industrie
Auto Industry
Automotive Industries
Automotive News (AN)
Automotive News: Market Data Book
Blick durch die Wirtschaft
Business Week
Chilton's Automotive Industries
Computerwoche
Daily Labor Report, The Bureau of National Affairs
Employment Gazette
Financial Times (FT)
Fortune
Frankfurter Rundschau
The Guardian
Handelsblatt
Hard and Soft
Industrial Engineering
Industrial Robot
Iron Age
Manager-Magazin
MVMA Facts and Figures
Production
Solidarity
VDA-Pressedienst
VDA Tatsachen und Zahlen
VDI-Zeitschrift
The Wall Street Journal
Ward's Automotive Reports (WAR)
Ward's Automotive Yearbook
Work in America
WT-Zeitschrift für industrielle Fertigung
Zeitschrift für wirtschaftliche Fertigung

Index

Abegglen, J. 43
Abernathy, W.J. 2, 12, 23, 42–3, 82
absenteeism 43, 105, 119–20, 270, 286, 329, 383
age of workers 119–20, 216
  and training 307, 308
AGVs (automated guide vehicles) 362–9
Akkordschere (piece rate squeeze) 228–9
alarm, defect 161–3
allowances 264
Alpha Project 81–2
Altmann, N. 127, 334
Altshuler, A. 7, 23, 24, 39
Amalgamated Union of Engineering
    Workers 93, 100, 191–2, 194, 225
American Motors 28
ANABES system 235
Anlagenbediener 212, 405
Anlagenführer (automated system
    controller) 195, 197, 201, 205–14,
    360–1, 405
  and labor productivity and changes 296–
    7, 304–5
Antwerp 56, 73
apprenticeships 307–22
  see also training
area management concept 339–41
Armstrong, P.J. 96
Armstrong, R. 96
Aronwitz, S. 104
Aspern 85
assembly areas: automation strategies
    69–74
assembly line 2, 19–20, 44, 345–69, 374–5,
    408
  balancing 247–8
  control *see* process control
  conventional, alernatives within
      framework of 346–53, 368
  crashes 358–60

high technology, risks of 353–62
  and quality control 159
  stationary workplaces *see* off-line
      production
assembly plants
  development of 55
  as units of study 10–11
Association of German Automobile
    Industry *see* VDA
Astra *see* Kadette
Athos, A.G. 42
Atlanta 81
Atzert, L. 399
AUDI 36, 61
  automation 68, 77, 79, 212, 214
Auer, P. 118, 390
AUEW *see* Amalgamated Union of
    Engineering Workers
AUJ 30
Australia 54, 56, 275
Austria 85
automated guide vehicles (AGVs) 362–9
automated system controller *see*
    Anlagenführer
automation and new technology 2, 42, 105
  and assembly line 353–62
  low level in Sweden 392–3
  and regulating work performance 239–40
  and skilled workers 18–19, 173–214, 402
    and industrial relations *see*
        demarcation rules
    new job profiles *see under* job
  strategies 52, 63–82, 90
    in assembly areas 69–74
    company-specific differences 79–82
    computer integration 74–9
    in stamping and body welding areas
        63–9
  and training 311–14, 319–20
  and trends towards new forms of work

428

374, 377–80, 383, 389, 394
work regulation problems 255–60
see also robots
automobile industry *see* restructuring of
    world automobile industry

Bailey, D. 261
Bangemann (EEC High Commissioner) 389
Barnes, R.M. 4
Batstone, E. 96, 113
Bayer, K. 85
Beer, M. 40
Beetle 79
Belgium 36
    automation 81, 197
    benchmarking 261
    quality control 147
    strategies 54, 56, 73
benchmarking 217, 260–79
    fear of losing jobs 277–9
    labor efficiency league 262–9
    off-standards in Britain 272–6
    in USA 262–72
Berggren, C. 82, 384, 392, 408
Beynon, H. 398
Bhaskar, K. 40, 112, 401
black-ball system 137
Bluestone, Irving 83
BMW 36, 388, 402
    strategies 59, 60, 61, 68, 78
Bochum 73
body welding areas: automation strategies
    63–9, 79, 81
    see also WEMR *and* skilled workers
        under automation
Bradley (Alan) 78
Brady, R.A. 223
Braun, S. 70
Brazil 27, 54, 56, 261
breaks *see* free time
Britain *see* Great Britain
British Aerospace 33
British Leyland (now Rover) 1, 3
    changing markets and rise of Toyotism
        31–3
    industrial relations 110, 111–15
Brown, W. 96
Brumlop, E. 23, 116, 408
buffers
    and assembly line 356, 357–8, 362
    and benchmarking 264
    and flexibility problems 253–4
    and mechanization problems 259
    minimizing 44–5
    see also just-in-time
Buick 54, 58, 399

Buick City 68, 85
bumping effect 94, 347

CAD (computer aided design) 75
Cadillac 58, 85, 399
Cahill, J. 325
Caldwell (president of Ford) 87
California 84
CAM (computer aided manufacture)
    75–6
Canada 68, 261, 403
capital investment 23–4
Cappelli, P. 108
captive imports 27, 32, 35–6
car industry *see* restructuring of world
    automobile industry
Carlson, H.C. 83–4
cascade princple 239
Cassino 71
Central America *see* Latin America
Central Policy Review Staff 110–11
centralized control *see* Taylorism-Fordism
certificates, markers and stickers in quality
    control 136–7, 140–1, 143–4
change-over time 64–6
changing markets and rise of Toyotism 17,
    21–51, 399
    impulse for change in 1970s 22–3
    Japan 37–40
        work and social organization 40–51
    in USA, Britain and Germany 24–37
Chaplin, Charlie 4
Chevette 54
Chevrolet 58, 399–400
Chicago 81
Child, J. 96
Chrysler 1, 388
    automation 68
    changing markets and rise of Toyotism
        26, 27–9, 34, 40
    industrial relations 107–8
    see also Talbot
CIM *see* computer integrated
    manufacturing
Clark, K.B. 42–3, 82, 282
Clark, R. 43
CNC (computerized numerical control) 64
Cole, R.E. 43
Cologne 55
    automation 68, 69, 73, 78, 81
Columbus 66
company strategies 17–18, 52–91, 399
    automation *see under* automation
    people-related 52, 82–91
    product diversification and upgrading 52,
        59–62

company strategies (*contd.*)
  and quality control *see under* quality
    control
  and trends towards new forms of work
    379–84
  world car 52, 53–9, 90
company-specific differences in automation
  strategies 79–82
  see also individual firms *in particular*
    AUDI: British Leyland; Ford;
    General Motors; Nissan; Opel;
    Toyota; Volkswagen
  competition between factories 372
  Competitive Edge Committees 109
  see also benchmarking
computer aided design (CAD) 75
computer aided manufacture (CAM) 75–6
computer aided quality control (COS)
  159–72
  and people-based quality feedback units
    166–72
computer integrated manufacturing (CIM)
  75, 77, 90, 395–6
computerized numerical control (CNC) 64
computerized production planning and
  control system (MRP) 75
computers 372, 390, 395–6
  and assembly line 359
  and automation strategies 64, 74–9, 90
  and line balancing 247–8
  and quality control 75, 159–72
concessions contracts 108–9
conflicts 104–5, 110–11, 112–15
  see also industrial relations; strikes
control structure changes *see* work
    performance *under* regulation
conveyor belts *see* assembly line
Copp, R. 398
core sites 55
Corsa 56
costs
  assembly line 366
  differential (USA and Japan) 42
  efficiency *see* work performance *under*
    regulation
  and industrial relations 111
  strategies
    automation 62
    product diversification and upgradiung
      59, 61
    world car 53, 57–8
  see also investment
COS *see* computer aided quality control
Craft, J.A. 108
craft unions 93, 100, 328
  and automation 180–1, 191–2, 194

and quality control 146
crashes, assembly line 358–60
Cray, E. 23
Cummings, T.G. 4
currencies *see* exchange rates
Cusumano, M.A. 38, 50
cycle times 244, 247–8, 346–51

Dagenham 81
Daihatsu 30, 395
Daimler-Benz 36, 388
  strategies 61, 76–7
Daniel, W.W. 96
De Lorean 105
decentralization
  decentralized agreements 96, 103
  see also group principle and team plants;
    worker participation
defect alarm 161–3
delivery quality 126–7
demarcation rules
  and quality control reorganization 135–6
  and skilled labor and automation 175–84,
    187–8, 191
    Federal Republic of Germany 182–4
    Great Britain 179–82
    Japan 46–7
    USA 175–9
Demes, H. 48
Denise, M.L. 53
Dertouzos, M. 389
Detroit 54
Deutschmann, C. 49
developing countries 27, 32–3
Diamond Star 30
Dieckhoff, K. 36
Digital Equipment 78
direct interest representation 96–7
direct production 47–8
  and indirect functions combined *see*
    integration; quality control
    reorganization
  personnel changes 289–97
  and regulating work performance 270–1,
    273–4
  and training 312–16, 321
  see also assembly line; automation
disability 119–20, 216, 240–1, 383
dismissal *see* personnel reductions
Dohse, K. 397
  on industrial relations 93, 94, 97
  on robots 67
  on Toyotism 46, 49
  on worker participation 336
  on world car 53
Dombois, R. 97, 98, 116, 402

Donovan Report 111
Dore, R.P. 43, 398
doubling up 113
dream times 65
Dubois, P. 398
Düe, D. 37
Dunnett, P.J.S. 112
Dyer, D. 24

early warning systems for overload 253
Eastern Europe 121, 393, 395
Edwardes, M. 32, 112
EETPU *see* Electric, Electronic,
     Telecommunications and
     Plumbing Union
efficiency 42
  and automation 177, 197
  costs *see* work performance *under*
     regulation
  league 272
  loss *see* loss of time
  measurement *see* work performance
     under regulation
  plant *see* work performance *under*
     regulation
  see also quality control
EI *see* Employee Involvement
Eichner, H. 398
EIT (Employee in Training) 307–8, 311,
     314, 315
EITB (Engineering Industry Training
     Board) 308, 316, 406
EITS (Employee in Training Seniority) 308,
     315
Electric, Electronic, Telecommunications
     and Plumbing Union 93, 100, 180,
     191, 194
Elger, T. 113
Ellesmere Port 68, 73
Employee Involvement program, 7, 82, 87–
     90, 95, 109
  and regulating work performance 216,
     279
Employee Participation Group 84
Employee in Training (EIT) 307–8, 311,
     314, 315
Employee in Training Seniority (EITs) 308,
     315
employment 25, 26, 31, 33–6, 46, 47
  life-long 46, 47, 108, 117
  skilled *see* skilled workers
  see also Employee; job; personnel;
     unemployment; worker
     participation
EMUG (European MAP User Group) 78
Engineering Industry Training Board 308,

     316, 406
EPG (Employee Participation Group) 84
ergonomics and work measurement 233–8,
     241
Erika 54, 57
error card system 141
Escort 54, 57, 58
Europe
  automation and skilled labor 174
     demarcation rules and industrial
        relations 175, 182–4
     new job profiles 185, 190–214
  changing markets and rise of Toyotism
        21, 23–4
     development 34–7
     and Japan 38–42
  Eastern 121, 393, 395
  industrial relations
     new 109–11, 116–17
     traditional 92–3, 95–103
     see also automation *above and* quality
        control; regulating *below*
  labor productivity 282–305, 387–9
  quality control
     computer-aided 160–4, 171
     strategies and industrial relations 127–
        8, 138–42, 143, 147, 149–59
  regulating work performance 215, 403,
     404
     benchmarking 261, 262, 273–6, 277–9
     industrial engineering and industrial
        relations 219–20, 223–32, 236–7
     new challenges and approaches 238,
        240–3, 244, 249–55, 258–9
  skill levels
     new work and management concepts
        324, 325, 326–7, 331–6, 407
     vocational training 307–14, 316–21,
        406
  strategies
     automation 62–4, 68–74, 76–82
     people-related 85, 87–91
     upgrading and diversification 59–61
     world car 53, 54, 55–7, 58–9
     see also under quality control *above*
  worker participation 336–44
     see also Federal Republic of Germany;
        Ford Europe; General Motors
        Europe; Great Britain
European MAP User Group 78
exchange rates 22–3, 32, 40, 42, 53
expenditure *see* costs
exports 27, 32, 35
  see also competition *under* Japan
extra performance 228

Facharbeiter (skilled workers) 373, 383, 392
　and automation 173, 195, 213
　and industrial relations 100, 122
　and quality control 155–6, 241
FEBES (integrated production disposition
　　and procurement system) 76–7
Federal Republic of Germany 10–14, 380,
　　397
　assembly line
　　conventional 345, 346–53, 408
　　high technology 353, 354–62, 374, 394,
　　　395
　　off-line module production 362–8
　automation and skilled labor 174, 393
　　demarcation rules and industrial
　　　relations 175, 182–4
　　new job profiles 185, 190–214
　changing markets and rise of Toyotism
　　　21, 23–4
　development 34–7
　and Japan 36, 41–2
　exports 399
　future 384, 385–6
　industrial relations 41, 117–25
　　major union *see* IG Metall
　　new 109, 116–17
　　and quality control 138–42, 149–59
　　traditional 92–3, 95–103
　　and trends towards new forms of work
　　　378, 382–3, 391, 400, 402
　　see also automation *above and* quality
　　　control; regulating; skill levels
　　　below
　labor productivity 387, 391
　　differences and trends 282–9
　　direct and indirect 289–305
　quality control
　　computer-aided 160–4, 171
　　strategies and industrial relations 127–
　　　8, 138–42, 143, 149–59
　regulating work performance 403, 404
　　benchmarking 261, 273–6, 279
　　industrial engineering and industrial
　　　relations 219–20, 223–32
　　new challenges and approaches 238,
　　　240–3, 244, 249–55, 258–9
　skill levels 122, 166, 307–14, 316–22, 373–
　　　4, 383, 392, 406
　　new work and management concepts
　　　342, 325, 326, 331–6, 407
　skilled labor *see under* automation *above*
　strategies
　　automation 62–3, 68–9, 70–1, 73–4,
　　　76–80
　　people-related 90
　　upgrading and diversification 59–61

　world car 54, 55–6
　　see also under quality control *above*
　worker participation 331–5, 336–44
feedback, quality-related 159–60
　units 166–72
feeders *see* automation *under* non-skilled
　　workers
Fiat 3, 11
　automation 68, 71, 79, 81
Fiesta 57
firing *see* personnel reductions
flexibility 216
　and assembly line 350, 351
　flexible technology strategies 62–82
　production increased 242–55
Flint (USA) 54
Flynn, M.S. 282
Ford, Henry 43, 44, 218
　see also Taylorism-Fordism
Ford Europe and Ford Germany
　changing markets and rise of Toyotism
　　24, 33, 35–6, 37
　industrial relations 99–100
　strategies 60, 61
　　automation 68, 69, 73, 77–8, 79
　　world car 54, 55, 57
Ford UK: changing markets and rise of
　　Toyotism 24, 32–3
Ford USA 11, 388, 389
　changing markets and rise of Toyotism
　　24, 26, 27–30, 40, 44
　industrial relations 108, 109, 110, 245
　strategies
　　automation 80–3
　　people-related 218, 261
　　　EI 51, 87–90
　　world car 53, 54–5, 57–8
foreign workers *see* migrant workers
FORS system 76
Fox 57
Fraser (union president) 108
free time 292–5
　see also loss of time
Friedman, G. 4, 216
front-wheel drive 23
　production as object of study 11
future development 386–96
　models for 384–5

Gallie, D. 398
Gastarbeiter 116–17
Gemini 54
General Electrics 78
General Motors Britain *see* Vauxhall
General Motors Europe 32, 33, 55
　Opel *see* Opel

General Motors USA 393, 395
changing markets and rise of Toyotism
24, 26, 27–30
closures 388
industrial relations 104–5, 109, 110, 390,
399–400
strategies
automation 62, 66, 68, 74, 75, 77–8,
79–83
people-related *see under* quality of life
world car 53, 56–7, 59
Genk 81
Gericke, E. 63, 70
Germany 393
see also Federal Republic of Germany
Glaser, E.M. 4
Glueck, W.F. 4
GM *see* General Motors
Goldschmidt, N. 42
Goldthorpe, J.H. 4, 6, 105
Golf (Rabbit) 68, 71–2, 79
Granada 81
Great Britain 1, 3, 10–14, 380, 397
assembly line 368
automation and skilled labor 173
demarcation rules and industrial
relations 175, 179–82, 183
new job profiles 185, 190–205, 210
changing markets and rise of Toyotism
20, 23–4
development 32–3, 34, 37
and Japan 33, 39
future 385–6
industrial relations 110–16, 124, 408
new 109, 118–20, 122
and quality control 136–8, 145–9
traditional 92–3, 95–9, 100–3
and trends towards new forms of work
378, 381–2, 383, 401
see also automation *above and* quality
control; regulating; skill levels
below
labor productivity
differences and trends 282–9
direct and indirect 289–95, 298–305
Nissan in 388, 391, 395
productivity 387, 388–9
quality control 164
strategies and industrial relations 128,
136–8, 139, 141, 143, 145–9, 150,
151, 159
regulating work performance 404
benchmarking 261, 262, 272–6, 279
industrial engineering and industrial
relations 218–20, 222–4, 227, 229–
32, 236–7, 280

new challenges and approaches 240,
242, 244, 248, 250–1, 257–8
skill levels 103, 138, 307–9, 311–13, 315,
318, 320, 374, 406–7
new work and management concepts
325–31
skilled labor *see under* automation *above*
strategies
automation 68, 73, 76
world car 54
see also under quality control *above*
worker participation 336–44, 390–1
greenfield sites 107
group principle and team plants, 46, 48, 306
and automation 196–7, 204–5, 211–14
and industrial relations 95, 103, 106
and labor productivity and changes 296–
7, 304–5
and quality control 141, 156–7, 172
and quality of work life program 83,
84–5
and regulating work performance 251
and trends towards new forms of work
375–6, 377–80, 384–6, 388–92
and worker participation 323–4, 331–7
see also quality circles

Haas, V. 85, 86
Hackenberg 67
Halberstam, D. 399
Hall, J.L. 42
Halle 54 71–2
Hamtramck 74
Hannover 79
Harbour, J.E. 43
Hayes, R.H. 282
Heizmann, J. 212, 213
Henn, J.M. 43
Hennig 398
Hentrich, J. 37
Hesse, R. 363
Hickson, D.J. 398
high-tech workers *see* skilled workers *under*
automation
hiring 47, 288–9
preferential 106–7
see also seniority
Hofu 68, 69, 269
Honda 26, 30, 33, 38–9
horizontal intregration 75, 372
hours
training 307–8
working 49, 121, 286
per car 63, 270–1, 389
see also loss of time
Hubert, T. 261

Human Relations School 42
human resources development *see*
      personnel; skill levels; worker
      participation
humanization of work life programs 118–19
Hutchinson, J.G. 219, 403
Hyman, R. 113

IBM 78
idle time *see* loss of time
IE (industrial engineering) *see* work
      performance *under* regulation
IG Metall 93, 101, 102, 118, 121
    and industrial engineering 223–4
    and skill levels and worker participation
      319, 334
illness 119–21, 286, 288, 383
image, quality 61
imports 26–7, 30, 32, 35–6, 104
    protectionism 39, 389
    see also competition *under* Japan
improvement, work 238–42
incentive wages 218–20
    see also wages
incidental work 176
indirect production
    and direct functions combined *see* quality
      control reorganization
    personnel changes 297–305
      maintenance 303–5
      quality inspection 302–3
    and regulation of work performance 270–
      1, 273–4
    standards in work measurement for
      231–3
    and training 321
industrial engineering *see* work
      performance *under* regulation
industrial relations 1, 3, 18, 92–125,
      399–402
    and assembly line 348, 353
    and automation 106, 173, 186–8, 191–2,
      194
      see also demarcation rules
    changes: events and impetuses 103–25
      Federal Republic of Germany 117–23,
        124–5
      Great Britain 110–16, 124
      USA 103–10, 124
    Japan 49–50, 117
    and new work and management concepts
      325–36
    and quality control reorganization
      169–70
      Belgium 147
      Ferderal Republic of Germany 143–4

Great Britain 136–8, 145–9
    USA 129–36
and regulating work performance 220–
    38, 280, 404–5
    benchmarking 261, 264, 266–8
    job design and ergonomics 233–8
    new challenges and approaches 245,
      249–51
    rating levels of performance 226–8
    shop stewards or works council
      representatives, participation of
      230–1
restrictive practices 98, 113, 179–82
traditional system 92–103
and training 317
and trends towards new forms of work
    381–4, 390–1
unions, major *see* craft unions; IG
    Metall; UAW
and work measurement *see* standards
and worker participation 323, 325–6
see also shop stewards; works councils;
    and under Federal Republic of
    Germany; Great Britain; United
    States
Ingram 325
inspection workers 127–8
    reducing *see* quality control
      reorganization
integrated production disposition and
      procurement system 76–7
integration 372–3, 377–8
    of production with inspection and repair
      work *see* quality control
      reorganization
    and regulating work performance 273–4
    reversal and automation 195–6
    and strategies 57, 75, 85–6
    see also group principle and team plants;
      worker participation
interest representation 96–7
inverse seniority 109
investment 7, 23–4, 389
    see also costs
involvement *see* worker participation
Isuzu 54, 56
Italy *see* Fiat

Janesville 56, 68
Japan 5, 14, 17
    assembly line 374
    and Britain 33, 38, 388, 391, 395
    competition from 2–3, 7, 14, 24, 30
      see also changing markets
    future 384, 385–6
    and Germany 36, 41–2

group concept 172, 336
industrial relations 49–50, 117
just-in-time 44, 65, 76, 86
productivity 388, 389
quality control 128, 132, 159, 163–4, 172
regulating work performance 236, 254,
    264
  benchmarking 269–72, 277–8
skill levels 331
strategies
  automation 64–5, 68, 69, 72, 76, 79, 81,
    82
  people-related 83, 84, 85–6
  upgrading and diversification 60
  world car 54, 56, 58–9
transplants 30, 40, 387–8, 389
and USA 26, 27, 30–1, 39–40, 41–2, 51,
    387–8, 389
worker participation 336, 375
J-car 54, 56–7, 58
Jetta 72
JIT see just-in-time
job
  awareness program 107
  control 116
  description and classification
    and assembly line 352, 354–5
    and automation see demarcation and
      industrial relations 95, 98, 102,
      109
    and labor productivity and changes
      296–7, 303
    and quality control 134–5, 141–2, 156
    and regulating work performance
      242–3
  design 98, 99
    and work measurement 233–8
  enrichment 337
    see also quality control reorganization
  fear of losing 277–9
  integration see integration
  mobility see mobility and promotion
  new profiles and automation 184–214
    Federal Republic of Germany 190–214
    Great Britain 190–205
    USA 185–90
  protection 136–7
  see also employment; personnel
joint management and union committees
  109
Jones, D.T. 16–17, 38
Jürgens, U. 397, 408
  on industrial relations 93, 94, 97, 116,
    223
  on Japan 24, 38
    group principle 48, 336

'Toyotism' 40, 46, 49, 51
  on robots 67
  on work performance regulation 243, 404
  on world car 53
just-in-time 44, 65, 76, 86

Kadette (Astra) 54, 57, 73
Kaiserslauten 56, 402
Kaizen 48
Kalmar 408
Kamata, S. 50
Kantrow, A.M. 42–3, 82
Katz, H. 107, 108
Keller, M. 74
Kern, H. 158, 174, 211
Koch, H.C. 63, 70
Kochan, T.A. 108
Kohl, H. 390
Köhler, C. 93, 94
Kolonnenführer (group leader) 197, 204–5,
    296, 321, 405
Krafcik, J.F. 362, 389, 405
Kujawa, D. 398

labor
  efficiency league 262–9
  productivity 19, 281–9, 405
    see also productivity
  regulation
    and industrial relations 93–8, 109, 112,
      119
    see also legislation *and* work
      performance *under* regulation
  relations see industrial relations
  see also employment; personnel
Landen, D.L. 83–4
Laser 54
last in, first-out principle see seniority
Latin America 27
  benchmarking 261
  world car strategies 54, 56
Lawler, E.E.III 4
Lee, S.M. 43
Leeds (USA) 56
legislation
  in Germany
    Plant Constitution Act 119, 365
    Works Constitution Act 97, 123, 150,
      223, 232
    see also regulation and rules
Leibenstein, H. 5
Leidecker, J.K. 42
levels of performance, rating 226–8
life-long employment security 46, 47, 108,
    117
line see assembly line

Livonia 85
lock-outs 114
Lordstown 56
loss of time 365–6
    cycle loss time 244, 247–8
    and labor productivity and changes 286,
        288
    and work measurement 229, 243, 255–60
    see also absenteeism; free time; hours;
        illness; strikes; vacations
Lünzmann, F. 70
Luton 56
Lutz, B. 398

MacDuffie, J.P. 389
McGregor 42
McKersie, R.B. 108
maintenance workers
    and labor productivity and changes
        303–5
    see also skilled workers under automation
Malmö 393
Malsch, T. 397, 398
    on production standards 232
    on robots 67
    on Toyotism 46, 49
    on worker participation 336
management
    concepts, new 322–36
    information systems (MIS) 75
    and personnel changes see personnel;
        quality control reorganization
    relationship with workers see industrial
        relations
    reports and quality control 161, 162–3
manning levels and automation 175, 181–2,
    199–200
manufacturing automation protocol (MAP)
    75, 77–8
MAP see manufacturing automation
    protocol
Marchington, M. 96
markers in quality control see certificates
Marsden, D. 32, 112
Marsland, S. 40
Maurice, M. 398
Mayer, G.E. 282
Mazda
    changing markets and rise of Toyotism
        26, 38–9
    as measuring stick 269
    strategies 54, 68, 69
measurement of work see work
    performance under regulation
measuring stick, Japan as 269–72, 277
mechanization see automation

Meister (supervisor) 243, 252, 332, 334, 337,
    367–8, 404
Mercedes Benz 393
Methods Time Measurement see MTM
Mexico 27
Meyer III, S. 218
migrant workers 116–17, 394
Milkovich, G.T. 4
Millward, N. 96
Mintzberg, H. 397
MIS (management information systems) 75
Mitchell, D.J.B. 108
Mitsubishi 68
mix see model mix
mobility and promotion 94–5, 153, 157, 209
    see also seniority
model mix
    and assembly line 350–1
    and labor productivity and changes 282–
        3, 291–4
    and regulating work performance 242–55
    'Modern Times' concept 4–7
    changes see restructuring
modularization 71–3
module production see off-line production
Molloy, E.S. 4
Monden, Y. 43–4, 45
Motomer project 76
motor industry see restructuring of world
        automobile industry
MRP (computerized production planning
        and control systems) 75
MTM (Methods Time Measurement) 224,
        225–6, 228, 234–5, 238, 403
Müller, F.U. 331, 334, 391
Munich 68
Mutual Growth Program 88–9, 109

national affiliation, influence of 379–84
    see also Federal Republic of Germany;
        Great Britain; Japan; United
        States
National Committee for Work
        Measurement see REFA
new technology see automation
New United Motor Manufacturing
        Incorporated 30, 84–5, 395
new work and motivation (NW&M) 52, 82,
        84, 322–36, 406–7
    in Federal Republic of Germany 122,
        166, 320–2, 331–6
    in Great Britain 103, 138, 325–31
    and industrial relations 94, 95, 103, 122,
        124
    and quality control 138, 166
    and regulating work performance 216,

225, 255, 267, 269
and training 306–7, 317–18, 320–2
in USA 95, 124, 317–18, 322–5
newly industrialized countries (NICs) 27,
399
Brazil 27, 54, 56, 261
Nissan
in Britain 388, 391, 395
changing markets and rise of Toyotism
30, 38–9, 50
as measuring stick 269
in USA 30
Nixon, Richard 22
non-skilled workers (and semi-skilled)
and assembly line 351, 361
and automation 173, 174, 178, 194–5,
196, 202, 208, 211–14
and industrial relations 100–2
in Sweden 392
and training 318–19
and worker participation 324–5
Norman, G. 104, 105
norms
and industrial relations 95–6
normal performance and work
measurement 219–20, 226
Norsworthy, J.R. 282
number of vehicles per worker 282–5, 289,
299
NUMMI *see* New United Motor
Manufacturing Incorporated
NW&M *see* new work and motivation

OD *see* Organizational Development
Oelker, K.-C. 363
off-line production 71–3, 349, 362–9, 374–5,
377–80, 383
off-standards in Britain 272–6
Ogden, S.G. 96
Ohno, Taiichi 43, 44
oil crisis 23, 28, 33–4
Okazaki 68
Oklahoma City 105–7
Oldsmobile 58, 399
Olle, W. 76
Omega 57, 73
on-the-job training *see under* training
Opel (GM) 393, 402
changing markets and rise of Toyotism
24, 35–6
strategies 60, 61, 73, 76–7
Open Systems Interconnection 77–8
option packages 60
Organizational Development (Design)
projects 7, 83, 106
OSI (Open Systems Interconnection) 77–8

Ouchi, W.G. 42
overcycle work 248–52
overload 253

pair formation concept 155
Panther 57
parallel production
on assembly line 348–9, 356–60
at different sites 55, 57, 262, 273–4, 372
Parent Area System 269
Parker, M. 324, 391
participation *see* worker participation
Partridge, B. 96
Pascale, R.T. 42
PEG (Permanent Employment Guarantee)
108
Peninou, G. 398
people-based quality feedback units 166–72
people-related strategies 52, 82–91
see also human resources
performance report 263
see also work performance *under*
regulation
Permanent Employment Guarantee 108
permanent maintenance workers 181–2,
188–91, 195–214
personnel
reductions 98, 118, 265
and automation 175, 197–8, 200
goal *see* quality control reorganization
and labor productivity and changes
286–91
and regulating work performance
278–9
and skill levels and worker
participation 318, 327
see also seniority; unemployment
structures and change 19, 289–305, 405
changes in direct production 289–97
changes in indirect production 297–305
see also labor productivity
see also employment; industrial relations;
job
Peugeot (and Talbot) 33, 78
piece rates 218–20, 228–9
Piore, M.J. 59
Plant Constitution Act 119, 365
Plant Vehicle Scheduling 78
Poland 395
Polo 68, 79
Pontiac 58, 399
Porsche 36
Port Elizabeth 56
Portugal 408
preferential hiring 106–7
privatization in Britain 32, 33

process
  automation strategies
    assembly areas 69–74
    process flexibility 66
    see also robots
    stamping and body welding 63–9
  control 43–6, 50, 216
  planning and work improvement 238–42
product diversification strategy 52, 59–62
production
  cycle times 346–51
  flexibility increased 242–55
  integrated with quality inspection *see*
            quality control reorganization
  management 42, 43–4
  schedule 246–9
  see also assembly line; parallel
            production; productivity
productivity
  agreements 108–10
  changes since 1970s
    cycles in USA 25–31
    decline in Great Britain 31–3
    increase in Japan 37–51
    worldwide 25
  labor *see* labor productivity
  regulating *see* work performance *under*
            regulation
profitability of motor industry 29, 34, 37,
            39
promotion *see* mobility; seniority
protectionism 39, 389
Przeworski, A. 10
Pugh, D.S. 398
PVS (Plant Vehicle Scheduling) 78

QDC (Quick Die Change) 64–5
qualifications *see* training
Quality Audit Representation 267
quality control 43, 302–3, 390
  and computers 75, 159–72
  and labor productivity and changes 292–
            3, 296, 299–300, 302–3, 305
  quality circles 48, 83–4, 138, 323, 325–7,
            332–4
  quality feedback units 166–72
  quality image 61
  quality inspection 302–3
  quality upgrade program (QUP) 131–5
  and regulating work performance 249,
            267, 276
  reorganization 18, 126–72, 402
    company strategies and industrial
            relations 128–59
      Federal Republic of Germany 138–
            42, 149–59

      Great Britain 136–8, 145–9
      USA 128–36, 142–5
  computer-aided and its limits 159–72
    people-based 'quality feedback
            units' 166–72
  and skill levels and worker participation
            323, 325–7, 332–4, 342
quality of life
  humanization of work life programs
            118–19
  Quality of Work-Life program 4, 7, 52,
            82–7, 90, 95, 106, 109, 115
Quick Die Change (QDC) 64–5
quitting
  forced *see* personnel reductions
  voluntary 105
QUP (quality upgrade program) 131–5
QWL *see under* quality of life

Rabbit *see* Golf
Rastatt 388, 393
rating systems 48–9
rationalization *see* restructuring of world
            automobile industry
Rausch, J. 256
recruitment 47, 394
  see also hiring
redundancies *see* personnel reductions
REFA (*Reichsausschuß für
            Arbeitszeitermittlung*) 219, 223,
            226, 228, 230, 234, 403
Regensburg 388, 402
regulation and rules
  work performance and plant efficiency
            19, 215–80, 403–5
    assembly line 349–50
    competition *see* benchmarking
    and industrial relations 220–38
    new challenges and approaches
      increased mechanization 255–60
      increased production flexibility
            242–55
      process planning and work
            improvement 238–42
    task areas 217–20
    see also industrial engineering; labor
            regulation
  see also demarcation rules; labor
            regulation; legislation
Reichsausschuß für Arbeitszeitermittlung see
            REFA
reliefmen 292, 294–6, 305
Renault 393
repair workers 292–3, 296, 305
  and assembly line 359
  and automation 177–9, 181, 188–91

integrated with quality inspection *see* quality control reorganization
responsibility
 quality *see* quality control reorganization
 separated *see* demarcation
restrictive practices 98, 113, 179–82
restructuring of world automobile industry 1–20, 397–9
 see also assembly line; automation; changing markets; company strategies; industrial relations; labor; quality control; regulation; skill levels; trends; worker participation
retooling 64–6
Riegler, C.H. 390
robots
 assembly 69–70, 73, 353
 costs 62
 failure 74
 and industrial relations 106
 introduced *see* skilled workers *under* automation
 and quality control 153
 stamping and body welding 66–9, 79, 81
 and world car strategy 57
 see also automation
Roos, D. 16–17, 39
Rosow, M.P. 11
Roth, S. 390
Rothschild, E. 28, 104
Rover *see* British Leyland
rules *see* regulation
Rüsselheim 55, 56, 73

Saab 393
Saarlouis 68, 78
Sabel, C.F. 59, 108
Sable 81
Saginaw 81
St Louis 68
Sakuri, T. 65
Sao Gaetno 56
Sao José dos Campos 56
Saturn project 81, 86–7
Savoie, E.J. 88
Schäuble, G. 118
Scheinecker, M. 85, 407
Schonberger, R.J. 43
Schultz-Wild, R. 98, 116
Schumann, M. 158, 174, 211, 297
Schweizer, W. 71
Schwendiman, G. 43
Scorpio 57, 73, 81
security *see* life-long employment

self inspection and self-regulation 44–6, 50, 371
 and quality control
  Federal Republic of Germany 138–41, 151–2, 154
  Great Britain 136–7, 145–6, 148–9
  Japan 172
  USA 143–4
 see also group principle and team plants
Sellie, C. 215, 404
Sengenberger, W. 94
seniority rules 93–5, 96–7, 98, 109, 347
 and quality control 135, 153
 and training 308
Serrin, W. 83
service hours 49
Shingo, S. 43, 65
shop stewards 96, 97, 103, 111, 408
 and quality control 138
 and regulating work performance 230–1
 and work measurement 230–1
 see also industrial relations
Siemens 80
Sierra 57, 81
skill levels 19–20, 306–44, 405–8
 new work and management concepts 322–36
 see also skilled workers; training
skilled workers
 and assembly line 351, 360–2
 job classification 95
 and labor productivity and changes 292–3, 296, 299–302, 304
 and new technology *see under* automation
 numbers of 122–3, 310–11, 315
 and regulating work performance 216
 status and wages 99–103, 123
 and training 318–19
 and trends towards new forms of work 373–4, 377–80, 383–6, 392
 see also skill levels
Slaughter, J. 324, 391
smaller cars, demand for 23
Smith, Roger B. 80
Sorge, A. 398
South Africa 54, 55
South America *see* Latin America
South Korea 27, 399
Southeast Asia 54, 56
Spain 36, 261, 408
SPC (statistical process control) 137–8
SPC (stored-program controls) 64
specialization *see* skilled workers
speed-up 104, 258, 347
Sperling, H.J. 120

stamping areas-automation strategies 63–9
standardization *see* Taylorism-Fordism;
    world car
standards in work measurement
    determining 224–6
    for indirect labor 231–3
    temporal limitations for revision of
        228–30
stationary workplaces *see* off-line
    production
statistical process control (SPC) 137–8
status 46, 99–103, 123
    see also skilled workers
stickers in quality control *see* certificates
stored-program controls 64
Straßenführer (system controller) 212–13,
    405
strategies *see* company strategies
Strauss-Fehlberg, G. 118
Streeck, W.
    on employment levels 37
    on industrial relations 116, 117
    on production changes 23, 62
    on vocational training 316
stress and strain
    and industrial relations 119–20, 127
    and regulating work performance 222–4,
        272–3, 394
strikes 3, 114–15, 288, 403
    and regulating work performance 222–4,
        271–3
    see also industrial relations
Strömel, H.-P.
    on Japan 46, 48, 51, 336
    on work performance regulation 243, 404
Studebaker-Packard 219
substitution effect *see* automation
Sunderland *see* Nissan in Britain
Sweden 408
    industrial relations 118
    production organization 390, 392–4
    strategies 82
synchro-control 65–6

Tahara 69, 269
Taiwan 27
Takezawa, S. 43
Talbot (Peugeot) 33, 78
Taurus/Sable 81
taxation 42
Taylor, F.W. 43, 44, 215
Taylorism-Fordism 2, 3, 4–7, 370, 371, 376
    comparison with Toyotism 50–1
    and regulating work performance 217, 218
    regulatory mode and functional alternatives
        5, 376

and strategies 59
    see also assembly line
team plants *see* group principle and team
    plants
technology *see* automation
Tenne, H. 10
Terry, M. 96
TGWU *see* Transport and General
    Workers Union
time
    change-over 64–6
    cycle 244, 247–8, 346–51
    loss *see* loss of time
    studies *see* work performance *under*
        regulation
    taken to build car 63, 270–1, 389
    temporal limitations for revision of
        standards 228–30
    utilization 120–1
    vacation and illness 49, 108, 119–21, 286,
        288, 383
    working hours *see* hours
Tolliday, S. 6, 96, 218–19
Toyota
    as measuring stick 269
    strategies 65, 69, 84, 86
    Toyotism 40–51, 237
        see also changing markets and rise of
            Toyotism
training (mainly vocational and on-the-job)
        47, 306, 307–22, 324
    and assembly line 360–1
    and automation 173–5, 189, 191–4, 206,
        208–9, 211, 213–14
    further 317–22
    and industrial relations 100, 122
    and labor productivity and changes
        292–3
    and regulating work performance 241
    trends towards new forms of work 373,
        382, 385, 389
transplants (Japanese firms in Western
        countries) 30, 40, 387–8, 389
Transport and General Workers Union 93,
        146, 180, 328
trends towards new forms of work 20, 370–
        96, 408
    company strategies 379–84
    directions of change 371–6
    future development
        in 1990s 386–96
        models for 384–5
    national affiliation, influence of 379–84
Tsuda, M. 48
Tsutsumi 269
Turner, L. 325, 390

turnover per vehicle 59–60
two-trade responsibility 203–5, 197–8

UAW (United Automobile, Aerospace and
    Agricultural Implement Workers
    of America) 93, 398
  and automation 176
  and captive imports 27
  and Japan 41, 42
  and new industrial relations 104, 107–8,
    124
  and people-related strategies 82–3, 87–9
  and quality control 129, 136
  and regulating work performance 221–2,
    245, 249, 264, 267, 268, 404
  and skill levels and worker participation
    317
  and skilled and non-skilled workers
    100–1
  and Southern Strategy 105, 107
  uncoupling work from line pace see off-line
undermanning 199–200
unemployment 26, 116, 122, 278–9
  see also personnel reductions
unions see craft unions; IG Metall;
    industrial relations; shop
    stewards; strikes; UAW; works
    councils
United States 1, 3, 10–14, 380, 397
  assembly line
    conventional 345, 346–8, 351–3, 374
    high technology 345–5
    obsolescence 368
  automation and skilled labor 173
    demarcation rules and industrial
      relations 175–83
    new job profiles 184, 185–90, 210
  changing markets and rise of Toyotism
    21, 23–4
  development 25–31, 37
  and Japan 26, 27, 30–1, 39–40, 41–2,
    51
  future 385–6
  industrial relations
    major union see UAW
    new 103–10, 113, 115, 118–21, 122
    and quality control 128–36, 142–5
    and teams 383–4
    traditional 92–103
    and trends towards new forms of work
      378, 381–3, 391, 399–400
    see also automation above and quality
      control; regulating; skill levels
      below
  labor productivity
    differences and trends 282–9

direct and indirect 289–305
  productivity 387–9
  quality control
    computer-aided 164–5, 395
    strategies and industrial relations 128–
      36, 139, 142–5, 151, 158–9
  regulating work performance 215, 403,
    409
    benchmarking 261, 262–72, 273, 275,
      278–9
    industrial engineering and industrial
      relations 218, 219, 221–5, 227,
      229–30, 232, 236–7, 280
    new challenges and approaches 240–2,
      244–5, 249–50, 258
  skill levels 95, 124, 307–14, 316–18, 320,
    374, 391, 406–7
    new work and management concepts
      322–5
  skilled labor see automation above
  strategies
    automation 64, 66, 68, 75–82
    people-related 52, 82–7, 90
    see also under quality control above
  worker participation 336–44
upgrading strategy 59–62
utilization time 120–1

vacations 49, 108, 121, 286, 288
Vauxhall (GM Britain)
  changing markets and rise of Toyotism
    24, 32, 33–4
  strategies 68, 73
VDA (*Verband der Deutschen
    Automobilindustrie*) 76
vertical integration 57, 75, 273–4, 372–3
  and labor productivity and changes 281–7
Vertrauensleute (shop stewards) 196
Vizemeister (supervisor) 207, 243, 247, 404
vocational training see training
Volkswagen 388, 393, 395
  changing markets and rise of Toyotism
    23, 24, 26, 28, 35–7
  industrial relations 116–17
  strategies 55, 60
    automation 67, 68, 70–1, 72, 76–7, 79–
      80, 81, 394
    diversification and upgrading 59, 61
  VW-AG 36–7, 41, 77
Volvo 82, 392, 393, 408

wages 42, 373, 402
  and assembly line 351, 352–3, 368
  and automation 175, 178, 192, 196
  and industrial relations 98–103, 107–8,
    118, 123

wages (*contd.*)
  and quality control reorganization 142,
    145, 150, 156
  and regulating work performance 218–
    20, 228, 233, 258, 275
  and skill levels and worker participation
    407
Ward 408
warranty cases 126
Weißbach, H.-J, 78
welding *see* body welding; WEMR
WEMR (welding equipment maintenance
    and repair) 178–9, 181, 186–90,
    312, 313
Whitehill, A. 43
Whitman, M. 52
Wickens, P. 391
Widick, B.J. 4, 104
Williams, K. 32
Willman, P. 32, 96, 112
Winch, G. 32, 96, 112
Windsor (Canada) 68
Wolfsburg 55, 68, 71
Womack, J.P. 16–17
  on buffers 254
  on Japan 39, 50
  on labor productivity 282, 389, 405
  on regulating work performance 272
  on worker participation 337
women 14
Woodcock, L. 398
work
  concepts, new 322–36
  improvement and process planning
    238–42
  measurement/performance *see* work
    performance *under* regulation
  systems 352

  see also employment; job; labor;
    regulation
Work in America Institute 118
worker participation 306, 336–44
  and industrial relations 106, 109, 119
  and regulating work performance 241–2
  and trends towards new forms of work
    375, 377–80
  see also group principle; new work and
    motivation; quality circles
workers *see* employment; industrial
    relations
working hours *see* hours
Works Constitution Act (FRG) 97, 123,
    150, 223, 232
works councils 97–9, 334, 382, 403
  and automation 182–3, 195–6, 205,
    210–11
  changes: events and impetuses 103, 117,
    119, 122–3, 125
  and quality control reorganization 139–
    40, 150–1, 157–8, 163
  and regulating work performance 230–1,
    235
  and work measurement 230–1
  see also industrial relations
world car strategy 52, 53–9, 90
Wright, J.P. 105

Yamamoto, K. 50
Yates, B. 24

Zabala, C.A. 282
Zager, R. 11
Zama 269
Zeitlin, J. 6, 96, 218–19
zero-buffer-principle 44–5
zero-error-principle 44